THE EARTH, THE TEMPLE, AND THE GODS

Greek Sacred Architecture

REVISED EDITION

VINCENT SCULLY

NEW HAVEN AND LONDON, YALE UNIVERSITY PRESS

Set in Garamond type.
Printed in the United States of America by
The Murray Printing Company, Westford, Massachusetts.

Library of Congress Cataloging in Publication Data

Scully, Vincent Joseph, 1920–
    The earth, the temple, and the gods.

    Includes bibliographical references and index.
    I. Temples, Greek. I. Title.
NA275.S3 1979   726.1'2'08   79–12717
ISBN 0–300–02431–2
ISBN 0–300–02397–9 pbk.

Acknowledgment for quotations and illustrations used is made in the Notes and List of Illustrations and here also to the
following: A. and J. Picard, Paris; American School of Classical Studies at Athens; Art Reference Bureau, Inc., Ancram,
New York; A. Asher and Co., Berlin; Atlantis Verlag, Zürich; Batsford, London; British Museum, London; F.
Bruckmann K. G. Verlag, München; Witter Bynner, Santa Fe; The Clarendon Press, Oxford; Deutsche Archäologische
Institut; Direktion der Antikensammlungen, München; Editions Cahiers D'Art, Paris; École Française d'Athènes; Faber
and Faber, London; Heinemann and Co., London; Vittorio Klostermann, Frankfurt-am-Main; Librairie Générale,
Paris; Macmillan, London; The Mansell Collection, London; The Metropolitan Museum of Art, New York; Ministry of
Works, London; New Directions, New York; New York University Press, New York; M. Parrish, London; Penguin
Books, Harmondsworth, Middlesex; Princeton University Press, Princeton; Spazio, Rome; The University of Chicago
Press, Chicago; Verlag der K. B. Akademie der Wissenschaften, Munich; Verlag Gebr. Mann, Berlin; Kurt Vowinckel
Verlag, Heidelberg, Berlin; Mrs. Alan Wace, Athens; Walter de Gruyter & Co., Berlin.

11 10 9 8 7 6 5

THE EARTH, THE TEMPLE, AND THE GODS

Paestum. Second Temple of Hera with eastern hill

For F.E.B. and E.V.
and
Daniel, Stephen, and John

The Gods.
Resolved by the Council and the People on the motion of Themistokles, son of Neokles, of the deme Phrearrhoi: to entrust the city to Athena the Mistress of Athens and to all the other gods to guard and defend . . .

Michael H. Jameson, "A Decree of Themistokles from Troizen," *Hesperia*, 29 (1960), 198–223.

TABLE OF CONTENTS

PREFACE TO THE 1979 EDITION

I AM AGAIN grateful to the Yale University Press for a new printing of the revised edition, to Marian LaFollette Scully for her editorial assistance, and to those many readers whose correspondence has been so gratefully received over the years. I am also somewhat exasperated by recent publications of Greek sites.[1] The landscape still does not exist so far as their authors are concerned, despite obvious human identifications with landscape in Greece and elsewhere throughout history.[2] Such obdurate blindness now seems hardly less than humanistically irresponsible.

This is not the place to renew observations made in earlier prefaces or in the text. But it should be emphasized once more that human beings see selectively, not empirically. They see what the conceptual structure of their culture permits them to see, and they only see new things when that existing cultural model is broken. Therefore I am not surprised that some people have found it difficult to see in this book what I saw at the sites. Photographs contribute to the problem, insofar as they are weak reflections of landscape's physical reality. Easy enough, though gratuitous, to say, "Go there and see for yourself"; but books can hardly be written only about forms that can be convincingly reproduced on the printed page.

Yet it is undeniably difficult to write or to read about such forms. Landscape is the most difficult of all visual experience to "handle."[3] The boredom of children confronted with "views" is proverbial. A word should therefore be said about the problem of language. A by no means unsympathetic sociologist once asked me why I had not regularized the descriptive language in this book in order to codify the descriptions, especially those of landscape, in a more "scientific" way. While I do agree that such codification has some merit as an exercise in conceptualization,[4] and while my descriptions in fact tend toward various verbal repetitions which reflect the frequent visual repetitions to be found in sacred sites and temples alike, still my concern for the individual work of art prevents me from believing that useful art history can be written in artificially deadened language. Such computerization may help to categorize phenomena (a real though minor virtue), but it is helpless before the complex and ambiguous problems of intellectual and emotional meaning, which is what works of art are all about. The art historian must explore those meanings with language which is as flexible and resonant as he can command, reaching out toward his subject, hoping to touch its level rather than to demean it.

1. For example, R. A. Tomlinson, *Greek Sanctuaries* (London, 1976).

2. In my *Pueblo: Mountain, Village, Dance* (New York, 1975), I discussed sites shaped by sacred mountains remarkably similar to those found in Greece and, as one cannot do in Greece, described the ritual dances which are still performed in them. Unlike Greek temples, American Indian architecture is mimetic of natural forms, as Egyptian and Mesopotamian architecture was. Close analogies can also be drawn between Pueblo courtyards and their rituals and those of Minoan palaces. *The Earth, the Temple, and the Gods*, fig. 3, and *Pueblo*, figs. III.41–III.48).

3. As in George H. Mead, *The Philosophy of the Act* (Chicago, 1938), pp. 107 ff:

"The reality of what we see is what we can handle." (Cited by Meyer Shapiro, "The Apples of Cezanne, an Essay on the Meaning of Still-life," *Art News Annual* 24 [1968]:34–53.) By this token the perception of landscape should probably be regarded as the most demanding of visual skills.

4. An interesting attempt, made partially in response to my book cited above, to achieve a general code for the descriptive language about, and the graphic presentation of, the relationship between man-made and natural forms in human settlements has been made by city planners Robin H. McCaffrey and Janet Needham-McCaffrey in their forthcoming study of New Mexican pueblos and Spanish towns, *Old as the Hills*.

PREFACE TO THE 1969 EDITION

I AM GRATEFUL to the readers of this book, whose interest has occasioned a paperback edition, and to its reviewers for the generosity with which it has almost universally been received. It is not easy to set aside firmly seated preconceptions in order to look at old material with fresh eyes—hardest of all to face facts which, if true, are so obvious and simple that they should patently have been recognized long before. Many scholars have apparently been willing to extend such recognition now. This is not the place to take issue with those who may have been unprepared to do so. The reader interested in polemic is referred to my letter in the *The Art Bulletin*, 46 (March, 1964).[1] Still, a serious problem of method apparently exists here for those classical archaeologists who were trained to catalogue data according to positivistic criteria based upon a contemporary or, more likely, a nineteenth–century model of reality. Landscape shapes, for example, simply do not exist for them artistically in other than picturesque terms. Hence they are blind to their sculptural forms and insensitive to their iconography, and so can neither trace their series nor assess their meaning for the Greeks. There is nothing strange in this. Human beings perceive pragmatically only within a framework of symbolic prefiguration. For this reason the human eye always needs to be trained and released to see the meaning of things. It can usually focus intelligently only upon what the brain has already imagined for it, and it faithfully reflects the timidity of that culture–bound, sometimes occluded, organ.

Modern culture has little connection with the earth—or, rather, normally fails to perceive a connection with it. But for the Greeks the earth embodied divinity. We, on our part, must make the effort of historical imagination that is required if our eyes are to see according to some dim approximation of the Greeks' inner no less than their outer light.

Here the Americanist archaeologist, with his anthropological intention and avoidance of ethnocentricity, can be of help, both generally in the intended completeness of his interpretive method (Walter W. Taylor, *A Study of Archeology*, Carbondale, 1967), and specifically in terms of the recognition of sacred landscapes (John Peabody Harrington, *The Ethnogeography of the Tewa Indians*, in the *29th Annual Report of the Bureau of American Ethnology, 1907–1908*, Washington, 1916).

I should like to express my thanks to the Yale University Press for proposing this edition and to Praeger for carrying it out and for including in it my later articles on Aeolic capitals and some additional sites, which originally appeared, respectively, in *The Architectural Review* (February, 1964), and the *Journal of the Society of Architectural Historians* (May, 1964). My sincere thanks are also due those publications for permitting reprinting here. The book, with a few corrections, rephrasings, and new photographs, has otherwise been left much as it was. The quotations used as chapter headings and so on have been retained, though they were chosen in part for their grace of expression in English and have therefore been criticized for their comparative freedom of translation. The interested reader may consult the Greek in any event, though where a Greek word is central to the topic it has of course been translated as strictly as possible. Yet it should be obvious that the structure of my thesis is, and has to be, fundamentally visual rather than philological.

I wish, it is true, that I might have been able to rewrite more of the text. The argument would have remained the same, but some sites, such as Olympia, could have supported a much more extended discussion of their sculpture and associated painting and literature. I should have particulary liked the chance to analyze a number of archaic temples in direct sculptural comparison with a number of kouroi. More references to sculpture and painting would have been useful throughout, since I think that one of the results of this study has been to illuminate the significance of the general development of Greek art from its early sculpturally "real" to its later pictorially "illusionistic" premises. There is, I believe, a good deal to be learned along this line about the relationship between art and nature in general.

The sections dealing with landscape and with the sanctity of the earth seem to me more germane than ever. They can help us to see and to respect the world, which is something of permanent value at any time. Further experience has shown that they have historical meaning not only in Greece and throughout Asia but also in areas as far apart as dynastic Egypt—where the Valley of the Kings lies in the fold of its breast–shaped mountain, rising like a natural pyramid above Deir–el–Bahri—and pre–Columbian America, where the axis at Teotihuacan runs straight to the crest of its own mountain mass and, as elsewhere in Mexico, the constructed forms repeat and abstract the shapes of the enclosing hills; or where, in the tall and articulated temple bases of Classic Petén Maya, the mountains, like Hymettos echoed in the sculpture of the Parthenon's east pediment, indeed become humanly conceivable, standing on their platforms in gracious companies like the lords of the Mayas themselves and breathing out the chill rain breath of their companion clouds.

Finally, the architectural concepts developed in this study, especially those dealing with relationships between elements both natural and man–made, have proved to be reliable touchstones for fundamental reality in the complicated problems of contemporary architecture and urban redevelopment with which we all have to deal. The heroic mood which Greece suggests cannot be sustained forever; nor should it be. But it can never be forgotten. The palpable presence of the gods, once felt, is always remembered and can, when we need it, place a heavy spear in our hand.

New Haven, 1969   V. S.

---

1. It is a pleasure to note the similarity of approach in Heinz Kähler, *Der Griechische Tempel* (Berlin, 1964). Most recently, a paper, "Minoan Palace Planning and Its Origins," read at the Sixty–

eighth General Meeting of the Archaeological Institute of America (Toledo, 1966), by Donald A. Preziosi, reinforces my thesis of landscape orientation as it does Graham's of the Minoan foot. Preziosi, who makes a strong case for a solar as well as a landscape focus, stresses the diagonal axis at Knossos as well as at Mallia (cf. my figures 2, 3, 13, 16). He has also pointed out to me an identically oriented diagonal axis running through the court of the newly discovered palace at Kato Zakro, which I have not been able to visit since excavation began. The axis is defined by an altar, as at Mallia, and is apparently directed toward a splendid rugged gorge, a great gash in the earth, crowded with cave sanctuaries, which runs down through the hills to the site of the palace on the shore. One is again reminded of Mallia. So far unique at Kato Zakro, however, is the stone rhyton, discovered there, upon which the gorge itself is, in effect, represented. It shows a great V of cleft, like a typical double peak, charged with an elaborate shrine of the goddess, rising in stepped façades multiply horned and crowned with a heraldic grouping of wild goats. For Kato Zakro: *BCH,* 86 (1962), 887–893; 88 (1964), 833–843, fig. 13; 89 (1965), 888–895; 90 (1966), 919–928. With special reference to the rhyton: N. Platon, *Crete* (New York, 1966), 87–89, 169, pls. 47, 48, 105; and idem, "Der minoische Palast von Kato Zakro," *Du* (January, 1967), 49–59.

As a Bronze Age representation of a sacred landscape, the vase from Kato Zakro is as rare and important as the well-known cup, now in the Hermitage in Leningrad, from a tomb at Maikop in the Caucasus. There the landscape is vast and distant, showing a whole escarpment of mountains, perhaps, as the cup's discoverer wished to believe, the Caucasus range itself. Whatever the case, the range shows two double-peaked mountains rising above a hedge of conventionally pyramidal peaks, while two rivers converge to an inland sea before them and animals, most conspicuously huge bulls, march across the foreground. Cf. Pharmakovsky in *Transactions of the Russian Imperial Archaeological Commission,* 1897; and Franz Hancar, *Urgeschichte Kaukasiens* (Vienna, 1939), 292–310. Also: Henri Frankfort, *The Art and Architecture of the Ancient Orient* (Baltimore, 1955), 114–115, fig. 45, pl. 124A. The concept of the Caucasus as a boundary range is stressed by Gaster, who identifies the Caucasus with the mountains "which hem in the earth" in Near Eastern mythology, and their "twin mounds" with the "Breasts of the North," mentioned in Jewish texts. He points out that the Caucasian word *m–kh–r* means both "breast" and "mound." Theodor H. Gaster, *Thespis: Ritual, Myth, and Drama in the Ancient Near East,* 2d rev. ed. (New York, 1961), 197–198. Also, on sacred mountains in general: ibid, 183, where Gaster cites Dunbar, *Antiquity, 3* (1929), 408–413; and Canney, *Journal of the Manchester Egyptian and Oriental Society,* 20 (1936), 25–40. I should like to take this opportunity to thank the scholars and officials of the Hermitage for their heartwarming kindness to me when I visited there in 1965.

PREFACE

THIS BOOK TOOK SHAPE from the belief that Greek temples needed to be looked at afresh in terms of their own forms and meanings and in relation to those of the landscapes in which they were set. It is intended to be a critical history of Greek sacred architecture, an argument as complete as practicable in its consideration of extant monuments but avoiding complete descriptions of them in order to focus upon those topics which arise from a study of Greek temples as physical embodiments of the gods in sacred places. In it, consequently, as much space must be given to the landscape as to the buildings, and the latter must normally be treated in broadly sculptural terms. As such, it is by no means designed to replace general handbooks, like those by Dinsmoor and Robertson, to whom the reader is initially referred for basic data and bibliography. But the histories of Greek architecture so far published have largely treated the monuments dismembered, as items in a series, as technological problems, or as isolated objects, and no comprehensive study of Greek temples as formal expressions of their deities or in relation to their specific sanctuaries and settings has hitherto appeared.

This book attempts to remedy that lack, and therefore tries to describe each site and its temples in at least two ways: first as they embody the specific presence of their god, and second as they participate in the historical development of Greek architecture. For that reason, each of the chapters in this book, most of which bear the name of a divinity, necessarily has an interlocking organization which attempts to arrange the sequence of sites so as best to explore the character of the deity in question and, at the same time, to set up a roughly chronological framework through which the larger development of architecture and site planning, and of form and meaning in general, can be kept in mind. The chapters, too, are arranged in a roughly chronological sequence so far as the growth of Greek art and thought is concerned, though each may be read as a unit within the larger frame. So posed, the problem resolves itself into a journey of definite stages but many turnings, since the out-of-the-way places must be visited and described as well and most available Greek temples analyzed anew and reinterpreted in these terms. So pursued, the topic itself comes to reveal a wide and fundamental structure of Greek intention in terms of which all Greek art has to be understood.

In that pursuit I have visited (with the exception of Assos, seen only from a distance) all the some hundred and fifty sites discussed or mentioned here, and the conceptual framework of the book is that suggested by them as I tried to consider them all. The photographs are intended only as a notational record of them and, within the severe limits of photography, as the closest possible approximations of the way I believe them to have been seen in antiquity. Regrettably, few of the thousands of existing photographs of Greek temples in landscape, most of them technically excellent but picturesque in conception, could help in this or could remedy various losses that were suffered, as, for example, of the clearest views of the tumuli at Pergamon and of several other sites in Asia Minor. Reconstruction drawings, often useful but necessarily imbued with the spirit of the age which made them, have for that reason been employed as little as possible, since, when the temple is photographed with its landscape, remarkably few fragments of it are normally required to suggest at least the main outlines of the experience of the site as it was originally intended to be. The method of transliteration for Greek names is hardly consistent, since it attempts to keep closely to the Greek where it can reasonably do so but also leaves some familiar names as they are commonly recognized; hence, Troezen, Mycenae, and Bassae. The footnotes do not exhaust the literature on Greek architecture and religion. They have been kept to a minimum and are intended only to give proper credit, to chart some related topics, and to define the subject in its major ancient sources and modern publications.

There can be little doubt but that I have made some errors. If so, they are mine and not those of any of the kind and generous people who have aided me in this study. I owe special debts of gratitude to Professor Frank E. Brown of Yale University and Professor Eugene Vanderpool of the American School of Classical Studies at Athens. Both assisted me in ways too many to enumerate, shared their knowledge freely with me, and made many excellent suggestions toward the revision of the original manuscript. I am also indebted to Professor John Caskey, then Director of the American School, and to Mrs. Caskey, for their hospitality in Athens during 1957–58, while I was an associate member of the School, and to Mr. Peter Topping of the Gennadeion Library and Mr. Colin Edmonson, secretary of the School, for generous help with references and illustrations. Sincere acknowledgement for many helps and courtesies must also be made to Professor Homer Thompson, Miss Lucy Talcott, and Miss Alison Frantz of the Agora excavations, to Mr. Charles Segal of Harvard University, to Mr. Christophe Clairmont of Yale, and to Mr. Laurance Roberts for many years of unfailing kindness while he was Director of the American Academy in Rome. During my work in Paris I was most graciously aided by Mlle. Raimonde Frin of UNESCO, and in London by Mr. John Pope-Hennessy of the Victoria and Albert Museum and Mr. Peter Corbett of the British Museum. I am also grateful to the late, sorely missed Professor Karl Lehmann of New York University for his conversation with me on this subject, to my colleagues Erwin Goodenough, Bernard Knox, George Kubler, Charles Seymour, and Paul Weiss, for their interest shown, and to Dottoressa Paola Zancani-Montuoro for her many courtesies at the Sele.

The members of my graduate seminar at Yale University reviewed the text with me during 1958–59 and worked on its annotation. They were Messrs. Richard Carrott, William Kane, Spiro Kostof, and Sheldon Nodelman. Special thanks for assistance in the final stages are due Miss Helen Chillman, while Mr. Richard Brilliant, Mr. Winston Davidson, and Mr. Paul Finney were also of help. Mr. Der Scutt drew the maps. Mrs. Martin Price made the Index. Grateful acknowledgement is made to Professors Phyllis Lehmann and George M. A. Hanfmann,

Miss Phyllis A. Reinhardt, Drs. William MacDonald and Robert Koch, and Mr. George Lewis, for sending me prints for publication. Other acknowledgements to those from whose works I have quoted or reproduced illustrations are made in the notes and List of Illustrations. I must, finally, acknowledge the assistance of my sons. The eldest, Daniel, took most of the photographs of Delos.

This work as a whole was made feasible through the generosity of many persons and institutions. A Fulbright grant to Italy first brought me to classical sites in 1951–52, and a Billings Memorial Fellowship from Yale University enabled me to travel and study in Greece during the summer of 1955. During that of 1956 travel through South Italy and Sicily was made possible by a George A. and Eliza Howard Foundation Fellowship, administered through the Graduate School of Brown University, and for which I was most kindly nominated by Mr. G. E. Kidder Smith. A Bollingen Foundation Fellowship allowed me to live in Greece from August, 1957, until July, 1958. The bulk of the work was done and the text written during that year, with the added help of a Paskus Fellowship in History from Jonathan Edwards College, Yale University. Finally, a generous subvention from the Bollingen Foundation assisted in publication.

V. S.

Athens, 1957—New Haven, 1961

LIST OF ILLUSTRATIONS

The Illustration Section will be found following page 273

All photographs by the author unless otherwise credited

xxix

ILLUSTRATIONS ADDED IN THE REVISED EDITION

THE EARTH, THE TEMPLE, AND THE GODS

Chapter 1

LANDSCAPE AND SANCTUARY

As for this place, it is clearly a holy one.
Sophocles, OEDIPUS AT COLONUS (Fitzgerald)[1]

THE MOUNTAINS AND VALLEYS of Greece were punctuated during antiquity by hard, white forms, touched with bright colors, which stood out in geometric contrast to the shapes of the earth. These were the temples of the gods. Unlike the Roman Pantheon, with its ideal "Dome of Heaven,"[2] or the medieval cathedral, a "Celestial City,"[3] the temples were not normally intended to shelter men within their walls. Instead they housed the image of a god, immortal and therefore separate from men, and were themselves an image, in the landscape, of his qualities. Because they offered no comforting interior space, the temples have been catalogued by some modern critics as non–architectural.[4] Because their forms were also simple, abstract, repetitive, and apparently canonical, others have seen them as creating a purely hermetic order and thus as overly restricted in expressive variation and conceptual breadth.[5] Yet it is our critical opinion which is restricted, not the temples. A romantic desire, paradoxically classicizing in intention, to see them as static, perfect shapes, pure and so divorced from the problems of life, has been tenaciously held since the beginning of the modern age in the eighteenth century, as it also was during later antiquity; it has so doubly played its part in obscuring the much greater facts of the intellectual and emotional engagement which produced the temples and of the specific kinds of force they exerted.[6] They in fact functioned and, in their fragments, still function as no buildings before or since have done. They not only created an exterior environment—which it is one of architecture's primary functions to do—that was wider, freer, and more complete than other architectures have encompassed, but, as sculptural forces, peopled it with their presences as well, in ways that changes of outlook and belief generally made inaccessible to later ages. They were capable of embodying states of being and, sometimes, of action, by whose character and results they are to be judged. Therefore, in order to know them it is necessary to know what they were intended to be and to do.

All Greek sacred architecture explores and praises the character of a god or a group of gods in a specific place. That place is itself holy and, before the temple was built upon it, embodied the whole of the deity as a recognized natural force. With the coming of the temple, housing its image within it and itself developed as a sculptural embodiment of the god's presence and character, the meaning becomes double, both of the deity as in nature and the god as imagined by men. Therefore, the formal elements of any Greek sanctuary are, first, the specifically sacred landscape in which it is set and, second, the buildings that are placed within it.

The landscape and the temples together form the architectural whole, were intended by the Greeks to do so, and must therefore be seen in relation to each other. Edith Hamilton echoed Choisy and put the problem in simplest visual terms when she wrote:

> to the Greek architect the setting of his temple was all–important. He planned it seeing it in clear outline against sea or sky, determining its size by its situation on plain or hilltop or the wide plateau of an acropolis. . . . He did not think of it in and for itself, as just the building he was making; he conceived of it in relation to the hills and the seas and the arch of the sky. . . . So the Greek temple, conceived as a part of its setting, was simplified, the simplest of all the great buildings of the world . . .[7]

This point of view, though it may seem obvious to most of those who have visited Greek sites, has not gone unquestioned by criticism. One objection which has been widely raised is that the Greeks of the archaic and classic periods are not supposed to have cared much for landscape, since they did not carve it or paint it or describe it at length in their literature. The statement as it applies to literature is of course not strictly true, especially as certain landscapes are described in the Homeric Hymns and many other places as appropriate to or expressive of various gods. The quotations with which this book is sprinkled attest to that, and there is, beyond a few quotations, a deep sense of the action and effect of landscape to be found among most Greek writers from Homer on. Similarly, the very absence of landscape background in most, in the larger sense all, vase paintings and reliefs may better be taken as indicative of the fact that the archaic and classic Greeks experienced the landscape only as it was, at full scale. Indeed, one might go on to say that all Greek art, with its usual sculptural concentration upon active life and geometry, may be properly understood and adequately valued only when the Greek's counter–experience of his earth is kept in mind. In this way the forms he made can be seen in their uncompromised logic and true dimension: as compact images of act and will—of what, that is to say, men are and can make—nakedly separate from the natural environment but to be understood in balance with it. The landscape should therefore be regarded as the complement for all Greek life and art and the special component of the art of Greek temples, where the shape of human conception could be made at the landscape's scale.

Such a supposition can be defended in terms of the history of ancient and modern culture as a whole, because it is only when the older, more intense belief in the gods tends to flag by the fourth century B.C. that romantic, picturesque poetry, nostalgically descriptive of landscape delights, like the idylls of Theocritus, makes its appearance, to be joined later by some tentative landscape painting. Again, it is only when the gods finally begin to die completely out of the land and when many human beings begin to live lives totally divorced from nature—at the beginning, that is, of the modern age—that landscape painting, picturesque architecture, and landscape description, like that of the romantic rediscoverers of Greece itself, become the obsessive themes of art. Because of this shift the Greek's view of the earth and his ritual use of it have become opaque to us. Therefore, any intended relationship between temples and landscape has been ignored by most modern critics and denied by others. One highly competent historian, for example, dismissed the subject of temple–landscape relationship by writing:

> First, as to topographical considerations in Greek design, it is so difficult to form any conclusions that we must practically dismiss the question. Hellenic lands abound in effective natural locations for the display of buildings; of these many were utilized, and others were ignored while less appropriate places were chosen. Furthermore, in view of the rigid tradition of type forms of building, we find no variation in design that could be related to natural setting.[8]

The fallacy implicit in this statement has been maintained by many of the sensitive and informed persons who have studied Greek architecture during the past two hundred years. They, too, have looked at landscape (and, as in the quotation above, architecture as well) with the contemporary picturesque eye, seeing it as simply a more or less "effective" picture, devoid of specific shapes and integral meanings. But, despite certain partial movements in that direction which can be detected in architecture and painting during the post–classic centuries, that is not the way the Greeks basically saw it.

In point of fact, the historic Greeks partly inherited and partly developed an eye for certain surprisingly specific combinations of landscape features as expressive of particular holiness. This came about because of a religious tradition in which the land was not a picture but a true force which physically embodied the powers that ruled the world, and although it may be objected that some of the landscape forms I shall define as holy are common in Greece, still the temples are many also, and their consistent appearance in relation to the sacred forms in question is never coincidental. Steps have already been taken by other scholars toward the elucidation of this fact. Lehmann–Hartleben, in a crucial article of 1931,[9] identified certain general combinations of features such as mountains, caves, springs, and so on as characteristic of Greek holy places, and Paula Philippson, in a beautiful short work of 1939, which does not deal with architecture, attempted to describe her informed impressions of a limited number of landscapes as embodying particular aspects of the goddess of the earth and of the relationship of men to her.[10]

We must now go further to recognize that, not only were certain landscapes indeed regarded by the Greeks as holy and as expressive of specific gods, or rather as embodiments of their presence, but also that the temples and the subsidiary buildings of their sanctuaries were so formed in themselves and so placed in relation to the landscape and to each other as to enhance, develop, complement, and sometimes even to contradict, the basic meaning that was felt in the land. From this it follows that the temples and other buildings are only one part of what may be called the "architecture" of any given site, and the temple itself developed its strict general form as the one best suited to acting in that kind of relationship. But in order to act to the full, it too had to become an embodiment, not merely a construction, or an abstractly perfect shape, or a pictorial element. Therefore, the specific variations in form which each temple exhibits derive both from its adjustment to its particular place and from its intention to personify the character of the deity which it, too, is imaging there. So each Greek sanctuary necessarily

3

differs from all others because it is in a different place, and each varies from the others in certain aspects of the forms of its temples and in their relation to each other and to the landscape. This had to be so, because Apollo at Delos, for example, was not exactly Apollo at Delphi, nor Hera at Paestum Hera at Olympia. On the other hand, a deep general pattern runs through all sites, both in the chosen shapes of their landscapes and the constructed forms of their temples. A profound repetition, at once the echo of ancient traditions and the syntax of a new art, informs the whole and sets off the specific statements which irradiate it and which, by the classic period, produce an unmatched dialogue between oneness and separateness, men and nature, men and the facts of life, men and the gods. So Apollo at Delos shares characteristics, in his landscapes, his temples, and their arrangement, with the Apollo of Delphi in his. So too does the Hera of Paestum with her of Olympia, while the Zeus there differs from, but is related to, him of Dodona.

My insistence upon a willed form in the organization of the sanctuary as a whole brings us to another point which has received considerable discussion. It involves the question of whether or not the relation of the buildings to each other in Greek temene of the archaic and early classic periods can be considered as having been consciously planned. Diametrically opposing views have been advanced. Von Gerkan, who begins his consideration of Greek town planning with the development of the Hippodamian grid in the fifth century, sees the earlier sanctuaries as unplanned conglomerations of buildings,[11] and this view is more or less shared by other authorities.[12] Von Gerkan's denial of planning to the archaic and most of the classic temene would seem partly to derive from a restricted idea of what architectural planning may be conceived to be, in which those solid elements that are regularly disposed in space are planned, those disposed irregularly being considered unplanned and haphazard. This criterion, certainly a foreign one to the Greeks, who did not conceive of solids and voids in such easily mutual terms, as we shall discuss later, can be carried to absurd lengths, as by a recent writer who remarks of Olympia:

> buildings were sited without concern for any niceties of relation, among an outrageous multiplicity of statues of all periods. Yet the layout dates more from the fifth than the sixth century and the site is flat, two circumstances which should have encouraged a better ordering.[13]

Such pallid judgments, based upon a priori conceptions of "order," can be destructive to our perception of the depth of Greek intentions, as when the same writer says of Delphi: "the layout . . . was complicated by the steep slope of the ground."[14] The answer is clearly that the steep slope did not "complicate" the "layout" for the Greek. Instead, it was the occasion for it; it created it.

Doxiadis, to go to the other extreme, has worked out a system of Greek temenos planning which he sees as consistently in use from the seventh century and which was modified but never entirely superseded by the tendency toward axial regularity that developed from the fifth century onward.[15] He works out his system according to the views of buildings offered from the propylon of the sanctuary, and he sees it based upon the Greek conception of the universe as circular and of human vision as extending across a 180° arc of that circle, as it in fact does. Building solids are then set within the arc for maximum individual visibility and at rhythmically

4

order or
not / planning -
Doxiadis - yes -
according to individual
in relation to
circular
universe

related intervals, the latter based upon an Ionian ten–part and a Dorian twelve–part divisioning of the circle as a whole. According to Doxiadis the system had further refinements and some development, but the essentials remained as I have rather crudely outlined them above.

Doxiadis' theory has much to recommend it: first, insofar as it insists upon the wide arc of vision, thus removing Greek sanctuaries from criticism based upon the restricted, rectangular window of Renaissance perspective, with which Greek conceptions had little to do—indeed, until the fourth century, nothing to do; second, as it asserts that the eye of the participant is normally led out of the temenos toward the landscape beyond it. As he rather beautifully puts it:

> So fühlt jeder Mensch, der eine Anlage betritt, sofort ihre Struktur, er wird unvermittelt zu seinem Ziel geleitet, klar und rein sieht er alle Formen, das Ganze vor sich, seinen Weg kann er erkennen, frei bleibt er aber, sich zu bewegen; sein Weg führt zu keinem Gebäude, er ist nicht durch die schwerste Masse betont, er ist frei, und nach der Natur ist das Ganze ausgerichtet, natürlich ist die Anlage gebaut.[16]

On the other hand, Doxiadis' presumed lines of sight within the sanctuary are sometimes blocked in actuality by subsidiary monuments, such as statue bases at Olympia, or, more seriously, fall across contours, as at the Acropolis in Athens, where the reference points are masked from sight by rises of ground. Moreover, the important experiences of most sites, as again at Olympia and the Athenian Acropolis, come from walking through them and penetrating to their hearts, into areas where Doxiadis' system does not precisely apply and which he does not adequately consider. Nor does Doxiadis deal with differences of meaning as embodied in the varying arrangements of different sites. Stillwell, who coolly summed up in 1954 most earlier opinions on the question—and who advanced his own sound and unexceptionable views, which will be referred to again—gave Doxiadis fairly short shrift in his article.[17] Yet, since the rather abstract observations of Martienssen,[18] Needham,[19] and Smithson[20] (who attacks Choisy) have added little to the clarification of the problem, Doxiadis' theory remains the most challenging one which has yet been advanced. What we may derive from it as most useful is its implication that the system of arrangement, if such in fact existed, was intended to appear to be no system at all. Because of this, the individual buildings were able to act upon each other as free and aggressive solids, and the eye was allowed to move beyond them, as it was clearly meant to do, toward those landscape elements outside the temenos which were essential components in the meaning of the site as a whole.

I shall refer to these points later (most systematically in *Chapter 4*), but it will not be necessary to enter into the planning controversy again. Instead, the buildings in Greek temene should be regarded as phrases in a developing language. Each makes a statement which is joined by others as new buildings are added, sometimes over many generations. The landscape is normally a constant, but its meaning too is developed as the buildings are placed within it. Each temenos is complete at any stage of its growth, but what it is attempting to say about the place, the god, and human life will constantly become fuller and more precise as the phrases are made clearer and joined to each other and the great sentences take form. Therefore, "planning," in the sense that we have come to know the word, is perhaps too static a term to apply to the process. A language is being created, speaking through visual form as specifically as does Greek itself. Especially as each temple is a unique presence, belonging to a common family but shaped and placed according to its own needs and meanings, is this most true. Once again it is the Greek conviction of the special character of individual things which makes possible the dramatic eloquence of the whole. Consequently, in site organization, as elsewhere, we must enlarge, not diminish, our conception of the meanings which Greek architecture was able to express and must beware of judging it by standards that are less meaningful than those upon which it was based.

In that architecture the action of buildings and landscape was fully reciprocal in meaning as in form, and this too is an essential fact, that the form and the meaning were the same. Therefore, no study of Greek temples can be purely morphological, of form without theme, nor purely iconological, of theme regardless of form, since in Greek art the two are one. The form is the meaning, and indeed the classic Greek mind, with an integrity of perception lost by later cultures which separated the two, firmly identified them.[21] Similarly, nineteenth–century technological determinism, which continues to engross some critics, can no longer be considered central to the problem, since it was clearly not central to the Greeks. Instead the problem is a sculptural one, of the counter–relationships between solid landscape and temple shapes in the clear light of every day. Since those shapes embodied the gods, it is mandatory that we approach them through the gods. If we do so approach them as the specific personifications of Greek religion (for which the Greeks themselves had no such generalizing, social word), we must clearly understand that we do so in order to see and understand Greek architecture, which, rather than a reappraisal of Greek religion, is the object of this book. Clearly enough, there are many manifestations of the Greek gods we cannot come upon in this way, and we need not expect to find revelations of them differing from those known through other sources which we cannot explore fully here. We can, however, expect Greek architecture to act in relation to those sources and as if it belonged in the same culture with them, as it has not always seemed to do in the past. Possibly we can also expect something more, because so far as the essential "being" of the gods is concerned, where, as Otto notes, "all is inexplicable,"[22] the temples in their landscapes, if correctly read, should help us more than any other form of Greek visual or literary art can be expected to do. Because here the gods, as the hard wrought facts of nature and of human life which they were, are more complete than they can be anywhere else, since here their mysterious beings were made determinate, localized, through the unique union of the natural and the man–made.

It is now our pressing need to try to bridge the gap which separates us from a comprehension of those beings, despite the insuperable difficulties for total understanding which time and distance pose. Herman Melville, a modern man like ourselves, may have perceived the essentials when he wrote his poetically questionable but conceptually exact four lines, entitled "Greek Architecture."

> Not magnitude, not lavishness
> But form, the site;
> Not innovating wilfulness
> But reverence for the archetype.[23]

Perhaps it is less of a paradox than it seems that Melville, who saw more profoundly than has anyone else into the depths and flux of the sea, should also have been able to state so succinctly the counter principles of clarity and permanence in a fixed and sacred landscape upon which Greek architecture was formed. The deeps which called to Melville were the measure of his own loneliness in the world, and the mighty creature, the object of his search, which had returned to them could only rise in the end to destroy a humanity which sought mastery without reverence and victory without compassion or joy. The hatred of Ahab for the nature of things as they are had brought Zeus' lightning stroke upon him, but his ultimate diabolism, in drinking the death of nature out of the sockets of iron weapons, demanded a vengeance which could only be worked by an older divinity, the white power rising out of the sea. Therefore, when Melville, as a typically absurd and querulous modern traveler, mounted the Acropolis of Athens one day in 1857,[24] he was able to understand all at once the miracle of reconciliation between men and nature which rose before his eyes. A white presence stood before him, high on its platform of rock above the long view to the sea. The cones and horns of the mountains lay behind it, fixed by its solemn permanence but uncompromised by it, and around it the whole horizon swung in a single arc. The world became simple, articulate, and known, with the ultimate harmony of the temple at its center: an organism as complex in its parts but as serenely whole in its action as any creature of the earth, but also totally abstract, as geometric as Melville's ships, a work of man. This was "form," as Melville knew it, "not magnitude, not lavishness," but the singleness of life, and as he scanned the horizon of land and water with his sailor's eye he recognized form's active complement, "the site." Somehow he was able to perceive the reciprocal relationship between the two; he knew that this was "reverence," and he divined that something deep and essential to human life upon the earth was being celebrated there.

The double issues of "form" and "site," of the human identification of the self and of reverence for that which is outside the self, of acting alone but at the same time being at home in the world, are much more cogent problems today than they were in Melville's time, of which we are the heirs. It is with these issues that Greek architecture deals, as it balances the man—made and the natural, nature and the human will. Indeed, Greek temples and their sanctuaries express concepts which embrace the whole of the larger issues of life as the western world has most realistically come to know them, since they were the result of an attempt to grasp reality whole, not to transcend but to understand the apparent truth of things. They formulate the perceptions of a religious attitude in which the divine, as Otto says: "is neither a justifying explanation of the natural course of the world nor an interruption and abolition of it: it is itself the natural course of the world."[25] Doing so, Greek temples and their sanctuaries in fact gave form to concepts more balanced and complete than western civilization has normally been able to grasp in any of its post—Greek phases. It was possible for them to do this because, intellectually uncompromising as they were, they still embodied the oldest traditions of belief which had been handed down since the Stone Age. They therefore stand, like the Greek culture which imagined them, at a central point in human history: at the moment in time when the deepest past, with all its instinctive intuitions, fears, joys, and reverences, was brought for a while into harmony with the hard challenges of a new and liberated thought—at the moment, that is, when the self and objects outside the self were alike identified as objective realities. At their best the

Greeks brought these opposites into equilibrium with each other and made a peace between them, a peace like Pindar's *Hesychia*: contentment, gentleness, wise action, justice, and calm. That moment can never come again, but the double wisdom it possessed has left a permanent record in the temples it placed upon the earth. The temples themselves came late. First, as the Greeks knew, was the earth: "well–founded Earth, mother of all, eldest of all beings . . . Mother of the gods, wife of starry Heaven. . . ."[26] It is therefore with the holiness of the earth that we must first be concerned.

Chapter 2

THE GREAT GODDESS

Long ago, the Mountain Mother
Of all the gods...
　　　　　Euripides, HELEN (Lattimore)[1]

THE LANDSCAPE OF GREECE is defined by clearly formed mountains of moderate size, which bound definite areas of valley and plain.[2] Though sometimes cut by deep gorges and concealing savage places in their depths, the mountains themselves are not horrendous in actual size. Nor are the plains, south of Thessaly, ever so wide that the mountain barriers fail to define them decisively. The empty steppes of Asia, where the individual human being is cast adrift in an undifferentiated world without fixed points of reference, and the engulfed valleys of the Alps, where the villages of men are sunk under the shoulders of tremendous and complicated peaks which are clothed on their slopes with forests like the pelts of bears, are alike antithetical to the harmonious valley to mountain relationships of the Greek land. Even Italy, where the mountains split the peninsula in a central chain, is different. There, men are generally either closely hemmed in by the earth or relatively free from enclosure on the long seaward slopes or in the plain. Only rarely is the bowl of a plain clearly defined by mountains or islands on all sides. The valley of the Arno comes close to being so, as do some other places, but in Greece all the famous districts are so formed. These include Attica, Eleusis, the Megarid, Boeotia, a portion of Phocis, Corinth, the Argolid, Arcadia, Laconia, Messenia, and part of Elis. (*Sketch Maps 1, 2*) In those harmonies of mass and hollow a sea full of islands almost always plays a role. The glittering shield of its surface contrasts with the tawny land but is itself contained within the plain through the continuation of the mountain boundary by the island chain. The forms of the earth are precise in Greece, but they vary in the Greek light. In summer the hills will be lighter in tone than the opaque blue sky, and they will seem to step forward, blooming white as silver gilt over their undertones of brown, green, and lavender. At summer midday they may dissolve in the blaze of the light itself, but at evening they will shift flat into the dark silhouettes of pure contour, tight–drawn as wire. In winter they will be shadowed in purple and rippled with cloud, and, above valleys green with the new wheat, they may be touched with snow. (*Fig. A*)

Because of the ordered variety, clarity, and scale in the landscape, the human being is neither

9

engulfed nor adrift in Greece. He can come close to the earth to experience either its comfort or its threat. His experiences will never be so bland as to be easily ignored or so overpowering as to be better so. Whatever they are, they will be both strong and welcome: strong as the Greek sun is strong or as the autumnal winds at the Scironian cliffs are strong, both dangerous forces, to be respected, but which can be faced and borne; welcome because they will never, by sheer brute power or monotonous insistence, batter down the senses or brutalize the soul. Each experience will soon find its balance and its opposite, as the white glare of the summer day gives way to the cool of evening with its star, and this to the night sky crowded with constellations and they fading in the stillness of the early dawn. With the changing of the light, the mountains advance or recede; their clefts flatten out or yawn, while the plain slides away to the sea with its islands. The relationships are inexhaustibly changing, but the forms are simple and few. They are as visually economical as the scanty yield of the Greek earth itself is materially so, where the vine, the olive, the wheat and the clear water balance each other in a harmony as spare and complete as that of the landscape forms. All human experiences of the shape and content of the earth are therefore peculiarly pure in Greece. Each is definite, whole, bounded, and comprehensible, and all have their own measure, their balance, and their inevitable form. (*Fig. B*)

Yet the hunters of the Old Stone Age apparently found little to attract them in this landscape. Its sea–bitten valleys and rugged mountains could hardly support the vast herds of grass–eating animals which they followed, as killers, across the northern plains. Only one small find of paleolithic implements has been made in Greece, in a shallow cave by the shores of the ancient Lake Copais in Boeotia.[3] Others may come to light, but it seems apparent that the great formulations of paleolithic art and religion were achieved elsewhere, as in the deep caves of southwestern France and the Pyrenees. The nature of those fundamental creations of the human consciousness has been studied by many scholars.[4] Briefly summarized, the essential belief seems to have been in the earth as a mother, especially as the mother of the herbivorous animals—all, except the horse, horned—upon whose continued presence human life depended. Therefore the deep caverns of the earth were holy places; upon their walls and ceilings the revered and desired beasts were painted or incised in the splendid movements of full life, and the earth was thus impregnated with them. The forms of the paintings themselves, which create an image of the living beast more persuasive and directly sympathetic than any later art has been able to do, seem to show that the necessary death of the animal, partly induced by magic, was dignified by human respect and admiration for the creature itself and even by human gratitude to it. The totemistic beliefs of later primitive peoples indicate that such was probably the case in fact, and that the paleolithic hunter was humble enough, or wise enough, to hope that an element of consent brought the quarry to his spear. Stone Age man thus focused his major attention upon objects outside himself. His own acts were of no consequence per se; meaning resided in the life of the animals which were the objects of those acts. He himself was simply one of the many creatures to whom the earth gave life and death. Later he aggrandized himself, but at first the animals were the gods, unchanging in their battalions, one with the earth, immortal.

Yet it now seems possible that a more complicated metaphysic was also embodied in the running, weapon–threatened, animal forms: one which developed balanced themes of fertility and death, movement and extinction. So, too, the caverns came to be conceived in spatial hierarchies, defined by certain species in various groupings and with critical areas indicated by abstract signs. Movement through the labyrinthine passages which led to the caverns seems also to have formed an essential part of the ritual, and schematized representations of the labyrinth itself can be found in some of the caves. In these ways the arts formed themselves, founded upon wish fulfillment but infused with reverence and, through the very process of use and making whereby they were realized, with love. The path of the labyrinth became a dance and the natural architecture of twisting passageway and swelling cave a personalized, familiar setting, while the painted beasts began to lead their own huge and symbolic lives. In sculpture, the most ubiquitous objects extant are female figures, generally regarded as images of the earth mother and certainly, despite differences in style and possibly in intent, carved as the child knows the mother, all breasts, hips, and *mons Veneris*, full and round, with the head often inclined forward.

It is not necessary to trace here the images and symbols of the goddess, the labyrinth, and the horns through the art and religion of the Neolithic period and in the civilizations of the Near East and Crete. Levy has done so with considerable success.[5] Instead I should like to suggest that the siting, orientation, and design of the palace architecture of Bronze Age Crete clearly made conscious use of exactly those images, some of them derived from the forms of the landscape itself, others constructed. The Cretan palaces and their use of the site represent a late and full ritualization of the traditions of Stone and Bronze Age culture. From roughly 2000 B.C. onward, a clearly defined pattern of landscape use can be recognized at every palace site. More than this, each palace makes use, so far as possible, of the same landscape elements. These are as follows: first, an enclosed valley of varying size in which the palace is set; I should like to call this the "Natural Megaron"; second, a gently mounded or conical hill on axis with the palace to north or south; and lastly a higher, double-peaked or cleft mountain some distance beyond the hill but on the same axis. The mountain may have other characteristics of great sculptural force, such as rounded slopes, deep gullies, or a conical or pyramidal massing itself, but the double peaks or notched cleft seem essential to it. These features create a profile which is basically that of a pair of horns, but it may sometimes also suggest raised arms or wings, the female cleft, or even, at some sites, a pair of breasts. It forms in all cases a climactic shape which has the quality of causing the observer's eye to come to rest in its cup. Though there are many overlaps in shape and probably many unguessed complexities in their meanings, still the cone would appear to have been seen as the earth's motherly form, the horns as the symbol of its active power. All the landscape elements listed above are present at Knossos, Phaistos, Mallia, and Gournia, and in each case they themselves—and this point must be stressed—are the basic architecture of the palace complex. They define its space and focus it. Within that space the constructed elements take their form and create four complementary types of enclosure. These are: the labyrinthine passage, the open court, the columned pavilion, and the pillared cave. All these forms, both the natural and the constructed, can be shown to relate to what we otherwise know of Minoan religion and its dominant goddess, so that the natural and the man-made create one ritual whole, in which man's part is defined and directed by the sculptural masses of the land and is subordinate to their rhythms.

From the old harbor of Knossos, where the traveler of antiquity would have disembarked, the notched peak of conical Mount Jouctas can be seen rising directly to the south. (*Sketch Map 4 and Fig. 1*) Upon it, in Minoan times, was a cave sanctuary of the goddess, in Greek times a sanctuary of Zeus which was supposed to mark the place where, in terms which are those of pre–Olympian religion, the god was buried.[6] Jouctas, then, was a holy mountain, like those of the Hebrews, the Mesopotamians, and the Hittites, like those, indeed, of all the religions of the Near East. Most of all, it existed in fact as a focus for ritual; it did not have to be constructed, like the Ziggurats of Mesopotamia.[7]

The way toward Knossos from its ancient harbor winds in a serpentine movement through the lower hills that lie between the palace and the sea. Finally the sea is left well behind; the valley widens and the hills on both sides rise up to define it clearly. Directly ahead, enclosed within the valley, and indeed pushed up close to the point where the valley itself is closed by a mounded hill, lies the palace and beyond it Mount Jouctas. The ceremonial entrance would seem to have been on the north. (*Fig. 2*) Here are the doubled stairs of the so–called "theatral" area, approached along pavements marked by raised stone paths which are so narrow that they must be walked upon in single file. Thus a procession into the palace must have taken on something of the character of the ancient processions into the caverns of Paleolithic times: a long file following a narrow way. Perhaps spectators were massed upon the steps of the "theater" to watch the ritual approach, as they later stood upon similar steps inside the Telesterion at Eleusis and at other mystery sites. The paths diverge at the steps. One moves east, enters a pillared hall, turns south, mounts a ramp, and comes into the open court at its north end. From here the eye travels directly down the long axis of the court and sees beyond it (though the lower part of this view might have been blocked by buildings in Minoan times) the mounded hill which closes the valley and the split peak of Jouctas in the distance. (*Fig. 3*) The reason for the elongation of the court on a north–south axis now seems clear: it directs the eye toward the sacred mountain of the goddess and emphasizes the natural order which derives from her. The sculptural solids are natural ones. The constructed palace opposes no counter sculptural presence to them. Instead it is essentially a hollow which receives and is controlled by their massive force.

Yet the court at Knossos is not precisely on axis with the mountain; in order to discover that axis the second, more labyrinthine ceremonial route must be followed. It moves south from the theatral area and directs its narrow path along the west flank of the palace with the mounded hill and Jouctas in view ahead. Arriving at an open space, the "west court," it divides again and is joined by a path from the west; in this area was an altar. Directly ahead was the west porch, with a single column enclosed between its walls. The cylindrical wooden column between walls was itself a symbol of the goddess' presence and a feature of her shrines.[8] (*Fig. 5a*) It might be argued that the column, thus enclosed, as later by lions at Mycenae, may have been considered especially expressive of the goddess since it joined to its tree symbolism a specific description of a female state of being. Thus the whole palace became her body, as the earth itself had been in the Stone Age. So, beyond the west porch at Knossos a corridor, narrowed down almost to the width of the footway and lined with processional frescoes, took the actual processions into a dark place; beyond it, in the light beyond the south terrace, the softly mounded hill and Mount Jouctas form the view. Here a ramp joined the façade at a lower level, bridging the ravine between the palace and the hill. Perhaps this façade of the palace was crowned by horns, as Evans thought.[9] The pair at present set up near the propylaia are his restoration based upon a rather small fragment. (*Fig. 4*) With them in view, however, it can be understood how the Minoans could have seen Jouctas as horned and why it is probable that it was the epithet *keratos*, "of the horn," that Strabo used to describe Knossos as a whole.[10] The cave shrine of the goddess was upon the horned mountain, and her shrines—as we know from Minoan gems and frescoes, and from the altars with horns upon them at Knossos—were horned with what Evans has called the "Horns of Consecration."[11] Thus the horned mountain itself defined the consecrated site where the larger ritual of ceremonial kingship under the goddess could best be performed.

In any event, it is the propylaia which, at Knossos, is directly on axis with the mountain. Thus, turning left and left again, the processions had Jouctas directly to their back, passed through the propylaia on that axis, and mounted the stairs toward the shadowed volume of the main columnar hall. Beyond this a narrow stairway, divided below by another single column, led downward toward the east, and took the processions into the bright light of the court. (*Fig. 2*) Here, as Graham has shown, the bull dance took place.[12] In it, the old Stone Age ceremonials achieved a new and beautiful form when, in the presence of horned Jouctas, the young men and girls, facing death in the bull, seized the horns sacred to the goddess and leaped, propelled by the power of the horns. (*Fig. 5b*) In this unilinear dance there was none of the complication of form and meaning to be found in the modern Spanish bullfight and its circular arena. The bull charges straight, down the long court designed for him as he embodies the mountain's force, and no baroque or spatially aggressive figures are made by a cape around him. Nor, though the bull was probably sacrificed to the goddess later, does there seem to have been any blood involved in the game itself except that shed by the dancers, surrogates for all mankind, if they failed to grasp the horns. The unilinear Minoan dance, therefore, did not dramatize subtle man making his own shapes around and finally killing the unreasoning power of nature but instead celebrated both men and women together as accepting nature's law, adoring it, adding to their own power precisely insofar as they seized it close and adjusted their rhythms to its force. The love for the free movement of the beast which is demonstrated by the paintings of the paleolithic caves now broadens its conceptual base and grasps the beauty of the movements of man and beast together and indeed of all creatures and things in the world. The final sacrifice of the bull to the goddess should itself also be seen, like the later sacrifices of the Greek world, as an act of reverence to the animal, since it dignified with ceremony and hallowed with gratitude the everyday deaths of his kind.

Turning right off the court at last, the processions might have entered the low, dark, cave-like shrine of the goddess with its enclosed stone pillars, flanked by offering pits and marked with the double axe. Therefore, the processional movement from light to dark to light and dark again—culminating as it does in the innermost cavern shrine where were found at once the hollow earth of the goddess and the pillar which both enters and supports the earth and is thus also hers—makes of the Minoan palace as a whole that ceremonial labyrinth around the secret place which the Greeks remembered in their myths. The space, though organized by rectangles, is fluid and moving, like the bull dances themselves and the frescoes on the walls. Through it ran the water which was the goddess' gift and which was collected in lustral basins wherever it found its level in her hollows. All is constant motion up and down around the central court, alike in the domestic apartments culminating in the Hall of the Double Axes as on the other side. There, movement is again labyrinthine, down lighted stairways to semi-cavernous apartments which open outward between pillars, first to columned porches and then to open courts. The exterior profiles of the palace, like its rubble, timber–tensioned structure, simply enclose that movement and shift inward or outward with it. They are not required, for purposes of coherence, to define a clear exterior shape, precisely because they themselves are within a defining shape, that is, the valley as a whole. Thus Minoan planning, possibly owing something of its labyrinthine quality and its courtyard system to the East and the axial propylaia to Egypt, was still neither derivative nor incoherent, as some rather impatient contemporary critics would have it be.[13] Instead it would seem to have fulfilled its elaborate ceremonial function exactly and with deeply expressive power. It can make even the modern observer at least dimly perceive what it must have been like to feel wholly in harmony with nature and at peace with it.[14] In the Minoan palace itself harmony with the land was at once profoundly religious, knowing, and, one senses, even romantically conceived. The palace complex richly reorganized in new and communally satisfying ways what must have been the most ancient of traditions, as it directed its unilinear courtyard upon the landscape forms. It wove its dances of the labyrinth and the horns within the larger hollow of the protecting valley which was the goddess, and in view of the mounded hill which was her gentleness and of the horned mountain which was her splendor and her throne.

Yet once again we should beware of assuming that a form such as the horned mountain could have had only a single symbolic meaning. There is evidence, for example, that the V cleft was associated with the female parts of the goddess in Paleolithic and Neolithic times, and that the same V was a stylized form for horns.[15] One may therefore legitimately surmise that the cleft or horned mountain may sometimes have been seen as embodying the *mons Veneris* of the earth. This could especially have been so at Knossos, where Mt. Jouctas is both conical and cleft. (*Figs. 3, 4*) No assumption of a personal preoccupation with sexual symbolism in the Freudian sense on the part of the Cretan people, and no Jungian preoccupation with the concept of a collective unconscious on our own, is necessary for us to understand how they might have hoped to endow Earth, "mother of all," with such an essential attribute and to have believed that those sites dominated by it were closest to the center of life and ultimate power. The horned mountain would thus have been conceived of as the goddess' lap, like the lap of horned Isis upon which the Pharaohs sat (*Fig. 6*), her symbolic throne for the king whose palace was focused upon it.[16] He, like the hollow courtyard of the palace, receives the earth power wholly and is subordinate to it although, bull–masked, he may wield it. His own throne at Knossos is set deep in the palace behind the goddess' crypt. It rises from its bucket seat to a high back carved in undulations like those of an earthquake tremor, and, like the propylaia, it faces exactly on axis toward the horned mountain from which those tremors came.

Similar formations, each of which also has its own specific characteristics, dominate all other Cretan palace sites. The road south from Knossos to Phaistos climbs across the broken hills of central Crete. At the highest point of the pass is the wild Dorian site of Prinias, close under the somber flanks of the Ida massif and ringed in rain and cloud. It was not the kind of place

14

the Minoans chose for their palaces. To the south the road descends from the badlands into the comparatively broad but evenly defined plain of the Mesara, which runs generally east and west. Toward the western end of the valley the hills begin to close, and on one of them, set forward from the others and lower than they but considerably higher than the slight elevation upon which Knossos is placed, is the palace of Phaistos.[17] Opposite it rises the peak of Mount Ida to the north, but, from the stream which runs through the valley below Phaistos, Ida is hidden behind a closer hill. From the palace, however, Ida rises majestically into view, a horned mountain behind a mounded hill. (*Fig. 7a*) Ida, too, was sacred, with two cave sanctuaries near its crest, the Kamares of the goddess and the Idaean, both later sacred to Zeus and the latter indeed regarded as one of his birthplaces.[18] Ida is all that could be asked in the way of a sacred mountain, especially as it is seen from Phaistos, and it is a spreading shape, unlike the closed pyramid of Jouctas. That mountain is austere and lonely, shaped like a high tomb, suggesting alike the Cretan Zeus who came to sleep within it and the demanding destiny of the king who faced it. Ida, widely horned at the crest, is embracingly female, and it descends in rounded, spreading slopes which are cut by dark clefts. Around it stand its subsidiary peaks, escarpments, and cones, and the whole is thrown into the scale of deep space by the low arc of the hill in the middle ground, beyond which the *mons Veneris* opens in birth.

It has been suggested that the original entrance to the palace at Phaistos may have been at the south, where the hill is now eroded away.[19] (*Fig. 8*) If this was true Ida would have come instantly into view across the court as does Jouctas from the northern entrance at Knossos. However, the southern entrance seems unnecessary, since the present one on the northwest works so well. It is also the natural entrance from the southern sea, and on the approach to it the long axis of the palace comes into view, lying athwart the extended megaron of the Mesara, at once stressing the valley's width and completed by it. (*Fig. 7b*) From the northern stairway the view is carried directly across the west façade of the palace as finally completed and comes to rest among the hills across the valley, at the point where another mounded hill is backed by a double mountain. Moreover, the north–south stairway gives the impression of being on axis with the horns of Ida, so that the whole axis from Ida across the Mesara is controlled. (*Fig. 9*) (The photograph must be taken from the side because of the trees. This view of Ida may never have been partly blocked by buildings, though it would be, as at Knossos, from part of the court.) Here is another theatral area with its single–file pathways. One path comes in from the west and ends at a crosswalk which runs from the northern bank of steps or seats diagonally toward the southern extremity of the palace. It is as if the cross–axis which is the essence of the plan of both palace and landscape were being acted out before the entrance. (*Fig. 10*) That cross–axis is doubly important because of the two Ways which make it, one from the land, the other, coming eastward, from the sea. The latter, approaching from Phaistos' own port, must have been the major way, so that here as at Knossos (and also at Mallia and Gournia) the site expresses engulfment by the earth after leaving the sea and the palace is a forecourt for the fertile Mesara.

The propylon at Phaistos leads forward into the gloom of a narrow stair which turns right and downward toward the light and finally comes out into the court. To the right once more are the columns between walls and behind them the dark pillar shrine of the goddess. In the view northward from the south of the court Ida stands splendidly dominant on a continuation of the court's axis, and it rises directly over the entrance from the court to the northern apartments of the palace. (*Fig. 11*) This doorway is beautifully flanked by engaged columns and niches and, if the southern end of the court was, as the excavators believed, left open to the valley, then this entrance affirms another clear axis from Ida to the hills at the south. This may be why the niched and columned wall on both sides of it is, uniquely in Minoan planning, symmetrically balanced around its void. The walls frame the sacred natural object, and their columns stand in their niches before the cleft of the mountain. It is from the southern part of the court (where later a small Greek temple was placed) that the observer can best appreciate another of the qualities of Phaistos: the brilliance with which the builders solved their double problem of at once setting the palace so that the whole broad Mesara valley, running east and west, could be felt as one enclosing shape despite its size, and at the same time of keeping the main axis of movement under the control of horned Ida to the north. Thus the hill on which Phaistos is placed is high enough to keep Ida in view, and is indeed felt as high in relation to the plain directly below it. But when the whole great valley is viewed from the hill its elevation seems not dominating at all, but merely high enough to allow the entire enclosure of the valley to be perceived from it. The totality of the earth's fullness and the full sweep of its sky can therefore be felt at Phaistos, since two continuous landscape axes have been resolved into harmony. That harmony is especially compelling here, since, not containing the primary seat of power, Phaistos could aim the bull dance court directly at the horns of the mountain and celebrate that special gift with its columned wall.

Yet it is easy to understand why Knossos was traditionally the Minoan king's site: Knossos is single, set in a valley just wide enough for it, with a unique mountain both conical and horned, and with one axis clearly fixed by that presence, while Phaistos at once expands, clarifies, and elaborates the pattern, bringing the natural images of embracing divinity into union with what may at first seem almost a conscious desire for a liberating view. In that sense it is understandable that Phaistos has constantly been referred to as a "summer palace," but the term does not adequately describe its haunting power. Knossos is supremely official, a swarming town complex brought into order through the ritual of kingship; it is urban and does not brood. But Phaistos, above which dark Ida lowers, seems purposefully stretched out as an act of worship for all the land. Its contacts are wider and it gives itself wholly to them, possessed by the invincible mystery of the earth, praising the valley's breadth, the mountain's terror. At the same time one can comprehend why Agia Triada, between Phaistos and its port of Matala on the south coast, has generally been called a "villa" rather than a palace by most scholars.[20] It is backed against a curving hill and, after the addition of the east wing under Mycenaean domination, opened like a hinge to provide a ninety degree view which is anchored to the northeast by the horns of Ida and swings to the west beyond the coastal headlands toward the cone of Paksimadhia in the sea. (*Fig. 12*) Under Ida is another strong cone, more visible here than from Phaistos. Between Ida and the sea, Agia Triada invokes them both as a kind of spiritual dependency of each and a way station between them. Entrance to it would seem to have been by a stepped ramp along the north side of the southern wing or by the road from Phaistos which runs behind the eastern hill and approaches the villa from the south. Both these routes meet at the large stairway which acts as a spatial pivot for the two wings. The later Mycenaean megaron is set down in the south wing and oriented generally toward Paksimadhia. There seems to be no proper court, and, while the building is carefully adjusted to its balancing position between Ida and the sea, the final ensemble does not have the palatial completeness of Knossos or Phaistos. The reason for this now seems obvious, i.e. there were only so many places made ritually complete by the landscape, and only in those places would or could true palaces be built.

The supposition that palaces and their supporting towns were built at sites which most closely approximated the holy landscapes of Knossos and, secondarily, Phaistos, is borne out by an examination of the two "provincial" palaces of Mallia and Gournia. Traveling east from Knossos along the coast road, one comes into the curving plain of Mallia, with mountains to the south and the sea to the north. The plain is comparatively broad, long, and unprotected. Almost its whole length must be traversed before, at its eastern extremity, the hills begin to close ahead and a mounded hill with a split mountain behind it rises up to the south of the road. By this time the observer is used to the pattern. It is the site of Mallia;[21] but it has its own particular qualities as well. The approach toward the entrance to the palace, from the associated town to the west and north of it, shows at once that the plastic advances and recessions of its west façade are echoed almost exactly by the peaks and clefts of the mountains beyond it to the east, with a pyramidal peak conspicuous behind the largest central projection. (*Figs. 13, 14*) Another narrow pathway appears, approaching the palace from the west at its northern tip. The same pyramidal peak is on axis ahead. Within the entrance the way turns south, (*Fig. 15*) follows a fairly direct path (almost blocked at a later period by a shrine) and finally emerges at the northwest corner of a long court. Directly ahead lies the mounded hill and diagonally behind it the split mountain, opening into a deep cleft and enframing a second peak like a horned brow. It is Mount Dikte, a mighty bastion, and it contained a cave sanctuary of the goddess which was later to be celebrated as the refuge of the infant Zeus.[22] The diagonal line of sight from the entrance of the court at Mallia dramatizes the greater diagonals of Dikte's cleft as these open like hinged portals to reveal the godly summit. (*Figs. 13, 16*) The sight line itself falls across and is focused by a small offering table which is placed near the court's center. This table lies also directly between the pillared shrine on the west side of the court and the pyramidal mountain to the east, which was noticed earlier behind the main projection of the west façade and on axis with the entrance path. Moreover, the east wing of the palace was made up only of one–storied storerooms, probably not much higher than the low excavators' building which occupies part of the area at present. Thus the pyramidal hill to the east, and indeed that whole serrated range, would probably always have been visible from the west wing. The latter, on the other hand, behind which are no mountains but only the long, open coastal plain, was at least two stories high, with its shrine below and a wide stairway leading to the floor above, which must therefore have been of considerable importance. It may have contained the typical second story which was common to many Minoan shrines above their pillar crypts. Thus the west side of the palace would have formed one side of an enclosure and the eastern hills the other. Similarly, there were apparently also two stories in the northern wing. In this way the site, made holy by the mound and Dikte to the south but too open to the uninflected west and north, would have been given the desired enclosure with the constructed buildings completing a shape suggested by the eastern mountains themselves and, indeed, probably echoing their basic masses. In order for the scheme to work, the axis of the court had to be set parallel to that range, necessitating the diagonal line of sight toward Dikte. But the dynamic of that line, as we have seen, was also integral to the mountain's receding, opening fastnesses. Similarly, the small group of buildings which new excavation has laid bare well south of the palace are generally in line with the palace's west wing, and their courts seem also to be closely related to the mound and cleft to the south and the pyramid to the east.[23]

If the site of Mallia seems to require assistance from the building masses in order to create an adequate enclosure, the same can hardly be said for Gournia, where the natural megaron can be seen at its most closely embracing.[24] Gournia is located near the southern shore of the Gulf of Mirabello, in a pocket of landscape not far to the west of the horrid precipices and clefts which rise beyond Vasiliki. The town itself occupies a low ridge in the center of a deep valley. (*Fig. 17*) To the north the arms of the surrounding hills open to the gulf, and to the south rises a rocky knoll, directly behind which are two horns of hill. (*Fig. 18*) The small palace in the center of the town is oriented in this direction, again, like Knossos, toward the closed end of the natural megaron. It looks across the so–called "agora" of the town directly at the conical knob with the horns on exact axis behind it. To right and left of the horns in this view are sharp clefts, from which the hills rise up again on east and west and continue to the sea. A small shrine in the northern part of the palace complex is oriented generally toward the single direction where the enclosure dips slightly toward the northwest, behind which point a decidedly conical hill projects above the nearer ridge. This seems secondary, however, and at Gournia the sense of absolute enclosure by the earth is almost overpowering upon the observer.[25] I have again called Gournia's double hills "horns," but their image is at least ambiguous. They bear little relation to the far–off, splendid, and sharp peaks of Jouctas and Ida. Instead they are so close and rounded that a more proper analogy would seem to be directly to the female body itself, and they do closely resemble the uplifted breasts of the "goddess of the horizon," topping her horns or crotch beneath, as she was depicted in Egyptian art.[26] (*Fig. 19*) Indeed, at Gournia one has the inescapable impression that human beings are conceived of as children who lie upon the mother's body, enclosed by her arms and in the deep shadow of her breasts. One thinks of neolithic Seskoulo in Greece, to be referred to later, but Gournia has the deep space of the megaron valley, as well as the typically Minoan clarity of ritual focus and precise control. It seems to celebrate the power of the goddess of the earth, of whom man, like all other animals, is simply an adjunct, and to whose rhythms his whole desire must be to conform. In fact, to have come ashore at Gournia from the quarter circle of the harbor and to have walked from that point into the land toward the town, must have been an experience for ancient man comparable to that created by entering the roughly contemporary megalithic sanctuaries built in the shape of the goddess on the island of Malta.[27] (*Fig. 20*) It should perhaps be noted that three of these, the cluster at Mnaidra, seem to have some relationship to the island called "Filfla," which lies farthest out of the islets off the coast at that point and has a double–peaked profile. Similarly, the Maltese island of Gozo, containing the Gigantea, illustrated here, has been traditionally regarded on Malta itself as Calypso's island, the place of immortality in her cavern. Entering either the Maltese temples or the site of Gournia would doubtless have meant a return to the goddess and issuing forth a kind of renewal or rebirth. To sleep within such a goddess shape, as the votaries apparently did at Malta and as the whole population obviously did at Gournia, would itself have been a ritual act, an analogy for the actual death which would have implied its own kind of immortality since it meant a return to her. Such return and renewal, clearly celebrated by the Minoan burial chambers which culminate in the breast–shaped tholos tombs of the Mycenaean period,[28] must have been a constant reality in the everyday sleep and waking of Minoan Crete. Gournia is therefore one more indication of the Minoan capacity to form the whole of human life in accordance with nature by using the appropriate forms of the land to create meanings for which other peoples in other landscapes were impelled to construct special buildings.

Another problem is implicit in the Minoan system of landscape use, natural symbolism, and the forms of art. It is the possibility that specific landscape features were sometimes seen as the recognizable images of organic creatures, man, animal, or god, going far beyond, that is, the simpler and more generalized perception of a hill as "horned" or "breast–shaped" or of the earth as enclosing. The topic is a tricky and unsatisfactory one at best, but an insistence upon the recognition of such images in landscape is common in all popular folklore, crops up occasionally in Greek myth and landscape identifications, and was introduced into the literature of Cretan archaeology by Evans himself. He noted how, from the general direction of Tylissos, the profile of Mount Jouctas suggests that of a man's face turned toward the sky, and he tells us that the local population referred to it as "the head of Zeus."[29] (*Fig. 21*) There is no reference to it as such known from antiquity, but Evans surmised that the tradition might have gone back that far. It is true that the exterior corner of the L–shaped plan of the villa or villas at Tylissos, which otherwise opens in the opposite direction upon the foothills of Ida, much as does Agia Triada, is oriented directly toward this apparition, seen across the gently rolling hills between. With this in mind, one should return to Knossos and look briefly at three late Minoan monuments (all of them heavily restored, not to say rebuilt) which are nevertheless oriented directly at the only three unusual formations to be found on the slope east of the palace. All these formations might also have been read as images. Beginning from the south, there is built into the mounded hill before the palace the important funerary monument and temple known as the Temple Tomb.[30] We should remember that it is across the hill which contains this and other tombs that Jouctas is seen from the palace itself. Within the building a swaying axis leads from the exterior pavilion into a pillar crypt, beside which is a sepulchral chamber. A stairway leads to the shrine of the goddess above, now marked and possibly marked in antiquity with her horns. From this upper chamber, like a place of resurrection above the tomb, a view is afforded directly across the narrow valley toward a natural formation in the rock which looks something like a profile turned to its right, the observer's left. (*Fig. 22*) It is probably unprofitable to attempt to relate this ambiguous image to any specific forms in Minoan art (although an elusive secondary image, suggesting the head of a beaked creature like one of the griffins flanking the king's throne at Knossos, can be seen in it as well). However, one should point out that the shape as a whole formidably resembles a hatted man's head thrust aggressively forward, like those found in Hittite rock carvings, especially those which celebrate the king's yearly ritual death and resurrection in the gorge of Yasilikaya near Hattusas.[31] If there was a connection, as is certainly possible, between the Late Minoan rituals of Knossos and those of the Hittites, the recognition of such an image might have made the present location seem an eminently appropriate one for the tomb of a king. It would also furnish yet another example of the Cretan exploitation of natural features to express meanings achieved elsewhere by carved or constructed forms.

Slightly north of the temple tomb and also built into the mounded hill, is the so–called "High Priest's Tomb."[32] From its restored table altar, like those found in representations of the goddess' shrine, the view falls across the valley toward a natural formation of which the main outlines, at least, cannot have changed much since antiquity and for which the parallels in Minoan art are not difficult to find. (*Fig. 23*) The inclined head, the raised arms, the sinuous body, the flaring, tiered skirt, all resemble the figure of the goddess descending to her shrine or dancing with her votaries on Minoan gems.[33]

The last of the three monuments is the "Royal Villa."[34] Here again was a two–storied shrine with columns in antis, a niche with a table altar, a pillar crypt, and a view across the valley, at least from its upper floor. And elusively but unmistakably imprinted upon the surface of the facing hill is a contour which resembles a flaring set of bull's horns. (*Figs. 24, 62*) Minoan and, significantly enough, Hellenistic burials are grouped especially thickly in that area of the hill. It is just possible that its formation was in fact seen as expressive of the sacred horns during Minoan times and later. Certainly it would seem to have been holy. It is further possible, therefore, that the natural configurations themselves may have suggested some of the forms of Minoan art and have played a considerable part in creating the image of the goddess as she came to be portrayed. I do not insist upon these specific identifications, as I do upon the broader issues discussed earlier. But the formations in question are so striking when seen on the spot, and the precise orientation of the three special monuments upon them seems so much more than coincidental, that the points in question must be raised.

In a larger sense, the availability of sites such as Knossos and Phaistos, and secondarily of others such as Mallia and Gournia, must itself have been an important factor in creating the character of the goddess herself as the Minoans knew her. The horror which could surround some of her aspects as other civilizations imagined her would seem, from the available evidence, not to have been of much importance on Crete. Certainly she could shake the earth and may have so destroyed Knossos more than once.[35] But to the neolithic peoples who first came out of their caves to settle Knossos, and to whatever immigrants from Asia Minor may have arrived, the seemingly miraculous combination of natural megaron, mounded hill, and sacred horned mountain must have gone far toward creating that atmosphere of reverent security in which the free and joyful actions of men were for the first time ritually encouraged among the high civilizations of the ancient world. That freedom would of course have been a relative one and would have depended entirely upon an unquestioning acceptance of the goddess' power and of the dominant rhythms of her earth. It is exactly this acceptance which the great Minoan palace sites celebrate, as do the fluid, continuously curving forms of their figural art. In them the deepest traditions of Stone Age religion would seem to have been civilized, preserved, and renewed; neither frozen into a lifeless pattern nor twisted into diabolism. They could therefore be handed on from the remotest ages as a living legacy to the Hellenic world, and as the first component of its civilization.

One could wish to know more of neolithic and early Bronze Age landscape use in Greece itself before 2000 B.C., prior, that is, to any possible influence from the Minoan palaces, and prior to the arrival in Greece of the Indo–European peoples. When neolithic men, for example, first moved down into Greece as shepherds and farmers, did they already sense patterns in the landscape which could cause them to build in certain places and in certain ways for purposes of psychic rather than simply of physical security? The excavated remains are still too scanty to allow that question to be definitely answered now. It is true that more or less scanty evidence of neolithic and early Bronze Age habitation has been found in sites where important cities or cult places were later to develop: at Delos, Aigina, Corinth, the Argive Heraion, Mycenae, Tiryns, Nemea, Pylos, Boeotian Orchomenos, Athens, Brauron, and elsewhere. Yet in northern Greece the plains of Thessaly are dotted with scores of tiny mounds, not yet excavated but apparently demonstrating no special pattern of landscape use. It would seem, on the other hand, that settlements such as Seskoulo[36] in Thessaly and Malthi[37] in Messenia were deeply set into mounded and enclosing landscapes not so different in character from the small figurines of the goddess which their artists modeled and carved. Similarly, the site of Dystos[38] in Euboea, where there was later to be a classic and Hellenistic town, consisted of a purely conical hill concealed in a marshy valley surrounded by double peaks. (*Fig. 25*) Other sites, such as those of Dimini[39] in Thessaly and Lerna[40] and Asine[41] in the Argolid, are also related to landscape features of a type similar to those which were holy on Crete. The citadel at Dimini (*Fig. 26*) occupies a low mound in the plain within the embracing arms of the southern hills among which a conical height rises. Northward across the valley, which also sweeps eastward toward the gulf below Pagasae, two conical hills can be seen. At Asine, the town, containing Mycenaean and Hellenistic remains,[42] occupies a jagged height at the head of a deep bay, beyond which lie the islands of the gulf. Inland a strongly conical shaft of rock stands behind the gentler hills in which Mycenaean burials have been found.[43] At Lerna there may even be evidence of a cult in the gravelike tumulus, ringed with stones, which was raised over an early Bronze Age palace, the "House of the Tiles," after it burned.[44] Other sites, such as those of Agiorgitika and Asea in the central Peloponnesos, of Rafina and Askitario on the east coast of Attica, and of Melos, Naxos, and Paros among the islands, might be considered, but the evidence they offer is too scattered in place and time and too scanty in physical remains for any conclusions to be drawn from it. Among the neolithic and early Bronze Age settlements in Greece and the islands, therefore, no coherent pattern of landscape use can as yet be determined, although certain similarities to the method of Crete can be found.

The problem is well demonstrated by the siting of Troy.[45] Here was a site in continuous use from the Neolithic period onward and whose history was to bulk large in the Greek mind. Troy is set at the western tip of a finger of higher ground which projects into the flat valley of the Scamander. From the elevation of its citadel the whole wide arc of the horizon is visible, formed by low and gentle hills which define a full circle, in the center of which the town is set. Far to the southeast the western extremities of Mount Ida, tented and horned, can be seen in clear weather rising beyond the circle of the hills. Westward from the citadel the flat arc of the plain opens toward the Hellespont, beyond which the low, extended ridge of the Thracian Chersonese keeps the circle of the horizon complete. Farther in the distance two other greater forms rise beyond the arc: first, the long, serrated ridge of the island of Imbros, and behind it, seen only in the clearest weather but sometimes looming up unexpectedly large at sunset, the doubled peaks of Samothrace, the summits of Phengari, Mountain of the Moon. (*Fig. 27*) Phengari and Ida lie approximately opposite each other along an axis upon which the citadel is placed, and both were, or were to become, sacred mountains. Ida, in the Homeric Hymn, was Aphrodite's place, where she lay with Anchises of the Trojan royal house and produced the child, Aeneas, who was later to be claimed as its founder by Rome. The Homeric Hymn makes it clear that Aphrodite on Ida was the great goddess, deity alike of mountain and sea, of the wild beasts and of men.[46] Samothrace was to become the home of the Great Gods and the center of the mystery cult which was guarded by the Kabeiroi.[47] There, too, the central figure was the great mother herself. The site of Troy therefore lay within a vast but clearly formed circle beyond whose outer rim two great mountains sacred to the goddess rose. Yet no specific relationship can be found between these mountains and the remains of the architecture of any of the many periods of building at Troy: whether of the Neolithic period or the Early and Middle Bronze Ages, or of the Late Bronze Age of Priam's citadel. It is true that some of the Hellenic buildings of the post–Mycenaean periods, like the geometric pillar "house" and the Hellenistic theater, seem to bear some relationship to the farther forms, especially perhaps to a horned peak near the site of Neandria which is a conspicuous formation among the hills to the south. Otherwise, there are no indications in the orientation of the pre–Hellenic gates in the massive walls or of the various megara behind them that any relationship with the mountains was being sought. Because of this one cannot say surely that the site itself of Troy was considered holy during the pre–Hellenic, Neolithic and Bronze Age periods. Yet Troy certainly became a place of meaning and reverence for the Greeks, and it would seem to have been the primary symbol for them of the old order which their hero ancestors had overthrown. For them it was clearly the old city beyond all others, and the city of the goddess most of all: not of the new Athena who first deserted and then destroyed it, but of Aphrodite, once the great goddess of the earth and the waters, who defended it to the last and sent its seed to Rome. Clearly Troy was set in the center of the pure circle of her world with the heights of her horned mountains rising on favored days out of the haze beyond the hills and across the sea.

Another set of observations should be made concerning Bronze Age religious practice and landscape use outside of Greece, and these are relevant to an understanding of later Greek temple orientation. The significant point is that the shapes of the Cretan landscape offered both shelter and focus for ritual buildings. A revealing contrast can be made between their earth-focused orientation and the sky–focused holy places which were built elsewhere during the second millenium B.C. The stone and wood circles constructed by neolithic and Bronze Age peoples on the downs of southern England are contemporary with the Cretan palaces.[48] Certain evidences of similar cult traditions would further seem to link these monuments with the same ancient impulses out of which the religion of Crete had grown. In the concentric circles of Stonehenge, Woodhenge, Avebury, and elsewhere, for example, a labyrinthine principle would appear to have had at least something to do with the design.[49] (*Figs. 28–33*) Axe blades or daggers have been discovered incised upon some of the stones of Stonehenge,[50] and there, too, the antlers of deer, used for digging and for trimming stone, have been found buried in the surrounding ditch.[51] The avenue of menhirs which marches across the downs from the embracing stone circle of Avebury to the tight grove of stones and posts which has been called the "Sanctuary," (*Fig. 30*) moves across the contours in such a way as to form a shape which has suggested, perhaps wrongly, a flaring horn to some observers.[52] More obviously, the Sanctuary and the raised bank of earth around Avebury both have in view the coned tumulus mound of Silbury, the largest artificial tumulus yet discovered in Europe. (*Fig. 29*) From the rings of Avebury itself the tumulus is out of sight, but from the Sanctuary, reached through the serpentine curve of the menhir avenue, the mound rises into view out of a gentle cleft in the downs, and its flattened top is now set exactly at the level of the western horizon. (*Fig. 30*) Such placing of architectural elements in order to bring the distant, empty horizon into focus from the holy place is characteristic of the sacred architecture of the downs and seems to bear only a distant relationship to that focus upon the slot of the horned mountain which was typical of the palaces of Crete.

We may speculate here upon the meeting of northern and southern traditions, in which the megalithic structural methods of the Mediterranean, which had been used there, as at Malta, (*Fig. 20*) Sardinia, and elsewhere, to create earth sanctuaries and tombs, and which had been carried to the north in this form and for these purposes by Bronze Age "missionaries,"[53] were now being used for other purposes as well by a northern people who had developed a religion dominated by the sky. Certainly the English downs form a landscape which celebrates the power of the sky, and they create the ideal setting for religious monuments which, unlike those of Crete, seem intended to invoke not only the earth but the heavens. From the heights of the downs the whole horizon swings in a circle, with no mountains rising up to seize the vision and arrest its swing. The earth seems to arch up gently, wholly open to the sky. (*Fig. 31*) It is true that whole villages, unsuspected from the heights, can lie concealed in the folds of the downs, embraced by the earth, but for these, too, no special focus will be offered; they are set in simple bowls. For all these reasons attention is directed toward the sky, and the sacred places of Stonehenge, Woodhenge, and Avebury's Sanctuary are set upon the mounded platforms of the higher land. It is true that great Avebury is set lower, but here the principle of the bowl, to be found later in Greece at sites sacred to Zeus, would seem to have been consciously developed. (*Fig. 28*) The wide outer circle of stones, covering an area vaster than that of any other site yet excavated, was set upon a platform above an encircling ditch, the earth from which was used to ring the whole site with a high mound. The labyrinthine circles within the vast outer ring of stones could thus all have been seen from above, but from the platform among the shafts nothing could have been visible but the clear circle of the mound and the sky above it. Yet out of this contained universe of purely human geometry, visually related only to the rhythmic paths of the celestial bodies above, a procession could have passed through the curving avenue to reach the height of the Sanctuary, with its man–made grove around its conical hut, and have had visible from that place the mound of Silbury and the wider circle of the natural horizon.

That circle of the downs seems widest and purest when seen from Stonehenge. (*Figs. 31–33*) Upon the mounded height at that place the stones are grouped in ever–tightening rings, until the vertical menhirs of the great trilithons are set so close together that the human body can only edge between them, rubbed on breast and back by the stones. The U–shaped group of trilithons faces northeast, slightly south of the point on the horizon where the sun rises on mid-summer day, and a flat altar stone is set in their embrace. (*Fig. 32*) From this the eye is led out between the circles toward the so–called "Heel Stone" far out in the avenue beyond the outer ditch, and this lonely menhir, itself leaning forward toward the sanctuary, is of such a height that its top also lies exactly upon the horizon, close to the point where the sun rises on midsummer day. (*Fig. 33*) It is true, as Atkinson has pointed out, that the sun could never have risen exactly at that point on the day of the summer solstice. It would always have risen there, then as now, a few days before and a few days after midsummer day itself. This, in fact, might lead to the conclusion, not that the axis from altar to Heel Stone was of no celestial importance, but instead that it was intended to mark the days which began and ended a festival of some duration—as any festival which was celebrated by a large gathering of cattle raisers and agriculturists would have had to be. Similarly, looking from the Heel Stone in the op-posite direction, the eye of the participant is led over the altar to the narrow opening in the great trilithon behind it, which may have framed a sacred sunset.[54] Other relationships at Stonehenge with sunrise and sunset on equinoctial days have been discovered between stones 91 and 93 and mounds 92 and 94. These are all set close to the outer ditch, and lines drawn connecting them would intersect the central altar.[55]

The orientation of the neolithic and Bronze Age monuments of the English downs is thus more to the sky than to the land, and they are set as man–made circles in the center of a circu-lar universe. The earth around them is as unfocused as the sea, except where, as at Silbury, con-structed points of focus are made, and it is among the heavenly bodies that they seek their larger pattern of order. The palaces of Crete, on the other hand, though oriented roughly north–south, their courts thus flooded with winter sun, seem directed not primarily toward the sky but toward the eye–fixing forms of mountains, and they are placed in a landscape which is not circular but, in its natural megara, essentially oblong and unilinear. Consequently, these two forms of reverence, while related to each other in their common impulse to adjust to the natural order of things, are apparently opposite to each other in their fundamental preoccupa-tions. The Greeks, as should be obvious later, were to attempt to adjust the orientation of their temples in relation both to the forms of the earth and the patterns of the sky, and were to place an oblong sacred building in a world which was felt as essentially circular[56] but which also had two points of focus, the rising sun and the sacred landscape shape. Two ancient forms of reverence and conceptions of the universe were, in this way, to be combined in the Greek tem-ple, and the reconciliation of these opposites, as of others, was to play a part in the wholeness of its expressive life.*

---

* But see now Preziosi for a union of solar and landscape orientation in Minoan palaces. Above, note to Preface, pp. x and xi. Preziosi's *Architec-tural Design in Bronze Age Greece* will be pub-lished shortly by the Connecticut Academy of Arts and Sciences.

Chapter 3

THE GODDESS AND THE LORDS

See there, see there! Keep from his mate the bull.
Caught in the folded web's
Entanglement she pinions him and with the black horn
Strikes...

Aeschylus, AGAMEMNON (Lattimore)[1]

THE INDO–EUROPEANS, speaking an early form of Greek, who moved down into the Greek peninsula shortly after 2000 B.C., were soon in contact with the culture of Crete, and they may have sacked Knossos about 1550 B.C. and conquered the island as a whole about 1400 B.C.[2] It now appears that there was no true break between Middle and Late Bronze Ages in Greece, although a rising pattern of aggressiveness seems to characterize the later centuries of the second period, whose culture is generally referred to as Mycenaean and whose later phases were directed by the most aggressive group of all, the Achaians. Yet it is clear that the warrior heroes who were first the chiefs of the Hellenic war bands and then the lords of the citadels were profoundly receptive to Minoan culture, and it would appear that they were either eager to see themselves or were anxious that their subjects should see them as ritual kings who ruled through the power and under the protection of the great goddess.[3] Their cousins, the Dorians, who eventually overthrew them, were clearly impatient of the power of the goddess and strove to curb it. But the earlier groups may even have brought her worship with them, and obvious similarities between their culture and that of the Hittites of Asia Minor, a stronghold of the goddess, serve to reinforce that supposition. The colossal, seated Hittite goddess, carved in the living rock high on the side of Mount Sipylos within the horned cleft of one of its ridges, indicates the importance of her worship in Asia Minor and the kind of natural formation which was felt to be her proper abode.[4] In any event, the Middle and Late Bronze Age settlements on the mainland of Greece begin to show a pattern of placement and orientation in relation to landscape formations, similar to those sacred on Crete, which was to be developed further in later Greek sacred sites. At the same time, the tablets in Linear B characters from Pylos, Mycenae, and Knossos now tell us that, certainly after 1600 B.C. and probably earlier, many of the special Greek gods were already present.[5] Among these were Zeus, Hera, Poseidon, Athena, Artemis, Hermes and, it would now appear, Dionysos. Hephaistos is doubtful. Apollo as "Paiawon" (Paian) is probable; so too is Ares as "Enualios." The supreme deity, however, would seem to have been Potnia, so named the "Mistress," and invoked at Knossos as "Our Lady of the Labyrinth." At Pylos she was hailed as "Divine Mother," and most of the surviving dedications of offerings there are to her and Poseidon, apparently her consort and possibly identified with the living king himself. This curious anomaly, replete with creative tension for the future, of individual warrior chiefs whose Indo–European pantheon of gods was already in the making but who still wor- shiped the goddess of the earth and of peace as the dominant power, is amply demonstrated by their buildings and most of all by the sites where they placed them. These tell us why the Bronze Age lords were the hero ancestors of the later Greeks, daimonic intermediaries with the gods: first, because they made systematic contact with the sacred earth; second, because some of them were eventually forced, by their own necessity for action, to contest the goddess' earthly domin- ion with her and to seize her places of power for their own. Out of that tragic confrontation the richest fabric of Greek myth took form, and some of the greatest sites, like that of Mycenae itself, document it with their forms. Finally, the inevitable death of the heroes, defeated in the end by the earth, gave a new sanctity to the already sacred places where the terrible encounter had occurred. Having come to grips with the earth, they became—in return and though dead— the receptacles and transmittors of its powers.

The major house type of the Middle Bronze Age was a long rectangle, open at one end and closed in a semicircular or apsidal form at the other. Such houses, called "hairpin megara," can be found at Thermon in Aetolia, Olympia in Elis, and Korakou north of Acrocorinth, as well as at Lerna in the Argolid, and at other places.[6] Thermon is a remote, not easily accessible site, set in a protected bowl high in the formidable mountains above Lake Trichonis.[7] A rug- ged hill rises directly over the site on the east, but the bowl itself is a long ellipse running north and south and containing a sacred spring in its hollow. (*Figs. 229, 230*) Far to the north a high pyramidal peak can be seen; to the south the bowl closes in two low, gentle, conical hills. The megaron is set in the fold of the site under the eastern hill. Its long axis echoes that of the earth shape in which it is placed, its apsidal rear closed against the long view to the north and its open end oriented slightly to the right of the conical mounds to the south. (*Figs. 229, 230*) As at Knossos, the building is enclosed by the natural shape and focuses toward the nearer hills, which are also mounded. Unlike Knossos, however, the building is itself not labyrinthine but essentially single. Although there were apparently a few subsidiary structures, the great megaron is a separate unit, probably housing the individual head of the family or the tribe. Thermon is thus more personal than the major Minoan sites and does not express the same vast collective oneness with the goddess which was theirs.[8]

At Olympia the hairpin megara, all much smaller than the chieftainly example at Thermon, are again oriented north and south, like all the Minoan palaces.[9] (*Fig. 264*) This time the open end is toward the north, facing the conical hill which was always to remain the dominant natural feature of the holy precinct of the Altis. (*Fig. 263*) The later Greeks were to call it the "Hill of Kronos," father of Zeus, but they maintained a sanctuary of Gaia, the earth, on its western slope, so that, before the coming of Herakles, the Dorian or proto–Dorian hero, the whole hill was probably sacred to the goddess and the site was already holy.[10] A break seems to have occurred between the Middle Bronze Age megara at Olympia and the later Greek cult on the site. At Korakou,[11] near Corinth, the hairpin megaron faces south toward another of the symbols of the goddess, in this case the great sweeping horns of the north face of Acrocorinth. (*Fig. 170*) Upon Acrocorinth, too, and under it, several important Greek cults were later to make their homes. At Lerna,[12] with the old, burned "House of the Tiles" reposing under its tumulus and its ring of stones, the hairpin megaron faced generally toward the hill of Palamedes above Nauplion, to which we shall return later in our consideration of the site of Tiryns.

The sacred formations of the Greek landscape thus seem to have first been brought into human focus as such during Middle Bronze Age times. Consequently, before considering the citadels and lordly megara of the Mycenaean Peloponnesos, where there are architectural remains in abundance to discuss, we must know those other sacred formations which have some related Bronze Age remains or associations. (Aigina, Delos, and Delphi, which are included among such sites, can best be discussed in subsequent chapters.) Their natural symbols created the meaning of the Greek landscape as the later Greeks were to recognize, worship, and use it, and around them some of the greatest myths were formed.

Attica was favored by them most of all. On its east coast, north of Cape Sounion, lies Thorikos, made up of two conical hills, the southern one much the larger and seen from the south as a perfect single cone. (*Fig. 116*) But the profile of the two together can also be read from east or west as a pair of horns. (*Fig. 115*) Upon and under this double symbol was a Mycenaean settlement of houses and tombs.[13] It was obviously seen as a chthonic force of unusual potency, because under it, in the fifth century, was built a unique structure which was apparently a sanctuary of Demeter and Kore.[14] Greek tradition had it that Cretans themselves had built at Thorikos[15] and worked the silver mines at Laurion nearby.[16] The Minoans at home, however, in a state of profound peace, would never, like the Mycenaeans here, have built upon the goddess' symbolic hill but rather, as we have seen, below it and in view of it.

Attica's primary sacred mountain was Hymettos, and we shall move toward it first from the east and then from the west, the Athenian side. Thorikos was out of sight of its most critical formations, but northwest of Thorikos was the site of Mycenaean Spata,[17] in the center of an east Attic plain which was ringed with the symbols of the goddess. (*Fig. 34*) To the east, behind low hills, the horned mountain called Perati rises. Under it lies Brauron with its Early Bronze Age settlement, below which, in later times, was to be an important sanctuary of Artemis.[18] To the northeast, across the gulf, the horned peak of Ocha swims mightily into view whenever heat haze or cloud relax their hold on Euboea. To the west of Spata a long hump like a whale's back rises out of the plain, and directly behind it the northern part of the ridge of Hymettos is peaked up into a sharp and widespread pair of horns. (*Figs. 34, 35, 148*) Under the northern horn, on the side toward Spata, is a cave now used by shepherds and the subject of their legends. These connect the place with a Hellenistic marble lion, the remains of an otherwise unknown tomb monument, which rests near the church of Kantza on the plain below and whose lair the cave is supposed to have been.[19] Antique, primarily Roman, sherds have been found near its entrance, but the floor is deep in sheep droppings and has not yet been excavated.[20] The northern horn of the mountain, above the cave, has a natural and sharply pointed outcropping of rock on its peak. (*Fig. 35*) The southern horn had a less precise peak, but at some period a conical, solid tumulus–like structure of rough but well fitted stones was built on top of it, giving it thereby the pointed character of the other. Indeed the tumulus, small though it is, decisively affects the character of the southern horn as seen from across the plain. (*Fig. 34*) The date of the mound is difficult to determine. It now supports a concrete survey marker, and one might thereby be tempted to regard it as comparatively recent except for the fact that Hellenistic sherds can be picked up in and around it.[21]

The western slope of Hymettos, that looking toward Athens, sweeps back between the horns in a decisive arc, and in the center of that concave curve stands a large, menhir–like pier of natural rock. (*Fig. 35*) The relation of this natural marker and pillar to the horns which enframe it is striking. No signs of cuttings in the rock or of sherds have been discovered near the vertical pillar itself, and of course no precise conclusions can be drawn from it, but the curious and decisive natural juxtaposition of the Minoan pillar and horns seems worthy of note. It seems especially worth remembering when one mounts the Acropolis in Athens and discovers that the archaic temple of Athena Polias, of the middle of the sixth century B.C., is oriented directly between the horns and thus almost exactly upon the pillar, though the latter is not itself visible at that distance. (*Fig. 35*) Seen from the site of the temple, the profile and massing of that part of Hymettos somewhat resemble Mount Ida as viewed from Phaistos. Below the horns and to the south of them under the bulk of Hymettos a number of swelling, conical foothills are clearly visible from the temple. (*Figs. 36, 37*) Among them was later to be built the sanctuary of Aphrodite near the spring at Kaisariani,[22] so that they, too, were clearly sacred to the goddess from an early date. Thus, if Greek tradition was correct in placing the temple of Athena as guardian of the city—and, in this temple, in her more chthonian aspect—upon the old palace of Erechtheus, the mythical Mycenaean king of Athens, and if the two bases which are now on the site were in fact the stone bases for Mycenaean wooden columns in antis,[23] (*Fig. 36*) then the megaron of the early Greek chieftain was placed exactly as one would have expected it to be: to make the most of the view toward the conical hills and the sacred horns of the mountain, lioness and bull, that lay across his world.

More, therefore, than any other place in Attica, the site of Mycenaean Athens must from the earliest period have been both the physically and spiritually secure place in the Athenian plain, having as it did both the proud and defensible hill to hold and the sacred symbols of the earth to focus upon. Its Acropolis was never taken by the Dorians, so that the roots of Athens in the ancient sanctity of its place were especially strong and undisturbed. Therefore the growth which they nourished was apparently continuous and could come to a special kind of flower in classic times.[24] (*Fig. 37*)

Westward from Athens, reached by what was to become the Sacred Way through the pass of Daphni (which will be traversed more slowly later) opens the plain of Eleusis. Toward its western extremity is the low, mounded acropolis of the Mycenaean town and sanctuary of Eleusis itself.[25] This is set opposite a wide and sharp cleft in the hills on the island of Salamis, and directly beyond and above Eleusis to the west, the split peak of Mount Kerata ("horns") stands out against the sky (*Figs. 120–122, 127*) The site of what were to be the great Greek mysteries of the goddesses of the fertility of the earth and of the afterlife was thus clearly marked with the critical landscape symbols—here named as well—and it was a holy place in Mycenaean times, its tiny shrine facing east like the later Telesterion, toward the cleft at

Daphni through which the processions to it wound.[26] Similarly, the site of Mycenaean Minoa, farther west, where the name itself may again be of significance, is a low mound by the shore.[27] Its view to the north is focused by the twin, rounded hills of the later Megara, where there was also to be a megaron of Demeter and where the name, too, may once more be as significant as the form.[28] To the east of Megara the horns of Kerata and the notch of Salamis, from this direction supremely hornlike also, define Minoa's view. (*Fig. 38*)

North of Attica and the Megarid, beyond the high pass from Eleusis to Erythrai, lies the fertile plain of Boeotia which harbored Mycenaean Thebes, rich in legend and in the raw material of classic tragedy, about which the Theban landscape itself can tell us much.[29] The traveler from the south will not see the city until the last moment, even though from above Erythrai it had appeared that the whole Boeotian plain was clearly visible. Thebes is a hidden city, closely set into the deep folds of the land, as are Knossos or Seskoulo. On the northern side it is more open, but even when approaching from this direction one is finally surprised at the size of the city and the actual height of its acropolis hill, since intervening folds of the land had allowed only a small portion of it to be visible before. From the north, however, it can be seen that Thebes is set on a mounded hill near the southern end of its enclosing valley and that directly on axis to the south rise the notched cleft, the broad horns, and the rounded masses of Mount Cithairon, below which the Heraion of Plataia was later to be placed. (*Figs. 39, 111*) The siting of Thebes was therefore exactly Minoan, focused across the rolling hills toward the sacred mountain.

The acropolis of Thebes was the traditional site of the palace of the mythical Cadmus,[30] and later a temple of Demeter was upon it,[31] while the lower hill to the east received the oracular temple of Ismenion Apollo.[32] Upon the first view of the city from the south, it also becomes apparent that the problem of the specific image in landscape, a problem touched upon in connection with Cretan siting, must be considered once more. Directly north of the city is a hill which looks very much like a crouching Egyptian sphinx, headless, and looming over the city itself. (*Fig. 40*) The mountain, Phaga, which has been identified as the haunt of the Sphinx whom Oedipus conquered, lies, however, well west of Thebes above the southern shore of Lake Copais.[33] Its profile is that of a mighty pair of horns or wings, which loom over the lake when seen from that side but which are not to be seen from the direction of Thebes. (*Fig. 41*) They would thus have faced Oedipus as he approached Thebes from Delphi and could themselves have suggested the legend of the Sphinx who flew down upon men from the mountain, since they seem, in fact, to be rising darkly and taking wing. Indeed, all of southern Boeotia is haunted by mighty landscape shapes which are suggestive of the goddess and before which men were presumably helpless until Oedipus faced them down. In all probability such natural formations assisted in giving birth to the special legends of Thebes. The story of Oedipus takes on special point here, insofar as the female sphinx herself is an aspect of the power of the goddess of nature. The reading of her riddle by Oedipus thus becomes a typically heroic tale of the questioning of that power by the aggressive and critical faculty in men. Similarly, hero shrines of Herakles, whose struggle with Hera was continuous and who ruled Thebes until the goddess drove him mad, were to ring Boeotia, set into folds of the hills around the plain.[34]

Farther to the right in the view across Thebes from the south, Mount Hypatos stands over the city. (*Fig. 40*) Its rocky top is cleft and horned, and, Pausanias tells us, a temple with an image of Supreme Zeus was later placed upon it.[35] But the volume which the opening shape of Hypatos creates might easily have been seen as a chariot car, possibly identified with, or again even suggesting, the one in which the doomed seer Amphiaraus was standing when he was swallowed up by the earth before the gates of Thebes.[36] The mass of Hypatos has, moreover, the curious quality of seeming to yawn open and the shape at its top of sinking into it. Because of this Hypatos itself may be the landscape object which gave the name, Harma (chariot) to an ancient town on its southeastern flank which, so the Tanagraeans claimed, marked the spot of Amphiaraus' disappearance.[37] Again, south of Hypatos and east of Thebes stretches a range of hills which looks like a dead man lying on his back, his head toward Thebes, his skyward–pointing profile seen clearly from the plain.

Below Thebes, the plain of Boeotia opens in a flattened V–shape, its eastern arm stretch-ing toward Euboea, its western toward Lebadeia. Between the arms rises the mountain strong-hold of Mount Ptoon, the form of which suggests that it was the Boeotian throne of the great goddess, whose power was to be usurped there by Apollo.[38] (*Figs. 191–192*) Within the mountains lie hidden lakes, and during much of antiquity part of the western arm of the Boeotian plain was itself under water, forming Lake Copais. Here the wings of Pausanias' sphinx mountain rise with the horns of Ptoon to the east behind them, (*Fig. 41*) but if we re-turn to Thebes itself we can see that the lionlike mass of the other "sphinx" mountain lies di-rectly between Ptoon and the city, and its crouching body shelters the hidden lake of Trikeri, above which Ptoon rises. (*Fig. 40*) In this way the sphinx–lion and the winged female sphinx of the goddess both guard her place, and from both formations the horned notch of Cithairon can also be clearly seen to the south beyond Thebes. (*Fig. 39*) We can have little doubt that Mycenaean Thebes, set as it was among such forms, was holy and more than a little dread: the sacred, dark, and ominous Thebes of the legends, where the power of the goddess was en-compassing and awful and the struggles of the hero–kings with her especially severe.

On the northern shore of the ancient Lake Copais was the site of Boeotian Orchomenos, a "Minyan" site.[39] Here, too, antiquity seems to have seen images in the landscape, since the long ridge at the low point of which Orchomenos was placed was called Akontion, or Javelin.[40] (*Fig. 42*) It does resemble a tapering, leaf–shaped blade, but, such is the ambiguity implicit in attempting to identify images of this type, it also resembles the profile of a man with deep eye sockets and a long beard, at the tip of which the town lies. This image is equally impressive when the drowned head is seen from across the modern plain which was Lake Copais. (*Fig. 43*) Perhaps the legends of cannibalism which surrounded the mythical king Athamas of Orcho-menos related to the positioning of his town before the mouth of a Kronos image.[41] Yet the position of Orchomenos can be explained in the more usual terms. It looks up a gentle ridge toward the split rock ledges at the top, and its view across Copais includes the horned peaks of Ptoon and Hypatos. In this sense Orchomenos is in fact a javelin, and its head is thrust into the waters of the lake toward the holy sites to the southeast. If the very early Greek temple or megaron on the site of the present cemetery marks the position of the major Mycenaean mega-ron,[42] as similar structures were supposed to have done at Thebes, more or less do at Tiryns and Mycenae, and probably do at Athens, then the king's megaron itself was in the optimum position, at once dominating the town, under the rock ledges, and exposed to the southern view. The later temple of Asklepios was placed higher to increase the panoramic effect, and the walls of the Hellenistic town climbed all the way to the peak of Akontion.

The great "Minyan" fortress was on an island in a bay near the eastern shore of Lake Copais. It would seem to have been occupied for only a short period and then only in times of pressing danger. This is Gla,[43] of which the ancient name is unknown,[44] unless it can be identified, as Noack believed, with the Arne that was mentioned by Homer. Reasons of purely physical security would seem to have governed the placement of this huge citadel, whose walls enclosed the whole island to form an enceinte much larger than those of Tiryns or Mycenae. It is true that Gla, when approached from across the plain which was Lake Copais, can be seen as lying beneath the wide horns or arms of the farther mountains behind it. This great image may have been imagined as rising above the citadel like an earth presence which signaled the scattered population around the lake to the protection of the walls. But from the site the image disappears, and the defender is left alone within the rather mournful circle of the hills, (*Fig. 44*) close to the sacred Mount Ptoon to the south but not in view of its critical formations. Across what would have been the shimmering forecourt of Copais serrated ridges rise before Helicon to the west, and the snows of Parnassos gleam above the horizon. Yet the curious, double–ended palace, with its two megara, seems to focus upon nothing in particular, and the citadel as a whole floats—as its needs probably forced it to do—without links to the land. This quality of detachment, almost unique in Greece at Gla, seems to arise not primarily from the fact that Gla is an island but because, unlike sacred Athens or Thebes, its site was never conceived of as a permanent, holy place, and the sacred symbols of the earth were therefore ignored in its placement. Its mighty walls, and its watchtowers upon Ptoon and around the lake, could not protect it in the end from the iron swords of the Dorian invaders. When it fell, no other Hellenic buildings of any kind were built there, and its very name was lost. Though it stood in plain sight it was avoided through the centuries. Desperate and fated as it was, its very lack of touch with the earth may also have been regarded by the Greeks as making of it something unworthy and even shameful, better abandoned and unsung.

It was quite otherwise with the Mycenaean settlements in the Peloponnesos. We have already mentioned the Middle Bronze Age megara at Olympia and Korakou. The scattered groupings that were to become historic Sparta were all set in the great natural megaron of the valley of the Eurotas, with the aggressive masses, the gloomy clefts, and the widespreading horns of Mount Taygetus looming over them. (*Figs. 45–47*) There the human position is unmistakably stated: the rich land in the fold of the earth, from which the goddess gives forth her plenty, and the towering peaks above it where the terror and majesty of her presence are always manifest. The valley of the Eurotas essentially makes a single shape. It can hardly be divided, and under Taygetus any walled city would have looked absurd. The earth creates the form in which life must be lived, and the form there is unchanging but tense, juxtaposing as it does the hollow valley and the jagged peaks. Many of the elements which were to make Spartan life what it eventually became—agrarian, closed–minded, disciplined—are explicit in the Spartan landscape, and its goddesses are perennially present there: Helen, soft and giving but the caryatid who upholds the world, Artemis, harsh and free but demanding upon men.

The whole route into the valley of the Eurotas is a progressive experience of the power of the goddess. From the northern pass the heavy, somber masses of Taygetus which lie above the gorge of the Magoula first rise into view. They voice a pure threat. Beyond them, south of the gorge, the peaks rise higher into sharper forms, one of the most expressive of these being a pointed peak from which the ridge sweeps out like the embracing arms of the goddess herself enframing her high but tiny head as in Mycenaean figurines.[45] Below the head and arms the mountain makes a deep hollow, so that the image as a whole calls to mind those early Greek terracottas in which the goddess is herself a throne.[46] Below the peaks the forward masses of the mountain advance toward the plain, heavy and barren formations, separated by deep gorges. They are the aggressive guardians of the mountain's higher fastnesses, like lions before the throne. Medieval Mistra was to be placed upon one of them. (*Fig. A*)

The place called Therapne, from which the mountain and the valley of the Eurotas can best be seen, would also appear to have been the holiest spot in Laconia during Mycenaean times. It is the site of the Menelaion, where the hero shrine of Menelaus and Helen was placed during the early archaic period[47] upon the debris of Lakedaimon, Menelaus' seat of power.[48] Although the remains presently visible on the spot are of a small fifth–century temple set upon a high base and replacing an earlier archaic temple on the site, still the recognition of the potency of the place is Mycenaean in origin, and it should therefore be discussed now. The Menelaion occupies one of several mounded hills, heavy with bee sounds and the song of birds, which line the east side of the valley of the Eurotas. (*Fig. 45*) The hill of the Menelaion is not the highest or the furthest projecting of these mounds, but it is the central one and the most perfect in shape. The remains of the later temple upon its high, deeply stepped platform still give the impression, when seen from the valley or from the other hills, of a nipple on a breast.

Other considerations would also seem to have governed the choice of the central hill. It is exactly on axis with a tremendous cleft in the bastions of Mount Taygetus across the way. (*Fig. 46*) The cleft is edged with sharp ribbons of rock like the twisted horns of the goats which throng the foothills of the mountain itself and which were to be especially sacred to Artemis. Behind the cleft the high peaks of Taygetus rise in set after set of profiled horns. From the ridge to the east of the Menelaion the platform of the temple is seen as framed exactly in the V of the cleft, with the masses of Taygetus spreading out north and south from it to define the whole length of the natural megaron of the valley. The cult was thus placed opposite an appropriate formation of the mountain and in the spot where not only the maximum majesty of the whole range but also the fullest extent of the valley could best be experienced. In the terrible presence of Taygetus one can also understand the relation of Helen to Aphrodite, in whose aspect the old goddess was to retain during later Greek times her attributes of irresistible power. From the Menelaion, too, one can see down into the river bottom where the temple of Artemis Orthia was later to be placed under the especially embracing, throned section of the mountain's ridge mentioned earlier.[49] Beyond it is the low hill, the acropolis of historic Sparta, where the temple of Athena Chalkioikis was to be placed in a rather different relationship to the same formation.[50] But Mycenaean Sparta also had its centers well to the south, near the mounded hill of Amyklai where the colossal figure of Apollo was raised in archaic times.[51] (*Fig. 47*) The relation of Amyklai to Taygetus is again one of maximum acceptance of the power of the goddess.

Opposite looms the most horrendous formation of the range: a great mass which thrusts up between two savage clefts, behind which the highest peaks stand vertical and remote in their snow. To the south lies the flat–topped butte of Vaphio. Across all, the mountain casts early shadow, the plain darkling like its pottery from tan to soft black.

West of Laconia, near the southwestern tip of Messenia, lies the coastal valley which was the traditional site of the Pylos of Nestor.[52] The entrance to the valley from the east is dominated by a tremendous conical hill, really a mountain of extraordinarily regular form. Another range of mountains rises and falls behind it, and this lifts up out of its lowest ridge to terminate in a rocky peak. The whole mass is now called Mount Mathia. The approach to the site of the Mycenaean palace which its exacavators have attributed to Nestor,[53] caused this curious formation, now well to the south, to drop out of sight. But as the road rose up the long ridge where the palace was placed with noble Mount Aigalion heraldic behind it the conical hill and its backing of mountains rose clearly up as well, to form the dominant feature of the southern horizon. (*Fig. 48*) The symbols of the goddess were explicit: the cone or mound and the horns seen across intervening swells of land.

The axis of the megaron of Nestor's palace runs north and south, and the entrance faces south to a point slightly to the right of the horns. (*Figs. 48, 49*) It is not oriented precisely at them, but from the courtyard they are clearly in view. Within the inner chamber the lord's throne was backed against the east wall opposite the great central hearth. Thus the lord, like the king at Knossos, faced across the short axis of his megaron, here not toward the horns but toward his own fire, which itself burned roughly on axis with them. This is a fundamental difference from Crete. The lord's hearth, center of his personal household, is set as the counterbalance to the earth's forms. His Late Bronze Age megaron as a whole has now become wide and rectangular and has a vestibule and a porch with columns in antis. A court, as here, may serve to extend the entrance axis. The megaron itself is now embedded in the labyrinth but retains its identity as a separate shape. Its hearth room remains inviolable as the columned hall of the lord, but its vestibule is penetrated by side passages which run wholly around the megaron as labyrinthine ways leading to other cavelike enclosures. So the Mycenaean megaron–palace, adopting some of the methods of Crete, has changed them, and now celebrates its own more personal ritual of kingship under the goddess. She confirms the lord's power, but the promise of individual security which he desires of her seems equally clear.

That important theme can be carried further. Slightly to the east of Nestor's main megaron there is a small chamber which opens to the south and has an altar placed before it. (*Fig. 49*) It has therefore been identified by its excavators as a shrine.[54] From the chamber, the sight line across the altar places the great conical hill to the south directly on axis. (*Fig. 50*) (A tree is again in the way at present, but it is hoped that the schematic drawing can be accepted as indicating what the relationship of altar to mountain actually is.) The chamber, the altar, the conical hill, and the horns together form the architecture of the shrine. This seems a fact of profound importance, since the goddess as seen in the landscape is both mirrored and fixed by the chamber and the altar and is thus being brought as a kind of actual guest into the palace of the king: the "Divine Mother," whom he, with Poseidon, served. Moreover, a short distance farther to the east, beyond the palace confines, is the lord's conical tholos tomb, now repaired by the excavators.[55] (*Fig. 51*) It and the conical hill, which is still in view to the south as always, have the same shape. And we should point out once more that Mount Jouctas, south of Knossos, has it, too. Did the tholos develop from Jouctas, which therefore became, for the Greeks, the tomb of Zeus? The Cretan king had his natural cone, and late Minoan sepulchral chambers may themselves have been developing toward that shape before the dominance of the Mycenaeans in Crete, but the latter unmistakably imaged it in their own tombs. Thus, when the tholos at Pylos was mounded over with earth, as such tombs usually were, there would have been two breast–shaped mounds in view at once, the natural one in the distance and backed by the horns, the man–made one close by, in which the lord was laid to rest. Here the tholos tomb—whatever its relationship to the traditional, neolithic, conical hut of Europe and Africa alike, which may itself have been sacred to the goddess, as even the thousands of undetermined initial date which exist in Apulia and are marked with symbols resembling hers would indicate[56] (*Fig. 52*)—symbolized the body of the goddess, in whose hollow enclosure the Mycenaean lords hoped to find permanence and a kind of immortality after death. Unlike the later Dorians, who abandoned such comforting hope, the Mycenaean would–be kings, despite their warlike pride, held on to the old Cretan oneness with the earth, its shapes, and its continuing rhythms, but sought to make them more personally their own. Certainly the site of Pylos is sweeping but somnolent and calm, and the myths of Nestor's long life, respected old age, and peaceful death seem especially appropriate there.[57] One might even go further to surmise that Nestor had the character he assumed in myth because of what the landscape which nourished him was.

When, finally, we consider the plain of Argos, around which the great legends were to gather in later times, we find a clearly defined valley, enclosed on three sides by spectacular hills and mountains and opening south toward the bay, which is itself safely enclosed by mountains beyond it. From the Neolithic period onward the most sacred place in this valley would seem to have been the spot which was later to become the Heraion of Argos.[58] This lies southeast of the twin peaks which mark the site of Mycenae, to be discussed later. Seen from the plain, the mountain of the Heraion, Mount Euboea, decidely recalls Mount Ida as seen from Phaistos. (*Figs. 7, 86*) Here are the same sweeping double peaks, full lower slopes, and deeply shadowed clefts. Below the mass of the mountain is a low, rounded foothill upon which the buildings of the Greek Heraion were to be placed. Before this two gentle swells of land rise left and right and define the axis of the view. This holy spot may have had a palace on its mound below the peak, and it contains scattered evidences of Bronze Age habitation, primarily tombs and votive offerings. It was not fortified and was thus a settlement like a Minoan one, placed under the sacred peak, not a citadel itself.[59] The second natural formation of symbolic nature in the Argolid lies directly southwest across the valley from the horned mountain of the Heraion. This is the complementary shape of the conical hill of Argos, which was also to receive one of Hera's temples.[60] The site actually comprises two hills, but the northern one is much lower and flat and is called Aspis, the Shield, because of its shape.[61] From any distance across the valley the southern cone, called Larissa, appears as single. Here again the main Mycenaean remains which have been discovered are of tombs set between the two hills, although there was certainly a prehistoric town on Aspis, with the rocky cone of Larissa towering above it. (*Fig. 53*)

The large town of Dorian Argos was to be built on and below the hills, but no major Myce-naean constructions have been found.[62] The great citadels were placed elsewhere.

Foremost among these is Tiryns, lying like a stranded sea animal in the plain.[63] When the modern observer approaches the site, he at first finds it difficult to understand how such a for-tress came to be built where it is. The natural mound is low. The nearer hills to the east, though well out of bowshot, look down upon it, and indeed at first sight the citadel resembles a ship which has wallowed in blindly upon the highest wave and come heavily to rest among the marshes, entirely separate from the element which supports it, wholly self–contained. (*Fig. 54*) Further examination reinforces the sense of the ship analogy, but now of a ship still alive in the sea. The great V of the northern walls cuts deeply into the earth of Argos like a prow. Seen from the west, the bulk of the fortress heels over and out like a ship low down in the trough, and its eastern entrance ramp and tower, seen from below, heave up like a ship's poop with the send of the sea. One is reminded of the myth of Danaus who sailed overseas from Egypt and ruled in Tiryns.[64] But Tiryns was not placed where it was without method: through which an intruding body was firmly tied into the land. From the great east ramp it can be perceived that the curving profile of the Heraion of Argos (Mt. Euboea) is directly on axis to the north, with the hills toward Mycenae seen as a second pair of horns to the left of it. The east gate itself is opposite the forward slope of a nearly conical hill. Beyond the gate a labyrinthine way (*Fig. 55*) winds up the inner ramp toward the south, turns east through the outer propylon, and turns north once more to face diagonally across the inner courtyard toward the great megaron. From this critical angle the horns and masses of the Heraion are directly on axis behind the megaron of the king. (*Fig. 56*) The megaron itself would have blocked the distant view, but it is probable that the Mycenaean builders still laid out the climax of their labyrinth with the position of the Heraion in mind. The situation would be analogous to the Minoan blocking of parts of the ritual view by building masses, as we noted on the south side of the court at Knossos and else-where. Probably, as is common among many ritually dominated peoples, it would have been enough, if necessary, simply to know that the essential object was in the right place. The later Greeks, who were to develop a more human–centered view of experience, were to be-come impatient with this attitude, but the magical concept of participation in the goddess which dominates Minoan–Mycenaean planning would certainly seem to allow it, as the king at Knossos faced Jouctas from his cavern, not seeing it but knowing it was there. From the upper fortifications behind the megaron, of course, the Heraion would have been clearly visible beyond the pointed bastion of Tiryns' empty northern enceinte, which plunges down into the wider sweep of plain toward the north. Exactly the same situation arises in relation to the megaron's orientation toward the south. From its central chamber the long axis is directed precisely upon the twin knobs or small horns which rise in the center of the wide–browed ridge of Palamedes, above Mycenaean Nauplion. (*Fig. 57*) A nearer mounded hill, now called "Profitis Ilias," is also included in this view, and there many burials have been found.[65] Directly on the axis between the megaron's hearth and the horns was the round altar in the courtyard in front of the megaron. (*Fig. 55*) The whole axis obviously ties the king's house to the sacred symbols in the south. Yet these forms were again not visible from the megaron or the altar itself because of the southern colonnade of the inner courtyard which blocked the

35

view. Still, from the outer courtyard they would have been clearly visible over the structures in the lower, southernmost part of the citadel; and from this a speculation arises, since Palamedes would have been visible from the megaron's roof, as would the Heraion. There is every reason to believe that Mycenaean roofs were flat and that such roofs, as now, were used as open platforms, sometimes (Aeschylus, *Agamemnon*, 1–20) by watchers. Perhaps, therefore, the roof was a place of release, the upper floor, like those of Minoan palaces and shrines, (*Figs. 3, 22*) from which the sacred landscape shapes were wholly visible.

The megaron of Tiryns seems in all these ways to be set into the Argive plain with a conscious adjustment to the natural features which symbolized the presence of the goddess in the land. Upon its site, after its surrounding courts, passages, and subsidiary megara had been destroyed, a narrower later structure was built, retaining exactly the same orientation. (*Fig. 57*) Current opinion holds this to have been a last, restricted Mycenaean megaron rather than a Greek temple of Hera, although terracotta images suggestive of the worship of the goddess have been found in abundance around the site.[66] (*Fig. 55*) It is true that the more purely military structures of "cyclopean" masonry have a different character, aggressively massive, lordly, and proud—the works of giants, recalling those of imperial Hattusas.[67] Yet the corbeled vault of their labyrinthine passageways and magazines is the cone in elevation, so psychically comforting as well as physically protective. Thus for all its ponderous bulk and exaggeratedly virile masonry Tiryns as a whole seems an essentially reverent site. It is lower than the holy places which it invokes. The goddess' symbols are all unchallenged above it. The conquering intruder, the war band chief, Danaus and whoever his Achaian successors may have been, here clearly acknowledges the power of the goddess and strives to orient the seat of his own power with respect to hers, and all the myths of the kings of Tiryns, from Danaus to Menelaus, serve to reinforce this view.[68]

Yet, as mentioned earlier, there was an inherent contradiction between the concept of the conquering war chief and the worship of the goddess. Leaving aside the question of a conflict between matriarchal and patriarchal systems of society, a question which was later to fascinate the Greeks and which certainly fascinates many mythographers now, the problem can be posed again in relation to our own subject of landscape use. That is, the worship of the goddess, as read in Minoan sites, was essentially one of peace, in which the rhythms of the earth directed life, not the aggressive attitudes of men. Thus the Minoan palaces were more or less on low ground and unfortified, and the symbols of the goddess were on high. To her was given the proud place and the major throne, and the king took a secondary role, perhaps as did the stripling son or suitor who is the consort of the goddess upon some Minoan gems.[69] (*Fig. 65*) In the worship of the dominant female deity, as developed most embracingly on Crete, there was little room for the aggressive restlessness of male ambition and mind. The male was son and lover rather than lord. The Dorians were to refuse to accept those conditions—being willing to forego with them the hidden promise of immortality they held—and to attempt to subjugate the Mother to their own lordly Zeus. The Mycenaean lords, though actively wishing to worship the goddess, as we have seen, were still constantly being driven, by their own lordship and by their active competition with each other, toward the goddess' place. The citadel of Mideia,[70] for example, though it offers a good view of both the Heraion and the cone of Argos, is still set itself upon a high and dominating hill. Myth had it that Mideia was fortified by Perseus.[71] That hero seems to have been one of the first to be aided by the primitive Athena who may have been the household deity of the Mycenaean princes.[72] He had slain the Gorgon, who was an aspect of the goddess' chthonic power to ward off evil. Her head, the seat of that power, he gave to Athena, and she wore it thereafter on her aegis. Seen from the west, his Mideia stands out across the valley as a massive cone, and from the north its attendant hills fall away left and right, a little like those of the Heraion, while the central mass rises up as a lofty throne. (*Fig. 58*) It is a height which in Crete would have been reserved for the goddess. Upon it, with the help of his specially manufactured personal goddess but essentially through his own daring, sits the male hero. We may ask if we are not involved here with one of the results of the Indo–European concept of *areté*, later fundamental to the Greek mind. That is, the Indo–European male, the Achaian, the epic hero, attains the high place through his own will to excel, his areté. Does he, then, unless he is most careful, offend the natural powers that govern the world? A later age, under the guidance of Apollo's "Know thyself," and "Nothing to excess," was to fear most of all the danger of *hybris*, an interior change, in such a victor, but for the Mycenaeans it can only have been an external power, that of the earth, he had to fear. Yet that power was real to them, and deeply respected, as their sites have shown. Therefore, something tense and revolutionary must have been felt as the lords mounted the goddess' hill, and the best visual and mythical indications that something was indeed felt and remembered are offered by the site of Mycenae.

Mycenae is, above all else, a seat of pride and power.[73] It is the holiest in appearance of all the formations where citadels were placed. As the holiest place it must have been both the strongest in a magical sense and, in the same sense, the most dread: the ultimate weapon which only the most reckless dare to use. From the pass into the plain of Argos from the north the two peaks of Mounts Marta and Zara, themselves peaks of Mount Euboea, rise mightily into view; below them stands the citadel of the fortress. The lords of Mycenae thus had a clear view of the major pass and controlled it, as they also sat upon a secondary pass to the east. From farther south in the valley the full splendor and menace of the site become apparent. A long, gentle hill rises out of the plain, and behind it, on a farther hill, the citadel can just be seen. (*Fig. 59*) Its own armored, conical shape, projecting as it does just barely over the nearer hill, inescapably suggests to modern eyes the turret of a tank, hull down in defilade. To left and right the flanking peaks form one huge pair of horns, so that the site as a whole rises as a mighty bull's head above the valley. (*Fig. 62*) Yet the horns also suggest here the raised arms of the Mycenaean goddess as she is shown in the many terracotta figurines found at Mycenae and elsewhere.[74] The arms themselves, in such figurines, make a horn shape with the head of the goddess between them, much as the citadel rises between the peaks here. Consequently, the formation as a whole can be seen as rising out of the earth like the goddess herself appearing in majesty: the mounded hill, the now terrible horns or arms above it, and in the place of the goddess' head the fortress of the lords. But there are again multiple images here, and the one which probably dominates is of a tremendous lap. The horns, for example, can also be seen as widely spread legs with the two rocky ledges in the hollow between them gaping, distended. (*Fig. 59*) Upon this most devouring of thrones the king dares to put himself, and the built-up cone of his citadel occupies its center.

The town of Mycenae was on the lower hill, and the acropolis citadel dominated it, as the whole formation of which it is a part dominates the plain. From it the Heraion of Argos is not visible, although a ceremonial way connected the two along the base of their common mountain range. But, as seen, Mycenae's formation is self-contained and alone. As the entrance road moves up toward the acropolis through the narrow entrance gorge at the southwest, the rock precipices of Mount Marta stand directly behind the citadel. Upon the face of the mountain is a savage natural formation in the rock which need hardly be read as an image but which flaunts above the palace like a banner. In contrast to this is the royal tholos tomb, the so-called "Tomb of Agamemnon," which flanks the entrance road to the west. (*Fig. 60*) Looking southwest along this road, one can see the mound of the tomb and the conical hill of Argos in the distance. Once more, as at Pylos, the goddess' symbol in the distance and the tomb shape in the foreground are juxtaposed across a long view. From higher up another formation appears across the valley to the right of Argos. It is a suddenly opening cleft within which a conical hill is framed. Directly behind this another cleft in the far mountains signals Mount Artemision, later sacred to Artemis. The cleft with enclosed cone will be shown later to be characteristic of several Artemis sites; the one most resembling Mycenae, that at Mukhli, indeed lay on the southern slopes of Mount Artemision itself (*Fig. 143*). It should perhaps be noted that a similar formation occurs at the sacred city of Hattusas, the capital of the Hittites, with whose megalithic corbeled architecture the Mycenaean citadels show close affinities.[75]

From the entrance road past the royal tomb at Mycenae the truncated cone of the citadel itself looms up with almost muscular force, and the two slopes of the mountains flare up and outward from it, now more than ever like great horns crowning the forehead of a bull. (*Figs. 61, 62*) Another significant juxtaposition occurs at Mycenae's lion gate. To reach this, the entrance road has turned to the right, away from Mount Marta, and now approaches the gate with Mount Zara behind it. (*Fig. 63*) From this point the latter has a purely conical or triangular shape, and this is echoed by the triangular slab which fills the space between the relieving corbeled arch and the lintel of the gate. Once again a relationship between corbeled construction and the conical symbols of the goddess seems apparent. This impression is reinforced by the complementary symbol of the goddess, the column between lions, which is carved on the slab, so that, at the entrance to the citadel, the goddess stood both up on her mountain above and on her gate below. In this way, too, she is brought into the town. (*Figs. 63, 64*) Conversely, the view out from the lion gate focuses exactly upon a notched mountain to the north. Whatever the arrogance of its position, Mycenae was thus intended to be placed under the protection of the goddess, and the darkest kings of the House of Atreus hoped equally to lie under her protection after death. Like all the Bronze Age lords, they seemed to hope to have life both ways, to act and be protected all the same. In this, especially, they must have seemed to the later Greeks as tragic ancestors whose fate demonstrated the grand folly of attempting to hold on to such irreconcilable dreams. The cult of the heroic dead was already strong at Mycenae. The position of the grave circle is therefore of considerable importance. It long antedated the lion gate and its walls and lay well outside the original citadel on the crest; it is thus backed by the main cone of the citadel and by the great horns. From its entrance, however, the view sweeps south and west. The cone of Argos is clearly visible in the distance, and to the right of it, now directly on axis behind the tomb of Agamemnon, the far cleft with its cone and Mount Artemision behind it appear once more. (*Fig. 67*) The grave circle thus seems to sweep all the near and far symbols of the goddess together, but to be especially oriented for the optimum holy view, across the nearer mound with the royal tholos toward the horned mountain in the distance. This organization recalls the similar view from Knossos: across the mounded hill, in which the Temple Tomb was placed, toward the horns of sacred Jouctas. (*Figs. 7, 10*) The cult of the ancestors which took place in the open air of the grave circle, surrounded by its standing menhirlike stones, must therefore have been central to the life of Mycenae. Once more, the significance of the cone should be pointed out; it was apparently more important in Mycenaean sites than it had been in Crete, as was its echo, the tholos tomb, fully developed only late in the millenium and by the Mycenaean lords. These facts probably mirror the basic difference between their preoccupation and that of the Cretan king. He made contact with the earth for his people, and was a part of it; they sought personal continuation for themselves.

On the mounting roadway above the circle another dominant feature of a later Artemis site can be seen in the distance across it. These are the clefts and lifting arms of Mounts Kyllene and, probably, Sciathis, which rise above the Stymphalian Lake, where the Dorian Herakles killed the terrible birds which were sacred to the goddess.[76] (*Fig. 68*) Their effigies in wood were to hang in the temple of Artemis there.[77] Because of the fatal connections in myth between Artemis and King Agamemnon, the double evocation of Artemis sites from Mycenae acquires considerable significance in indicating the specific cult of the goddess which was practiced there: a cult which now seems to have had in it something of violence and terror. Reinforcing this supposition is the fact that the placement of Mycenae itself between the horns is recalled by the somewhat similar placement of the later temples of Artemis at Mukhli and Aulis.[78] Higher up within the citadel the surviving megaron of the palace, slipped into the side of the hill above the deep cleft on the south, was oriented fairly exactly toward Stymphalia, although its view in that direction would, as at Tiryns, have been blocked, here by the structure which is taken to be the throne room. (*Fig. 68*) Yet here again the possibility that the roof was used as a viewing platform should be kept in mind, and on line with the megaron's hearth Stymphalia's mountain was another cone between its horns, like a cloudy mirror image of Mycenae itself. (*Fig. 68*) Upon the summit of the citadel was a shrine of some sort, and this faced across the mound of the tholos tomb toward the cone of Argos and the notch of Artemision once more. (*Fig. 69*) The later, archaic Greek temple of Athena was placed upon the shrine and purposefully retained its southerly orientation. Indeed, it swung south until it finally lay but a degree or so east. (*Fig. 66*) It was thus held to its sky orientation only by a thread, while it sought to make the most of the sacred formations to the south and west, possibly so that it and they could both be seen from its altar. So turned, its long flank would have been seen from the plain below, lying athwart the cone of the acropolis between the horns and now civilizing the savagery of the place into a new kind of Olympian force.

Finally, the summit of the citadel of Mycenae creates a sensation of physical and spiritual dominance over the landscape. (*Fig. 69*) The rush of brutally triumphant exultation which many observers have noted in themselves there would seem to arise from that sense of double command.[79] The mounded hill of the lower city again plays a role in this, since it affords a barrier between the viewer and movement on the plain but at the same time allows him to see over it as king of the hill, "monarch of all he surveys." (*Fig. 59*) For these reasons it can well be imagined that the kings of Mycenae indeed felt themselves to be in the goddess' place, having assumed her natural power for their own.

It may be for these reasons also that Mycenae, from its founding by the hero Perseus[80] until the deaths of Agamemnon and Clytemnestra within its walls, was the chosen setting for the most terrible of myths, all of them having to do with the punishments consequent upon the human lust for power. So the murdered Agamemnon, who had taken his wife by force from her first husband, slaughtered Artemis' protected animals, sacrificed his daughter to Artemis in order to advance his own kingly will, and finally brought down Aphrodite's Troy, is himself later treated by Aeschylus as a slaughtered bull, whose death constitutes in part a reprisal by the goddess for his pride.[81] Thus the site of Mycenae itself, the hero ancestors who dared it, and the fate which overcame them at the hands of the Dorians may all have had much to do with encouraging those peculiarly Hellenic trains of thought out of which mature classic ideas of justice and balance were to evolve. More specifically, as the most awesome of horned bull's heads rising in menace out of the earth and the most challenging of thrones assumed by a king, Mycenae already seems to suggest in its own dark way that double theme which was to become central and luminous in Greek sacred architecture: the theme of what rightfully belongs to the natural order and what to man, of what the human act may dare to be in the face of nature's law.

Chapter 4

THE TEMPLE. HERA

There is one
race of men, one race of gods; both have breath
Of life from a single mother. But sundered power
holds us divided . . .

Pindar, "Nemea 6" (Lattimore)[1]

A DECISIVE GULF in intention divides the latest Mycenaean megara from the archaic Greek temples. Many centuries separate them, and many complex developments in thought at which we today can merely guess. Initially, an enormous cataclysm brought a Dark Age. Into the domains of the Bronze Age lords burst the hardy Dorian tribesmen, descendants, so it came to be said, of Herakles: no men for compromise. The invaders broke up the old order of ritual kingship under the goddess, and thus the megara of the kings disappeared. The Dorians seem also to have attempted to suppress the old concept of the dominance of the goddess of the earth herself, seizing the sovereign power by virtue of their own thunder–wielding sky god, Zeus. Certainly the Dorians went farther than the Achaians before them toward destroying the old, simple, almost vegetable unity between man and nature, apparently refusing to accept the comfort of the goddess' tomb and instead proudly burning their dead before burying their ashes. Their early cities, too, tell us that they must have seen the earth and the goddess herself in very different terms than their predecessors had done. On Crete, for example, their strong-hold sites of Dreros,[2] Lato, and Prinias[3] are set on or under savage heights, not in the gentle megara of the valleys. On the island of Thera they occupied a high headland, forward of an awesome cleft in the volcanic mountain, (*Fig. 114*) with a black beach curving under their city far below, the islands falling away to left and right and exposing the city to the open sea.[4] From all these places the goddess of the earth must herself have been felt as threatening and dark. Nature could now be conceived of as hostile to human desires, inimical to the human will, pitiless. A new tension between men and the natural order thus arose.

We can hardly tell what the beliefs of the eleventh to ninth centuries actually were, but by the time they received formulation in the *Iliad* the many old Hellenic gods have acquired personalities, are engaged in strife with each other, and seem to differ from men only in two particulars: they have power and they cannot die. Only Zeus, despite his vagaries, already stands above such a description, since he alone knows the future and is thus the god of things as they are and must be. The female Olympian divinities seem to represent the goddess firmly subdivided into the several aspects of power her old sites already suggest: Hera, Artemis, Athena, Aphrodite, and so on; and these are coupled with male divinities of various kinds: Apollo, Poseidon, Ares, Hephaistos, Hermes.[5] Dionysos, later to be god of the dying and reviving vine and probably already present during the Mycenaean age, is now conspicuous by his absence. As each of these deities is a power he or she is impersonal and beyond question, except as that power may come into conflict with other forces. But Homer already puts those inevitable conflicts between powers in directly human terms, so that they sometimes seem merely the squabbles of jealous women and erratic men. In their warring natures the old world order lies in ruins, and the early Greek appears to stand alone and unaided against ultimate fate, his *Moira*. The essential point, as Simone Weil has so movingly pointed out,[6] is that the *Iliad* is the most realistic statement ever made of the helplessness of the individual before the facts of force, and the noblest statement as well, since it recognizes that all men, native or foreign, Greek or Trojan, suffer the same. This is the measure of the greatness of the Greek and of the Homeric gods, each of whom is the embodiment of a certain kind of natural and/or psychological force, as human beings can identify forces. Each is the recognition of a fact, and it was precisely this willingness to recognize the facts as they could be learned which was to distinguish Greek civilization beyond all others. So the gods had not created the world but were its mightiest children, the quintessential products of its nature. And it was apparently because Homer brought those facts of things together, undisguised as human beings could recognize them at their most true, that the Greeks were to regard him as their first great religious teacher and his poetry as the bible of their civilization.

As Homer presents the facts, they are pitiless. Men die, and their shades go wailing down to Tartarus. In the *Odyssey* the epic hero even consciously chooses such a fate: Odysseus rejects the immortality he is offered in the island cave of Calypso, which may perhaps be equated with the old tholos tomb of the goddess but which has now become a place of rather shameful escape and withdrawal, and chooses instead to play out to the full his human destiny in mortal life, which means the choice of mortal death as well. These formulations of belief seem possible only after several centuries of Dorian influence, or after a long period of Achaian–Ionian contemplation of the fate which had overcome them at Dorian hands. Thus there must have been in the Dorians of the Dark Ages, and in their impact upon the other Greeks, something hard and splendid which left a permanent mark upon Greek thought as a whole: a realistic view of life, an incapacity for self-deceit and, perhaps most of all, an intuition that the inevitable human conflict with nature and with fate could not be resolved at the last by any easy reconciliation between them, as in the old religion. Everything was to be thought through again, now keeping not only the relationships but also the differences between men and nature and men and the gods in mind. At the same time the beauty of the old way of peace with the earth was never wholly forgotten, although its forms had apparently at first been thrust brutally underground, so that a strain of haunted memory was henceforth to give a further dimension to Greek thought. In a sense there was laid here the foundations for a new piety more profound than the old, and the new reconciliation, when it came, was to involve a deep sense of the terrible oppositions and alternatives which had gone into its creation.

The great Athenian grave monuments of the ninth and eighth centuries, the Dipylon jars, contemporaries of Homer, were the first monumental embodiments of the new attitude. (*Fig.* 70) Man–sized, sometimes with horned handles, they were already sculpture and architecture in one and were constructed, like the figures upon them, of separate, abstractly geometric parts, so totally rejecting at last that Minoan continuity of organic flow (*Figs.* 5, 15) which their Achaian ancestors had already done their best to stiffen. Unlike the Minoan jars, their forms, though hollow, were treated not as spreading containers but as active masses, and all their profiles and surfaces were formed to this end, from the upward spring of their structural patterns to the gestures of their mourners. Standing in the open above the ashes of their graves, and moistening them with their slowly dripping oil, they celebrated the family cult and contrasted in all major ways with nature's forms around them. They were monuments to the gulf between human wishes and nature's demands as, in the face of all, they raised above their dead a harsh shout of grief and defiance. (*Fig.* 70)

Then, apparently by the early eighth century also, the new temple appeared in its most primitive form: it too an actively geometricized container, with a high, upward thrusting, perhaps already sacred gable. (*Fig.* 72) It now stated the oppositions at full scale but, in so doing, already took a step toward their reconciliation. The very places where the temple finally appeared indicate that the Greek of the darkest ages was still aided in his attempt to face reality by that tradition which upheavals of belief had never entirely been able to take away: the tradition, that is, of the essential holiness of the land. Despite the specific breaks caused by the Dorians, this tradition, as the earliest Greek sites will show us, must be regarded as having been generally continuous and always capable of specific renewals. Man and human social life were in the grip of hazard. The land remained, the special Greek landscape with its abundance of sacred symbols, its sculptural clarity, and its unexpected resources of expression. First the land received its altars. But now the more complete Greek view of divinity required something else: the temple enclosing its image. Thus the temple placed upon the earth was no longer the house of a chief or king but the house of a god. As such it took on an absolute qualitative difference from the old semi–sacred megaron of the hero ancestors which its form partly recalled, and which it may appropriately have revived. More likely, it began by assuming a house type still common in the eighth century, since apsidal and even long rectangular houses of early date have now been found. The temple retained the type and developed it monumentally; the house seems soon to have diverged from it, since no late archaic or classic examples are known.[6a] Convenience may have dictated that development, but it seems equally likely that, once the temple had fully assumed this plan and developed its gable, the house was soon constrained to avoid both. Because the temple was not a simple human habitation, or even a viewing platform in the protected spot from which a ritual king represented his people or a lord seized the land as his own. Instead it represented to all men the presence of a god and was itself the monument of that presence. However, the fact that the first Greek temples followed by many years the open–air altars which were built on their sites clearly shows that it was still the site which first suggested the presence of the god: the site at whose exposed altar the dedicated beasts were sacrificed. The temple added another element to the place, a geometrical form, man–conceived, different from the natural landscape but complementary to it.

There are eight general points which should be made relative both to that complementary action of temple with site and to the development of the temple form itself. (1) A majority of temples are oriented toward the east, sometimes—as Dinsmoor has most dedicatedly worked it out with the Parthenon and some other temples—toward the rising sun of the deity's feast day in the year of the temple's dedication.[7] Such orientation toward the eastern sky is counter alike to the Minoan north–south orientation toward a landscape feature, to the Mycenaean focus upon such features on any available bearing, and to the apparent Etruscan and Roman indifference to celestial orientation, although the latter also often seem to seek the south. The tendency of the Greek temple to focus where possible upon the east recalls the sky orientation of the prehistoric stone circles and of the temples of the Ancient East. Yet in Greece such orientation, whether or not the inspiration for it came from contact with the East, was clearly post–Dorian in date and, it would seem, in meaning: indicating a conflict between the sky and the earth powers or, perhaps more justly, a partial liberation of the god from the earth and a consequent enrichment of his character. However, some sure contact between the temple and the sacred landscape shapes, often, though not always, an axial one, was clearly desired, too. At a great many sites, where the sanctuary had already been placed, or could be placed, more or less west of the formation, or in some other favorable relation to it, as at Delphi, Perachora, Samos, Paestum, Olympia, and so on, no compromise with a sky orientation seems to have been necessary. On the other hand, in some of these places, Perachora and Delphi among them, it is clear that the earth shape entirely dictated the placement. At favored Athens, as already noted in the Temple of Athena Polias, the concordance between sun and earth was exact. Elsewhere, a compromise was apparently worked out, and the temple swung off its desired sunrise enough to assume a coherent position in relation to the shape in question and to the topographical conformation of the site as a whole. Such adjustments can be sensed, for example, at Calydon, Eretria, and elsewhere. Sometimes the landscape demanded that the temple be faced almost due south, as at Mycenae, already mentioned, and at Thermon, Marmaria, and the temple of Hera at Delos. In most cases of this kind—though not at Thermon, where the god faced a bit west of south—the temple conformed to the topography as closely as possible but still held, as at Mycenae, to a token easterly bearing. Yet at Bassae, for special topographical reasons, the orientation of the temple body as a whole was almost due north. Therefore, the reason for the placement and orientation of any Greek temple can probably be understood in the following terms: first, through the sacred character of the landscape itself, which caused it to be built where it was and with which it was seen; second, through the tension which may or may not have existed at each place between the special terrestrial and celestial points of focus. Indeed, it would appear that such tensions were sometimes conceived of by the Greeks as making the temple appropriately active, both of the earth and free of it, a true personality and a force. The reconciliation of opposites so involved is again between pre– and post–Dorian attitudes. Consequently, some of the greatest Ionian deities, in whom such tension existed least, or not at all, might face due west, like Artemis at Ephesos and Magnesia and, apparently, Apollo at Delos.

Or, to take another approach: many deities whose particular character in a place involved an especially close link with the earth seem more likely to face the earth's cones or horns directly: Hera at Paestum, Athena Polias at Athens, Artemis at Magnesia, Despoina at Lykosoura, Apollo at Delphi and Ptoon, Asklepios at Kos. True enough, as noted at Athens, the earth and the sky may work together in some cases, to the extent that one might speculate upon the possibility that such concordance fixed the feast day in the beginning. But again, some such temples will face far south or north to find their form, as their landscape may require: Athena at Marmaria and Pergamon, Hera at Delos and Pergamon, Asklepios at Kos, the oracular Zeus at Dodona. So, further, in the most fully chthonic divinities the clear dominance of the earth form over the sky orientation may be surmised, even when the building in question faces the east as it can.

(2) So far as the placing of temples in relation to specifically sacred landscape features is concerned, a double point must be made, involved with the culturally pivotal question of "god–centered" or "man–centered" design. First, as indicated above, the temple may sometimes be oriented directly toward such a feature, as the long axes of Minoan palaces had been. In these cases one might now doubly assume that what the god is supposed to see rather than what the human observer sees entirely determines the temple's placement. But this may be too categorical an assumption, since, even when the temple faces the sacred object, or the sunrise, or both at once, the relationships seem to be so handled that the human participant at the site can himself usually see the temple and the landscape form together as a single architectural whole of contrasted shapes. The original placement of the open altars, as we can tell from those which still exist, was probably critical in this, since they were obviously sited in the ideal position from which the whole sacred landscape could be grasped and the ritual, even of the sky, best performed. Human movement to them would thus have been to a culminating point, with the temple, when built, taking up its related position with equal appropriateness both to the site and to the worshiper's path of movement toward it and his use of it. In many places, for example, as again at Delphi, Samos, Magnesia, Paestum, archaic Athens, classic Olympia, and so on, the major altar is in one way or another between the temple and the essential landscape form, which thus balance each other on either side of the worshiper. Or the altars may be so placed or the approaches so arranged that the temple carries the eye east, west, north, or south toward a significant shape and can be seen with it. Such occurs at Bassae, the Himera, Paestum, Olympia, Athens, and elsewhere. Indeed, multiple combinations, specific and unformularized, occur almost everywhere, are developed most eloquently during the fifth century, and can be grasped only through the direct experience of each site as a 360° whole. It must therefore be closest to the truth to assume that, whatever the relationships are, the psychic and physical sensations of the human participant as he would have approached, used, and perceived the site and the temple in the site were normally taken into account from quite an early period; they clearly became of increasing importance to the Greeks as time went on. Vitruvius (IV.5.1) was later to enunciate a purely man–centered principle when he suggested that temples should

face west so that the worshiper might face east and see the gods coming toward him from that direction. The Greek was never to go so far toward pure theater. His view of reality was larger, and it also involved a reconciliation, that between the intrinsic nature of the god of the place and the view of him which might be made apparent to human eyes. The form of the Greek temple itself contributed to this double end.

(3) Some temples, for example, bring to completion or climax the natural enclosure of the site or offer a special, distinct enclosure for their deity in an open site. The simple megaron or temple in antis does this; and such temples without peripteral colonnades tend to remain characteristic of sites where a deity, usually a goddess, is being celebrated in an essentially chthonic, non–Olympian aspect. It remains especially typical of mystery sites, where the basic cult act takes place inside or invokes interior, cave experience. (4) The temple, like the dipteral Ionic examples, or some of the earliest peripteral Doric, may go further and create what might be called a complex inner landscape, an especially appropriate environment for its deity within the larger site. The most characteristic Ionic temples, for example, make wide spreading groves on low, flat ground. (5) The temple, on the other hand, and especially the Doric temple, may become a fully sculptural entity, placed in many kinds of terrain and expressing its god by its own sculptural qualities: so making his character, otherwise hid, externally visible. The rapid exploitation of the Doric temple form throughout the sixth and early fifth centuries seems directed mainly toward this objective. Once the major members and features are evolved and organized, as in the creation of a species, they are always retained but infinitely varied, thus forming the bodies of recognizable individuals. From this it becomes apparent why all Greek temples had to make use of the same basic forms, of the "archetype" which Melville hailed and some other critics have deplored. It is precisely because differences of character between individuals can be fully perceived and absolutely evaluated only when they belong to the same species, in this case, "one race of men and gods." In this they resemble the archaic Kouroi and Korai, each of which is much like all others but also embodies a particular potency of its own at a scale peculiar to itself. Here we find the most intense expression of the special Hellenic quality, in which the temple, like most Greek prayers, normally asks nothing unreasonable of the god but describes him. It does not seek to indicate that the body of his temple can contain and protect human beings. The body is his own, inviolate, not a shell but complete, separate from nature and men alike but related to both. (6) At the same time the Doric temple is involved with all Greek art in a remarkably coherent formal development, thus in a tendency toward generalization which is always in vital tension with the specific variations occurring at each site. By the later fifth and fourth centuries and thereafter, this tendency leads the temple toward a high, abstract, less "physical" massing, and toward a certain loss of individualization. Out of this derive the Hellenistic and Vitruvian formulas, in which distinctions between Doric and Ionic types themselves tend to lose their earlier point. (7) The temple, finally, tends in later centuries to reassert enclosure rather than the exterior and uniquely Greek sculptural presence which some of the Doric temples of the periods noted above strove to embody. The temple, therefore, first develops toward a unique kind of sculptural image in the landscape, and then, though never entirely losing that quality, becomes more of a simple "building" again, less sculpturally exposed in space and more pictorially framed.

(8) The character of the relationship between temple form and landscape also changes from site to site in accordance with the meaning of the deity as it is recognized at a given time at each place. Thus, though there is, as in sculpture and painting, a chronological development to be found, it is constantly enlivened, as there, by special considerations.

From the point of view of the double reconciliation of man with nature and of the old goddess with the Olympian order, no deity seems more significant than Hera, the wife of Zeus. Jealous and embittered as myth tells us she was, and cold and difficult to understand as modern historians of religion find her to be, Hera as mother and queen can indeed come most fully alive for us when her hard and regal character is read at her holy places. A consideration of the most important of these also affords an excellent cross section of various temple types, landscape usages, geographical variations, and chronological developments, so that it seems doubly reasonable to begin a general examination of Greek sacred sites with hers.

One of the earliest Greek temples was built at the shrine of Hera Akraia, Hera of the cliffs, at Perachora.[8] Seen from Corinth, the tapering headland of Perachora projects far into the gulf, and is clearly marked off from the land behind it by a deep break in the cliffs which comes down to the water's edge. (*Fig. 172*) Seen so, Perachora already has a definite shape, like an archaic bronze image lying on its back by the sea. Hera is above all the goddess of the headland at this place, of the rising solid earth above the water. Therefore, seen from shipboard approaching the Isthmus of Corinth, the rocky mass of Perachora projects into the gulf like a prow and then widens behind in a strong V of two arms above which a conical peak rises. (*Fig. 71*) Behind and above these shapes looms the mass of Mount Loutraki like a guardian animal, and its western face terminates in a single, vertical horn. Loutraki is only the western bastion of Mount Gerania, upon whose summit Megarus, guided by the crying of the cranes, found refuge from the flood. (Pausanias, I.40.1) So Hera's headland itself announces the earth in the sea–flooded heart of Greece. Southward across the water lie the great formations, to be discussed later, which signal places sacred to Artemis, Zeus, Aphrodite, and Apollo. Eastward, the long body of the Isthmus holds Poseidon's shrine, while to northeastward Hera's own horned Cithairon rises above Boeotia. To north and northwest Helicon and Parnassos tower. The sanctuary at Perachora is set below the southern face of the headland cliffs, laid out beneath the precipices behind the almost perfect ellipse of a tiny harbor. (*Figs. 72–76*) About in the center of the narrow shelf of land between the cliffs and the sea, but set close against the cliffs, was placed, possibly in the ninth century, a small apsidal temple, like an abstracted version of the hairpin megara of Middle Bronze Age times. This faced east, parallel to the harbor. A small terracotta model found at Perachora probably shows us what its form was: an enclosing, volumetric shape with an open, gabled porch to the east. (*Fig. 72*) It may be taken as the first type of Greek temple built, a type which starts all over again, whether by accident or design we are not yet sure, with something resembling the earliest kind of megaron form used by the ancestral heroes. But it no longer has a flat roof and so cannot be stood upon; its sloping roof enforces its own integrity, and its eastern gable signals the major line of force emanating from the divinity it encloses. During the sixth century a long rectangular temple in antis, really a large megaron but now with two gabled ends, two true pediments, was built to the west of the older apsidal temple, (*Figs. 75, 76*) and along the harbor curve at that side some kind of subsidiary enclosure was created. A triglyph altar, its frieze of triglyphs and metopes seeming to rise out of the earth as does that of the oracular altar at Corinth, was built close to the older megaron, (*Fig. 75*) and in the fourth century a stoa was cupped under the slopes to the east.

From the hill to the west the whole shape of the site and its meaning become clear. (*Fig. 73*) From this point it can be seen that the temples are oriented toward the rocky cone which rises to the east, and which is so conspicuous from shipboard, and that the great arms of the hill stretch out from the cone to north and south, funnelling down toward the narrow waist of the harbor, which is then enclosed by hills behind. The whole site is one goddess shape, clearly recalling the particular form of the goddess in some of the terracotta figurines found at the shrine.[9] (*Fig. 74*) The conical peak is the high, richly caparisoned head, while the wide neck and broad, sloping shoulders also find their counterparts in the configuration of the site itself. In the body of this shape the temples are set. Since the meaningful approach to the sanctuary in antiquity was from the sea, the pilgrim would have been aware for some time of the goddess-like shape of the land, and he would have been completely enclosed by her body as soon as he entered the harbor. In this warm and quiet place under the cliffs his view, like that of the image in the temple itself, was focused eastward toward the goddess' head, the conical hill which rose above the raised arms or horns of the land. From the position of the earlier apsidal temple the conical hill to the east could not be seen. The building was thus thrust completely under the upraised arms. From the entrance to the great temple in antis, however, the conical hill looms above the lifting arc of the arms, and the orientation of the temple upon it is exact. (*Fig. 76*) Here is a case where an easterly orientation is precisely in accord with the forms of the landscape. Given the shape and obvious meaning of the site, one can understand why the sixth-century temple did not make use of a peripteral colonnade. On the one hand, there would have been little room for it on the narrow shelf by the harbor, but beyond that the peripteral colonnade would have externalized the shape of the temple so that it would have become a sculptural object crushed in the embrace of the land. Without a colonnade, however, and with a closed west end, the temple remains a clearly volumetric element, three walls and a gable roof—the pediments themselves probably indicative of divinity and, so Pindar tells us in Ol. 13, a Corinthian invention—enclosing a certain amount of space. As such it completes the body of the natural site, on axis with the proudly conical hill and under the uplifted arms. There is in this way a full reciprocity in design between landscape shape and constructed building at Perachora.

Another point should be made, insofar as Hera is so much of the earth at Perachora, so enclosed by it, that she cannot have a peripteral colonnade and uses columns only in antis. The column enclosed, by the walls of a shrine or by lions or other beasts on gems and in relief sculpture, had been a symbol of the goddess in Minoan–Mycenaean times, as we saw at Knossos and Mycenae. The exposed columns of the peripteral colonnade—especially and perhaps exclusively in Doric architecture, that is—while not necessarily ruling out any chthonic association in a particular site, nevertheless seem to have had Olympian connotations. But at Perachora as at Cretan Gournia, (*Fig. 18*) the impression is inescapably one of being enclosed by the goddess herself, and the Greek continuation of the ancient Cretan way of using a landscape shape to define the essential form, is again made clear by contrast with the megalithic sanctuaries on Malta. (*Fig. 20*) Perachora, in its harbor, even offers a more or less horned entrance to the body, like those constructed at the Maltese shrines. Higher up at Perachora another early sanctuary was set, to Hera as Limenia, of the Harbor,[10] in the hollow between the goddess' arms, (*Fig. 73*) and here a great cistern was dug. So the shrine at the harbor itself is of Hera Akraia, since she faces the cliffs there, while the shrine above, less dominated by the cliff, takes the name of the harbor below it. The high rock, the water basins in the earth, the enclosing horns and arms, the complementary temple shape, all together make Perachora complete and holy in a tradition that must have gone deeply back into time. The jagged cone at Perachora is bitter, like the Homeric Hera, but the site as a whole tells us clearly what Hera fundamentally was at this place: the old earth mother who embraced all. She thus clearly persisted into archaic times as the essential goddess, resisting whatever attempts to subordinate her may have been made, and, though pushed roughly in among the Olympians, she was still a chthonic deity, whose altar rose oracularly out of the earth and whose body— no longer every day and night or for time everlasting, but only during the period of purposeful communion with her—was the complete refuge for men.

Perachora thus demonstrates a restricted, sharply focused, and densely massed site with the temple in antis used as an enclosed shape within it. The Heraion at Samos, on the other hand, offers a sweeping site of great size, a tremendous temple, and the use of the dipteral Ionic colonnade.[11] Here the temple was placed near the western end of a long coastal plain, defined by hills which swing from the site of the ancient town of Samos (now Tigani) to the east, enclose the plain on the north and west, and are then continued in a sense by the far arc of the Dodecanese which define the sea horizon to the south. It is sited at the point from which this whole landscape may best be experienced. Its main focus of view is toward the east, and it is oriented toward the strait between Samos and Mount Mykale on the mainland of Asia Minor. (*Fig. 77*) Mykale itself is clearly breast–shaped on this side, with a hard cone of rock at its summit. Other considerations as well may have directed the placement of the original altar here, long before the first of the many successive temples were built. The approach to the site on the ancient sacred way along the curving shore from Samos, for example, shows the temple to be exactly on axis with a familiar formation to the west: two gentle hills which enframe a third hill between them, with a serrated ridge line rising behind. (*Fig. 78*) The temple is also placed opposite the single spot where the hills to the north are cleft into a dramatic gorge. (*Fig. 79*) A great triangulation thus gave the temple its place between mounds, cleft, and far Mykale. In the sanctuary, holy since the Bronze Age, was tended the goddess' willow, reputed to be the oldest tree in the world.[12]

Samos tells us once more that Hera was the mother of the earth, here not closely enclosing us as at Perachora, but instead defining the great circle of land and sea. Samos is a world view, stabilized by the breast–shaped mountain. The spaces involved are vast. The first temple on this site, crowded up to the altar, also received the first peripteral colonnade which can be dated with any confidence. The cella, long and narrow and with a central spine of columns, may have been built first, apparently as early as 800 B.C., and the colonnade of seven columns across the front and only six at the rear added later, certainly within fifty years of that date. A simple megaron, whose exterior mass was sharply defined by planes of wall so that the building became a simple enclosing shell, as at Perachora, would have had little power to make its presence felt in the sweeping landscape or, most of all, to set up the kind of visual rhythm on its exterior which could make the very size of the setting measurable to the human eye. This the colonnade did, making the building active enough to balance Mykale.

It is useless to attempt to trace the idea for it to any earlier architecture, either Minoan, Asiatic, or Egyptian. Insofar as its columns stand outside the walls there are no parallels, although an analogy might be drawn with an Egyptian courtyard temple which had been turned inside out, the external columns now liberated from enclosure by walls. It is also misleading to attempt to see the peripteral colonnade as simply a ring of porch; it is much too narrow at the sides for that. Nor can it have been intended simply to support roofs to shelter the mud brick walls of the cella; it would have been easy simply to overhang the roofs for that purpose.[13] Instead, this first of peripteral colonnades can only be imagined as having been intended to serve a visual and plastic purpose. What that purpose was seems clear: to articulate, penetrate, and extend the exterior envelope of the building so that it should become a true mid–space element, at once bounded and boundless, masking its enclosing surfaces, opening to space and receiving it, setting up with its columns, most of all, a regular standard of measure whereby distant horizons could be grasped. And this device, throughout the whole of Greek history, was used only for temples. It was therefore holy and partook, once invented, of the sanctity of the gods whom it both protected and imaged. All of these qualities of the exterior colonnade can be better considered when we have, as we shall shortly, a standing example before our eyes, but they should be mentioned at this point because they may have been first imagined at Samos and because the innovation itself seems closely related to the nature of the site which the temple there was required to complete.

Once the temple received its colonnade the whole landscape seen from it or in relation to it was pinned into place with characteristic Greek definiteness. What was the nature of the temple itself, as viewed from outside, conceived to be? First of all, as we have seen, it was a mid–space element, not primarily a space–enclosing shell, and this quality was to remain characteristic of most peripteral Doric and Ionic temples throughout the archaic and classic periods. Beyond this, however, was the temple to be conceived of as a sculptural body or as an open pavilion? The colonnade in wood could hardly be other than the posts of a pavilion, but once transposed into stone it might be developed toward either effect. The Doric temple was generally to move toward the sculptural body, the Ionic toward the open pavilion surrounding a deeply enclosed cella. The steps in that direction can be traced at Samos. A new temple was built in exactly the same place early in the seventh century. (*Fig.* 80) This, which itself apparently underwent some transformations, eventually had a dipteral colonnade of six columns on the east end and a wider span between the flanking columns and the cella wall. Inside, the earlier central rank of columns, which necessitated an off–axial placement of the image, was abandoned in favor of two rows engaged in the side walls. A third temple replaced the second during the first half of the sixth century, and this, like the more or less contemporary temple of Artemis at Ephesos, had a double colonnade all around. This third temple burned, and a new one, so large that it was never entirely finished and its columns were left unfluted, was begun under Polykrates about 530 B.C., in a position somewhat westward of the others. It had three rows of columns at front and rear and two along the sides. (*Fig. 81ab*) Those at the rear numbered nine across, while those at the front were kept to eight, in order to allow a central doorway to the cella. Behind the entrance columns two rows penetrated a deep pronaos, and here a knowledge of Egyptian temples on the part of the builders may legitimately be surmised. The interior thus retains the unilinear space common to Egypt, while the columned exterior opens out to a radial space defined by any number of features on the circle of the horizon, toward which the vision was encouraged to expand, even though the exterior colonnades themselves could direct the eye only in one or at most two directions from any single point.

The west end of the cella itself created closed wall planes behind the western colonnade. There was no opisthodomos, and from the western side the cella was thus read as an enclosing shell, though this character was deeply masked from the exterior by the triple colonnade, now equal in depth to that in front, as that on the second temple, for example, had not been. In this way two opposites were juxtaposed: the columned pavilion of the exterior and the walled enclosure of the interior, the latter a cavern for the goddess if roofed, a precinct if "hypaethral." It is difficult to know whether the largest temple at Samos was roofed or not. It would certainly appear that the earlier temples were intended to be so. It is true that the Ionic temple of Artemis at Ephesos may possibly have been hypaethral, but the only temple that we know surely to have had a cella open to the sky is the Hellenistic temple of Apollo at Didyma, and this, as we shall mention later, had a small closed shrine inside the open cella to house the image of the god. Around the cella the Ionic columns in stone were high, comparatively slender, and widely spaced. (*Figs. 81b, 157*) At the same time the deep grooves which came to be carved in them elsewhere, separated as they are by narrow vertical planes, are purely in function with their upward thrust, while the shallow concavities of Doric flutings, fewer and separated only by the sharp edges of their intersections, are, as we shall see, in function not only with that column's verticality but also with its sculptural rotundity. One can therefore understand why the Ionic column, like the later, even more treelike Corinthian type, had for that very reason to be given a base if it was to be adequately defined as structurally separate from the stylobate and so avoid an overly botanical appearance of growth from it. The Doric shaft, so solidly compressive as its own form makes it, needed no such device and could be set upon the stylobate's edge, which the other's base prevented.

The Ionic columns leap upward from the compressed cushion of their bases to form a manmade grove, an ambient within which the sacred cave is set. Thus the dipteral Ionic temple, though sculpturally defined, becomes a constructed environment rather than a purely sculptural unit. This may be another reason why interior columns were dispensed with in the final version at Samos: because the temple was not conceived of as a necessarily integral body whose exterior and interior should embody the same laws, but as a surrounding. Its columns rise as a forest of trees on the marshy plain, and why they must so rise in a broad, flat, low place seems obvious. Spread in such a numerous group, they cannot logically crown a restricted hill or ridge. They create a wide, spreading space themselves, and so cannot draw together into a compact crowning body. (*Figs. 81b, 157*) One recalls the willow tree of the Samian goddess, a spreading form growing in well-watered ground, and these columns, too, speak of water, growth, bounty, exuberance. Their number, of nine at the rear and eight across the front, is too great to be easily grasped from near at hand as forming a single unit rather than a group.[14] The Doric Parthenon was to exploit that very limitation of the human eye for more complex meanings, but in the great Ionic temples the intention seems primarily to have been to form a grove. Seen from the far distance, as at vast Samos, the Heraion would have been a single gleaming object; closer to, a man–made, covered forest which, from its altar, opened up into its separate trees. Finally, the widening of the intercolumniations in front of the cella would have tended to pull the worshiper in among the shafts. From this it would appear that the Ionic temple was meant to envelop, and its scale, unlike that of the Doric temples, remains primarily that of a building, of a constructed environment, of columns set upon a broad platform, rather than that of a single piece of sculpture. Similarly, the great roofs of the Ionic structures, whose huge pediments— now probably reserved for sacred buildings alone—stretched high above eight widely spaced and equally sacred columns, must have added considerably to the engulfing effect. The shape of the pediment, which visually held the whole together, seems to have suggested an eagle's wings, heraldically spread, so that the Greeks called it *aëtos*, "eagle," while they called the wide colonnades across which it stretched, *ptera*, "wings." So, whether Ionic or Doric, the temple was seen as opposing the mountain's mass with actively complementary forms. (*Fig. 77*)

The special qualities of the Ionic temple are enhanced by the nature of the Ionic capital. The main line of its development seems clear. Its Aeolic prototypes, like those from Larisa and Neandria, may evoke horns but express plant growth in the sap–filled coils of their volutes.[15] At Samos the volutes are compressed in section and rolled out laterally as if opening under the weight of the gable. (*Fig. 81b*) They have, as restored, no organic connection with their echinus. At the more or less contemporary temple of Artemis at Ephesos (whose siting will be discussed later) the capitals achieve their most telling late archaic form as their mass thickens and swells, and abacus and volutes respond to each other and to the fluted shaft. (*Fig. 159*) Now the whole works together as a force, rising up and rolling richly out and under to lift entablature and pediment into the air. So developed, the Ionic capital visually culminates the thrust of upward energies. Its volutes, whether originally based upon ram's horns or plant forms, now become beautifully mathematical expressions of the action of forces, akin to those of hydraulics. A paddle stroke will create an Ephesian Ionic capital and its fluted shaft in the water, reminding us of Thales, the first Ionian philosopher, who taught geometry and regarded water as the essence of all forms, or of Herakleitos, to whom reality was motion, or even of Aristophanes, who, parodying Anaxagoras, remarked (*Clouds*, 828) that these men had replaced Zeus with *dinos*, "whirl." Thus the columns gush up, and so springing could invoke many ancient symbols and holy things: the horns, the sacred tree, water itself. They create thereby a secondary holy landscape within which the deity can be housed and through which her labyrinthine processions can wind. It is therefore significant that the temple at Samos was called "The Labyrinth" in antiquity.[16] But it was a different kind of labyrinth from that formed by the Cretan palaces. Now it was an abstract setting, a frame for the movement of the labyrinthine dance. (*Figs. 81a, 158*) Thus it provoked the labyrinth but did not guide it, as the Cretan palaces had done. In this way the labyrinth itself became no longer a directed flow but a principle of choiceful action, picking its way around the solid, interrupting column shafts.

The principle of action informed the organization of the temenos as a whole. This organization changed over the centuries as the temples succeeded each other on the site, but the main lines remained generally similar.[17] Entrance to the temenos was always from the north. In the earlier one the angle of sight toward the temple from the propylon was fairly acute and was partly blocked by the pre–existing altar. (*Fig. 81*) In the later one the temple and the propylon were shifted west to allow the line of sight to run out between temple and altar in an expanding arc. At an early date the extension of this arc to the southwest was blocked by a long stoa, the earliest known in Greece. This ran generally northeast–southwest and directed the view primarily toward the sea and, eventually, Mount Mykale. Other stoas and subsidiary buildings eventually took their places in the temenos, closing it in but never, so far as one can determine, so placed or so high as to block the view of Mykale from the raised platform of the temple itself. Between the front of the temple and the subsidiary buildings an irregularly triangular space was defined, echoed to the north by the diagonal cleft in the hills. (*Fig. 79*) The irregularity of the intervals between buildings in the temenos has—always, and at every stage of its growth—several positive reasons.[18] First, its irregularities allow each building within the temenos (all of regular shape) to act as the unique elements and thus to retain positive plastic dominance over the intervals between them. The only exception to this, an intended one, is the stoa, which is meant to define the spatial enclosure. Second, the asymmetry of the near spaces around the great symmetrical shape of the temple ensures that no echoing rhythms within the temenos itself will visually tie the temple too closely to the ground inside the temenos enclosure and thus prevent it from fulfilling its primary function, which is to bring the whole far landscape into focus by being seen in relation to distant natural forms, as here to Mykale, the western hills, the northern cleft, and the southern islands. Therefore the apparently anarchic grouping of the buildings in archaic temene is neither thoughtless nor regrettable. It is simply a "mass–positive," "space–negative" method of building placement. Space is merely a void, a true interval, between masses. This method does not represent a lack of perception on the Greeks' part, as some critics—familiar, as they tell us, with the opposite criteria in Baroque planning—have claimed.[19] Instead, it was not only reasonable rather than mystical, since space is in fact a void defined by solids, but also essential, as the Greeks obviously knew, in order to release the great shape of the temples and the smaller shapes of the other buildings for the kinds of plastic action they had in mind. In this way the environment which had been created by the old labyrinth and courtyard of the Bronze Age was fundamentally modified; solids now acted on each other, confident in the open, clear in the light. The environment was now defined by a counterplay of forces. This quality, though with many expressive variations, remained characteristic of Greek temenos groupings for a long period, and will be seen at a number of Doric sites better than it can be at Samos. A recognition of it as deliberate serves to show where the Greeks' primary attention was focused: upon the active relationships between solids; upon those between temple and landscape and, as we shall see, between temple and temple. Yet with those the Greeks would later shape some voids uniquely alive.

At restricted Perachora and wide–spreading Samos alike, conical hills form an important element of Hera's motherly sites. The same is true at Olympia, (*Fig. 263*) but there Zeus, as king and father of kings, always held the dominion, and the cone was clearly the sacred tholos tomb of the old god, Kronos, and symbolic of that of Pelops as of all hero kings.[20] The present temple of Hera was originally of Zeus with Hera beside him.[21] It dates from the late seventh century, and under it are the foundations of two earlier ones. The first of these, according to Dörpfeld's reconstruction, was a simple expression of its structure and its interior space. (*Fig. 82*) It was non–peripteral, may have had only an eastern pediment, used clerestory windows, had no opisthodomos but instead a man–scaled door at the west. In all these ways it revealed its character as a container, and each of the elements or lacks noted above was scrupulously avoided in the subsequent rebuilding. Why they were avoided here, as in almost all subsequent Doric temples, is a question which can best be answered by a consideration of how the temple was meant to function on its site. We must leave aside at this time any consideration of the placement of the fifth–century temple of Zeus, and we cannot speculate upon whether there was a much earlier temple of Zeus on the same spot, its remains now deeply buried under the massive foundations of the fifth–century building.

One of the main entrances to the temenos in the fifth century was well to the southeast of the temple of Hera, whence the conical hill of Kronos lay directly on axis to the north. Just in front of that hill, as we have seen, the Bronze Age apsidal megara had been placed, and near them was the conical altar of Zeus. Defining this area and with the capitals of its eastern columns on line with the slope of the hill, stood the early temple. (*Figs. 270, 272*) Seen from this point of vantage, its long east–west length would have flattened out the hill slope, and its heavy, gabled, unbroken roof would have complemented and emphasized the geometry of the cone. The temple was set in as close a relationship to the hill as possible, and the two together made a coherent union of separate forms, one constructed, one natural: the new king and the old, later the daughter and her father, together. The basic necessity here was not for the completion of an enclosing site, as at Perachora, but for the juxtaposition of two objects closely in space. This relationship now involves two new elements of the second and third temples' design: the peripteral colonnade and the "opisthodomos." (*Figs. 82, 83*) The first, as we have already seen, externalizes the temple as a space object and makes it difficult for the viewer to read it as simply a shell enclosing a volume. (The columns were, of course, originally of wood and were replaced with stone over many centuries.) The second element, the opisthodomos, has a similar function: to deny any wall intersection at the corners, since it is precisely the meeting of two planes at an exterior corner which expresses space enclosure in a rectangular building. The pronaos already served the function of externalization naturally at the eastern, entrance, end. Now at the western end a false pronaos is added, and the generalizing name "opisthodomos," simply "the work at the rear," perfectly describes its primarily sculptural function. Other functions, such as that of an occasional treasure house, were secondary and arrived at after the plastic decision had been made. Moreover, the false pronaos, once fully developed, was normally confined to peripteral temples, and this fact alone indicates that it was intended to act sculpturally and not, for example, as weather protection for the rear walls, as the projecting side walls of the Bronze Age megara of Troy had probably done. (Chapter 2, Note 45)

By means of the opisthodomos the temple was effectively made double–ended as viewed from the outside, and any angle view of it would always seem a complete, never simply a back, view. In this way the temple became even more an abstract exterior object in the light of nature as well as a dark megaron for its deity, now conceived in depth.

One recalls that the final Ionic temple at Samos used a triple colonnade to mask its closed west end, but the earlier Doric solution seems more integral. The purposeful elimination at Olympia of the first temple's low door and clerestory windows, both expressive of contained space and its uses, was especially cogent. Thus the Greek temple, by the middle of the seventh century and exactly at the moment when Greek monumental sculpture first began to take form, dedicated itself to similar sculptural ends. Indeed, the problem of making the temple one integral whole was to preoccupy Doric architects for several centuries, since only by becoming fully integral could its sculptural rather than its spatial or structural character be stressed. That is to say, even the final Heraion at Olympia was not yet fully integral and thus sculptural insofar as its columns are still so far apart as to emphasize its pavilion quality. (*Fig. 84*) They are also comparatively short in relation to the deep overhang of the cornice and the height of the gable above them. The terra–cotta akroterion, not sculpturally active itself, rounds over and caps the whole. Thus the effect is of posts supporting a great weight, a structural not a sculptural effect, and one emphasized by the triglyphs which appear only over the capitals, clearly express-ing beam ends and too spread out to form simply a complementary textural pattern. These are the qualities Etruscan temples were to exploit: the skeletal, spatial, and "heavy–headed." The Heraion is also long in relation to its width, and this makes it difficult for the eye to grasp its exterior mass as a compact whole. These points are important, because, so long as the Doric temple could be read purely as a constructed container of space, its opportunities for expression were limited to those possible for constructions and containers, but, when it became sculpturally integral, it could transcend those normal architectural limitations and become a body, an organic though wholly abstract unity, a potentially active image at architectural scale. The Heraion at Olympia was not yet an integral force by itself, although, by contrast, it may be felt to have become one when the later temple of Zeus was built nearby.

These and other related questions can be considered in greater detail at the site of the temples of Hera at Paestum, but in order to understand the temple–landscape relationships at Paestum itself it is necessary to look first at the Heraion of Argos.[22] This, too, had been sacred to the goddess during the Mycenaean period, as we have already seen, and in archaic times it claimed, with Samos, the honor of having been Hera's birthplace. Indeed, Hera at this spot, ox–eyed Argive Hera, is clearly the old goddess herself as queen. It was here in myth that Zeus came to her in the form of a cuckoo and, taking advantage of her kindness, ravished her and brought her under his dominion.[23] The Heraion of Argos is therefore Hera's uniquely holy spot, upon which she sits as "golden-throned Hera"[24] and from which she is able to view her ancient world.

As noted earlier, the Heraion lies northeast across the valley from the conical hill of the Dorian city of Argos. On the slopes of that hill stood a temple of Hera, and nearby were sanc-tuaries of Aphrodite, Apollo, and Athena.[25] (*Fig. 53*) But the Heraion was the supremely holy place, and it was to the Heraion that Cleobis and Biton dragged their mother's chariot across the plain from Argos.²⁶ The story of their subsequent death through the favor of the goddess as they slept in her temple obviously derives from the old, pre–Dorian tradition of sleep, death, and oneness with the goddess which we mentioned earlier. We have also discussed the embracing horns and mounded foothills of the site of the Heraion. In the archaic and later classic organization of the site two phases can be traced. (*Fig. 85*) In the earlier phase, attention seems concentrated upon the great formation itself, below which the temple was placed. (*Fig. 86*) In the later phase a subtle duality is developed, in which the spectator's attention seems to have been doubly directed: first, toward the backing formation, second, in the opposite direction toward the valley and the sacred objects across it. (*Fig. 87*) A certain shift in attitude can be seen in this partial reorientation and enrichment of the experience of the site, since the first phase seems to concentrate upon the immediate objects of the cult seen close to each other, the second upon a broad sweep of relevant objects in space. The earlier temple, probably dating from the seventh century, already had an opisthodomos and occupied the top of the mounded hill that lay before the mountain. Thus it was in an excellent position to be seen, as one approached across the valley, directly in long profile under the mountain's horns and standing just east of a deep cleft in the body of the mountain. (*Fig. 86*) It, too, had an opisthodomos—just as the terracotta model of the Geometric Period found at the site was rectangular with side walls slightly projected at the rear, so contrasting with the apsidal model from Perachora (*Fig. 72*) and probably representing a further step toward that full Doric form with whose initiation the Argive Heraion was later associated. (Vitruvius, IV.1.3.) The opisthodomos looked west across the slope, and there may have been a lustral basin on this side, in front of the cleft, although this is by no means certain. No trace of an altar has been found to the east of the temple, and the platform would indeed have allowed little room for one there. Instead, its splendid, cyclopean elevation offered a fine position from which to look down upon the lower terrace, where the main altar may always have been, and beyond it across the valley toward the cone of Argos and its accompanying cleft to the north. Again, the altar was between the temple and the cone, but there was no place from which the temple itself could be seen against the valley view, since its own platform occupied the highest available ground. So the early temple as experienced—a little like Hera's temple at Olympia—was itself a complement to the closely sheltering sacred mountain behind it, not to the cone of Argos.

In 423 the early temple burned, apparently through the carelessness of a priestess. The new temple which was then built was not placed upon the still solid foundations of the old one, but instead on the terrace below it. From across the valley, therefore, it stood out slightly less well than had the other against the mountain backdrop. On the other hand, the old platform now allowed a view of the new temple against the valley and the cone. With the steps, stoas, and the possible Telesterion which were then added to the site, we are already in the realm of rather regularized and axial planning, sometimes to be found in the fifth century, but more characteristic of fourth–century and later practice. All of these elements reinforce the new double experience. Left of the steps, a stoa directed the eye northwestward far up the valley. (*Fig. 85*) Directly ahead, in the middle of the top of the steps, was the main altar, now on a cross axis with the new temple, whose eastern range of columns stood, in this perspective, next to the mountain's western horn. Diagonally ahead, the cyclopean masonry of the old platform directed the eye, and under it, on that axis, the enclosed building called a Telesterion was placed. Its presence, like that of the enclosure at Perachora, would seem to indicate a continuance or revival of the rites of the old goddess, practiced inside. The lower terrace funnels toward the Telesterion and, in the view backward from it across the valley, the space funnels outward in the opposite direction in a wide arc. The temple took the eye in a long perspective toward Mount Kyllene above Stymphalia to the northwest, and its east front marked a line of sight to the cleft above Argos. (*Fig. 87*) The altar, in this same view, directed the eye across space toward the Argive cone. Its present position is marked by the ruins of the former caretaker's hut, of which it need hardly be said that the resemblance to horns is purely an accident of decay. From the altar itself the participant in the ceremony must have looked toward Argos, unless he stood on the steps below, which seems unlikely. The view from the altar swept of course beyond Argos across the bay, and, from the stoa behind the temple, a line of sight from the temple across the corner of the stairs toward Palamedes and the pointed hills above Tiryns was set up. Thus, the double orientation of the later site seems complete. Indeed, we have treated the stairs as primarily an entrance feature, but one can imagine a ritual which moved in the opposite direction: that is, through what was possibly a propylon to the west under the cleft, past the new temple, up the central flight of stairs to the holy site of the old temple, and from that elevation turning away from the sacred mountain behind to look across the new temple toward Argos. Descending again to the lower terrace and the altar, one would then have had a final climax as the stoas opened out and the stairs spilled down toward the far view.

One fact is clear: the planning of the Heraion, like that of all the sites we have seen so far, consciously makes use of the landscape elements as integral parts of the overall architectural design, and the elements chosen as pivotal are those which had always been the old potent symbols: the horns and the cone. As developed at Argos, the planning of the site controls the whole visual horizon, and the entire world as seen is drawn into the focus of the human eye. This is the Greek reconciliation with nature in terms of broader experience, a new and more complex "pact of friendship" with the world. At the same time, Argos again presents a Hera who embraces the whole earth, still holding in her nature a memory of the identification of the animals with her, "ox–eyed," like the beasts sacrificed at her altars.

When, from the eighth century onward, the Greeks began to plant colonies around the Mediterranean basin and the Black Sea, it is apparent that their yearning for the goddess as a mother was intensified. The reasons for this were probably many, and similar reactions have been traced among colonials elsewhere, notably in America. In fact, the American analogy, though it obviously should not be pressed too far, is in many ways a good one. It is especially cogent as it relates to landscape. That is, the American comes from the comparatively small, definite, clearly defined landscapes of Europe, hallowed by long associations and fenced off into stable units by centuries of cultivation and building. He then journeys with trepidation across the primal indefiniteness of the sea. He is cut off by it from his known world, and he comes at last to a landscape which is bigger, wilder, more unfriendly, most of all less bounded, than that of his European home. Especially as he moves westward does the size of the land increase, until he finds himself at last adrift in a new kind of primal flood: the "sea of trees," the "sea of grass," the empty desert with its mirage, the phantom mountains which come no nearer throughout a long day's march. (*Fig. 88*) South Italy and Sicily are not Kansas, but emigration to them must have meant at least three related things to the Greeks of archaic times: a hazardous journey across the sea, a considerable enlargement of landscape scale, and a comparable relaxation of custom and tradition in the face of a larger world of opportunity and change. In that new world, wider and less stable than the one he had known, the Greek seems to have reacted much as the later European in America was to do: with ebullient invention up to a point and, beyond that, with an extraordinarily pressing desire for security. The strength of the Greek goddess cults in South Italy and Sicily is therefore not to be explained away by the existence of pre–Greek cults of that kind in those regions, although such certainly existed in many places.[27] On the contrary, the problem that faced the Greek in the new lands was precisely the one we might expect, in view of the landscape forms we have been considering: the problem, that is, of finding sacred sites where the landscape spoke, or could, through the placing of temples in it, be made to speak, of the gods. The problem is complicated by the fact that the Greek was primarily founding not sanctuaries but cities in Italy, and his temples there were generally city temples. Out of this fact grow types of temple–landscape association which can best be discussed later, when we briefly consider the question of the temple in the planned town. And it should be pointed out that colonial cities were gridded very early. But the problem in architecture that underlay all others for the Greek in Italy and Sicily was the problem of landscape scale, and this was integrally related to the aforementioned need for finding security in a new place. Both these problems the Greek attempted to solve by the placement and form of his temples. Such attempts can be recognized at the sanctuaries of Hera at the river Silaris, in southern Campania, and at the town of Poseidonia close by. (*Sketch Map 3*)

When the Greeks from Chalkis landed at the mouth of the Silaris, now Sele, they dedicated the spot to their goddess.[28] Beyond the temenos the valley opens widely northeast toward the interior of Italy, and from a position close to the shore the temple of Hera faced the vast expanse. (*Fig. 89*) Seen from a landing boat, a condition now impossible because of the building–out of the shore line, the long temple with its peripteral colonnade must have pointed like an arrow into the heart of the land. The exaggerated projection of the colonnades beyond the adyton on the west and the cella on the east enhanced that effect and provided a deep shelter for the goddess in an alien place. Beside the temple stood its treasuries in an active rank, and before it a long altar was set at a perceptible angle, creating once more an irregular spatial interval and thus leaving the eye free to move over it into the distance. In these ways the sanctuary at the Silaris expresses a will to command the land and to bring what must have seemed to the Greeks its miraculously wide expanse under the eye of their own goddess of the earth and under the eyes of the worshipers at her shrine. The land is celebrated at the Silaris, as is the long valley of the river which waters it, and colonists and goddess take possession of it together.

The town of Poseidonia,[29] the Roman Paestum, was placed seven kilometers to the south of the Silaris, at a point in the long coastal plain where a range of the mountains of the interior closes in to form a decisive barrier. The valley is still fairly wide by Greek standards, however, and the town itself was so laid out as to group its gods and its agora within a long rectangle through its center. (*Fig. 90*) It was fortified during the fifth century, and from this period at least a long avenue ran along the sacred central rectangle from north to south, parallel with the coast and the mountain barrier. Near the southern end of the rectangle, and east of the long street, between, that is, the street and the mountains, was a temenos enclosure, and near the northern end was another. The latter contained a temple of Athena and will be discussed later; the former had two large temples of Argive Hera. The earlier of these, which used to be called the "Basilica," dates from about 550; the later, which used to be called the "Temple of Poseidon," from about 450.[30] Perhaps forty yards separates these two temples, and apparently this interval was always left open. From the main road to the west, it is clear that both temples are oriented in the same direction: eastward toward the strongly conical and notched hill which terminates the nearer range and behind which the clefts of the farther mountains can be seen. (*Figs. 94, 95*) Indeed, both temples face exactly toward the notch formed by the northern slope of the cone and the southern slope of the rest of the range. (*Figs. 92, 98*) We are instantly reminded of the Argolid, with the conical hill of Hera which focuses the view from the Heraion, and we surmise that the conical hill, which meant the goddess and home, had something to do with the placing of the town itself or, at any rate, permitted the town to claim Hera as its link with the earth and dictated the place of her temenos within the town.[31]

Long altars stood before each temple on the east, and across these the conical hill with its attendant clefts was the dominant feature of the goddess' view from her cella. But, as we have already noted at Argos, the larger visual function of a classic Greek temple was to complement the landscape features which it brought into focus for the worshiper. From the altars at Paestum, as they were originally placed before the houses of the town grew up to the east of them, both hill and temple could have been seen, but not together. This means that the placing of the road to the west, from which temples and hill could normally be seen together, was of the utmost importance in developing the character of the deity as the human participant might be made to see it as a whole. (Of course, the original approach from the sea, whatever that was, would always have shown hill and temples together.) The Doric temple, so perceived with its landscape, was made to play a more complicated part in the total sculptural expression of its divinity. A study of the two temples at Paestum, concentrated on the essential points of how effectively they focus the view and how fully they embody an unmistakably sculptural expression in contrast to that of the hill, can demonstrate an extraordinary development in the Greek understanding and command of the possibilities latent in this double relationship.

The older temple is so wide as to be read primarily as a spatial enclosure. (*Figs. 90, 92*) Its nine columns, with the central one expressive of the single row which runs through the center of the wide cella as a spine, can never be seen at once as a unit; they constantly demand to be counted and thus cannot unite their quality of an additive colonnade with the counter quality of seeming to be a single form. Their shapes, too, express the structural separateness of the parts of the temple. Their pronounced entasis, the decisive thinning of their sections below the capital itself, the wide, flat swag of their echinus, all express the flattening and bulging of vertical supports which are gallantly upholding a tremendously compressive weight. (*Fig. 93*) Their form itself is, of course, profoundly sculptural, and they have the power to make the human observer feel in his own body, as Ionic columns do not, what it is to stand upright and support a great burden. The human being can thus identify with them empathetically, and, precisely because of their abstract form, the image of the human body standing upright is insistently evoked by them. In this way they embody the beginnings of the whole tradition of humanistic architecture in the west. Above them we must visualize the strong plastic entablature and the high, very wide gable, stretching across the nine–columned façade. (*Fig. 92*) Its effect must have been both deeply sheltering and weighty: a deep canopy supported by short and compressed shafts. The forces thus weigh down upon the tensely balanced uprightness of the columns, and these seem, as their numbers multiply, to stretch out laterally in order to distribute the weight; in this way they further emphasize the quality of spatial enclosure. Like the Ionic temples which may have had some influence on its design, the first temple of Hera at Paestum is a building made up of separate parts and spreading widely into space. As such it is expressive of shelter and enclosure in a new land, but precisely as such, it does not stand as a single sculptural force in the void. Because of this, too, its capacity to carry the eye past it would constantly have been interrupted by the tendency of the eye to slip around the narrowed shafts of its columns into the deep volume of space under the entablature and between the columns and the deeply set back cella walls. (*Fig. 94*) For these reasons the view of the first temple and hill from the western road is not so unified as that created by the second temple. If, as seems likely, the earlier temple also had a closed adyton behind its cella and no opisthodomos, the west would have had a further quality of "backsidedness," like that of Ionic temples. It, like them, is an ambient, though without the grovelike quality of the Ionic colonnades. Instead, the echinus, always carved in a single block with the abacus slab, here sags, heavy with the body of the goddess (*Fig. 93*); elsewhere it may start to lift (*Fig. 316*), or stolidly compact (*Fig. 189*), or, approaching a more perfect conoid, bulge with energy (*Fig. 96a*), or expend it upward (*Fig. 324*).

In the second temple of Hera at Paestum we are dealing with the Doric temple at the height of its sculpturally expressive powers. The first impression the eye retains is of an absolute unity and balance. (*Fig. 95*) It then sees, without ever losing that first impression, that the unity is made up of totally separate parts and that the balance is between completely dissimilar units. The columns of the front and rear are six; one may count them if one wishes, but the eye takes them in at a glance as forming a single shape. Accepting this as one, the eye then feels the whole shape to be taking on direction as the side columns recede into space. The temple is both open and closed. In the optimum angle view the eye can slip between the columns of both the front and the flank, but, moving, it may be prevented, for example, from entering between the columns of the side, which thus form one plastically rhythmical wall. As the observer changes position these relationships change; the eye will penetrate at the side and will slowly slide out along the columns of the front until they in turn become an impenetrable façade. (*Fig. 91*) Great care is taken with the corner columns; they, like all the others, are slanted inward, but more decisively. In order that the angle view through the corner will not be too open the intervals between the corner columns and their neighbors are contracted, and this contraction tends to make the corner column appear thicker, almost elliptical when viewed diagonally as it encroaches upon the void and stands solid at the angle. (*Fig. 96a*) All stand at the steps' edge, drawing them into the temple body as a whole.

Immobile, the columns will be seen in varying relationships to their backgrounds: along the side in variations of relief against a solid plane of wall; from either end (now that there is an opisthodomos) (*Fig. 97*) as the forward rank of a group of cylindrical elements through which the eye penetrates literally step by step between the wall ends into the hollows of the temple, while it can at the same time be moving down the outside of the cella wall between it and the columns of the flank. The temple is therefore both open and closed, solid and void, interlocking inside and outside in a splendidly measured rhythm of column and wall; drawing the human observer toward its unilinear interior even as it is inviting his eye and his feet to move down its ptera avenues and through its intervals toward landscape space. (*Fig. 96b*) Overhead were closely spaced timber beams with coffered or "slotted" wooden ceilings, capping the rectangular voids and concealing the skeleton members of the built–up gable roof, this too most often statically compressive rather than a truss.[32] Beyond the central void the doors of the cella will be closed, except on the deity's special feast days, but they stand deep in the body of the building within the shadows of the pronaos and behind the columns in antis. In this way the temple always allows itself to be penetrated for a certain distance, on its hard pavement between the shafts of noble bearing, but it also keeps, behind the closed doors of its inner recess, its own special being and its integrity. Therefore, when the doors are opened that act is itself special and marks a particular occasion, the rare moment of full contact when the inner image is shown. So the temple both invites and sets a limit. It is a true being, separate from the human beings who come to it and with its own selfhood different from theirs. It is the fact of the deity: approachable but inviolate. For all these reasons, the emphasis, in the wholly integrated plan and elevation, is all upon the placement of solid cylinders and planes, drums and blocks. The temple is thus designed not spatially but sculpturally. Inside, for example, the scale dwindles as the columns are doubled, one above the other, to support the roof. (*Fig. 98*) The image of the Argive goddess of childbirth, now facing at Paestum out of her dark house directly toward the cleft beside the conical hill, is set in this way within a building fabric which has itself the character of a body made up of many parts (*see also Figs. 304–312*). Because there are two rows of interior columns, the body can now have a hollow center and a single doorway, in contrast to the older temple of Hera whose central axis was taken up by a single row of supports, as was that of her earliest temple on Samos. These both made it difficult for the image to occupy the center and split the temple into two halves, internally and externally. In the second building, as in all later Greek temples where interior columns were required, the principle of the esophagus took precedence over that of the spine.

The space conception of the temple as a whole, however, is based entirely upon the effect of tangible objects upon each other in an essentially modular relationship. Space itself is negative, the solids positive, both inside and out. But the general impression is of a balance between objects and intervals. This is especially true of the exterior, where the columns themselves are so spaced and proportioned as to give the impression that their cylindrical masses and the space between them are in an almost one–to–one relationship with each other. (*Figs. 95, 96*) Therefore, the temple cannot be viewed as a structural web, like a Japanese or, in a different way, a Gothic building; nor, on the other hand, as a solid mass, like an Egyptian or Mayan pyramid; nor, to go further, as a shell which encloses a space, like a Roman, Romanesque, or Renaissance building. Instead, the temple interweaves qualities characteristic at once of the skeletal pavilion, the volumetric shell, and the solid mass, and thus escapes being defined as any one of these so that it can be seen purely as an articulated sculptural body. Other balances occur: the temple is an essentially prismatic form, a joining of flat planes which are more horizontal than vertical, but it is defined to the eye by vertical cylinders which deny the two–dimensionality of the bounding planes and give the mass three–dimensional depth. The verticality and rotundity of the cylinders are alike emphasized by their flutings, but these also serve as a purely surface contrast with the horizontal flat plane of the entablature. Above this appears the sharply horizontal shadow line of the taenia, but this is broken by the small cylinders of the guttae, above which are the clearly vertical shadows of the triglyphs. These, in turn, are arranged in a horizontal sequence, occurring over the column capitals and between them, over, that is, both solids and voids, and shifted over enough to join in a tensely stretched articulation of the planes at the corners. Between the triglyphs the flat slabs of the metopes may come alive with sculptured groups, usually representing, as Kähler and others have pointed out, the triumph of human will, assisted by the Olympian gods, over the beast power of nature and the old goddess and forming a "diadem" for the mathematically ordered form beneath.[33] But, more than this, the relative visual complexity of the sculptural groups can only have been intended to heighten the subtle order of the architectural forms. The shadow of the cornice is deep over this zone of activity, and above is the shadowed triangle of the pediment, a final contrast to the cylinders and rectangles below. In the pediment a sculptural group at larger scale may appear, rising above the diadem of metopes in a further burst of freer action. Above this the hard profile of the raking cornice will, however, hold the sum of the building's sculptural forces calm and steady. But above the cornice the moldings of the roof will flare, and down the flanking roof edges the alternating water spouts and antefixes make their own quick and colorful movement, reflecting the images in the sculptural groups below but abstractly disciplined in their profiles. So actively heraldic akroteria, floral, monstrous, and human, now burst upward from the gables. For them the temple is no mere space platform, as the Veiian Etruscans, by turning them into gods and exaggerating their size, tended to make it, but their generating force, as they crown, release, and vaunt its own bodily power. (*Figs. 109, 344*)

In that personification of force the base, now integrated with the overall mass, is profoundly important. (*Figs. 95, 96a*) The three steps set the temple clearly off the ground as a detached object; yet they also lead the eye gradually up to the temple and away from it, thereby uniting it with the ground and with surrounding space. Similarly, they, like all the other elements in the temple, are scaled in a proportional relationship to those other elements, not to human use. This fact, coupled as it now is with the absence of those other features, such as windows, which make the observer read most buildings primarily as containers for human activity, means that the temple's scale is purely abstract, thus purely sculptural. We saw the necessary eliminations toward this end taking place at Olympia. (*Figs. 82–84*) Where doors are used they are set deeply within the planes of the pronaos walls and are also scaled to the building, not to human size. Therefore, the developed temple totally avoids the kind of identification with human use that would limit its sculptural abstraction. But its form is not only abstractly scaled; it is also sympathetically proportioned as an integral being which, more than any other kind of building, evokes an image of permanent human force. Because of these two qualities it can attain considerable size without crushing the human observer under a grandiose environment. Instead, it magnifies into the beings of the gods the best of what he himself can identify as his own.

It is important to note that this kind of scale, and the quality of appearing as a single body made up of many parts and therefore potentially active, would not have been possible if the Greeks had complicated the simple form of the temple by the introduction of asymmetrical elements into it or the addition of subsidiary masses to it. Its singleness as one integral force and as a jointed body with its own symmetrical balance and clear contour would have been fatally vitiated thereby. The solitary exception to this rule is the Erechtheion in Athens, which is asymmetrical and additive in massing for specific reasons, which will be discussed later. It should also be apparent why the temple could not have been built in an arcuated structural system. Arches between the columns would have set up a curvilinear rhythm in which one part would have run into the next to produce an effect primarily spatial rather than sculptural. Similarly, the swelling forms of arcades, apses, and domes would have caused the temple to be seen from the exterior as a shell of space, indeed as inflated by it. One can test this, for example, by looking at the pediment, with its solid and quiet diagonals, and trying to imagine the effect if it were curved in the profile of a barrel vault. The moment such pressure had been felt upon the parts each would have lost its quality of seeming to rest with absolute stability and without strain. Instead of a balance between solid and void, in which the position of each solid is determined simply by its relation to other solids, interior space and its expression would have become dominant, and the temple would have lost the primary tools of sculptural density and precise articulation whereby it makes its presence felt in the landscape and keeps its scale personal to itself.

At the same time, the temple can act as it does precisely because the structural oppositions between the elements which compose it can no longer be felt in terms of struggle. Each is separate, but all make one. The columns rise, swell, contract, cushion out into an upward–thrusting echinus, and stiffen into the slab of the abacus upon which the weight of entablature and pediment is placed. This weight, though solid, no longer appears to press down upon the columns unduly, nor do these any longer dramatize their support of it. The resolution between the forces is so exact as to remove a sense of conflict but not so precise as to preclude variation. That is not to say that the structural forces are denied; quite the contrary. The temple is supremely *built*, and thus architectural. But the craft of the architect here is to convince the observer that the sculptural form assumed is the one the structure must inevitably have become. So the temple, load and support, becomes one thing. The whole rises, and the word here must be rises, out of the ground, rises upon the stepped base, which is itself swelling upward also, so that one force is acting through the whole. This force then raises the center of the entablature in a slight but perceptible arc, bends it inward at the narrow fronts and outward along the long sides. These refinements are clearly not intended to correct optical distortions (otherwise they would not be visible) but to create positive effects of life and vitality.[34] Yet as its vital force pushes upward, inward, and outward, the temple, and this is perhaps the finest of its balanced paradoxes, still exerts a solemn pressure upon the ground. The base is again important here. Because of it the columns do not rise singly out of the earth but are part of one solemn unity which weighs upon it. In this somber pressure we are made more fully aware of what the Greek temple represents in terms of the general development of human culture. It is megalithic building, its metal clamps and reinforcing bars carefully concealed from view. At the same time it is megalithic building which has in this case been turned to very late by a highly developed people with long experience of the skeletal forms of wood construction behind them, so that, as we have seen, many traditions have fused in the final form. Again, it seems a reconciliation between old and new ways. The stones, once reaccepted, are treated with a conscious sense of their special dignity. No mortar intervenes between the pressures of the blocks and drums upon each other. Drum by drum the columns rise, and as the heavy individual units are added, slowly and carefully over many months and years, the point loads increase, building up a concentrated weight upon the earth which is distributed by the foundations and expressed by the outward–spreading stairs. The visible surfaces are then carved, fluted, and rubbed. No more conservative or reverent kind of building can be imagined: it is not timid building, as many critics, imbued with a rather naive nineteenth–century technological positivism, have asserted. But it is ritual building, the process itself measured and holy, as slow as Stone Age time itself and, indeed, a kind of ultimate refinement of Stone and Bronze Age tradition. All the more remarkable, therefore, is the Greek union of such reverent conservatism with the complex and subtle optics and mathematics which inform it. Since these are based upon the effects they will have upon the human eye, they are the product of careful observation and cool application of principles which had been arrived at through experiment. Similarly, all the carefully cut and treated surfaces of the stone were covered at last with a hard coat of blazing white stucco, and the details of frieze and cornice were picked out in strong blues and terra–cotta reds, the colors of earth and sky intensified, while the sculptural groups were gilded and painted in reds, blacks, browns, yellows, blues, and greens. Respect for the material and the process, therefore, was not allowed to stand in the way of the utmost clarity and brightness of optical effect. This was a union of the most ritually conservative, intellectual, and physical of attitudes, and it makes the Greek temple one of the most illuminating products of that dialogue between mind and matter through which all works of art are created.

The union is, however, more complete than this. We have seen how the temple is at once closed and open; it is also wholly self–contained and yet capable of carrying the eye far into space. The second temple to Hera at Paestum can be observed to do this in several ways. The stylobate and the entablature set up a strong perspective which carries the eye rapidly toward the conical hill. (*Figs. 95, Frontispiece*) Even when the perspective created by the stylobate was blocked by the massed houses of the town the entablature alone would have done this. Moreover, the entablature leaps out in a strong arc as we have seen, and when one looks along this profile its active line creates a trajectory for the eye which projects it even more rapidly toward its objective. (*Fig. 99*) Yet as the eye is projected rapidly by the continuous line of the cornice the triglyphs and metopes below that line set up a choppy, metrical beat which tends at once to slow the movement and to divide the space between temple and hill into measurable units of distance. (*Figs. 95, Frontispiece*) A rather different effect is created by the shafts and capitals of the columns. The unit of measure which these set up is so insistent, and the gravity of their march is so profound that, when they abruptly stop at the far end of the temple, the eye must snap across the dizzy void which is thus created and come to rest upon the next solid object of comparable scale, in this case the conical hill. The temple and the landscape are thus one architecture here. Once again, the space created is that of the intervals between objects. It is the solid bodies in space which are important; space itself is a void within which the bodies are free and across which the eye can move from one to the other. At the same time, while the temple can direct the eye to specific landscape objects, its whole body remains a regular rectangular unit within the irregular but more or less circular landscape shape; within the circle, that is, of the natural world. If it were itself circular it would essentially merely echo that world—as Stonehenge, for example, does (*Fig. 32*)—and its special quality as a dense, potent, and unique presence in the landscape would be seriously reduced. Similarly, if it were square rather than rectangular, it would lose potency and become static. As it stands, each element remains supremely itself, nature in its own whole and permanent form, the temple clearly man made, forceful, and abstract. True enough, beneath the temple's abstraction and because of it there are latent images and echoes: obvious echoes of landscape like the clarification of far hill profiles in the gable shape,[35] (*Fig. 95*) hidden but tenacious images of the human body, as in the vertically standing, muscular forms of the columns. (*Fig. 96a*) Therefore, when a Doric column falls and drums and capitals divide, it is somehow a human back, the human neck, that breaks. (*Fig. 107*) Still, it is the abstraction of the temple which is its most human quality, and it is this which brings into the natural landscape a dignified image of man. Once seen together, both landscape and temple will seem forever afterward to be incomplete without the other. Each ennobles its opposite, and their relationship brings the universe of nature and man into a new and stable order, creating the most complete and realistic environment ever imagined by men as their own. The Dorian insistence upon human separateness is thus brought into union with the full sanctity of the land in terms of the double character of divinity. The contrast with Minoan form and meaning is exact; there is no longer the spread–out, protective hollow of the palace, dominated by nature's massive solids, but, as in all Greek art, the compact sculptural body of the temple, balancing them.

At Paestum, also, the two temples of Hera create together a special perspective toward the sacred landscape feature. (*Figs. 90, 99*) This becomes an urban device of great power. The eye is taken out of and beyond the town in a directed expansion of vision to the surrounding land. Similarly, the temples stand together, in the view from the east, against the sky, below which, out of sight, lies the empty Italian sea. Thus the temples not only focus upon the critical landscape object but also free the eye to investigate the whole arc of the horizon, even as they create their own interior landscape in the center of the town. That town order is then carried far out to space. The strong profiles of the entablatures are like the *kanones aëros* of Aristophanes' Meton, inscribing straight lines across the ovenlike half–sphere of the sky and furnishing a measure for its expanse.[36] So colonial cities built many temples, extending their grid to the sky as well.

We have used the classic temple of Hera at Paestum to illustrate qualities which are held in common by many Doric temples during the later archaic and early classic periods, but each temple is specific as well. Each, as read with its landscape, expresses a special set of experiences and embodies its own special meanings. At Paestum the meaning seems clear. Everything about

Hera's second temple there speaks of permanent, fixed, heavy, and earthbound values. (*Figs. 96a, Frontispiece*) These effects are so pronounced that various critics have attempted, despite the extraordinary refinement of the temple's design, to place it much earlier in time.[37] And a sensitive modern architect, not an art historian, has said: "Paestum marks the great event in architecture when the walls first parted and columns became."[38] The columns at Paestum do indeed seem to be of great bulk and weight, as if they were the first columns ever made, but this quality is not necessarily characteristic of earlier Greek columns. Many archaic examples are much thinner and less heavy, and even those of the first temple of Hera at Paestum give the impression of being so. (*Fig. 93*) The effect of the second temple of Hera at that place is therefore calculated to express the meaning its builders intended. This meaning is entirely appropriate to the landscape, reminiscent of Argos, to the colonial town, and to the Argive Hera and the Hera Eileithyia whom it celebrates: namely, that the Greek and his goddess had been on the land a long time—indeed, with the triumphant illogic of art, forever—and that they belonged there.[39]

Many temples in South Italy and Sicily were certainly built for Hera as Lacinia, as, that is, the goddess who holds the land for men as their fair share. One was built on the headland at Croton, where the gulf of Taranto curves around to its western landfall.[40] Here again it was a great arc of shore and sea, like that at Samos, but now an empty sea, which the temple culminated, defined, and thus made Greek. Across the gulf, the columns called the "Tavole Paladine," which faced the vast and empty plain at Metapontum, may have been Hera's also. (*Fig. 88*) Air photographs now show that the placement of this temple, of c. 510 B.C., was—from some early period, perhaps from the beginning—integrated with an extensive grid of landholdings that stretched out across the plain like American quarter sections.[40a] The temple called of Hera Lacinia at Akragas in southern Sicily may be hers in fact, but here, too, the identification cannot be sure.[41] The temple is placed at the spot where the curve of the southern ridge line both rises highest in its arc and is at the same time farthest from the acropolis mass which looms far to the northwest. (*Fig. 100*) To the east, in view from the temple's altar on the point, the land outside the city bubbles with many hills, and to the south the long coastal plain slopes down to the distant sea. As one approaches by sea or land from the east this temple is the first seen of the many at Akragas. It is placed at the exact spot from which most of the arc of land and sea which forms Akragas and its approaches can best be grasped. (*Fig. 101*) The temple is almost contemporary with the second of the two Hera temples at Paestum, probably dating from about 460–50 B.C. Unlike the solemn presence there, it is a tight, stiff, hard form as befits one placed upon a rocky eminence as a spatial pivot. (*Fig. 102*) Yet one senses that it cannot act as a pivot for the great space enclosed by the ridges of the city themselves. (*Fig. 103*) Only the mighty and unusual temple of Zeus, to be considered later, comes close to doing that. Indeed, Akragas itself apparently had a grid plan by the late archaic period, and one of its long streets led straight to Zeus' temple.[41a] Thus the problem of the temple in the city, and particularly in a huge Sicilian city like Akragas, is a special one. It involves the placing of temples of deities in landscapes which are not peculiarly appropriate to them. In fact, the Greek gods were in the landscape of Greece, but they had to be imported to Sicily. In this a special problem arose for Greek temple architecture, in which the temples were intended to play a reciprocal role with the land. It involves in part the placing of temples with respect to what might be called city landscapes rather than natural ones; the implications of this question, as noted before, can best be considered later. Therefore, while one must consider the landscape relationships of the temples of the Sicilian towns, yet the problem is often not one of sanctuaries with identifiably sacred forms but of urban adjustments, which involve another kind of relationship of man with his gods. It is clear that the temples along the southern ridge at vast Akragas (*Fig. 103*) were so placed and so designed as to define the confines of the town: taut "Hera" on the point; dense, high–stepped "Concord" set solidly between land and water like a bench mark halfway down; (*Figs. 104, 105*) thick "Herakles" (perhaps Apollo) rising like a fence above the main gate. However these temples were in fact dedicated, they clearly set between the acropolis and the coastal plain a sure semicircle of Greek gods. (*Fig. 103*) In accord with this, the temples of "Hera" and "Concord" both have rising stylobates and entablatures at the sides but are straight across the front.[42] They are thus firmly static laterally, in terms of the ridge, but they carry the eye longitudinally along it—so connecting themselves with each other and projecting beyond their own bodies their godly palisade. (*Figs. 104, 105*)

A similar problem arises at Selinus, which will also be discussed as a whole later.[43] Here is another landscape at great scale but, unlike that at Akragas, generally flat, gently rolling, essentially featureless. (*Figs. 106, 107*) No ring of hills forms the plain close enough to make its presence strongly felt, nor do any islands bound the sea. The land itself moves in long fluid waves, upon two of which the temples are set. The later Temple ER on the eastern hill, the early megaron, and the splendid, gaudy Temple C (*Figs. 108, 109*) on the western acropolis may all have been dedicated to Hera. Temple C had an adyton and no opisthodomos, a quality shared by many other Sicilian temples throughout the sixth century. Similarly, Temple C, like many other temples in Sicily, has what Dinsmoor quite rightly calls a "double front" of columns, a deep porch projecting forward from the otherwise simply peripteral colonnade.[44] Behind the deeply sheltering volume of space so created, a deep pronaos leads into a long and narrow cella which has a closed adyton at the end. The whole axis so set up is further emphasized by the stairway at the east, where a falling away of the ground level necessitated a multiplication of the steps of the base. These are again doubled to form true stairs, thus vitiating the sculptural quality of the exterior and emphasizing its character as a shelter. Everything about the temple expresses deep engulfment; it is an enclosing shape, something like those of the great Ionic temples but not, like them, primarily a grove. Its axial stairway, porch, and cella without opisthodomos were to affect the form of Etruscan temples, and, like those temples, Temple C is a great pavilion expressing shelter. It is possible that the very strangeness and openness of the landscape of Sicily tended to force the Greek to expand and project the interior space of his temples, almost as it had caused him to revalue his goddess. (Something similar happened in American architecture.)[45] The Greek certainly attempted at the same time to develop the exterior details of his temples in Sicily in order to make them function in the larger landscape, the more golden and less blinding light, the larger scale. Therefore rich and bold invention in detail took place, and daring compositions in metope sculpture, as at Temple C, where Perseus strikes off the gorgon's head in one of the first of the great figural programs celebrating the conquest of nature which are characteristic of Greek metope sculpture. The lavish and outscaled terracotta cornice decorations, revetments, and moldings took their form. These too the Etruscans were to imitate and exaggerate, as they were to develop as well the character which these details assisted in creating in many of the early Greek temples in Sicily: the character, that is, of decorated pavilions rather than of purely sculptural unities. Into the landscape at Selinus, as elsewhere, the great early pavilions were set, but the problem of focus was great. Far to the east of Selinus, near Cape Sciacca, a large conical hill does rise up by the sea, and the buildings in question are oriented in that direction. The east–west crossroad of the eastern acropolis, whose colonial grid plan itself would now also appear to date from as early as 500 B.C.,[45a] is also oriented directly towards it. Yet the hill is distant and hardly forms a spatial unity with the temples as does that at Paestum. Moreover, temple after temple stands side by side with the ones we have already mentioned, and there is no significant variation in orientation among them. Though the colonists at Selinus may have wished to invoke the Hera who meant earth and home, still their colonial landscape and its sea were too big for them and her, and they used their temples for other plastic purposes: on the interior to form a sheltering volume for their goddess, on the exterior to create what might be called a bounded "landscape" for themselves. So Temple C lifted its massively contoured upper works on dramatized echini, and each of the two hills above the harbor received its hedge of temples, defining the psychic defences of the town. (*Figs. 106, 107*) This is an urban problem, and one of gods in a land which is not their own.

The problem faced by the Spartan king, Pausanias, at Plataia was a different one. Herodotus tells us that the Spartan phalanx stood near the sanctuary of Demeter, on the eastern flank of the battle line. To its left was Plataia itself, below the slopes of Mount Cithairon and with some sort of sanctuary of Hera near its walls. Mardonius has attacked and the Spartans, preparing to engage, offer sacrifice beforehand:

> The victims, however, for some time were not favorable; and during the delay, many fell on the Spartan side, and a still greater number were wounded. For the Persians had made a rampart of their wicker shields, and shot from behind them such clouds of arrows, that the Spartans were sorely distressed. The victims continued impropitious; till at last Pausanias raised his eyes to the Heraeum of the Plataeans, and calling the goddess to his aid, besought her not to disappoint the hopes of the Greeks.[46]

The spot where the sanctuary of Hera, probably at that time containing only a small temple or shrine, was placed is no higher than the spot where Pausanias was apparently standing; nor could it itself have been an object conspicuous enough to hold his eye at the distances involved. But the point on the ridge of Cithairon below which the sanctuary was located was indeed higher than Pausanias and a clearly legible form to him: two mounded hills like breasts, a cleft between, and above it all the mountain's horns. (*Fig. 110*) These were the setting for the Festival of the Daedala, the marriage of Zeus and Hera as a wooden bull and a cow. A great fire consumed them both, flaring above the mountain's cleft.[47] This deep notch was visible from Thebes, as we noted earlier, and focused the view south from the mounded hill of that Mycenaean city. (*Fig. 39*)

The whole sacred formation rises directly above the city of Plataia. From Plataia itself the form is full and enclosing. (*Fig. 111*) Great arms of the mountain embrace the plain below; a rounded slope slides down toward it, and above the slope the two conical hills are tightly pressed together within the mountain's folds. Above the cones the cleft of the ridge is decisive, and its profile opens wide in fluid curves to left and right. It is one of Hera's most characteristic and splendid formations, and its presence can be felt across all of southern Boeotia. This presence itself, now legible to us as to Pausanias, must have been the "Heraeum" to which he "raised his eyes." Herodotus tells us the result:

> As he offered his prayer, the Tegeans, advancing before the rest, rushed forward against the enemy; and the Lacedaemonians, who had obtained favourable omens the moment that Pausanias prayed, at length, after their long delay, advanced to the attack . . .[48]

In this way the victory at Plataia, which ushered in the classic age, was won under the sign of Hera and in the shadow of her mountain forms. It can hardly have seemed surprising to the Greeks that this should have been the case, because, as her temples show, Hera had become the mother, austere and grand, who was strong enough not merely to protect but to release her sons and who affirmed the propriety of their solid grip on the land they claimed as their own.

Chapter 5

DEMETER

But now, let all the people build me a great temple ...
upon a rising hillock.

Homeric Hymn II, "To Demeter" (Evelyn–White)[1]

DEMETER'S SITES, like those of all Greek divinities, make use of the same general language of sacred landscape forms. They are related to all others but, like all others, they have their own special character. Hera's sites, for example, celebrate the majesty of the surface of the earth, but Demeter's evoke its interior, life–giving, death–bringing forces. Demeter, as goddess of the fruitfulness of the earth with its seasonal resurrections, is especially close to that aspect of the goddess which both nourished man and promised him a certain continuity of existence after death. As such, Demeter is an Olympian only by courtesy, and the rising importance of her Mysteries from the late archaic period onward would seem to show a growing renewal and reinterpretation of older rites which the Dorians had thrust underground. Euripides associated Demeter with the old earth mother and apparently found in her search for Persephone a focus for his own religious anguish:

> Long ago, the Mountain Mother
> of all the gods, on flashing feet,
> ran down the wooded clefts
> of the hills, crossed stream–waters in spate
> and the sea's thunderous surf beat
> in wild desire for the lost girl
> not to be named, her daughter ...[2]

He accepted, too, the tradition that placed Demeter on Mount Ida, which may be taken as either Mysian or Cretan Ida, since their myths had clearly come to overlap: (*Fig.* 7)

> she crossed the place where the mountain nymphs
> keep watch in the snows of Ida,
> and there cast the blight of her grief
> across the stone and snow of the hill forests.[3]

70

Once again it cannot be our task to delve into the religious and mythological complexities involved in Demeter's character.[4] It was always bound in mystery, and the architectural remains at her sites—some of which, along with those of related mystery cults, can best be discussed in our concluding chapter—were always different from those of more fully Olympian divinities. They therefore create an elusive image for us, one which, historically speaking, is constantly slipping backward toward pre–Greek and forward toward Late Antique times. This is so because they tend very soon toward "space–positive" rather than "mass–positive" building placement and interior design, thus directing, protecting, and enclosing men in ways that the Olympians did not do.

Yet when the Spartan king, Pausanias, sacrificed at Plataia he was standing near Demeter's shrine, which was probably at the site of the present church of Agios Ioannis, on a gentle swell of land under its own focusing projection of the ridge of Cithairon.[5] (*Fig. 110*) The softly rounded hill of the shrine is surrounded by other rolling hillocks, and all of them are densely covered with grain today. They seem to form the most fertile area in the southern Boeotian plain: embodying the bounty of the earth which is Demeter herself, the breeze sweeping through the wheat of the "rich–haired" goddess.[6] Pausanias looked toward Hera's formation, which is somewhat to the west along the ridge, but when the omens proved favorable and the Spartans advanced, they had in sight to the north the horned peak of Hypatos, rising in that direction over the hidden hills of Thebes and opening like an engulfing force. (*Fig. 112*) Under this image appropriate to her chthonic nature, and upon the mounded hill of the Theban acropolis, stood another sanctuary of Demeter. It was supposedly upon the site of the palace of Cadmus and in all likelihood enjoyed a tradition of holiness which went back to Mycenaean times.[7] (*Fig. 40*) As the Spartans advanced in their disciplined thousands toward the sign of the goddess, breaking the Persian Immortals whom they had previously feared, may we suppose that some among them remembered that the small band of their comrades at Thermopylai had died near another shrine of Demeter and with her same mountain symbols before their eyes? Just a few hundred yards forward of the narrowest part of the pass at Thermopylai, where Leonidas had taken his stand behind the wall, was the shrine of Amphictyonic Demeter at the place called Anthela.[8] This shrine was the meeting place for an important league of Greek cities. It was placed upon a gentle mound under a great opening cleft in the hills. Westward from it, bounding its sky horizon, looms the mass of Mount Oeta, where the funeral pyre of Herakles had burned. (*Fig. 113*) The profile of Oeta is distinguished by a double set of horns, side by side. Even from Thermopylai, at the narrowest part of the pass, where Leonidas held until his flank was turned, the horns of Oeta are the dominant feature of the view. The present monument, despite its regrettable character, can still serve roughly to mark Leonidas' position in relation to the horns. Unlike the monument's narcissistic warrior, however, the King would have been facing west by north toward them as the Persians came down upon him. When, on the morning of his last day, and upon receipt of the news of Ephialtes' treachery, Leonidas sent his allies away and, as Herodotus tells us,[9] advanced from behind his wall upon the Persians in front of him, he must have come very close to Demeter's shrine. Somewhere near there he met his death. At Thermopylai as later at Plataia, therefore, the horns and clefts above Demeter's "rising hillock" were in the eyes of the Greeks as they fought for their land. Their ardor in its

71

defence can only have been spurred by the kind of passionate love with which reverence and no little fear were mingled, even as—so Demaratus told Xerxes—they feared the law.[10] At Thermopylai the element of fear and death can indeed be felt at Demeter's site, where the savagely marked wall of rock on the south rises beside the cleft to its wild ridges.

This dark aspect of Demeter who, with Persephone, goddess of the underworld, has a close link with death, can also be experienced at Thera,[11] where the niche of Demeter and Persephone together was set at the inland tip of the town's ridge, directly opposite a darkly clothed, horned, and tented peak which rises like a shrouded ghost across the gorge.[12] (*Fig. 114*) Again, a typical overlap with another divinity can be sensed here, since the peak's shape closely recalls a type often found at sites sacred to Artemis, who, as Hecate, is night and sometimes death, and who indeed had a votive column at Thera, but set well forward on the ridge near the temple of her brother Apollo.[13]

The worship of Demeter was believed by the Greeks to have been introduced into Greece itself at Thorikos, on the east coast of Attica.[14] There was, as we have seen, a Mycenaean settlement upon and around the conical hill there, connected with a tradition of Cretan colonization,[15] and the site was thus apparently sacred to the goddess from early times. Its main conical hill, (*Fig. 116*) as already noted, is backed by another beyond a deep saddle to the north, and seen from the west the formation as a whole makes a splendid pair of horns. (*Fig. 115*) Across the valley to the southwest the clefts and ridges of the encircling hills form another visual focus of a rather similar kind. Exactly between the cones and horns of Thorikos itself and the clefts of the southwestern mountains a curious, fifth–century building was placed. It consisted of a colonnade of seven by fourteen Ionic columns, with the narrow ends facing southeast–northwest. No traces of a cella have been found.[16] In this position the long axis of the building echoed the movement of the deep, narrow valley which is sheltered under the western slopes of Thorikos, contains a mounded hill in its fold, and opens outward toward the wider east–west valley and the sea. The flanks of the temple were offered to the horns of Thorikos and to the formations on the southwest. In the center of each of these flanks the intercolumnation was widened, providing in this way a cross–axis of vision which was controlled to the northeast by the horns of Thorikos and on the other side by the dramatic hills across the valley. If no cella was ever built, the building might have remained a pure pavilion, not enclosed itself but instead celebrating the deeply felt enclosure of the site and at the same time fixing the shape of that enclosure by emphasizing its dominant axis and focusing by a cross–axis upon its sacred symbols. The remains of this building have now been completely covered over once again, but an inscription found near it shows that it was dedicated to Demeter and Kore. It was apparently Periclean in date, and its curious and expressive form offers another example of the inventiveness of middle and later fifth–century Athens as it attempted to weld the chthonic deities firmly into the intellectual and emotional life of the city. Certain peculiarities which the building at Thorikos shares with other Attic monuments of that period and slightly later, and with buildings elsewhere which were probably designed by Athenian architects, point to this. Its columns, for example, were left unfluted. This was true also, as we shall see, of the later columns of the fourth–century exterior colonnade at Eleusis and of the contemporary columns of the Periclean temple of Nemesis at Rhamnous. (*Fig. 276*) Both of these were again sites of very special meaning. The temple at Segesta, (*Fig. 177*) where, as at Thorikos, no cella was built, and which also celebrates some goddess of the earth, has unfluted columns also.[17] The usual explanation offered for these phenomena is that all the monuments in question were left unfinished through the exigencies of war, and that they would otherwise have been completed in the usual fashion. This explanation may be partly true, but it is not satisfying, and a study of all these monuments in situ tends to create the impression that, while they may at first have been left unfinished by accident, they were allowed in the end to remain that way precisely because it was recognized that they fulfilled their unusual functions better in that form. A similar impression, though involved with different meanings, is created by the unfinished portions of the Propylaia on the Acropolis of Athens, but this and the other monuments mentioned above can best be considered in these connections when their sites as a whole are discussed. We recall, however, that not all the Ionic columns of the unfinished temple on Samos[18] were fluted, (*Fig. 77*) nor was the exterior colonnade at Hellenistic Sardis, (*Fig. 163*) to be discussed later.[19] At Thorikos, certainly, the unfluted columns, perhaps fulfilling a function very different from that of the usual peristylar colonnade, would have risen like the massive trunks of great trees, forming their own kind of grove within the shelter of the valley. The splendid linear abstraction and lively force of the fluted column would have been subordinated to a more earth–evoking shape, and something somber and majestic as the mysteries of the earth itself would have risen up to be crowned by its capitals' horns.

The larger conical hill at Thorikos had an unusual theater on its southern slope. (*Figs. 116, 117*) The masonry of this structure seems late and consciously unfinished.[20] Similarly, despite its late date, the theater has not taken on a semicircular form. Its seats are arranged in a kind of rough rectangle with rounded ends, and its orchestra, also roughly rectangular, is nevertheless bent into the sinuous curve of a bow from the rock–cut chamber on the east to the temple of Dionysos on the west. (*Figs. 116, 117*) A temple of Dionysos, as patron of the drama, was of course often so associated with theaters, but the relationship here seems a special one. The cult of Dionysos, apparently gaining in importance as it does during the late archaic period and at some time connected with Orphism, is regarded by most scholars as expressing a kind of renewal of the older religion of the goddess.[21] Indeed it now seems that Dionysos, if it is indeed he as a god who is twice mentioned in Linear B religious texts, was an ancient deity who now revives, equipped with an exotic new genealogy, after his Homeric eclipse. Invoked as Bromius, he was apparently celebrated as a newborn child at the Eleusinian Mysteries.[22] He was thus closely connected with Demeter and Kore, whose pavilion at Thorikos stood not far from the theater. All this brings us back to the theater's unusual form, an examination of which creates two impressions. First, if the theater had been semicircular it would, as placed, have ruined the hill shape, the perfect cone of Demeter. It is thus widened and flattened and complements the spread of the cone, into which it would otherwise have cut as a wound. Secondly, the shape, which implies rhythmic movement across the orchestra from the rock–cut chamber to the temple, (*Fig. 117*) coupled as it is with the total absence of a stage building, causes one to believe that some special type of cult was celebrated there. One remembers the processional pathways of Crete with their "theatral" steps and their labyrinthine windings, and one recalls the apparent connection of Dionysos, as well as of Demeter, with a reinterpretation and renewal of that tradition. The Greek theater, as normally finished after the fifth century, was rationalized, like all Greek architecture, into a perfectly geometrical shape, abstract and clear. Thorikos never achieved that abstraction. In all likelihood it was never intended to do so but was instead meant primarily to do just the opposite: to echo in its shape the curving path of the procession from chamber to temple, to sway itself in the Dionysian rhythms of the torches, and to celebrate, as does its shape within the conical hill, the power of those goddesses of the earth, "not to be named," who were its patrons.

Demeter's most important shrine was at Eleusis.[23] There the great Mysteries, based upon Kore's seasonal death and resurrection, were performed. The site of Eleusis itself is the culmination of a whole set of symbols of the goddess which form the surrounding Attic landscape. Under Hymettos, south of its horns, were the peaked mounds of Kaisariani. (*Figs. 36, 37*) Here there was an important shrine of Aphrodite's, to be mentioned again later, while low down off the northern slope of the Acropolis, near the corner of the Agora on the Panathenaic Way, was the Eleusinion of Athens, oriented due south toward the Acropolis height.[24] The image of Iacchos was kept in the Eleusinion, to be carried in sacred procession to Eleusis during the ten days of the festival of the Mysteries. Directly opposite Hymettos' horns, northwest of the Athenian acropolis, is the hill of Colonus, sacred to Athena and Poseidon and to the "gentle, All–seeing Ones,"[25] the Eumenides of the earth, as well. (*Figs. 118, 119*) In antiquity Colonus was well outside the city and a deme in its own right. (It is within the modern city and carries upon its crest monuments to the great classicists Müller and Lenormant.) This was the spot that Sophocles chose as the scene of Oedipus' final moments upon the earth, and somewhere nearby was the deep cleft into which the earth received him, as, witnessed only by Theseus, he passed between two worlds in a kind of death more splendid and fulfilled than any mortal had known before.[26] His preparation for this mystic passage was an ablution performed with water which his daughters brought for him from "the hill of Demeter, Freshener of all things."[27] This eminence is still a leafy mound, rising a few hundred yards to the north of Colonus, and the domed church which now completes its shape appears as the natural descendant of the goddess' tholos tomb. Far behind Demeter's Hill, to the north, the horns of Deceleia can be seen from Colonus, and south across lower Attica the cone of Zeus Panhellenios on Aigina defines the major axis of the view. A cross–axis is created by the horns of Hymettos to the east and, directly to the west, by the conical hill that marks the pass at Daphni along which the Sacred Way to Eleusis wound. (*Fig. 118*) Colonus and Demeter's Hill thus form a kind of center to southern Attica, and all around them, deeply embedded in the earth as they seem, the symbols of the goddess rise.

Another rite which took place at Athens during the ten days of the Mysteries was a procession of mystai to a shrine of Demeter on the sea near Phaleron. (*Fig. 145*) Pausanias mentions such a shrine,[28] but its exact location is unknown. Wherever it was in that area, however, it would have had the twin hills of Piraeus either close by or in profile view across the water. From that position Piraeus resembles Megara as seen from Minoa, discussed earlier;[29] and in Megara too there was a shrine of Demeter's.[30] But the climax of the Mysteries was the day–long procession which danced and sang its way from Athens, wound through the pass of Daphni, debouched into the Eleusinian plain, and circled the shore of the gulf of Eleusis, to arrive at Eleusis by night. Every step of this route is marked by the appearance, disappearance, and reappearance of the sacred landscape symbols. The first objective is the conical hill which guards Daphni on the Athenian side. Winding under its flanks, the procession would have come into the pass itself, and from the height of the pass the horns of Mount Kerata above Eleusis come suddenly into view. (*Fig. 121*) Eleusis itself, far off and low down by the sea, is not yet visible. As the Sacred Way winds down the pass between the arid, rocky hills, the horns of Kerata slide once more out of sight: the mystic object found and lost. Between the hills the way is hard and barren; no opening is seen, nor does any objective beckon to the view. After a time the hills to the left are burst apart, and a mass of rock thrusts up between them, backed by the lifting profile of the more distant ridge. Exactly opposite this dramatic and unexpected appearance a sanctuary of Aphrodite is placed upon the Way.

We cannot explore the possible relations between Demeter and Aphrodite; according to Euripides, in his *Helen,* Aphrodite induced Demeter, with music, to smile in her sadness for Kore lost underground.[31] In Aphrodite's sanctuary below Daphni are lustral basins and a megaronlike enclosure.[32] The goddess seems much of the earth in this place, and there can be little doubt that ceremonies of some sort, probably of purification, were carried out by the procession here.[33] Whatever the case, the shrine of Aphrodite on the Sacred Way is opposite the kind of irresistibly upthrusting rock which, as we shall see, is characteristic of Aphrodite's sites. It is also placed exactly at the point where the Way turns and the horns, now not of Kerata, but of Salamis, come suddenly into view. (*Fig. 120a*) These, very female in connotation, form a strong notch which fixes the eye, and the Sacred Way leads directly toward them down the opening pass. Salamis, as an island of sacred shape, may have been associated with Aphrodite as goddess of the sea. In the Homeric Hymn Aphrodite is hailed as "queen of well–built Salamis,"[34] but it is the town of Salamis on Cyprus which is being referred to. Yet Cyprian Salamis was mythically founded by Teucer and received its name because that hero had come from the island in question.[35] Its own association with the goddess may therefore be inferred. Clearly enough, as the hills fall away to left and right beyond Aphrodite's shrine on the Sacred Way, the long body of Salamis swings into sight and forms the seaward boundary of Eleusis bay. (*Fig. 120b*) Salamis in this view does resemble a body on its back with its head to the east, and it calls to mind the image of a female body to be seen in the mountains near Aphrodite's shrine at Troezen, to be discussed later.[36] Across the bay from Salamis the curving coast of Eleusis swings in an arc, with the winged cleft of Thria opening in the mountains to the north. Far ahead the split summit of pyramidal Kerata gestures at the western headland of the bay. (*Fig. 121*) Under it can now be seen the mounded hill of Eleusis itself. Curiously enough, the sacred formations once again marked a critical place of battle, since the horns of Kerata were far to the left rear of the Greek ships when they finally charged the Persian line at Salamis, while the ridge of Hymettos stood above their burned Acropolis before them.[37]

Eleusis is clearly that passage between worlds, that "Gate of Horn," celebrated in the Odyssey and by Virgil, about which Levy has written.[38] The landscape forms, with which Levy does not deal, reinforce her argument: so Kerata, horned in fact and in name, rises above the sanctuary which is Eleusis, a name usually taken in antiquity to mean the "passage" or "the gate."[39] The architectural and landscape evidence is precise, since the sanctuary is set under the horns and at the end of a tortuous labyrinth: one which first creates the drama of losing and finding along the

Sacred Way and then finally sways up toward Demeter's engulfing megaron within the sanctuary itself. (*Fig. 123*) The Gates are there. The two elaborate propylaia built by the Romans on the site of older Greek propyla, the smaller during the first century B.C., the larger during the second century A.D.,[40] are themselves so oriented in relation to each other as to enhance the swaying rhythm which must have been the essence of the procession's meaning. (*Figs. 123, 124*) Directly ahead of the outer propylaia is the grotto of Hades, (*Fig. 124*) a natural cave in the rock toward which the procession first directly leads. The cavern is partly masked by walls, however, and the procession would have been required to swing half left through the smaller propylaia in order to come to the grotto beyond it on the right hand. Having come first to the cave of death, the Way passes beyond it and curves snakelike upward to the left around the side of the hill. (*Fig. 124*) One can imagine the path of the torches, a sinuous trail of fire, as they approached the great hollow bulk of the Telesterion.[41] This building, after its Mycenaean beginnings, had at least five important enlargements from the very early archaic period onward during antiquity; but its essential character was always the same: a columned hall surrounded by windowless walls and pierced by narrow entrances. (*Figs. 123, 125*) The Mysteries were to take place inside, with the initiates crowded together by torchlight in a shadowy grove of columns. It is significant in this regard that the revolutionary Periclean project for the building, which used a minimal number of columns to support the ceiling of the hall and intended a colonnade around three sides of the exterior, was modified shortly thereafter by the multiplication of the interior columns and the elimination of the side colonnades of the exterior, leaving a portico only on the front, as in the sixth–century Peisistratid building which Xerxes had destroyed. It seems clear that as many columns as possible were desired inside, in order to create an interior more labyrinthine, mysterious, and grovelike, while the exterior was deemed better without the side colonnades which would have masked the fact that this building, unlike the normal temple, was intended primarily for interior experience and belonged to the chthonic rather than the Olympian goddesses. The columns of the exterior portico itself were left unfluted, possibly on second thought, as suggested earlier, to emphasize that same earthlike quality. Certainly the Romans, who poured money into the sanctuary for hundreds of years and who built the propylaia, would in all likelihood have been delighted to pay for the fluting of the columns if the priests of Eleusis had asked them to do so. One may perhaps conclude that all concerned were pleased enough with the solemn shafts as they stood.

The interior of the Telesterion represented the conclusion of the Way. (*Fig. 125*) Here the revelations that touched the ultimate mystery of death were to be made. As in Minoan palaces, therefore, the participant in the rite was drawn at last into the cavern and enclosed by the goddess' pillared shrine. So the axes of movement find a conclusion, an end. They do not remain free as in the Olympian sites. The Telesterion as completed had a bank of steps around its interior walls. These are too narrow for seats, so that the spectators must have stood densely upon them, feeling the rise of that unreasoning excitement which communicates itself so quickly through a crowd which is packed into a space slightly too small to hold it easily. Similarly, so standing, the spectators could instantly have changed into participants, flowing down suddenly from the steps among the columns, moving and dividing like a released torrent among the shafts. The famous Eleusinian relief of Demeter, Persephone, and Triptolemos, with the torchlighted flicker of its draperies across the tightly grouped columns of its figures, can enhance the present remains of the building by helping to conjure up its intended interior effects. (*Fig. 126*) What in fact went on among the columns we can only guess: whether a dramatization of Kore's birth, abduction, and reappearance; whether a journey through the underworld; whether, after a sacred marriage, the birth of a holy child related to Dionysos; whether, at the last, the reaping of a spray of wheat with a stone axe and in profound silence.[42] Certainly dancers wound between them. Euripides and others hint at much:

> The dappled dress in the deer skin
> is a great matter, and the ivy wound
> green on the sacred hollow reed
> has power; so also the shaken,
> the high, the whirled course of the wheel
> in the air; so also the dances,
> the wild hair shaken for Bromius,
> the goddess' nightlong vigils.
> It is well that by daylight
> the moon obscures her.[43]

There is of course much that reminds one of Cretan forms in such a description, and, like the Cretan shrines of the goddess, the Telesterion may have had a second floor around at least part of the interior. The stairways to the upper level of the site moved up the north and south sides of the building where it was cut into the rock. The interior experience now presumably completed, the landscape once again asserts the holiness of the spot as a whole. Along the rock–hewn terrace behind the building, the horns of Salamis, now joined by another set and widened out into curving, gentle, double arcs, defined the view to the south. (*Fig. 127*) In this direction faced the building that used to be called the "Temple of Demeter," a simple megaron enclosure of which the present foundations date from Roman times.[44] Beyond and above the acropolis of the town itself are the horns of Kerata, in this view strikingly female, consecrating the site. (*Fig. 122*) The Telesterion faces back toward the cleft of Daphni, and the whole landscape around Eleusis is thus focused by the sanctuary, which becomes the center of a clear circle of rich land and enclosed sea.

But the echo of Demeter's place continues on across the mountains into the Megarid. Here her megaron may perhaps be identified with a platform cut into the southern slope of the easterly of the two breast–shaped hills of Megara.[45] The horns of Kerata are behind her again, but the horns of Salamis and the mound of Minoa are both in the arc of her view. (*Fig. 38*) Demeter also had a shrine on the slopes of Acrocorinth,[46] but this awesome horned rock belonged to Aphrodite,[47] as did the double pair of mountain peaks which cut it off from the Argolid to the south. (*Figs. 170–172*) Demeter was again coupled with Aphrodite at Lerna, where Athena and Thetis were also present.[48] Humped and shelving Mount Pontinus comes close to the beach south of Argos and spews its water forth at that point to form a reedy marsh beside the shore. Here, where Herakles had killed the water monster, the Hydra who inhabited the marsh, there must have been felt a strangeness which spoke of underworld forces in the combination of hunched and spouting rock, haunted marsh, and sea.

The rich farmlands of South Italy and Sicily, more productive than any the Greeks had known at home, seem to have made these places centers of Demeter's cult. Enna[49] in Sicily and Hipponion[50] in Calabria each claimed, like Eleusis, to be the spot of Kore's abduction. At Hipponion the wheat still waves richly across the gentle hillsides, and the poppies which relate both to Aphrodite and Persephone grow with it. At Enna a perfect, still lake, believed like the oval cup of Avernus to mark a place of passage between worlds,[51] opens like a mouth within the secret hills that rise above the golden wheatlands of the Catanian plain. At Akragas, north of the so–called "Temple of Hera Lacinia," a fifth–century temple of Demeter and Persephone was placed,[52] (*Figs. 103, 128, 129*) high above the plain but under the steep side of the circling ridge at the point where it begins to lift toward the double acropolis behind. It is as the most important goddess of Akragas that Pindar invokes Persephone in the twelfth Pythian ode:

> Beloved brightness, loveliest of the cities of mortals,
> house of Persephone, you who keep by the banks of Akragas
> where the sheep wander, the templed hill,
> I beseech you, lady . . .[53]

Between the temple and the rock wall on its north side are placed circular rings of stones, thought to be chthonic altars into which libations to the earth could be poured. (*Fig. 129*) Their shape echoes that of the larger, wheel–like altars which are to be found at Akragas itself in the so–called "Sanctuary of the Chthonian Gods" on the lower part of the ridge below the Temple of Olympian Zeus.[54] The Temple of Demeter was, appropriately, without a peripteral colonnade and apparently had no columns in antis either. It was thus a simple megaron facing east away from the city. It looked toward several conical hills which rise out of the plain behind sweeping U–shaped swells of land. Its orientation essentially echoes that of an ancient rock–cut water sanctuary at the foot of the cliff below. (*Fig. 130*) Here, at a site possibly Minoan–Mycenaean, certainly pre–Greek in its origins,[55] the water which flowed out of the cliff was caught in basins behind a menhirlike façade whose square piers recall the goddess' pillars in Minoan shrines. This façade faces across a gentle valley defined by cup–shaped troughs of ground and mounded hills. Indeed, the axis of view is primarily focused by a dominant conical hill which rises behind a nearer cup. As in Minoan sites, an absolute calm and completeness is felt; cliff, water, pillars, valley, and female hills make a single, quiet whole.

The Sanctuary of Demeter Malophoros just west of Selinus also faces across a shallow valley, much narrower than that at Akragas and defined on its eastern side by the walled mound of the acropolis of Selinus itself.[56] (*Fig. 106*) As at Eleusis, the megaron of the goddess is cut into the side of a mounded hill, and there was a Way to it which wound from the north gate of Selinus down into the marshy plain and crossed the stream, so moving across water toward the sanctuary. (*Fig. 131*) This, like the one at Akragas, was very old, and its first megaron-temple was of apsidal form. The later rectangular building, throughout various reconstructions, retained a basic megaron shape, an enclosing volume partly hollowed out of the hill and without columns in antis, having only a door on the main axis. It, too, was a cavernous culmination for processional movement. During the Hellenistic period the entrance to its adyton was arched, recalling in elevation the plan of the earliest building on the site.[57] Such intention to conclude movement in a cup seems inevitably to have led the Greek mind toward a sense of the spatial axis which could conduct the participant toward the final enclosure. In the classic period, therefore, a propylon, with another round altar before it, was built before the shrine at Selinus, in front of the megaron and shifted slightly off direct orientation with its door. (*Fig. 131*) That is to say, an axis of entrance was set up but kept to a kind of dance rhythm, not allowed to stiffen into that absolutely straight line which would have had two effects: first, the destruction of rhythmic variation in movement, and second, the subordination of the buildings as positive masses to the space, for which their solids would then have become simple definers. (*Fig. 419*) A desire for the processional dance rather than the march, probably a traditional Stone Age sense and certainly Cretan, as we have seen, was to remain generally constant in Greek sacred architecture, even in its most axial Hellenistic groupings. So also the Greek mind was always to retain some special sense of the building as an active plastic unity. Yet the axis of movement for which building solids are merely shell–like containers and which leads to a closed, cavernous conclusion at the end, was to form the basic directing element in Roman architecture (*Fig. 419*) and was, of course, to culminate in the axial plan and thin wall construction of the Early Christian basilica. Its early though still flexible appearance in Greek sites dedicated to the goddesses who promised the security of the earth, and its growing importance throughout the Hellenistic period, indicate that it was the product of a rising desire for individual security. It reduced the alternatives of choice and provided an enclosed, sure end to any journey. In a perfectly complementary way the enclosed axis had, in Egypt, been a symbol of the unchangeability of an ordered world, while it had more imperative connotations for Rome. As such, the new axis disciplined and strictly refocused the old pre–Greek rituals and formed at the same time a sharp contrast to the challenge of movement in the open air, without fixed conclusions in the temenos itself, which was characteristic of most Greek sites.

On Crete the palaces themselves, whose niches, engaged columns, and columned screens prefigure Rome, had also been environing spatial hollows defined by a dominant directional principle, as the single axis which ran through their centers was fixed on the sacred presence. (*Figs. 2, 3, 11*) It seems clear, therefore, that Demeter's sites—differing, for example, from those of the related Hera in the character of their forms and their planning—formed a link which ran beneath the normal surface of Greek design and connected the older architecture of the religion of the goddess with the new architecture of Christianity.

Chapter 6

ARTEMIS AND APHRODITE

Over the shadowy hills and windy peaks she draws her golden bow.
Homeric Hymn XXVII, "To Artemis" (Evelyn–White)[1]

I am mighty among men and they honor me by many names,
All those that live and see the light of sun
From Atlas' pillars to the tide of Pontus
Are mine to rule.
Aphrodite speaks: Euripides, HIPPOLYTUS (Grene)[2]

IN THE GREEK ARTEMIS the facts of nature are not seen as an analogy for human salvation; in her power lurks a threat. Those of her qualities which insist upon the separation between men and nature, as well as the pitiless vengeance she visits upon those who transgress her laws, alike reflect a Greek sense for the reality of the free and elemental things of the world: for those forces which are not humanly controllable and which may indeed be hostile to human beings, but which, because they exist, must be recognized and revered. There can be little doubt that Artemis represented to the Greeks the old goddess in her aspect as mother of the wild beasts and guardian of the untamed wild lands.[3] She must therefore have been very close indeed to the oldest aspect of the goddess that can be surmised: the one in whose earth the horned beasts of paleolithic times were painted. The pendulous, many breasts of Artemis' cult statue in the great shrine at Ephesos might thus seem to indicate a continuing memory of her appearance in paleolithic figurines (although they may also represent a late elaboration upon an earlier, simpler motif), while the animals which mount two by two upon her columnar body recall those which flank the pillar symbol of the goddess on Minoan gems and at Mycenae. (*Figs. 64, 65*) Yet even at Ephesos it is possible that her earliest aspect was more purely as mistress of the beasts, with her spreading wings sheltering their forms. (*Fig. 132*) The Greeks, perhaps to bring her to the side of humanity, made Artemis a huntress herself and a guardian of gates with her bow—the ideal guardian, remote and incorruptible. So her virginity, in the most purely Greek view of her, is absolute, psychic rather than merely physical. She is the great mother who resolutely avoids marriage, as Hera could not avoid it, and who thereby remains free of domination by males and their law. Thus she protects the wild from rape by men, and her sites in Greece are haunted by that watchful, dangerous presence. She is everywhere in the untended lands, and for this reason the wider surroundings of her sites, the mountains, the beaches, and the swamps, must often be described at greater length than is necessary for those of most other deities.

One of the oldest of all rectangular temples was that of Artemis Orthia (Upright) at Sparta. The sanctuary was also called the Limnaion, the place of Artemis Limnaia, Lady of the Lake.[4] Here an eighth–century, megaronlike structure, with engaged wooden columns in its walls, was replaced by a temple in antis during the sixth century.[5] (*Fig. 133*) The temple is set close to the bed of the Eurotas river and is therefore at the lowest point in the valley. The place is marshy, and before excavation a small stream from the slopes of Mount Taygetus ran through the site itself. Three altars, of the eighth century, the sixth, and from Roman times, succeeded each other to the east of the temple and at the same angle to it. The temple itself is oriented roughly southeast in the general direction of the conical hill of the Menelaion. Its axis north-westward is defined by a decisive pair of horns which rise upon the ridge of Taygetus north of the gorge of the Magoula. (*Fig. 133*) But it is from the altars, where the Spartan boys endured the trials of their manhood rites, that the nature of the site as a whole is most fully experienced. It feels like the marshy bottom of the world, the deepest kind of cup. This sensa-tion is caused by the fact that the depression above which the necessarily high base of the temple rises is so low that the nearer hills blot out any sense of distance between it and that part of the ridge of Taygetus which lies most closely at hand to the west. There the forma-tion is the climactic one mentioned earlier: of the small, high head of the goddess and her em-bracing arms or wings, (*Fig. 46*) which also recall great horns or a horned bow. This mighty presence looms over the hollow and watches it. In the soggy pit the image of the goddess, from her closed house without exterior colonnade, witnessed during the late archaic and classic periods the struggle of the Spartan boys to seize, under the sting of whips, the greatest number of cheeses from her altar. By Roman times this ancient puberty rite had lost its mean-ing and become a stylized ordeal and a spectacle, in which the boys were sometimes beaten until they died.[6] A theater was built in an arc around the altar in order to provide for the tourists who flocked to this local attraction during later antiquity. The Spartan of Sparta's great age had found it possible to satisfy Artemis with less fatal results. Yet her site itself always cele-brated that double character of the earth which we noted earlier as the basic feature of the Spartan plain: its deep enclosure and its terror under the mountain's eye. (*Figs. 45–47, 133b*)

From the Messenian side of Taygetus another temple of Artemis, though now reduced to a few foundation stones, still invokes the mountain's wild presence and carries the observer's eye toward its horns.[7] This temple was placed on the slopes of Ithome, high enough up off the valley floor of Messenia so that it can face eastward across the bowed saddle between Ithome, to the left, and the mountain called Eva, to the right. (*Fig. 134*) In the far distance Taygetus fills the horizon, and directly on axis with the center of the near saddle, presents its own bow–shaped notch against the sky. The goddess herself faces her distant symbol, and the human eye too is carried in great leaps across tiers of rugged mountains into far space, as the temple's position directs it like an arrow.

At Calydon, where Artemis' brother Apollo shared the place with her, Artemis as archer is felt once more. The site as a whole, seen from the sea as the Gulf of Corinth is approached, forms an awesome entrance to Greece. A long, tented ridge, below which the temple is placed, slopes from north to south toward the mountain promontory of Varassova which thrusts out into the waters of the gulf and whose tilted strata culminate in a horned or winged profile. (*Fig. 135*) To westward, Ithaca, Cephellenia, and the farthest promontories of the Peloponnesos rise from the Ionian Sea. The Calydonian temple of Artemis Laphria is on a mounded hill which juts out into the Aetolian coastal plain.[8] (*Fig. 136*) It is connected by a long saddle with the higher hills of the city itself to the northeast. The notch through which the city's west gate opens out upon the saddle is itself a horned cleft, and beyond it further hills can be seen. The doubly curved profile of its opening can also be read as bowed, as at Ithome, or, as at Mukhli, to be discussed shortly, as winged, like the wings of the Lady of the Beasts noted earlier in Greek vase paintings and bronzes. (*Fig. 132*) An early apsidal temple on the site at Calydon faced northeastward across the saddle directly toward this cleft, but the placement of the later temples was more meaningful, that of Artemis oriented in a southeastward, that of Apollo in a more southerly direction.[9] As one came out of the city gate, the long side of the colonnade of the temple of Artemis would have been presented to the view, set on its mound rising in fluid profiles out of the plain. The temple would thus have been lifted high above the sea horizon and the islands, standing out against the double peaks of the Peloponnesos which can still be seen to the left of its position. The long axial movement along the saddle toward the temple was dramatized and stiffened by a stoa during the Hellenistic period. After this a propylon opened out toward the typically archaic angle view of the major temple itself. Beyond it was the smaller temple in antis of Apollo, so set with the temple of his sister as to block the spectator's view to the southwest and to direct it in an arc toward the southeast. Upon that bearing the only threatening formation of the whole view is to be found; it is the great cleft mass of Varassova's promontory rising out of the sea. (*Figs. 135, 137*) Again and again, as at Corinth and elsewhere, temples of Apollo are so set as to oppose formations similar to this one. So he joins his sister here. The two temples together open a fan of vision toward it, and the single altar on the site is placed between them. Conversely, the temples set up a funneled perspective northward, where a high conical peak comes into view in the distance. The whole prospect of broad plain, sea, promontories, and islands, sweeping in an arc of one hundred and eighty degrees, is thus stabilized in each critical direction by a powerful natural object. The exhilaration to be felt at Calydon arises from the fact that the temples seem to have been thrust forward, out of the winged cleft, into a vast space which demands action and poses definite objectives and challenges. It is no wonder that the water spouts of the temple of Artemis were in the shape of hunting dogs' heads, since Artemis is clearly Laphria, the huntress and sharer of booty here, and the myths of the chase, like that of Meleager and Calydon's boar, must have grown up quite naturally in this environment. The enclosing hills withdraw from the plain; the space sweeps outward from the platform, and the temples of the two archers, guardians of this western gate to Greece, begin to maneuver to left and right like disciplined huntsmen whose threatening quarry has just risen out of the sea.

Eastward within the Gulf, far along on the way to the Isthmus, Artemis watched the northern approach to the Peloponnesos. At Sikyon, west of Corinth, there was another of her temples.[10] This, oriented dead east but possibly with another cella to the west, was placed in the upper city during archaic times but was under the main acropolis height. As one moves upward from the Gulf of Corinth toward the site, the wild mountains to the south, also sacred to Artemis, can be seen against the sky. From the temple itself, however, these are no longer in view. Instead, the dominant forms to the east are Acrocorinth and the two horned mountains which rise to the south of it. Behind them the flat–topped mountain above Nemea is a conspicuous object. From above, the temple defines a landscape in which the double horns reverberate at one end of a line of vision, which sweeps from them down the curving horizon toward the Isthmus of Corinth and then rises again up the slopes of Mount Loutraki. (*Fig. 138*) It is once more an extremely wide view, a field of fire across the Isthmus, defined by horned masses in a bowlike arc.

Immediately behind Sikyon the pass into the Peloponnesos rises above eroded badlands. The view back across the site is through the V's of inhospitable gorges, with the horns beyond Acrocorinth evident once more. Thus the temple of Artemis at Sikyon is also placed at the entrance to a landscape most appropriately hers. To this terrible land the Isthmus and the Gulf are a forecourt in which the symbols of the goddess are conspicuously present but in which her full nature has not yet been revealed. She shows herself progressively on the way toward Stymphalia. Beyond the first passes a long, rather mournful valley opens ahead, and a tangled range of wild mountains can be seen. From the valley most of the peaks drop out of sight, but they reappear one by one as the southern end is approached. First a double–peaked snowy mound shows itself in the V–opening between the nearer hills. (*Fig. 139*) Then the first sullen glimmer of the Stymphalian lake is seen, and a strikingly tented peak, recalling the horns of Hymettos and the ridge at Thera, come into sight at the left. Beyond it the ranges of Mounts Kyllene and Sciathis, sacred, the Homeric Hymn tells us, to Hermes and his son, Pan, rise around the lake in dusky tiers, falling away behind their largest cone and lifting again toward the snow.[11] From the lake the whole mass of Sciathis at the southwestern end of the valley comes into direct axis ahead. Its central feature has a familiar shape: a flat central plateau with two low swinging saddles rising on either side to other peaks. (*Fig. 139*) But its images are multiple: horns, arms, or that shape like a composite bow or yoke which is placed above the goddess on some Minoan gems. To left and right heavy mountain masses frame the mighty apparition, and the whole range cups the valley in its arms. Somewhere within it (possibly related to the ruins of a medieval church which are on axis with the mountain's central horns) stood the temple of Artemis where the wooden effigies of the Stymphalian birds were hung.

It seems clear that Stymphalia was the domain of the "mountain mother," deep, lost, and dominated by her, and the religious explanation of its basic myth, that Herakles' killing of the birds represents a Dorian subjection of a special cult of the goddess there, has much to recommend it.[12] The birds, too, are the goddess' symbol and perch upon her shrine in some Minoan objects. Moreover, the goddess at Stymphalia is identified by the landscape as Artemis, mother of the wild, as on the famous Boeotian amphora: with the birds, snakes, bears, wolves, and fish all sheltered by her body or under her wide spreading arms, which are shaped on the vase like the mountain here. (*Figs. 139, 140*) She engulfed the city of Stymphalia as well, but her harsh–voiced birds must persistently have returned, as they do now, to the marshy lake beside it, since she formed most of all a protected enclave in the heart of the wild. (*Fig.*

141) Though traversed by routes in antiquity her place must always have had something of the quality of a preserve in which, despite Herakles, she still held the wild creatures of earth, air, and water in her arms.

South of Stymphalia is Mount Artemision, whose notched summit, visible from Mycenae, was also sacred to Artemis.[13] But the temple of Artemis which lay on the flanks of Artemision was deeply imbedded in one of its southern gorges. Although a modern road passes close by, the place is still one of loneliness and threat. Its position is marked by the purely conical and sharply pointed hill called Palaeo–Mukhli that rises at the northern end of a deep valley which is itself dominated by a single pyramidal and embracing mountain shape. (*Fig. 143*) Directly on axis with Palaeo–Mukhli and to the north of it, a gorge penetrates deeply into the mountain. (*Fig. 142*) The rugged mass of the conical hill and the deep void of the gorge make one strong architectural shape, beyond which the jagged ridges rise toward the peaks of Artemision. A torrent winds down through the gorge, and a kind of terrace juts out from the eastern slope above it. In this vicinity Frazer reported finding the cut blocks of a temple, and while nothing so clear can be made out there today, there are certain signs which may indicate the corner angle of some sort of building.[14] There was certainly a temple of Artemis somewhere in the gorge, and the terrace seems a likely place. It is directly on axis with the main cleft at the northern end of the gorge which, even more strikingly than that at Calydon, calls to mind the lifted, looming wings of the Mistress of the Beasts. (*Figs. 132, 142*) Through their opening the hard precipices of the depths of the mountain show themselves, and behind them the utter loneliness of the heights begins. In the view south out of the mountain from between the wings or from the terrace, the sharp cone of Mukhli stands between the sloping sides of the gorge. (*Fig. 143*) The shape so formed is exactly that of the cone of Astarte on her horned altar in the Temple Court at Byblos, as represented on a coin of the Emperor Macrinus.[15] (*Fig. 144*) So Artemis is especially the cone between the horns, the mother and the power. Once again it becomes inescapably apparent that the landscape image formed the holy place, and the shape of the cone of Mukhli itself recalls the "pointed hills" of Euripides' invocation of Artemis. The citadel of Mycenae (*Fig. 61*) between its mountain horns is also recalled here, so connecting the king's fortress with the goddess' refuge for the hare with young whom his eagles tore. So throughout the Peloponnesos, from Sikyon to Mukhli, Mantineia,[16] Tegea,[17] Sparta and, as we shall see, to Bassae, Artemis holds the wild fringes and dominates the fertile plains from her mountain homes.

The relationship between mountain symbols of Artemis and sea beaches is equally striking. Her sanctuary above the harbor of Munychia on the bay of Phaleron guarded the older sea gate to Athens. Her temple there was on the northern promontory above the port, the smallest of the three harbors of Piraeus.[18] It probably looked east across the curving bay of Phaleron toward the southern terminations of the ridge of Hymettos. Across the bay the ridge of Hymettos forms another of those complex horn shapes which resemble a bow or a yoke. This formation is intersected by a pointed conical peak. (*Fig. 145*) The enframed peak and the horns thus interlock to make the double symbol in one shape, much as it could have been seen above Stymphalia from the roof of the megaron at Mycenae. (*Fig. 68*) Well to the northeast the horns of that end of Hymettos are clear against the sky beyond the cone of Lycabettos, but the focus of the view is south of them, stepping in a strong rhythm across the exposed beach, enfilading it from the oval harbor to the distant mountain bow: which itself enabled the Athenians to place Artemis appropriately there, bringing any amphibious invader under her archer's eye.

A similar framing of a far cone within horns and across water occurs in the view which was offered by the temple of Artemis near Cape Artemision in the northwest corner of the island of Euboea,[19] where the jagged peninsula of Thessalian Trikeri advances in a line of tented peaks, smotheringly looming across the straits but splitting in one place to reveal the distant cone of Mount Olympos exactly framed in the cleft.[20] (*Sketch Map 1*) In the waters not far from here the Athenians' hundred ships fought the Persian fleet. Artemis is thus both a disturbing presence and a guardian of the Greek land who calls up the powers of the wild. The journey which can best reveal that double being will bring us back to Athenian Hymettos once more. It should properly begin at Aulis.

No aspect of Artemis' character more intrigued and perhaps disturbed the classic Greek mind than did her reputation for having demanded human sacrifice in the past. The sacrifice by Agamemnon of his daughter Iphigenia was the most famous of these occasions. We noted earlier that the invocations of Artemis' sites were especially strong at Mycenae—Mount Artemision, Stymphalia, and Mukhli being most directly concerned—and that the setting of Mycenae itself between its horns also somewhat recalled that of the temple of Artemis at Aulis, where the sacrifice occurred. The approach to the tiny harbor at Aulis from the southeast passes across low swampy lands and finally reveals two hills rising to the northwest. (*Fig. 146*) The harbor is directly behind the eastern hill. The profile created by the two hills and the valley floor is a perfect arc. It is exactly in that space that the temple of Artemis is located.[21] Once again she is low down in the valley within the horn of the hills. As at Sardis, to be discussed later, the temple is oriented across the valley, but here it is a simple temple in antis without an exterior colonnade and with a deep adyton rather than an opisthodomos. Emphasis is upon its interior, where there are two rows of columns in the cella and a great tripod base in the adyton. It is a house for a secret and withdrawn deity. Its pronaos faces the northeasterly hill, slightly off axis with its rocky peak. Within the entrance to the cella a cylindrical base is to be found. It is slightly off axis with the door and in such a position that it lines up, in a diagonal axis of sight through the door, with a sacred well and the peak of the hill. This base may have supported a tree trunk, mentioned by Pausanias as marking the position of the plane tree beneath which the sacrifice of Iphigenia took place.[22] If the Greeks who built the temple had such in mind they clearly took a more subtle way of marking the spot than would have been the case if they had simply lined the temple up with the peak and placed the base on axis between the two. As now arranged, the temple has the curious quality of action between the hills, turning slightly between them. The position of the base, emphasizing as it does a diagonal axis to the peak, serves to intensify the relationship and to give it a lively rhythm. Beyond the temple the glimmer of the harbor can be seen; Artemis is once again at an entrance as goddess of the gate.

There were two important temples of Artemis on the coast of eastern Attica. These sites are at the modern Loutsa and at Brauron.[23] A problem of cult is involved in the identification of these two neighboring places, and a reading of the landscape symbols can assist in solving it.

Euripides tells us that Iphigenia did not die at Aulis but was miraculously transported by Artemis to Tauris, on the Black Sea, where she acted for many years as Artemis' priestess and prepared unlucky travelers for sacrifice to the goddess. From this predicament she was rescued by her brother Orestes who was attempting to follow Apollo's order to seize the wooden image of Artemis at Tauris and return with it to Greece. Finally Athena intervenes, saves Iphigenia and Orestes from the pursuit of the Taurian king and orders Orestes, not Iphigenia, as follows:

> Take back your sister and the statue
> Safely to Hellas. Pause at God–built Athens,
> Then, passing through, continue to the end
> Of Attica, and find a holy place
> Close to Carystus' hill, a place called Halae:
> There build a temple. There set up the image . . .[24]

Athena goes on to tell Orestes that, in memory both of his deliverance and of Artemis' own "former ways," a knife should be held to a human throat in the festival celebrated at the new temple, and a few drops of blood should be drawn.[25]

Two facts should be noted in the passage quoted. First, Orestes is to go to the very border of Attica to find a holy place which is to be identified as the appropriate spot for the temple precisely because it is close to "Carystus' hill." The place is then named: "Halae," and Halae is to be identified with the modern Loutsa, also sometimes still called by its ancient name and on the shore of eastern Attica. But there is apparently no hill nearby. Because of this, and because Pausanias tells us that the Athenians believed the statue from Tauris was brought ashore at Brauron,[26] which is in fact under a hill a few miles south of Loutsa along the shore, it has been generally accepted by most scholars that Brauron itself was the place where the return of Artemis from across the sea was celebrated.[27] This belief has been reinforced by the fact that Euripides then causes Athena to mention Brauron. But the nature of the Euripidean reference should be noted. It comes a full eleven lines after Athena's order to Orestes to build a temple at Halae, and this time (a) it is embodied in an order to Iphigenia and (b) refers to an already established cult and shrine:

> Iphigenia! Steps are cut in rock
> At Brauron for a shrine to Artemis.
> You shall reside as keeper of the keys there
> And at your death you shall be buried there
> And honored in your tomb with spotless gifts,
> Garments unworn, woven by hands of women
> Who honorably died in giving birth.[28]

It would sound as if Euripides had intended to mention two different but neighboring places: Halae, where a new temple was to be built; Brauron, where a cult of Artemis having to do with childbirth was already established. But what about Pausanias? It is true that Pausanias' account of Attica is careless, jumbled, and confused. His mention of Brauron is indeed out of topographical order, but it does occur in a rather significant way. He is discussing Marathon, well to the north, and he says that Marathon is "equally distant from Athens and Carystus in Euboea."[29] Then, after finishing his account of the battle of Marathon but before going on to describe the temple at Rhamnous, which is connected with Marathon both topographically and in legend, Pausanias jumps south and interpolates his account of the image of Artemis and the Athenians' belief in its return to Brauron. He does not mention any hill, and he says that he himself does not believe that the image there is the one from Tauris and that he will tell us later who really has it.[30] He then jumps north again and continues a normal itinerary of northern Attica.

Can we guess that the sudden memory of Brauron, apparently forgotten earlier, may have been triggered in Pausanias' mind by his mention of "Carystus" in Euboea? Since the ancient Carystus may be identified with the modern town of that name and since Mount Ocha rises above Carystus, may we not assume that the place ordered by Athena was to be at the "end" of Attica so that it could be as close as possible to "Carystus' hill" in Euboea? And it should be pointed out here that, as noted earlier, Mount Ocha and Mount Perati above Brauron are both splendidly horned. Halae–Loutsa, finally, is one of the closest places in Attica to Mount Ocha.

The opinion that the temple of Artemis at Loutsa is in fact on the spot ordered by Athena and that it is indeed intended to relate to Mount Ocha in Euboea is borne out by its placement in the landscape. (*Figs. 147, 148*) The present temple dates from the fourth century, but there are earlier remains on both sides of it which still await excavation. It was a short and curious building with a peripteral colonnade of perhaps eight or more small columns along the front and possibly eleven down the sides. It apparently had no opisthodomos, a fact which is often characteristic of fourth–century and later temples, but especially appropriate, as we have seen, in temples of chthonic deities. It is placed just behind the dunes which line the beach and is itself very close to the shore. It is like a beached boat, and this impression would have been stronger when the low dunes in front of it were cut down, as they probably were in antiquity. Yet even if the dunes were not leveled, the setting of the temple would still have been appropriate, guarding, from a protected position, the most inviting of landing beaches. (Here, in fact, a famous Allied hoax during the Second World War was entirely successful in convincing the Germans that a landing was intended. Pillboxes still line the shore.) Behind the dunes lies the archer. Her temple faces directly out to sea, and Mount Ocha is clearly visible to the northeast. (*Fig. 147*) The axis of the temple is not directed toward Ocha, however, and any intended relationship between the two might have to remain conjectural except for a particular fact. At the southwestern corner of the temple's cella is a block not bonded into the foundations and apparently a statue base. A line of sight from this block through the door of the cella proves to be exactly on axis with Ocha's gnarled and twisted horns, visible at eye height over the dunes. One is reminded of the diagonal relationship between base and mountain at Aulis (with which of course the myth of Iphigenia as a whole, and the memory of human sacrifice in particular, would directly connect this temple) and recalls also the placement of the figure of Themis in the southwestern corner of her cella at Rhamnous, to be discussed later. At any rate, a definite axis is set up between the block at Loutsa and the horns of Mount Ocha. Similarly, when standing on the dunes east of the temple and looking west along its southern flank, an observer's eye is carried across eastern Attica to the horns of

Hymettos on the horizon. (*Fig. 148*) The temple thus sets up a splendidly active, sharply curving axis of movement between Athens and Ocha: "god–built Athens," where Orestes was to pause; "Carystus' hill," close to which his temple was to be built. The site of Loutsa–Halae itself was therefore one of the best places on the east coast from which Ocha and Athens could be visually connected. The fourth–century temple there is like a poetic and convincing organization of building and landscape after Euripides' description, and one may speculate whether this new temple at Loutsa might not have been built over the older shrine through a revival of enthusiasm for Artemis Tauropolis which had been at least partly aroused by Euripides' own graphic treatment of the myth.

Brauron is not far off, and the way to it from Loutsa is an expressive one. It follows the beautifully curving shore southward until Mount Perati blocks the view ahead and the shore recedes deeply westward to form a narrow bay. The path then turns in along the shoulder of the hill until the temple appears at the head of the bay, on marshy ground close under a jagged outcropping of rock. It is flanked to the north by its stoa, and the doubled horns of the southern ridge of Hymettos rise far behind it. (*Fig. 149*) This is the same formation which formed the focus of the view from the temple of Artemis at Munychia, (*Fig. 145*) and is now being seen from the other side.

It was at Brauron that Iphigenia was to be honored in her tomb with garments "woven by women who honorably died in giving birth." The site of Brauron was indeed sacred to Artemis as the protector of women in childbirth, in which she was also regarded as responsible for the pain.[31] Hera herself was Eilithiya, the guardian of childbirth (this was one of her aspects at Paestum), but Hera was also goddess of marriage, and childbirth for her had to do also with the family, with human increase, and with women in society.[32] Artemis was the protector of the woman alone, not of marriage, and of childbirth as the female faced it alone. Thus Artemis was also the patron of animal birth and of the young of animals, and it was as animals, as bears, that the women of Athens worshiped her at Brauron. Every fifth year they wound in procession alone, without men, from Athens to the site. They may have cut across the low northern saddle of Hymettos at the point where the monastery of John the Hunter now is. On this route they would first have had on their right hand the sanctuary of Aphrodite at Kaisariani—Aphrodite who got them into their fix. (*Fig. 37*) From the saddle of Hymettos the view opens in a wide sweep. Ocha, fiercely horned and looming, rises to the left across the sea beyond Loutsa. Brauron is ahead to the southeast across the flat bowl of the plain, and its position is marked by the sharp horns of Perati above it. The way must have moved down through the plain, and if it wound through the hills northwest of Brauron, the most direct route, it would first have lost the sacred mountain and then found it again as the hills opened before it. (*Fig. 150*) Certainly the last of the way would have been across the flat, marshy plain directly west of the site. From this point Perati itself is no longer horned, but the hills ahead which frame the site swing once again into an arc, somewhat as they do at Aulis. Upon a closer approach, the temple, its position marked in the photograph by the small white church of St. George, can be seen at the bottom of its jagged hill, like a frozen wave of rock rising out of the plain. (*Fig. 151*) Beyond this savage projection the higher hill to the left makes a V–shape with it, and in the V, somewhat as at Mukhli, Perati, now cone–shaped, is enframed.

Entrance to the site was probably to the left of the present temple, dating from the sixth century. Just to the left of the entrance, a fifth–century stoa was used to bound that side of the site and probably as a place where the women could sleep at the shrine.[33] (*Fig. 153*) If the entrance was in fact as I guess it to have been, the site would have opened into a fine arc, created by the angle of the temple and continuing to the flat U of the shoreline. (*Figs. 152, 153*) To the left Mount Ocha would once more have appeared upon the horizon, and its far horns would have been countered by the nearer cone between the horns of Perati, which is clearly visible from the temple to the right. From the temple itself, a closed megaron in antis, without a colonnade but with several adyta, as befitted the wild and withdrawn goddess here, the cone and the horns are the most significant objects in view. Close to the southern flank of the temple are the "steps cut in rock," which Euripides mentions, and the church of St. George sits squarely upon them: excorcising like Herakles, one supposes, the earth demons of the place.

Close to the steps and to the temple's corner, the rock of the hill is split into a broken cleft which may, in antiquity, have formed a true cave (*Figs. 154, 155*) Into this narrow slot was shoved a structure like a megaron, probably unroofed, and with an altar hearth inside it. Be-hind this, and unconnected with it, was another platform cut into the rock and facing across the valley toward the northeast. (*Fig. 153*) From whatever building occupied this cutting the temple itself was not visible, and the view was a soft and gentle one, defined by the rounded contours of the low hills to the north. The site thus has two aspects: the one to the south harsh and jagged, the one to the north soft and calm. (*Fig. 155*) We do not know how the cere-monies were conducted, but a procession can be imagined for which the young girls were robed in the prescribed bearskins in the withdrawn building last mentioned. If they then moved out along the foot of the rock toward the temple, the stoa with its projecting corners—later con-tinued all the way to the rock—would have blocked their forward movement at an appropriate point and directed it to the left toward the temple itself. Approaching the temple's entrance, and arriving near the spot in front of it at which offering pithoi can be seen in the ground, the partici-pants would have viewed the front of the goddess' house framed by a perfect, full, rounded hill across the valley. All up to this point would have been calm and softness, expressive of beautiful female bodies and a gentle life. But turning in front of the temple the girls would have seen and, the altar of burnt offerings tells us, entered the megaron crammed into the savage opening in the rocks. (*Fig. 154*) From this denlike place they would in time have emerged, and their exit would have been between rocks which seem to grind down upon the megaron in their cleft. This must have been the act which brought the women to Brauron, since no use of a natural feature could express the agony of childbirth more directly than this one does. The walls of the goddess' temple shielded the place from view. Across the valley the gentleness of the northern hills sup-plies a typical balance for the statement of woman's position in the world which the site other-wise makes. But the cleft clearly celebrates the special and unsharable female act, when the bears, witnessed only by their goddess, drop their young in pain among the rocks, alone.

Artemis' sites on Asia Minor show her to have been more all–embracing there than she was in Greece itself. In them her name was given to many aspects of the Asiatic goddess, and her cults often embodied practices which were Asiatic or pre–Hellenic rather than Greek. At her great shrine of Ephesos, for example, it is clear that she was the unchallenged goddess, ruler of all: "Great is Diana of the Ephesians," the people of Ephesos shouted at the followers of St. Paul, and it can be no accident that popular legend eventually insisted that the Virgin Mary had died at Ephesos, and that her house was indeed still to be seen high in the rugged mountains southwest of Artemis' shrine.[34] At Ephesos the first altar and image of Artemis, around which the great archaic temple grew, were placed on low ground at the head of a roughly semicircular bay. (*Fig. 156*) This has now been silted up well forward of the temple site, but originally the temple itself must have stood as a typically Ionic dipteral pavilion close to the water's edge. One is reminded of Samos, with the columns rising by the shore below the encircling hills. The resemblance is limited, however, by the fact that the temple at Ephesos is placed exactly on axis with the major line of movement. Its pavilion is itself an entrance to Asia, standing as it does at the end of a harbor, and fairly closely enclosed by hills except on the water side. The axis of the temple is reinforced by the doubly mounded hill mass directly behind it to the east. Out of the cleft between the mounds rises a pyramidal summit which attracts the eye. The formation as a whole is again somewhat similar to that behind the Heraion at Samos. Yet at Ephesos, with its western entrance, and where the temple was formed around a complex of altar and image which never changed position, it is possible that the building was in fact "hypaethral," as Vitruvius, (III.2.8) who does not mention Ephesos in this connection, describes such temples: open at both ends and with two interior rows of columns, between which the cella is open to the sky. If it was so unusually conceived as an airy ambient for image and altar alike it could of course have been unroofed only over the altar, forward of the columnar image, which would otherwise have been left unprotected, but it might, as Henderson thought, have had not an adyton but an "opisthodomos," in this case a true second pronaos to frame the eastern door.[35]

Ephesos may be approached either by land or sea. From the land the pilgrim would have crossed the wide plain of the Cayster and followed the river as it found its way between the coastal mountains. As the way winds with the river into the hills, an isolated mountain mass rises up on the right hand, a mountain with a sweeping ridge line like raised arms or wings, next to which is cut the cleft of a horned gorge. On this bearing the temple lies beyond the mountain, and in the sea approach, especially from the southwest as Strabo, for example, enters the bay, the mountain itself forms the first natural object which announces the site. In this movement around the headland and eastward within the now silted bay, the full splendor of the place becomes apparent. Hills, which recall in their shape the sphinx mountain before Thebes, and which would have been lapped by the sea in early antiquity, lie to left and right, facing out at an angle well in front of the temple. The latter, its position roughly marked on this bearing by a line of trees which can serve to recall its own grove shape, lay dead ahead between the hills, with a harsh gorge and the pyramidal mountain behind it. To the north rises the winged mountain noted above, and to the south the mountain which was to become Mary's rises above the lower hill, again doubly mounded, where the Hellenistic town was placed. Low on its flank toward the temple was an ancient sanctuary of Earth, "Mother of the Gods."

The temple itself faced out to sea, but at an angle which brought into the goddess' focus the great horns above Klaros across the bay, where an important oracle of Apollo's was to be found. The whole ample landscape opens widely around the temple, placed as it is at the exact position from which the once splendid bay and its defining mountains can best be experienced. Standing within her cella, the mother of all the creatures on the continent looked out through the shadows of her colonnade at the approaching traveler. (*Fig. 158*) Her temple was the largest built in antiquity, and the processional reliefs which were carved around the drums of its columns may express part of the reason for such size. (*Figs. 157–158*) As at Samos, the wide spreading colonnade must be seen as a forest through which the labyrinthine processions wound. The shafts of the columns would then have acted in the way that the reliefs upon them indicate and express: as the definers of a curving, unilinear movement which coils around them.[36] At the same time the wings of Artemis in the reliefs are echoed by the winged mountain profile that flanks the site. Once again it is clear that the dipteral Ionic temple was intended to be an inner landscape rather than a purely sculptural presence. The ground plane of that landscape was defined by a projected pedestal which here had only two steps, so that, in contrast to the high platform at Samos, (*Fig. 81b*) it was unusually low, like a flood of the bay's flat surface across the land. Samos both balanced Mykale and was a hub; this was at once a climax and a forecourt, a stone plantation on a broad stone ground.

Directly ahead as approached from the sea would have been the wider opening between the central columns, and their two rows would have led the eye deep into the grove toward the goddess in her shrine. (*Fig. 158*) Yet again there are so many columns that there must have been a tendency on the part of the participant to wander among them and an invitation for a procession to move in a ceremonial dance, a dance winding and sinuous until it was pulled, by the wider central intercolumnation, toward the cella itself. Finally, the doors, on their special days, would have directed the labyrinth into, and perhaps through, the hidden space where the image stood on the axis between Asia and the sea. As at Samos, itself called "The Labyrinth," the winding dance so tenaciously loved in Greece would thus have been encouraged and possibly made continuous here. Its line would have coiled through the temple and its participants turned in the stylized elegance of clear relief profiles as they moved—again like the profiles of the processional reliefs around the column drums. Circling so among the hard, high shafts of these Ionic columns, of which all the forces from base to voluted capital fully expressed upward thrust (*Fig. 159*), the supple horizontal patterns of the dance found their appropriate architectural opposite and their frame. But around the abstract white pavilion in which the dance took place rose the embracing arc of the continent's hills. Therefore, while the open altar, the image, the wide platform, and the grove of Artemis are down in the swampy lands, one feels that they are invoking not only the water forces from which they spring but also that presence who sits, as in the caves of Crete or like the rock–cut Hittite goddess on Mount Sipylos, high above and beyond them among the peaks.[37]

At both Greek Magnesia on the Maeander and at Lydian Sardis such invocation of the mountain goddess seems obvious. At Magnesia both the early peripteral Ionic temple and the Hellenistic pseudodipteral building by Hermogenes which succeeded it on the same spot were faced toward the west, exactly upon the pointed, conical mountain which bounds the site on that side.[38] (*Fig. 160*) Seen in the approach through the passes from Ephesos to the northwest, the mountain rises into a flat, peaked face and then sends a long arm out to define the site. The temple of Artemis Leukophryene and the public buildings of the city of Magnesia as a whole were set on low ground just north of that long, rumpled tier of foothills which descends eastward from the mountain into the plain. Just beyond the last hill a low, isolated ridge with a crumpled profile rises from the plain. In this approach, the temple is first seen at the end of the foothills and below this ridge, while far to the eastward, up the valley, the mountain profiles open up into a great chorus of horns. Deeply set into her low ground and with the shape of her other symbols behind her, the goddess of the wild beasts and here also, it is believed, of the moon and the night, turns her back upon the horns, which her worshipers saw behind her as they approached her temple from the agora of the town. She herself looked westward toward the mountain which exactly fits the invocation of her which is voiced by the chorus in the *Iphigenia in Tauris* of Euripides: "Artemis, goddess of the pointed hills."[39]

The present temple of Artemis–Cybele at Sardis dates from the fourth century and later, but it was built upon the site of a fifth–century structure which may have replaced Croesus' early temple, which the Greeks are supposed to have burnt in their revolt against the Persians in 497 B.C.[40] The siting and the temple itself can therefore be legitimately discussed now. The acropolis at Sardis, below which the temple is placed, rises among the foothills of Mount Tmolus, which borders the southern edge of the Hermos Valley, Lydia's chariot plain. (*Fig. 161*) The town of Sardis itself lay generally west and south of the acropolis, stretching toward the plain, while farther out yet, dotted across the horizon, lay the breast–shaped tombs of the Lydian kings. The height of the acropolis is seen for a vast distance across the valley, and it rises in deeply corrugated masses to the sharp peaks and tented ridges of its summit. Its appearance is magical and barbarous, savage in scale. (To the modern eye it recalls the fantastic, castled landscapes of late medieval painting, toward whose tortured gothic mountains the saints and prophets make their way.) It was what it seems to be: not a typical Greek acropolis but a holy mountain itself, the physical and mystical citadel of Asiatic Lydia. To the south of this formidable apparition rise the greater masses of Mount Tmolus, called by Strabo, "blest,"[41] and as one approaches the site it becomes apparent that the summit of Tmolus is itself horned. (*Figs. 161–162*) It rises to a double peak a little like that of Cretan Ida, and opens in great clefts to the acropolis below. Far out in the plain the largest tumulus of all, that of King Alyattes, toward which the smaller tumuli lead, stands almost on the axis of the acropolis and the horns. (*Fig. 162*) In its present eroded condition the acropolis itself, as seen from near the temple, also presents, rather disconcertingly, a precisely horned profile, with a sheer face below it from which a great piece of the hill must at some time have sheared away to deposit its soil upon the temple in the valley. (*Figs. 161, 163*) Whether or not the mountain was horned in antiquity is difficult to say, but it is likely that the erosion and earthquakes which gave it its present summit were post–classical, so that it would have had a more solidly pyramidal profile when the temple was placed directly under it, on low ground close to its western slope and deeply enclosed on north and south by its projecting arms.

The long axis of the temple runs roughly east and west within the hollow of the valley. The main approach must always have been from the northwest, from the plain and the town of Sardis, so that the temple was first seen with the horns of Tmolus beyond it among the clouds, while its long flank carried the eye in a decisive perspective toward the acropolis height, and the volutes of its Ionic capitals stood out against the farther horns. (*Fig. 163*) The worshiper's attention was therefore focused first upon Tmolus and then upon the acropolis, but upon arriving at the hill slope to the east of the temple, he saw that the western extension of its axis was formed by a splendidly domed peak, below whose sharp arrises the hard pyramids and cones of lesser hills could be seen. (*Fig. 164*) Among these was the necropolis of the town. A great arc of ridge, like an arm rising heavily out of the earth, swings from this mountain of graves to enframe the temple, which was thus a long, stretched pavilion lying in the hollow between two striking peaks. Each of these seems to represent a holy presence, since each has qualities of form which call up the symbols of the goddess. It therefore seems logical to assume that the unusual double–ended form of the later temple itself related to the fact that it faces two such presences, one, the acropolis, a citadel of life, the other a place of death, and it is therefore possible that the earlier temple was intended to be double–ended too. (*Fig. 165*) The temple as it stands clearly focuses attention upon its two entrances, the one on the west toward the domed peak opening out in elaborately baroque sets of stairs. Similarly, the flanking colonnades are deeply pseudodipteral, giving a wide passage from end to end and heavily shadowing the closed long walls behind them. Moreover, it is possible that, since no columns were used in the wide spaces between the dipteral colonnade at east and west and the entrances to the cella, those areas may in fact have been unroofed and a strong shaft of light may have flooded them.[42] This baroque device of casting the side walls into deep shadow and brilliantly spotlighting each entrance may have been characteristic only of the later temple, but it beautifully dramatized the temple's double–ended focus. "Artemis" and "Cybele" (or Aphrodite) may each have been one aspect of the Anatolian goddess worshiped here, and it is possible that each of the peaks may have stood for one of those aspects. Certainly the architecture of peaks and temple is unified into one sweeping plastic shape. The goddess here, full as her site is of terror and barbaric power, is more than the Greek Artemis. She is also Aphrodite, great goddess of Asia, and the savage dome which rises up on the west speaks of that being upon whose footsteps the wolves and panthers of Ida fawned, and whose lion of miraculous birth was carried in procession around the Lydian citadel.[43]

It may at first seem inappropriate to link the virgin goddess Artemis with Aphrodite, the goddess of love, but it is clear from Greek myth that they were in part two sides of the same coin. More than this, the Greek Aphrodite, like Artemis, was a direct descendant of some of the most potent aspects of the old goddess, and her most characteristic temple sites express a nature which seems, like that of Artemis, to be beyond the reach of reason or control.[44] But Aphrodite's most individual sites act upon men with sudden forcefulness. They are not so much grandly remote and disquieting, like those of Artemis, as disturbing with the directness of explosive apparitions. Aphrodite was certainly a goddess of the sea and was born in it. Her great Ionian and Asiatic shrines, of horned Cnidus, and of Cyprian Paphos, are located on strong masses that rise out of the sea, and their force is set off by the waters lapping below them. She was also a mountain goddess, especially of Mysian Ida beyond Troy where Anchises had promised to make her "an altar upon a high peak in a far seen place."[45] Ida, itself, as seen from the sea to the southwest, exhibits the characteristic tented profile, and its whole southern flank, deeply notched and gorged, was studded, so Strabo tells us, with many sanctuaries.[46] The shrine which Aphrodite shared with her son and agent, Eros, in Athens,[47] is so located on the northeastern slope of the Acropolis as to face toward the brutal cone of Lycabettos which rises in the middle of the modern city but was outside the ancient one. (*Figs. 328, 345*) Lycabettos seems to have been so disturbing to the Athenians that they invented the myth of Athena's dropping it there by accident upon hearing of the fatal disobedience of the Cecropidae. She had been intending to add her load to the Acropolis hill, and this itself is significant, since Lycabettos, though much higher than the Acropolis, is much too narrow at the top ever to have been used as an acropolis itself and may for this reason also have been seen as peculiarly unreasonable, potent, and intrusive. It is a naked force, especially as seen from the southwest, and it is as such that it appears from the Acropolis, with whose site organization, as we shall see, it was always intimately connected.

From Aphrodite's own shrine on the slope of the Acropolis the conical hills which enclose her greater shrine at Kaisariani[48] are just visible under the ridge of Hymettos and to the south of its horns. (*Figs. 166, 37*) But it should also be remembered that evidences of the association of Aphrodite with Athena have been found in the Erechtheion,[49] and may therefore have existed in the old temple of Athena Polias as well, in a temple which was exactly oriented upon the horns of Hymettos with the hills of Kaisariani also in view. (*Fig. 36*) Those hills, like Lycabettos, seem naked and full of force: forceful because they come up into tightly pointed, full, and solid cones; naked because, seen from among them or from above, the curious natural pigmentation of the sod which is confined to certain areas of their slopes by the rock outcroppings resembles a garment which has been flung across but fails to cover them. They indeed seem to be, as Aphrodite said of Ida to Anchises: "the deep–breasted mountain Nymphs who inhabit this great and holy mountain . . ."[50] Water gushes from between them as at "many–fountained Ida," and the main temple would seem to have been in the hollow near the place where the spring now comes forth in the entrance courtyard of the monastery of Kaisariani. From slightly to the north within the hollow of the hills the flank of Lycabettos is on axis between the V of the near slopes. (*Fig. 166*) Remains of what appear to have been Roman buildings are to be found in the churches which were later built on the promontory forward of the spring. (*Fig. 167*) From this point the largest conical hill is directly on axis ahead, while across the Attic plain the conical mound beside the Sacred Way to Daphni can be seen. We recall that another shrine of Aphrodite was set within that pass, exactly at the point where the Way came into sight of the horns of Salamis and opposite a massive, unexpected outcropping of rock.[51] (*Fig. 120*) In all instances so far considered, Aphrodite's shrines have had to do with the appearance of unexpected and irresistible forces, expressing a nature at once aggressive and triumphant.

Such is the character of the natural formation which rises above her shrine at Troezen on the coast of the Peloponnesos south of Epidauros, not far from the island of Poros.[52] At Troezen Aphrodite was associated with Hippolytos, clearly the Hellenic hero of the place, who, in myth as interpreted by Euripides, had been doomed to death because he had scornfully denied Aphrodite's power. Artemis, too, had her sanctuary at Troezen, as did Demeter, Poseidon, and Athena, the latter holding the acropolis of the ancient town, which stood slightly west of the modern one. There was also a sanctuary of Asklepios on the site,[53] as there was a temple of Aphrodite at his site of Epidauros, to be discussed later. But it is violent conflict and the victory of Aphrodite that Troezen most fully expresses. The hills above the town split into a savage gorge with twisted ridges on its flanks. To the right of the gorge as seen from the plain, the rocky masses of the mountain swing upward in an arc and culminate in a saw–toothed skyline which reads from a distance as sharply horned. (*Fig. 168*) The central feature of this skyline is a stiffly vertical projection which again, a little like Taygetus, resembles a small, high head held proudly up within the mountain throne. Artemis, too, is thus appropriately embodied here. Below this formation the mountain slopes steeply downward, and directly at its foot stood the temple of Aphrodite, with the sanctuary of Asklepios and the temple of Hippolytos close by. Its position is now marked by the white walls of the church of Palaeo–Episcopi.[54] To the left of the temple another arc of rock rises up the side of the mountain to form a snaky line of precipices. The shrine thus stood below the center of an awesome formation which burst out of the plain in an impressive manifestation of the earth's power: rising majestically at the center, deeply riddled by clefts, pushing its curving ridges out to left and right like encircling arms. From the shrine, with the active force of the goddess–mountain at its back, the view sweeps across the lowlands toward the jagged promontory of Methane in the sea and the island of Poros across the channel to the southeast. Northwest of the shrine, invisible from it but also serving as an identification for it from the sea near Poros, is the long formation of mountain ridges which create the image, so the inhabitants of the area claim, of a woman lying on her back. (*Fig. 169*) The resemblance is indeed persuasive; the head low on the north, a long neck, high breasts, arched stomach, long legs with the knees drawn up. The slanting shins define the northern slope of a great V which rises on the other side to the formation of Troezen. Perhaps it was not accidental that the story of the frantic lust of Phaedra was connected with an area defined by these formations. Certainly the whole landscape, whose forms must from earliest times have been considered uniquely expressive of the great goddess of land and sea, was particularly appropriate to the special Greek identification of her with Aphrodite. Equally clearly, the waters of the almost inland sea which her mountains dominate are haunted by the anguish of Phaedra, which the landscape shapes themselves may thus originally have suggested.

Acrocorinth, which was one of the most important centers of Aphrodite's worship, is haunting and terrible as well. Somewhere near the city, below its dominating bulk, she had a large temple, and her dedicated courtesans there were sought after and expensive.[55] Upon the peak of Acrocorinth are to be found the remains of another of her temples.[56] As one approaches Acrocorinth from the Megarid and passes beyond the Scironian cliffs, the bulk of the mountain suddenly rises beyond the long and apparently flat plain of the Isthmus with twin horned peaks behind its mass. (*Fig. 283*) It seems an irresistible and illogical appearance, a vision so solid as to enforce belief. A closer inspection does not diminish that impression of unreasonable force. The great rock sustains its dominance and its bulk. Its northwestern slope opens into a wide horn shape, and it is below those horns that the temple of Apollo is placed. This does not concern us for the moment, and the general effect of the mountain in most views is of a solid, rocky plug which thrusts up from the mounded slopes below, but which, from close at hand to the north, seems also to be attempting to lift widespread arms of rock out of the earth. It recalls

95

in this way the necropolis mountain at Sardis. (*Fig. 170*) On the summit of the rock fresh water welled from the Fountain of Upper Peirene.[57] Aphrodite's temple was upon the very peak, and from it the two horned mountains to the south (*Fig. 171*), mentioned earlier, loom up massively across the nearer hills, with further horns of mountains farther south lying in the cleft between them. From the site of the temple the whole landscape indeed seems to be bursting with irresistible forces and monstrous images. The crouching mountain above Nemea seems extraordinarily lionlike in this view, and may have suggested the myth of that place.[58] Beyond it are the lifting arms of Mount Kyllene above Stymphalia and the jagged peaks beyond Sikyon. Parnassos and Helicon are across the gulf, and Perachora seems more than ever a bronze figure sleeping on the water with the horned guardian of Mount Gerania above it. (*Fig. 172*) To the east the orientation of Aphrodite's temple appears to lie directly across the low Isthmus with its temple of Poseidon and to be directed across the Saronic gulf toward the headland of Salamis. The latter appears at this distance to be a purely conical hill, but a close inspection of it from the sea shows it to be tightly horned. The earth below Aphrodite's mountain is thus tense with the symbols of the goddess, and her view from its summit sweeps across the Isthmus to embrace two seas.

Aphrodite's great temple in the West was upon the top of the mountain of Eryx, which rises directly out of the sea on the western coast of Sicily. Like Acrocorinth, it is an unexpected and overwhelming apparition. The land around it is low and the farther hills are gently rolling and mounded. Suddenly the mountain arises and dominates the whole plain and the sea. This was Carthaginian Sicily, but the native and ancient goddess celebrated at Eryx was early recognized as the equivalent of the Greek Aphrodite.[59] While the site was in Carthaginian hands she was identified as Tanit. In Roman times she was called Venus, and Venus Erycina had her own temple in Rome.[60] The temple at Eryx was placed on a ridge of rock which sweeps out from the summit,[61] so that from the summit itself the temple could be seen poised above the tremendous view: to the right the long peninsula of Trapani, the sea, and the islands; straight ahead the interior of Sicily, all mounds and cones of hills; to the left other mountains which curve around to the sea on the northern side and erupt at the shore into a climactic conical mass.

The Carthaginian recognition of the sacred character of Eryx calls to mind the nature of the site of Carthage itself. There the city looked across its double harbors toward a great black mountain which looms upon the further shore of the bay. The mountain is grandly horned. In antiquity it was called the "Horns of Tanit," and the temple of that goddess, standing upon the height of the city—the Byrza, which was the place of original settlement—had it in view across the water. Its sacred shape continues to receive recognition, since in Arabic it is still called "horns," *Qurnain*.[62]

The setting of the main temple at Greek Tyndaris, on the north coast of Sicily, was much like that of Eryx. The place was colonized in 396 B.C. by homeless Messenians. Their eponymous deity was called Tyndaris, and her close identification with Aphrodite seems evident, since she was also named Helen and was, like Helen, associated with twin brothers, the Tyndaridae,[63] who took their name from Tyndareus, foster father of Castor and Pollux. The hill which was the acropolis of Tyndaris and upon which its theater was placed with a wide sea view toward Stromboli, rises as does Eryx out of the sea plain. Its dramatic isolation as a female force is

96

especially evident when it is viewed from the southeast, and it was upon the eastern summit, where the Basilica of the Black Virgin now stands, that its main temple was placed. (*Fig. 173*) Again the view sweeps wide toward a horned horizon, but the most expressive contrast is with the sea below. It washes in long shallows below the base of the temple's rock, and in so doing creates enormous swirling patterns in the sand. The scale of the view thus becomes strange and giddy; the high solid rock of the temple, the constantly shifting ebb and flux below. Once again it would appear to have been the unexpected violence of contrasting states of being juxtaposed which caused the site to be seen by the Greeks as expressive of a Helen–Aphrodite. Most obviously Tyndaris, however she may have acquired her name, was the old goddess of mountain and sea alike and, associated with Helen, was given a site which itself embodied an expression of the irresistible and terrible dominion of love and which was therefore entirely appropriate to the existing cult of the Messenians who were allowed to settle there.

For all these reasons one might have expected that the water sanctuary which is to be found high upon the slopes of Cefalù, not far west of Tyndaris on the north Sicilian coast, might also have been associated with the name of Aphrodite or one of her familiars. The mountain rises suddenly out of the sea, like Tyndaris and Eryx, and it sweeps around in a deep arc to thrust a massive buttress above the city below. (*Fig. 174*) Its water sanctuary, set forward on a grassy shoulder high above the sea, may be very old, but the architectural remains are Hellenistic and Roman, with romantically rustic cyclopean masonry.[64] (*Fig. 175*) On its rounded bluff, the sanctuary seems appropriate to the goddess of the thrusting mountain and the water, but its popular association has been with the name of Diana, thus Artemis.[65] This may have come about because the mountain is a lonely and disquieting place, close though it is above the town. In the dawn it is absolutely quiet, and its western clefts are in shadow. The slopes are full of holes and grottoes, inhospitable, dangerous ground. But Aphrodite has some share in this too. Like "many–fountained Ida, the mother of wild creatures," here is a place for the "grey wolves, fawning on her, and grim–eyed lions, and bears . . ."[66] The rock is hollow and full of water, deeply burgeoning with life. Many qualities of the goddess of earth are felt there: her fertility, her resources of power, her threat to careless men.

Because of its expression of a similar combination of qualities which in Greek lands might belong to Artemis, or Aphrodite, or even Demeter, the temple at Elymian Segesta should, I think, be discussed at this time.[67] Its complete colonnade stands in the center of a turbulent landscape like a stormy sea, with at least one pair of horns rising high among the hills to the north. Segesta was not a Greek city. It lay within the orbit of Carthaginian influence in western Sicily, and the name it gave to the goddess it worshiped is unknown. It was usually allied with Carthage against Syracuse and Akragas, and during the Peloponnesian war it therefore allied itself with Athens against the Dorian enemy. In all likelihood an Athenian architect designed its temple sometime during the 420's. As at Demeter's slightly earlier enclosure at Thorikos, its columns were left unfluted and, either through accident or by design, it had no cella. Probably also like Demeter's sanctuary it was left unroofed, and no cuttings for beams are to be found in its entablature blocks. This might lead to the beguiling conclusion, if we could be convinced that such cuttings were always made before the blocks were hoisted into place, that no roof or cella were ever intended, but this view would probably not be correct.[68] The build-

97

ing at present is thus a pedimented colonnade, an open rectangle of columns. (*Fig. 176*) As left, its unfluted shafts and the projecting bosses of the stones of its stereobate combine to create an effect of ponderous, uncivilized power. (*Fig. 177*) Above the cylinders of the columns, somewhat thicker in section than they would have been if fluted, the echini of the capitals seem to thrust up out of hunched and muscular shoulders. Such unrelieved solid geometry and powerful mass inevitably call to mind the fevered Romantic–Classic visions of the first and eighteenth centuries A.D. That analogy should not be carried too far, however, since the temple was designed with the most intensely Greek mathematical subtlety, its stereobate rising in a swift and tensile arc. (*Fig. 177*) The placing of the temple is of utmost relevance here. Seen from the higher ground of the theater to the southeast, it is exactly on the top of a fully mounded hill. The impression it creates is that of a nipple on a breast. (*Fig. 178*) Behind it a pyramidal mountain mass rises abruptly. So far as one can tell, even from the vantage point of the theater height, no unusual ground feature other than a slight depression would seem to separate the temple from the mountain. As the temple is approached from below, and on the east side, it seems to move forward itself to enclose the viewer. (*Fig. 179*) This effect is produced because the observer is mounting the hill slope and the columns thus swing forward toward the vertical as they begin to be seen with flat, rather than sloping, ground before them. In this approach the triangle of the pediment echoes the shape of the pyramidal mountain behind it, with the rear of the western pediment sliding between them. As one enters between the columns into the noble space defined by them, the back of the western pediment now covers or echoes the hill façade, and in this way the interval between temple and hill seems further diminished. Such is still the impression as one steps forward through the west columns toward the mountain, but suddenly the terrible and the unexpected occurs. The ground drops precipitously away before one's feet, and a gulf, tremendous in depth and width, opens between the temple and the mountain. It is hundreds of yards deep and almost as wide. The rock slopes down into it with a quick rush, and the scale as a whole is so great that a shepherd and his flock of sheep seem tiny far below. (*Fig. 180*) Now that the whole organization of the site is grasped, the reason for the fast rise of the temple's stylobate becomes apparent. (*Fig. 177*) It not only makes the structure a rising culmination to its mound but also carries the eye in a rapid trajectory toward the gulf. Seen from the gulf side the western columns dramatize that movement, because they have a pronounced inward lean themselves and are now also read against the sharply slanting fall of ground. (*Fig. 181*) In this way they seem actually to lean back against the gulf. The stereobate rises and hurtles forward, the side columns lift and march with it, and the whole comes to a violent stop just at the edge of the void. The somber, unfluted columns and the massive bosses on the stones now seem an appropriate setting for the kind of rite the landscape calls forth. One recalls the piglets thrown into Demeter's "megaron" cleft at Athens; here it is men one imagines swung—as if by inertia—out of the columned enclosure into the void. Segesta thus seems to celebrate some insatiable goddess of the earth, a primitive Demeter, Aphrodite, and Artemis all in one. Moreover, the temple is a monument built by an extraordinarily knowledgeable and skillful Athenian of the classic period, who seems to have manipulated the Greek vocabulary of architectural form in order to express the presence of a goddess whom he clearly saw as savage and barbarian, and to whom, therefore, he felt the typically civilized man's romantic attraction. He was an architectural Euripides. There is a kind of implicit archaism in the temple, somewhat related to what I believe to be the consciously manipulated archaism prac-tised at Bassae at almost the same time. Did Ictinos himself, if it is indeed he to whom we owe the major part of the work at Bassae, find his way to Sicily as well as to Arcadia? The question is asked without irony, since Segesta was clearly built by someone like Ictinos who was capable of pushing the formal elements of the Doric temple into realms of expression unreached before and never again attempted. Segesta is great because it is a strange masterpiece with a meaning that transcends race; it is Greek but embodies a presence not wholly of the Greek gods. Its columns crown the hill with solemn grandeur, but, rearing up at the edge of the abyss, it is the only Greek temple that screams.

This is not the place to discuss the temple of Apollo which was built by Ictinos (and perhaps others) in the mountains of Arcadia at Bassae. But above the temple there was a double sanctu-ary which does concern us now, because Artemis and Aphrodite were together there. Somewhere down below, in the gorge of the Nedda near Phigaleia, was the cavern which sheltered Horse-headed Demeter. The wild mountains then rise, and at their highest point a perfect, natural hairpin megaron is formed in a mountain peak which had in antiquity the name of Kôtilon, or cup. In this tightly enclosing space, curved like an apse to the north and open to the south, two rustic sanctuaries of Artemis and Aphrodite were placed together.[69] (*Fig. 182*) The site is high, and was overrun by wolves, and the view to the south is wide. It is focused, however, by the flat-topped mass of Mount Ithome, which can be seen far to the south directly on the axis of the natural megaron, with which it seems to form one great architectural shape. The two small sanctuaries were set well forward in their megaron enclosure, apparently to make the most of the view. In order to understand the meaning of that landscape vista we should prob-ably return for a moment to Mycenaean Pylos. From the palace of Nestor the dominant object of the southern horizon had been the great conical mountain, part of Mt. Mathia, at the en-trance to the coastal plain. (*Figs. 48, 50*) If we move thence northeastward to Mount Ithome, upon which the unfortunate Messenians were forever taking refuge and on the slopes of which was a temple of Artemis (*Fig. 134*) we find that a number of curious sanctuaries, be-lieved by some to have been chthonic in cult, are to be found upon its summit and are oriented southwest across the valley toward the selfsame conical hill south of Pylos.[70] A long landscape axis was thus set up, but if we move far north to Bassae the axis is prolonged. Seen from the natural megaron which Aphrodite and Artemis shared, Ithome looms behind the rising arc of nearer mountains as a unique and isolated force. We should not forget that Ithome, like Cretan Jouctas, Ida, and Dikte, was also made sacred to Zeus and that upon its summit was a sanctuary to Zeus Ithomatas, in which human sacrifice was apparently practiced until a very late date.[71] From their forward position in the megaron the two sanctuaries have Ithome directly in view and also look beyond it to south and southwest, where lie the Ionian and Aegean seas that bound the Peloponnesos. The megaron above Bassae would thus seem to have been the ultimate throne of the goddess. It is placed in the heart of the wildest and most primitive landscape of classic Greece. Out of that untouchable sanctuary Artemis looked across the bow of her lonely hills, and Aphrodite had in sight the irresistible thrust of her mountain and her double seas.

Chapter 7

APOLLO

A young god, you have ridden down powers gray with age.
Aeschylus, EUMENIDES (Lattimore)[1]

THE COMPLEXITY OF Apollo's nature and origins has engrossed the attention of many scholars. It is amply attested by the variety of his sites, as is his importance by their number. Yet beyond the complexity a pattern emerges: Apollo's most important places tell us that he was usually invoked by the Greeks wherever the most awesome characteristics of the old goddess of the earth were made manifest. Wherever her symbols were most remote, tortuously approached, and largest in scale, and where they seemed to open up the interior secrets of the earth most violently or most dominated a thunderous view, there the temple of the young god was placed, and generally so oriented as not only to complement but also to oppose the chthonic forces. Clearly enough, Apollo is intellect, discipline, and purity—central, as so many modern writers have insisted, to the archaic formulation of some of Hellenic society's most nobly human ends[2]—but, equally clearly, the sites tell us that Apollo is those qualities embodied in an implacably heroic force. Yet he, too, cannot come to grips with the earth without being touched by it. Therefore, god of the sun though he may be and, like his sister Artemis, incorruptible and a guardian of gates, he still takes on some of the darkness of the old cavern as he assumes the oracular power. Apollo's sites thus tend to embody grandeur, strife, and the development of a complex character. True enough, they seem primarily to celebrate, with archaic action and directness, an arrogant intrusion of the shining Hellenic male god into the central strongholds of the pre–Hellenic goddess. At the same time, many of his sanctuaries would seem to have been so organized as to create, out of that basic conflict, a conscious and humanly perceptible drama, in which the god's code of "Nothing to excess," which his terrible victories made more necessary to him than to any other, is finally shown to emerge in the teeth of nature's irrational power. Thus in many of Apollo's sites the abstract, mathematical order of the Greek temple is made to contrast most sharply with the roughhewn masses of the earth, dramatizing at once the terrible scale of nature and the opposing patterns which are the result of disciplined human action in the world—while, within, the secret darkness also receives special attention.

Apollo's two most important sites, Delphi, the seat of his greatest oracle, and Delos, the place of his birth, are extremely rich in buildings and can better be discussed later in this chapter. We have already mentioned the character of Apollo's site at Amyklai, where his colossal statue stood above the tomb of the local hero, Hyakinthos, on the mounded hill above the Sparta of Menelaus and Helen. (*Fig. 47*) This was the spot from which the forwardly aggressive power of Taygetus could be felt most fully, as distinct from Artemis' Limnaion, above which the mountain goddess watched enthroned. Therefore the young god must be placed here, standing with his bow before the clefts and rising, if the reconstruction of the curious monument is correct,[3] between the wings of the colonnades below him as the great mass rises near him between the double gorges on Taygetus itself. His columnar form, male and aggressive, would have stood out in sharp contrast to the cleft body of the mountain and as a counterforce to the shrouded presences of its peaks.

At the vale of Tempe, under Mount Olympos in Thessaly, where the worship of Apollo was supposed to have been introduced into Greece, we find a wild gorge defined by the horns of two rocky hills. "The eddying river Peneus," upon whose bank the swan sang for Apollo,[4] runs through the gorge, and just at the point where it breaks through the mountain a strong V–shaped cleft opens in the side of the gorge to the west. Somewhere in this vicinity Apollo's shrine was placed, among the laurels, and the landscape is typical of many of his sites: the great horns, the split gorge under the sacred mountain, the rushing water. It is the landscape described in the Homeric Hymns to Apollo as sacred to him: "wooded groves and all peaks and towering bluffs of lofty mountains and rivers flowing to the sea. . . ."[5] A modern road is now being pushed through Tempe, its presence ruining the scale of the gorge but emphasizing the fact that this is the direct route into Greece from the north. Tempe is a gate, and Apollo guards it. He was also the god to whom Zeus had given the gift of prophecy, which comes from the earth. Thus he had taken it away from the goddesses who had held it before. One of Apollo's oracles was at Pagasae, southeast of Tempe, across the coastal plain and bay from neo-lithic Dimini, and above modern Volos on the gulf.[6] Pagasae has all the characteristics of those sites in which the old goddess had been most completely embodied. Above the sea rises a strongly mounded hill. On axis behind it the mountain ridge dips down into a cleft, and directly behind the cleft a towering set of horns arises. This is now Apollo's oracular throne, horned in consecration and towering above land and sea: "All mountain peaks and high headlands of lofty hills and rivers flowing out to the deep and beaches sloping seawards and havens of the sea are your delight."[7]

These words of the Homeric Hymn equally well describe the site of the Panionion in Asia Minor.[8] (*Fig. 286*) This was the place where the Ionian cities met during archaic times to carry on the business and festivals of their league, but the Panionion, with the horns of Mount Mykale above it, was, as Herodotus tells us, sacred to Heliconian Poseidon, not to Apollo.[9] Herodotus does not say that Poseidon had a temple there, and the remains so far discovered at the site are clearly those of an open altar within a temenos wall, to be discussed later. However, there is certainly an overlap between Apollo and Poseidon at the Panionion, a site whose con-formation makes it appropriate to either. So Apollo's temple at Thera, for example, was placed well forward on the promontory of the town, sailing eastward above the black beach toward the open sea.[10] Vitruvius insists that the Ionian cities built a Doric temple to "Panionian" Apollo and were indeed the first to work out the proportions of the Doric order.[11] He does not specify that the temple was built at the site of the Panionian festival itself. It might, therefore, have been built on the higher ridge southwest of the hill that supported Poseidon's open altar, or indeed at several other appropriate spots along the Ionian coast. It may even have occupied the ridge that lies below the great double peaks, now called "The Two Brothers," which rise above a splendid cleft on the southern shore of the bay of Smyrna, east of Clazomenae. Just east of the peaks is a deeply folded gorge which contains warm springs, at a town now called Agamemnon, and which was the site of the hero sanctuary called the "Agamemnoneion" during antiquity. The placing of Apollo's temple below the peaks would thus accord with Strabo's description of the southern coast as he approaches Smyrna, noting as he does a temple of Apollo followed by a place of warm springs.[12] The two peaks stand like beacons exactly on the axis of the present channel into the bay, and the ridge where one would expect the temple to have been placed curves in below them to form a deep pocket above which the mighty horns tower. It, too, like the ridge above the Panionion, is a height below horns and above the sea. A temple placed there could not appropriately have been a spreading Ionic grove but rather a more compact Doric sculptural body, like the temple of Athena at Assos, the only archaic Doric temple in Asia Minor of which the remains have as yet been found.

Vitruvius also goes on to say that the proportions arrived at for the Doric order were those which best seemed to express the character of a male body.[13] His association of that order with a temple of Apollo is therefore of some interest insofar as it links that god with those qualities of abstraction and maleness in the Doric peripteral temple which most contrasted with the shapes of the earth associated with the old goddess. Vitruvius then tells us that the Panionians later worked out the Ionic order, with the proportions this time intended to express those of a woman, and the volutes of the capital the meshes of her hair.[14] This legend may have derived simply from the occasional use of caryatids in Ionic buildings. But it at least indicates a continuation of that association of the Ionic column with female properties, thus with the goddess, which we mentioned earlier in connection with its tree and horn symbolism.[15] Despite this association, not all Apollo's archaic temples were Doric. His archaic oracular temple at Didyma, destroyed by the Persians in 494 B.C., was Ionic, and one of the earliest examples of a developed Ionic capital was found on the site of his temple at Naucratis, in the delta of Egypt.[16] Again, it would seem to have been primarily the setting which, even in Ionian sanctuaries, determined the temple form. Thus the site at Naucratis, like those at Sardis, Ephesos, and Samos, is low and flat, while Didyma, to be discussed later, occupies a long, broad, and very gentle ridge in the center of a vast and open landscape. So at Locri Epizephyrii in south Italy the Ionic temple was down on the plain toward the shore, while the two other temples among the foothills above it were Doric.[17]

Apollo's temples could therefore be either Doric or Ionic, and the Doric could be used anywhere. At Actium it stood on a long and marshy promontory near the mouth of the Ambracian Gulf.[18] Surrounded by double peaked mountains, it too guarded an entrance to Greece. (*Fig.* 370) Above it, near the gates of Cassope and between two great mountain horns on the way northward to Dodona, another temple, possibly of Artemis, commanded the view to the gulf.[19] Apollo's temple on Aigina is also Doric and is placed in a landscape which again

102

shows affinities with sites sacred to Poseidon.[20] It is on the summit of a low promontory which projects from the western shore of the island. The site had been occupied since Neolithic times, and throughout the Mycenaean age, and the Dorian cult itself went back to the Geometric period. There can therefore be little doubt that the place was originally sacred to the goddess. The taut cone of Mount Oros, which became sacred to Zeus Panhellenios,[21] lies southeast of the promontory, and mounded hills and subsidiary cleft and horned ridges lie between. (*Fig. 183*) To the east rise the Artemis–invoking bow shapes of the ridges of central Aigina, and the promontory carried the compact body of the temple away from them into a bowl of sea that is encircled with the symbols of power, a drowned crater out of which cleft mountains rise. (*Fig. 184*) One imagines some sea goddess originally upon the spot, perhaps like the Aphrodite of Troezen whose mountain is just out of sight to the south. The light of the place seems especially important for the meaning, with the water shimmer and the island haze. The temple must have sailed like an explorer's ship into a sea of apparitions.

Such conscious intrusion by Apollo seems a cogent fact at Daphni. One recalls that the sacred way to Eleusis wound from Athens into the pass at Daphni, and that from the height of the pass it brought the horns of Kerata, insignia of hidden Eleusis, into view. (*Fig. 121*) At that point in the pass stood a temple of Apollo, guardian of the gate to Athens.[22] Its exact position is unknown, but since the present monastery is exactly over the Early Christian basilica which was built there, and since the logical foundations for the basilica would have been those of the temple, it is reasonable to suppose that the temple stood where the monastic church now is. If so, then the temple, as can be seen by looking west from the western façade of the church, was oriented on a direct line with Kerata's horns. Can the procession, which was to arrive at Eleusis by night and to celebrate there the hidden rites of darkness, have come to Daphni about at midday, when the sun was highest? The bright columns of the god of the sun, and of the rational order which is known in the light, may have consciously been used at Daphni as a typically Hellenic reminder of values other than those evoked by the goddess' ecstasies. Similarly, as the traveler progresses beyond Eleusis, past Megara with its innumerable sanctuaries, he comes to the rotting Scironian cliffs, a dangerous passage, haunted for the Greeks by legends of disaster. Considered as a whole, the many myths—not least among them the Euripidean story of the death of Hippolytos through the attack of a bull thrown up by the sea—seem to express the power of a mountain and sea goddess like Aphrodite, and an image of Aphrodite stood with those of Zeus and Apollo upon the summit of the cliffs. Pausanias, who records this fact, tells us also that the traveler, upon descending from the cliffs to the west, will "see a sanctuary of Apollo Latous, after which is the boundary between Megara and Corinth. . . ."[23] The remains of this sanctuary, if any, have not yet been discovered, but the appropriate landscape formation for it can be easily seen: a mounded hill behind which rise the horns of a gorge. The young god would again have stood not only at a boundary but also at the spot of entrance into or release from the threatening place of the dangerous goddess.

Farther west, at Corinth, a conscious opposition between the temple of Apollo and the mountain of Aphrodite seems manifest. As we noted earlier, the mass of Acrocorinth appears as a single, thrusting bulk when seen from across the Isthmus. (*Fig. 283*) As one progresses into the town of old Corinth, however, it becomes apparent that the northeastern precipices of the mountain swing open into a tremendous pair of horns. The ground slopes rapidly away beneath them for a long distance, flattens out into a wide plateau, and then mounds up into a low hill. Upon that slight eminence the temple of Apollo is placed.[24] (*Fig. 185*) The whole swing of land away from the mountain is stabilized by it, and temple and horns together, when viewed from the west, form one balanced shape. The way in which the temple would normally have been approached in antiquity would have further dramatized that relationship. Coming into the agora of Corinth along the main road from the north one would have been below and to the side of the temple's hill, and the mountain mass of the goddess would have dominated the view ahead. (*Figs. 170, 186*) Arriving at the agora one would have turned north again and mounted a steep flight of stairs toward the temple. This would then have stood out clearly against the sky. (*Fig. 187*) Only the columns of the southwest angle are now standing, but they are enough to show the effect of the temple as seen from the stairs. Its shafts are massive and without entasis, uncompromising and solid. From the stairs one comes out upon the temple's platform near the eastern altar. From here the columns would have stood against the long horizontals of coast and gulf, with the slopes of Mount Loutraki rising across the water. As one moved toward the altar the whole unusually long body of the temple would have swung into axis, and from further north it would have slipped into place against the hill slope below Acrocorinth's horns. (*Fig. 188*) As the temple now stands, one must move farther north than would have been necessary in antiquity in order for the relationship to be apparent. It can still be seen, however: the capitals of the columns rising against the distant hill slope, the great horns opening above, the temple standing steadfast below them.

The reason for the lack of entasis in the columns now becomes apparent. It is not because they are early, since others, such as those of Hera's first temple at Paestum, which have a great deal of entasis, are earlier still. Instead, it is because, with entasis, a column seems to swell and rise or, as at Paestum, to be compressed, but that was not what was wanted here. These columns, under the splendidly menacing horns, were intended to stand stolidly and immovably upright. (*Fig. 189*) Their slight diminution toward the capital and widening toward the stylobate, but total lack of swell between, give them an extraordinarily static stability. Each one is like a male body which is firmly planted on its feet, stoically upholding a great weight and attending strictly to business under the mountain's eye. Their capitals are correspondingly massive, chunkily set, with no elegant concavity between shaft and echinus to separate each from the other. Contrast should again be made with the swelling, spreading forms at Paestum. (*Fig. 93*) Enough of Apollo's colonnade is left to afford a view of the horns through it, and the effect is clearly of human and, in this case one must say, male order in contrast to that of nature.

This is not to say that Apollo's temple at Corinth denies its setting. The fact is quite the contrary, as we have seen; the horns are necessary for the columns and the relationship is fully reciprocal. It tells us here that, for the archaic Greek, human order and natural order were separate but complementary things, and that an understanding of each could be made most intense by seeing it in contrast with the other. Geometry itself was clearly a way in which the Greek attempted to make this double reality palpable. Thus it is the columns which make the great scale of the mountain unmistakably perceptible, just as it is the mountain which confers upon the columns their solemn nobility. A different use of geometry can be seen in the later Odeion and theater at Corinth, whose shapes emphasize the concavity of the horns behind them by repeating it in strictly geometric form. In this use hill and theater become a single space–embracing shape, as it was natural they should do, but the relationship between hill and archaic temple is essentially that of separate objects balancing each other across a void. In terms of the confrontation of Aphrodite by Apollo, it is the cylinders of the temple which stand against the mountain's open cleft. The expressive contrasts which the temple sets up are, however, not limited to that with Acrocorinth. From the rock–cut fountain of Glauke, for example, the hexastyle façade of the temple would have stood out in clear profile against the sky. (*Fig. 190*) The roughhewn cavern, from within which water wells, sharply sets off the elevation of the temple's form and its abstraction. Yet, detached as the temple so is, and contrasting as it does with the forces of hill and watery cavern, its northwest column (now gone, about where the church steeple appears in the photograph) would have risen in this view in such a way as to pick up the slopes of Gerania's Loutraki far behind, and its pediment would have brought them into focus. Or, seen from above, the temple itself is the focus of a sweep of sea and land: a node of human measure in the center of a view that looms with monstrous images, like those on the pottery of its city's greatest age.

The temple at Corinth was oracular, with two cellas, one facing west under the horns, and in the agora below its platform was a wall made up of triglyphs and metopes at ground level. This recalls the triglyph altar at Perachora and indicates, as does the latter, the expression of forces rising out of the earth, since in this case it guarded the entrance to a sacred spring from which prophetic utterances were apparently heard.[25] Similarly, Apollo's temple at Thebes, the Ismenion, was placed directly over an oracular cavern in the heart of a landscape haunted, as we have seen, by the images of the goddess and of her power.[26] In the view of Thebes from the south which we considered earlier, the site of the Ismenion is upon the lower hill, now covered with evergreens, which stands to the right of the acropolis. (*Fig. 40*) It is opposite the point in the draw below the acropolis where the sanctuary of Herakles was placed. As one moves down into Thebes along this route, which would have been the one from which the temple was first seen by travelers from the south, the hill of the temple slides into axis with the horned mountain of Hypatos, opening to engulf the chariot of Amphiaraus. The temple was oriented east and would once again have been seen against the mountain in a flank view. The later temple on the site, dating from the fourth century, offers an excellent example of an almost purely optical, barely sculptural, opisthodomos, now dwindled to a mere recess for its two columns. Such dwindling of the opisthodomos occurred in many temples built after the classic period. In some it came finally to a mere articulation of the wall planes or the indication of antae behind the cella. In others, as in the third–century rebuilding of the seventh–century temple of Apollo at Ptoon, it disappeared entirely, and in so doing seems to indicate a kind of return to the old interiority of the simple megaron type, though now set within the peripteral colonnade.

From the very beginning the temple at Ptoon[27] may have been specifically intended to turn its back decisively to the west. This theory is borne out by an examination of the site.

Mount Ptoon is one of the fullest expressions of the power of the goddess of nature into which the young god intrudes. Apollo's oracular sanctuary is set high on the slopes of that Boeotian mountain, which we have already mentioned in relation to the myths of Mycenaean Thebes. Entrance to the site may be gained either from the ancient Lake Copais or from Thebes. Both ways are labyrinthine and involve a preparation for the sanctuary which is psychic as well as physical and which seems to be especially typical of Apollo's greatest sites. Access to the Ptoon massif from Copais is guarded by the winged hill of Phaga that Pausanias associated with the legend of the Theban Sphinx[28] (*Fig. 41*) and which we discussed earlier. We must now pass beyond it to the toothed jaws of a rocky cleft which leads to the town of Agraiphnion. From across the lake the horned summit of Ptoon has been seen for some time to the far right of the cleft, but from the cleft itself the horns disappear. (*Fig. 191*) The way then turns south from Agraiphnion and mounts through a high draw toward the bulk of Ptoon, which slowly rises ahead. As the way mounts the shoulder of the mountain across from the summit, two opposites come into view at once: a hitherto hidden and unexpected lake far below to the south, (*Fig. 193*) and the whole rocky bulk of the summit itself, a great domed and pointed mass with a single outcropping like a rhinoceros horn jutting from its north face. Directly underneath the vertical cliff of the horn the temple of Apollo was placed. Yet the horned peak caps only one of two masses which open in a greater horn shape. In the tremendous V thus formed a further summit like a stretched and truncated pyramid is exactly framed. (*Fig. 192*)

The climax of opening is complete, yet it is even more striking if one has traveled to it along the route from Thebes. The major elements of this route can be seen from the passes of Cithairon far to the south and have also been mentioned before: the lion–sphinx mountain nearest Thebes, (*Fig. 40*) double conical hills behind it, the horns of Ptoon beyond them, with the deep blue of the enclosed lake gleaming below. One crosses the open plain and discovers that the inner secrets of the site are guarded on this side by the lion body of the sphinx. On this approach the hindquarters of the apparition are passed, and the conical hills mentioned above make a V shape with Ptoon's cleft beyond. If one looks back across the plain from this point it will be seen that the horns of Cithairon above the Heraion of Plataia loom almost on axis to the south. The way then winds between the hills and comes, almost without warning, upon the strange and quiet lake behind them, above which seabirds as well as eagles fly. The mountain of Ptoon lies in long slopes to the east of the lake, with the cleft of the site gaping like a sword slash in its body. The way winds around the lake's southern, western, and northern shores. From the slopes above it the head of the dead man east of Thebes can be seen, and from its northern banks the major conical hill to the south of it precisely complements its own still form. Far to the south the notch of Plataia's Heraion is still in view. (*Fig. 193*) The traveler must circle the lake—somewhat larger now than in antiquity because of the draining of Lake Copais—in order to arrive below Ptoon's cleft, which yawns, abandoned and painful. The taut rock divides as if split by the power of the sun, and it is through this opening, scarred by some monstrous birth, that the participant should climb to the shrine. (*Fig. 193*) The edges of the gorge are toothed, and a thin stream of water runs out between them. Only beyond it does the mountain wholly open, and the whole climactic sweep of pyramidal peak and flanking horns comes fully into view. (*Fig. 192*) It is another of the great thrones, a manifestation of the ultimate mountain presence behind the tortured clefts and above the lost seas. One can begin to understand the power of the great goddess of Boeotia here and to grasp the full terror of the moment when Apollo was first conceived of as striding, on his way to Delphi, into this place with his bow.[29] In summer the sky above the cup is brilliant with heat; in winter the clouds sail low over it, eastward from Helicon and Parnassos. (*Fig. 195*) Perhaps the goddess at this place may have been associated with that Hecate whose presence, so Hesiod wrote, was recognized by Zeus himself as potent over land, sea, and sky alike and who held the fortunes of men in her hands.[30] Similarly, her place at Ptoon looks westward, as if she might have been related, like Artemis at Magnesia, to the Hecate who was goddess of the night.

As one climbs up the mountainside toward the site of Apollo's temple at Ptoon another feature of the enframed pyramid beyond it becomes clear: namely, that its elongated ridge supports another and wholly unexpected pair of sharp horns. (*Fig. 194*) Toward these the temple, upon its flat platform and under its own great horn, is exactly oriented. The god faces east, away from the site's western view. The interlocking of natural and man–made architectures is extraordinary. The vertical face of the horn and the horizontal plane of the temple's platform make a perfect right angle, though their actual junction is prevented by the area of slope between them. (*Fig. 194*) Even so they create a tensely rectangular and precariously poised volume of space for the temple to stand in. Only the horn's cliff and the temple stand up straight. Everything else leans, but the dangerous ambient is given its anchor in the notch of the eastern horns. So the white, gleaming cylinders of the later colonnade stood against the rock, attempting to assert geometric permanence on one of two great slopes which look as if they had just opened up to reveal the focus of the farther mountain, and which, having opened, might at any moment close terrifically again, the cruel horn of one locking into the notched peak of the other. At Ptoon it is the earth which seems full of the ability to act and to surprise, offering for only a moment of unknown duration its precarious environment for human life.

The directed movement of the human viewer himself from a position in which he feels the overwhelming power of nature to one in which the new god heroically takes his stance seems to have been a calculated one. The participant was led up from the lower terraces—where the cult of the hero Ptous was embedded in the fold of the site—toward the west end of the temple along what may have been a curving ramp. (*Fig. 194*) The movement began at a hollowed cavern, connected with the sacred spring in the horn above and out of which the oracle may have been spoken. The participant's path thus curved up from the cavern along the mountainside until the moment when the temple to his left swung and locked into the focus of the eastern horns. Apollo thus binds himself into place at Ptoon, standing as a challenge to the flux of nature which might at any moment carry him away. It is he who is now enthroned, small in the terrible horns; and the compulsion is upon him to be far–shooting, death–bringing, full of threat. Behind him stretches a vast panorama across western Boeotia. (*Fig. 195*) The stoas of the sanctuary of Ptous which bounded the site below were set well down the slope, and would therefore not have blocked the human worshiper's view as he stood at the temple's altar and looked down its flank. The nearer hills heave and subside, and a glimmer of water shows beyond them. In antiquity there would have been the whole sheen of Lake Copais across the plain. Behind this lies the winged sphinx mountain and the serrated ridge that we noted earlier from Mycenaean Gla. Beyond its jagged profile, enveloped in cloud, rises Mount Helicon, enfolding the Valley of the Muses: that, too, once a cleft of the goddess and now Apollo's domain. But the god turns his back to this view, Hècate's view to the sunset, night–bringing west. Nor can he become an independent sculptural presence here. Instead, his temple must seize upon the horns of its site like a Minoan bull dancer, dependent upon them. It cannot exert a counter force to them, and this is probably why it received a peripteral colonnade only at a late date and never had an opisthodomos. Because of all this there is something young and unsure, too small for the circumstances, about Apollo at Ptoon. He is tense, offering himself up to his destiny, impotent to act except as the place he has seized may direct, as are the entranced kouroi which have been found at the site—who stand, like the god himself, with the terrible pressure of the place upon them.[31] (*Fig. 196*) Thus Ptoon tells us that in their challenge to nature the Greeks still clearly stood in awe of the might of the natural world and of its goddess and that they did not find it necessary to believe that Olympian order would always be victorious or that all men could wholly mature.

Apollo's greatest oracular sanctuary, that of Delphi,[32] where all the meanings implicit in his struggle with the goddess are fully developed, lies in the heart of the massif of Parnassos and is poised on the lower slopes of the mountain itself. Entrance by land into the citadel of Parnassos involves passage between horned clefts, that behind Lebadeia on the east, that behind Gravia on the north. In each case the way winds through stark passes; a fastness is being penetrated. The more direct road is that from Lebadeia, the way which Apollo himself seems to take in the Homeric Hymn.[33] This would have been the land route from Athens and Thebes and will be discussed later. It is, however, only from the Gulf of Corinth that the sanctuary signals its position from afar and from which movement to it is comparatively easy. From the port of Itea, at which pilgrims disembarked in antiquity, the view extends to the northeast toward the deeply shadowed cleft in the body of Parnassos, around which the nearer ridges seem to wrap, as if enfolding it, secretly, within their masses. (*Fig. 197*) Subsidiary horns can be seen beyond the cleft on the heights of the mountain, and the deep gorge through which the Pleistos river flows cuts under it. Up in the cleft is the holy spot as described in the Homeric Hymn: "Crisa beneath snowy Parnassus, a foothill turned toward the west: a cliff hangs over it from above, and a hollow rugged glade runs under."[34] The way from Itea crosses the olive–laden valley and winds up the gorge. It was by this route that Apollo led up to his shrine those Cretan sailors whom he, first in the shape of a dolphin, had kidnaped so that they might become his priests:

> So the Cretans followed him to Pytho, marching in time as they chanted the Ie Paean after the manner of the Cretan paean singers and of those in whose hearts the heavenly Muse has put sweet–voiced song. With tireless feet they approached the ridge and straightway came to Parnassus.[35]

The way to the shrine is thus followed with Cretan dance and song, and certainly the site had been holy long before the coming of the Dorians. There had been a Mycenaean sacred place below the horns, and we are told in the Homeric Hymn that Apollo had killed Pytho, a "bloated she–dragon," child of Hera and thus the snake of the goddess, who had been the guardian of the shrine.[36] Apollo had struck down the old earth power with the pitiless arrogance of the young god of human order: "Now rot here," he had cried, "upon the soil that feeds man."[37] In the *Eumenides* of Aeschylus, of the fifth century, a gentler version of the legend is told: Apollo had been given the shrine as a birthday gift by Phoebe, the last of three goddesses who had held the oracle before him, but the Furies, servants of the goddess, still revile Apollo in the old terms: "He made man's ways cross the place of the ways of god / and blighted age–old distributions of power."[38]

Delphi must therefore have seemed to the Greeks the place where the conflict between the old way, that of the goddess of the earth, and the new way, that of men and their Olympian gods, was most violently manifest. There can be no doubt whatever that it was the landscape itself which gave rise to this belief and which dictated the presence of the shrine. The light is continually shifting across it with the passage of heavy, thunder–laden clouds. (*Fig. 198*) Earthquakes shake it, so that Poseidon, once again closely associated with Apollo, had a sanctuary there as well. As one mounts the shoulder below the site the gorge itself opens in a great hollow under the cliff to the north, and it is now seen that this itself is splendidly crowned by tremendous horns that open thunderously against the sky. These are the twin peaks of the Phaedriades, the Brilliant Ones, and the holy Castalian spring gushes from the cleft between them. As the light changes across them they shift and swing, looming and fading. In these first views they are overwhelmingly triumphant, the majesty of the earth, sentiently upraised, the fighting horns. Above them, under the higher horns of the mountain, which are visible from Itea but invisible from below the Phaedriades, lies the sacred Corycian cave. This is "the Corycian rock / . . . hollowed inward, haunt of birds and paced by gods."[39] To the left, below the Phaedriades, the shining columns of Apollo's temple can be seen, precise and tiny under the cliff. (*Fig. 199*) To the left again, above the temple, a second cleft splits the cliff into another set of horns. As one moves toward the shadowy cliffs and the bright columns of the temple, the valley drops off far below, and the Pleistos is a long ribbon, like an earth snake itself, blindly nosing its way through the hollow. (*Fig. 198*) The scale of the drop is thus always clear at this point, defined as it is by contrasting natural objects: the high cliffs, the far river. Between the two the sanctuary still seems small and engulfed.

It is likely that even travelers coming up this route from Itea might have visited the shrine of Athena Pronaia at Marmaria before continuing on toward Apollo's sanctuary under the terrible cliffs.[40] There Athena, Before the Shrine, and probably later confused and so associated with forethought, was not only Polias, guardian of the place, but also the embodiment of the old earth goddess, and her sacred snake remained unkilled by her side. If, mounting the slope above the Pleistos, the pilgrims from Itea had come first to this shrine, they would have intersected at it the main route to Delphi from Athens, Apollo's own first way to his sanctuary, through the pass at Lebadeia. There the traveler would have had on his left another cleft of prophecy, the gorge of the Trophonion, sacred to the hero Trophonios and later associated with Zeus.[41] After the open, heavy, heatstruck or windswept plain of Boeotia, the deep gorge of the Trophonion offers a cool and sheltered refuge, an enclosing hollow full of the sound of water: an ideal forecourt for Parnassos but a profoundly holy place in its own right. It is an archetypal hero site, celebrating both an ancient daimonic power in the earth and a humanization of that power in the dead human hero who descends to the underworld but retains, through the will of the gods, a certain power to heal the ills of men. Somewhere in the precipice on the side of the Trophonion's V–shaped gorge, through which a stream flows down into the twin fountains of "forgetfulness" and "memory," was the shrine of the oracle. There the worshiper was pulled feet first through a hole in the ground and visited by a sacred snake in the dark caverns. Openings can still be seen in the side of the gorge near the springs, with a huge ear–shaped hollow in the rock beyond them. Whether these were connected with the rite is not known, but they certainly express that journey into the underworld which was the shock treatment offered to souls in need of it by the shrine. After his return to the light, the worshiper eventually regained, we are told, his ability to smile.[42]

Past this place of the daimonic hero and of the goddess' snake which is not killed but instead assumed by Zeus in the fullness of his nature, the road to Delphi winds itself snake-like among the mountains, which close around it. After a time they begin to open again, and the way, passing the high perch of Arachova, comes finally to a spot from which the mountains can be seen yawning widely open ahead in a great V. (*Fig. 200*) Beyond this lies the plain of Krissa, the waters of the gulf, and the farther mountains across the plain. No sign whatever of the Delphic sanctuary can yet be seen. Advancing further along the shoulder of the mountain, one comes finally to the spot across from which another horned cleft cuts through the mountain barrier on the south beyond the Pleistos. In all likelihood this is the gorge of the nymph Telphusa, who resisted the assumption of her sanctuary by Apollo and was punished by him through the overthrow of the mountain upon her.[43] Yet an earth goddess still haunts her place since, fronting her cleft, lies the sanctuary of Athena Pronaia. (*Figs. 200, 201*)

The two temples of Athena, the two treasuries, and the tholos are set in a row facing south upon a narrow plateau which confronts the double peaks, with the cleft between them, across the valley.[44] The dancelike rhythms of the buildings' placement causes the eye to move across them toward various points in the opposing formation, now toward the peaks, now toward the cleft. (*Fig. 201*) The feeling is of being imbedded in earth forces at this point, like Telphusa herself under the mountain. One of the treasuries, that of Massalia, dating from the sixth century, was Ionic. The capitals of its two columns in antis were not voluted, however, but carved into forms which were not only palm treelike but which also resembled opening jets of water spurting upward. (*Fig. 202*) The action of water as a force, which we noted as one of the characteristics of the Ionic capital, thus seems especially stressed here. Also significant as expressing the chthonic nature of the sanctuary are the forms of the two latest buildings on the plateau: the second temple of Athena, of the fourth century, and the tholos, a work probably of the very end of the fifth. The earlier temple of Athena, destroyed by a landslide in 480, had no opisthodomos but did have a peripteral colonnade. The second temple dispensed with the peripteral colonnade and emphasized its axis of enclosure: from a porch at the south to a huge base of some sort inside the cella at its north end. The form of the temple was therefore much like that to be found at mystery sites during the Hellenistic period, as at the shrine of Despoina at Lykosoura and at the Kabiria near Thebes and on Samothrace.[45] Facing its horned hill, it was clearly intended to invoke interior, mysterious, and non–Olympian experience.

Similarly, the tholos is so placed as to bring into focus both the nearer cleft across the way and the great cleft to the west through which the mountains open to the plain. (*Fig. 203*) The form of the tholos in plan is a radial circle, recalling the circular altars of chthonic deities, like those mentioned at Akragas. (*Fig. 129*) Its exterior ring of columns is Doric; within that ring is the closed cylinder of the tholos and within that an interior ring of columns. These were Corinthian, representing one of the earliest uses of the Corinthian capital known. We shall discuss its earliest known use, at Bassae, later. There, as here and as usually later except in votive monuments, the Corinthian column was used inside. Of all Greek capitals, the Corinthian, with its spreading leaves, is the most naturalistic, and it is therefore the most treelike. Rising inside the darkness of the cella the Corinthian column can only have been intended to express forces associated with the earth, like the sacred trees of the goddess in Asia and of Minoan times: trees which, as we shall see, came also to be associated with Apollo. As it appears in the later fifth century, the Corinthian column seems a new expression of the sacred grove, now growing within the cave of the cella itself, and its appearance once again announces that revival of various aspects of the old religion which marks the later classic and Hellenistic periods. More than this, at Delphi, the tholos which contains the sacred trees rises at a point which dramatizes the opening of the earth which the V of the hills so violently expresses. The omphalos, or navel, which was supposed to mark the center of the world, was kept in the adyton of Apollo's temple itself, but the tholos of Athena's sanctuary more clearly seems to evoke the navel of the earth than does any other building there. (*Fig. 203*) It is also placed at the point in her sanctuary from which the pilgrim who came by land from Athens first saw Apollo's shrine lying along the slope within the hitherto unexpected bowl of the hills to the northwest. As he moved forward along the way to it, the horns of Parnassos thundered above his head and the Castalian spring gushed forth between them. Whether coming by sea or by land, therefore, the traveler was at first impressed at every point, by architecture as well as by natural formations, with the power of nature and the smallness of man. (*Fig. 199*) Indeed, the place as a whole, though enclosed in its gorge, is extraordinarily potent over great distances and from many directions. The way from the west, for example, with Parnassos first seen, then lost, then approached from the lush valley below, offers an equally effective climax when the sanctuary is finally attained.

At the entrance to the temenos itself the scale begins to change: the man–made forms of Apollo's sanctuary grow larger, and they begin to act. (*Fig. 204*) From the entrance, which in the classic period was a simple gate in the wall at the southeast corner, the view is toward the temple high above, seen at the optimum sculptural angle and beginning to rise against the downward slope of the mountain behind it. (*Fig. 205*) It is true that the southeastern entrance to the Way marked the beginning of a natural movement up the hill contours, especially after ablutions at the sacred Castalian spring to the east, but it was not necessarily the most direct route to the temple. Such could have run in a straight diagonal from the west, and many visitors to the site today cut up that way as they approach the temple from the museum. One can therefore only assume that the eastern entrance was chosen because of the kind of view it offered of the temple and that the later turnings which the Way is forced to take are calculated ones. Directly west of the entrance, the temple was lost to sight, and the Way mounted the hill slope among the jostling treasuries and memorials with which the various city states had been encouraged to line it. The buildings rose and partly blocked out the valley view as well; the Way was here involved with purely human life, in which the individual was expected to be able to receive blows as well as to give them. If you were an Athenian you were forced to bear the monument put up by the Spartans after Aegospotami, and it was directly opposite your own monument to Marathon. If you were a Spartan you would have had to endure the partial blocking of your monument by the one set up by the Arcadians to celebrate your defeat at Leuctra. And next to your monument would be another intended to throw yours into the shade, set up by the Argives to celebrate the refounding of Messenia, your former hard–won possession. "Know thyself," which joined "Nothing to excess" as the god's motto at Delphi, clearly required a certain self–command here.

Farther ahead the islanders and the colonials jockeyed for position along the way. The Cnidian and Siphnian treasuries, with their caryatids, stressed the female aspect of the Ionic order, while that of Clazomenae, like the Massaliot treasury at Marmaria, used palm capitals and thus called upon the complementary aspects of vegetative and water force. Above the heads of the two Siphnian korai the lions of the goddess leaped heraldically upon the horned beast, while above them in the frieze the gods fought against the Titans of earth, and in the pediment the human hero, Herakles, struggled with Apollo for the tripod. Each treasury along the Sacred Way acts as a separate unit and makes its own solid presence felt as it seeks its desired position. The movement is like that of free persons in a crowd. (*Fig. 204*) It is therefore absurd for criticism to attempt to apply here the principles of later abstract, "space–positive" planning, in which the spatial module, not the building solid, is the determining factor in a building's placement. To attempt to do so, and therefore to see the organization of the monuments and treasuries at Delphi as "unplanned," or faulty, as some critics have done, is to fail to understand what was in fact taking place and wholly to lose the architectural experience which is offered. As we have seen, Greek sacred buildings, like the treasuries, which are simple megara in antis, can act as separate units precisely because they are simple and of purely sculptural scale. Thus, set off the slope by their platforms, they can "face," or turn a flank, or push in at an angle. (*Figs. 204, 206*) All these things the treasuries do along the Way. The spaces between them are simply voids which are not yet filled and which, because they are irregular in shape among the regular shapes of the treasuries, cannot prevent the eye from seeing the treasuries as lively objects which are acting out their city's will to witness the procession and to be seen themselves. Each of the little buildings is therefore an active individual participant in the life of the site.

In this jostle of human action the precarious footing of human existence in nature was temporarily forgotten, but the Way turned splendidly up the contour, and the cliffs heaved into view once again, grander than they had seemed at any point since the sanctuary had been entered, closer and more menacing even than they had appeared from the entrance to the gorge. The flank of the Athenian treasury directed the eye up the rising path where the Bouleuterion thrust its corner toward the roadway. Above the Bouleuterion the high Ionic column which supported the winged sphinx of the Naxians would have been seen: rising, appropriately treelike, near the cleft rocks which marked the sanctuary of Gaia, the Earth, out of which the Pythoness was supposed originally to have prophesied. (*Fig. 207*) Above the rocks was the temple, and above the whole opened the V of the cliff's smaller pair of horns. The man—made forms were now all seen and judged against the cliff, and the contrast was both intense and subtle. Up the path the elegantly polygonal masonry of the terrace upon which the temple's platform stands came into view. (*Fig. 208*) This is closest to the cliff face in pattern but not like it at all in any other way. Against the cliff's true irregularities it poses a studied and subtle irregularity; against nature's scarred greys, browns, and greens, it opposes the lucid brightness of its fine limestone. The delicately fluted columns of the Portico of the Athenians make a sharper contrast; frailty opposes crushing force. The columns of the temple itself offer their own sturdier contrast: big enough to have power, small in the face of the cliff, upright against the swinging horns, solid before the clefts. (*Fig. 207*) The temple was so placed that the top of the polygonal wall blocked its own pedestal from view. The columns therefore seemed to float free and the whole temple body to slide backward away from the horns as the pilgrim mounted the path. (*Fig. 208*) At the angle of wall where the path turned north, he must have felt that his journey was approaching its climax. If he looked back along the Way, he saw the space opening outward toward the Athenian treasury and the gorge beyond it through which he had traveled. Directly ahead of him the final stretch of the Way aimed at the cliff face. The temple momentarily went out of his sight behind the east wall of the terrace. As he climbed, however, the columns once more slid forward effortlessly just above the wall (which was on this side several courses higher in antiquity than it is now). In this view the cliff had disappeared, and the temple was seen against the open sky. (*Fig. 209*) At the top of the path the view of the temple was again completely blocked, this time by the high altar of Chios. Once again the eye may have strayed backward down the Way toward the depths. The labyrinth had led always upward, out of the engulfed valley and its river snake and through the places of human life. It had led into the very teeth of the cliffs, with the temple always growing in scale against them but now out of sight once more. Therefore, when the corner of the altar of Chios was turned and the temple at last opened up before him, the pilgrim must have experienced a moment of what can only have been intended as calculated triumph and release. (*Fig. 210*) The temple was now finally seen, not only against the sky, but also against the hills across the valley above which it rose. It now gave scale and definition to the Way which had been traveled; its position was high and proud. Its foundations lift its base high above the void, and the space, in the view from the altar, seems to drop off sickeningly under the splendid uprights of the columns. Because of this, the mountain across the void seems to come very close, as objects do across a deep depression, and the zigzag mule track up its flank helps to dramatize the scale of the temple near at hand. A ramp leads up to it, concluding the labyrinthine Way by a final climactic axis of movement into the enclosure of the cella. At the same time the inclined plane of the ramp avoids that vitiation of the temple's exterior sculptural scale which small steps would have brought about. The columns of the present fourth—century temple are higher and therefore seem slimmer and more effortlessly abstract than those of the older temple were or would have done. But the stiff older columns too, almost without entasis and supporting the frontal figure of Apollo, with his great horses, on the pediment above them, would have stood against the cliff as these stand; as the young god opposes, in Pindar's words, his "shining front," to the horns. (*Fig. 211*)

In this way too, around the temple, the images of other victors joined the god over the centuries: among them the charioteer, his feet gripping the floor of his chariot and his arms, still swollen with blood, lifting the slackened reins. His tucked–up chiton fell in folds like the flutes of the god's columns, but it quivered with a deeply interior tension as he held himself in tight, poised luminously between his godlike victory and his human fate, outfacing the abyss with the god whom at this moment in his life he most closely resembled:

> we have some likeness in great
> intelligence, or strength, to the immortals,
> though we know not what the day will bring, what course
> after nightfall
> Destiny has written that we must run to the end.[46]

But forward of the Prusias monument and to the right of the temple as seen from beside the Chian altar, one of the symbols of Apollo's own link with the earth would also have been in view. (*Fig. 210*) This was the bronze palm tree set up by the Athenians after their double victory on the Eurymedon in 460 B.C.[47] The tree, as we have seen, was an old symbol of the goddess, and in this case, as we shall discuss later, it was intended to symbolize Apollo's own birth to Leto on the island of Delos. One recalls the palm capitals of Massalia and Clazomenae. Inside the temple, which also had an externalizing opisthodomos, was the closed adyton of the god's own oracle, still uttered in classical times by a priestess. The cavelike adyton of this darker Apollo contained the stone omphalos, the navel of the world, and the basic form of this, too, as an adorned and sacred conical stone, must have derived from the old tree and pillar cult of the goddess. But the god, in the fifth–century intellectual view, will no longer allow his adyton to be thought of as a cave. His house is different from nature, and the rites which it expresses are those proper to civilized men. So Aeschylus has him speak to the Furies, as he tells them that his house is not for them, who love the sacrifice of human blood:

> the whole cast of your shape is guide
> to what you are, the like of whom should hole in the cave
> of the blood–reeking lion, not in oracular
> interiors like mine nearby, wipe off your filth.[48]

On the other hand, the depth of Greek religious experience brought Apollo, by the late archaic period, to share his shrine with Dionysos, whose haunt was the mountain fastnesses and who was associated with the mysteries of rebirth. As such, Dionysos was connected, as we have already noted, with Demeter at Eleusis and was invoked there as Bromius, and he roamed the peaks of Parnassos and took over Apollo's shrine itself for three months out of every year.[49] He is nature itself, in no way opposed to it, and when Apollo's priestess in the *Eumenides* invokes

Dionysos she connects him with the mountain's caves and horns: "the Corycian rock / hollowed inward / Bromius, whom I forget not, sways this place ..."[50]

Out of the dances and choruses of Dionysos the Greek drama had grown, and we see in the Greek theater, as noted at Thorikos and Corinth, an echo of landscape shape itself. At Delphi, when one mounts beyond the temple and comes to the theater, it can be seen that the arc of its seats is nestled into the earth and indeed echoes the hollow volume of space created by the mountain's horns above it. (*Fig. 212*) It is also placed directly opposite the point where the opposing cliffs across the Pleistos pour most aggressively down into the valley. (*Fig. 213*) Their convex shape is then cupped across space by the concavity of the theater, so that the natural and the man–made, despite the theater's geometric abstraction, are moving in the same rhythm and make one great shape together. Higher up, the stadium, with no seats until Roman times, was also in a hollow under the cliffs. Partly because of the theater, the view from above the sanctuary at Delphi back across the valley of the Pleistos is in the end a calm and contained one. A single person standing in the orchestra—where, in many theaters, an altar was placed— seems to have had the entire landscape constructed around himself. (*Fig. 213*) He is in the hollow of it, in that "fold" which Pindar was fond of referring to. The strife which had been an integral part of the earlier experience is no longer in evidence. The long slopes are seen from this angle as gentler than they had appeared before, and the shrine of Athena at Marmaria is in view at the shoulder of the mountain. (*Fig. 214*) In the circle of the hills and oriented south as it is, the site now seems a warm and sheltered place, even somnolent in the afternoon sun, and the temple, though high, is set in a calm and noble megaron of earth from which its oracle can speak wisely to the world. The site now takes on its permanent aspect; it is a throne, from which "excess," both natural and human, has been exorcised and where a grand gentleness reigns. So, returning through the temenos, in the looser patterns of movement off the Sacred Way which would have been natural after the first experience of the site, the pilgrim would have discovered echo after echo between architecture and landscape, as between the gables of the treasuries and the cones of the southeastern hills, (*Fig. 215*) to seal, in these descending views, a kind of treaty with the land.

Pythian Apollo and Dionysos are associated in many other sites. At the place itself called Dionyso, north of Mount Pentelikon in Attica, for example, the temple is Apollo's.[51] The ancient name of the place was Ikaria, where Dionysos is supposed to have given to the hero, Ikarios, the gift of the vine. Ikaria was traditionally the home of the semilegendary Thespis who is supposed to have invented the tragic drama by first introducing a protagonist with the Dionysian chorus.[52] The site itself is an amphitheater. The violently cleft and horned crags of Pentelikon on the south speak of Apollo; the high, curving bowl of the mountain to the north resembles a theater, its symbolic presence perhaps rendering unnecessary the unsuccessful efforts which have been made by archaeologists to find a man–made theater on the site. To the east the hills curve downward, splitting in a V toward Marathon and opening in a wide cleft toward Euboea. Exactly into this cleft, when the day is clear, swims horned Mount Ocha once more. (*Fig. 216*) This would seem to have been the focus of the site. One guesses that entrance was either from the west or from the south, facing the theater–mountain; in the latter approach one walked north toward the temple of Apollo, and Ocha moved into the cleft on one's right hand. From the north, next to the small temple in antis, the placement of which opens an arc toward the east, one looked directly out toward framed Ocha, with the distant landscape shapes once again echoed and abstracted by a choragic monument in the temenos itself which has the form of an exedra. Thespis' site thus focuses upon a perfect, almost geometric structure of sacred landscape forms and states in this way what Greek drama, inspired here, was intended to be: an act of natural inspiration and abstract discipline alike, a revelation to man of that link with nature's fact which gave dimension to his suffering, a reconcilement of his critical faculty with nature's ways.

The actual remains at Dionyso are late, though set in a site which must have been very old. The first temple of Dionysos Eleuthereus, below his theater on the south slope of the Acropolis in Athens, dates from the sixth century, his second from 420 B.C.[53] Just below was the shrine of Pythian Apollo. The temples of Dionysos are thus closer to the hill than is the Pythion. The sixth–century temple was in antis; the second had a cella with a deep porch, and this temple became the focus for a lateral movement across the theater's front, across, that is, the later stoa which lies behind the theater's stage. The architect of the stoa clearly lined it up with the axis of the fifth–century temple, running his stoa almost into the earlier temple in the process. The relationship of building mass to the space in which it is set thus begins to be regularized and stiffened, pinning the building into place and offering it as the complement of a space rather than so specifically as an actor in it.[54] The relation of Dionysos' temples and their complementary theaters also tends toward a distinctly cross–axial arrangement, as we noted at Thorikos. (*Figs. 116, 117*) Axiality, as we have also already seen, is shared by other chthonic deities, such as Demeter, whose roots go deeply back into Cretan practice, and it becomes more generally important for all kinds of planning throughout the Hellenistic period. A rather analogous arrangement is found at Eretria in Euboea. Here again the landscape is defined by the sacred symbols. Seen from Attica, from a point west of the shrine of Amphiaraus at Oropos, a conical mountain rises above Eretria, framed in the bow of its own hills. From the site itself the mountain is not visible, but the surrounding hills themselves are cleft and horned. A wave-like outcropping emerges out of the plain before them. It is the acropolis of the town, and the temple of Apollo is so oriented roughly southeast on the flat ground before it as to direct attention toward it and to dramatize its shape. (*Fig. 217*) The present temple dates from 510 B.C., but there was a much earlier hairpin megaron on the site.[55] The actively rising and breaking character of the acropolis hill is curiously echoed in the group of Theseus and Antiope which stood in one of the pediments of the temple. The group turns upward as Theseus lifts the Amazon queen, and her head bends down toward her future husband like the curling tip of a breaking wave. The later theater was excavated and built up under the acropolis itself, and the temple of Dionysos is placed on the same kind of cross–axis before it that had been used earlier at Athens. (*Fig. 218*) At Eretria, however, another path of movement is set up: from the propylon to the west along the flank of the temple and then in toward the temple exactly at the point where the tip of the acropolis hill would have come into view. The curve of that movement, defined by building and land, is facilitated by an unusual curving wall which is attached to the temple's southeast corner. These urbanities in design bring us into the realm of Hellenistic planning, and the theater and temple of Dionysos are themselves largely of the Hellenistic period. So also is the tumulus which crowns the hill to the west of the theater: a Hellenistic recollection of the tholos tombs of Mycenaean times. The whole site as finally worked out bears a long Hellenistic and Roman diagonal landscape axis superimposed like a phantom upon it—a slightly curving axis running from the tumulus through the propylon, the temple of Apollo, the temple of Isis, and coming to rest far off among the hills of Attica across the gulf. Such devices, however, common as they are to Hellenistic city planning, can best be discussed as a whole later.

Delos, the place of Apollo's birth, must claim our attention here, but Delos itself demands that we should first consider Cape Zoster on the southern coast of Attica, where legend said that Apollo had almost been born.[56] One recalls that the jealous wrath of Hera had prevented Leto from giving birth to Apollo and Artemis and that she had fled across the world seeking a place to do so. At Cape Zoster (girdle) she is supposed to have been able to drop her girdle but to have been prevented by Hera from accomplishing the birth. She then fled on to Delos. The temple of Apollo at Zoster is on a narrow sand spit which connects the cape with the mainland. (*Fig. 219*) The building lies athwart the narrow strip exactly like a girdle across a waist. It is an unusual, rough, enclosed structure, dating mostly from the fifth century and with a kind of forecourt.[57] It is so oriented northeast that the eye is directed by it to the strange cleft at Vouliagmeni, in which a warm salt lake is cupped next to the sea. The rock opens awesomely here to enclose the lake, and great reefs of the cliff have broken off to lie partially or wholly submerged in the water. The temple on the waist thus clearly invokes the earth forces which this formation so grandly expresses. Seen from the cliffs above the cleft, the position of the temple itself is especially expressive. (*Fig. 220*) It lies between the lake and the far headland at the point where the land tightens down to almost nothing. It is a string drawn tight across a waist, a girdle hardly dropped but instead suddenly constricted. The lake itself and the whole sweep of bay speak of opening and release; all the more in this setting does the temple on the waist tell us of the cruel agony of birth prevented.

Zoster, then, is a constricted gasp, but Delos is a widespread opening under the eye of the sun. Delos, like Delphi, had of course long been holy before the coming of the cult of Apollo, and had pre–Mycenaean and Mycenaean settlements, probably sanctuaries, upon it.[58] Small, barren, heat struck, windswept, and volcanic, it lies across a narrow strait from the larger and slightly more hospitable island of Ortygia. In the Homeric Hymn Delos herself expresses fear to Leto that Apollo, if born upon her, will spurn her for her ugliness.[59] Yet the elements which made Delos holy must have been felt for many centuries; its spectacular harshness and barrenness are perhaps among them, but the Homeric Hymn is specific, as it praises the birth of Apollo to Leto: "and him in rocky Delos, as you rested against the great mass of the Cynthian hill, hard by a palm–tree, by the streams of Inopus."[60] Here are the goddess' hill, her sacred tree, and her gift of water, set upon her island, like Calypso's, in the middle of the sea. (*Fig. 221*) There was also a cave on Mount Cynthus, dressed up with cyclopean corbel vaults during the Hellenistic period as a chthonic grotto with a statue of Herakles inside but probably sacred long before and an intrinsic part of the holiness of the island. (*Fig. 222*) Upon the summit of the mountain was a sanctuary of Zeus and Athena. Seen from the low ground on the northwest, where the sanctuary of Apollo was placed, the holy mountain rises up as a rocky cone above two mounded hills which open up to left and right before it. (*Fig. 221*) In the cleft so formed a Kabirion was placed, in the fold of the mountain exactly where one would expect to find it. Under the cone and oriented south toward it, (*Fig. 223*) was a temple of Hera, which offered also a splendid view across the island. The slopes of Cynthus are covered with broken boulders of great size and curious formation; some of them resemble skulls or the scattered fragments of colossal kouroi. (*Figs. 222, 223*) The mountain has a rocky subsidiary peak but is not noticeably horned. Well to the northwest of the mountain, on very low ground behind the northwest headland of the island, is the rush–grown marsh which marks the position of the sacred lake, probably very shallow and marshlike even in antiquity. (*Figs. 221, 222c*) Along its western flank is the seventh–century row of roaring lions, guardians of the goddess, and in the center of the lake itself the excavators have planted a palm tree. It is difficult to describe the heat of the sun for much of the year upon Delos. It is reflected in waves off the rock and draws heavy steamings from the marsh. Under the sun, and between the heated opposites of naked mountain rock and marsh, the sanctuary of Apollo was placed. As one of the most important Hellenic shrines, especially for Athens, the islands, and Ionia, the sanctuary received a great number of buildings. These are arranged in a manner which, of all active archaic groupings, some critics have found most anarchic and chaotic. (*Fig. 224*) It is true, as one examines the site, that the possibility of anarchy and chaos seems always to threaten, as the individual buildings crowd and jostle each other. Yet if one walks through the temenos it becomes apparent that the grouping here is not one of anarchy but of purposeful action—and of the same kind of reciprocal relationship with the landscape with which we have become familiar.

As the pilgrim's ship ground on the sand or came alongside the mole of the ancient harbor, it would already have been close to the gleaming columns and walls of the sanctuary itself, but the dominant object in view would have been the rugged, brown mass of Mount Cynthus. As the pilgrim walked toward the small agora from which the fourth–century stoa of Philip of Macedon led toward the temenos, the summit of Mount Cynthus would indeed have been directly ahead on the axis of his view. As he turned north along the Avenue of the Processions, however, Mount Cynthus would have dropped completely out of sight behind him, and his gaze would have been carried by the columns of the stoa in a measured beat toward the entrance to the temenos. Entering through the propylon, the pilgrim left the narrow, clearly directed alley of the entrance avenue and came into an opening, fan–shaped space upon whose void, nevertheless, the masses of buildings and monuments were actively aggressive. (*Fig. 224*) To his left was the bronze palm tree which was donated to the sanctuary by Nicias in 417: symbol of the god's birth and thus, with all its memories of the goddess, of the young god himself. It recalled the similar bronze tree set up earlier at Delphi. Directly ahead was a major altar, and beyond altar and tree was the Athenian building called the Keraton, the Place of the Horns. Here the horns of the victims sacrificed to Apollo are supposed to have been kept, and out of it the Crane Dance was performed, a dance to be identified at once with the invocation of birds, of swamp walking, and of the labyrinth.[61] The lack of obvious horns on Cynthus—though the mountain is, of course, cleft and has a secondary ridge—would thus seem to have been made good by the horns preserved in this unusual building in the sanctuary; a building, furthermore, around which a dance so reminiscent of the Cretan rites of the goddess was performed. Behind the Keraton was the temple of Artemis, and its south flank indeed almost touched the Keraton's corner. Up to this point the pilgrim had followed a labyrinthine way into Artemis' enclosure, but turning back out of it toward the main temenos once more, he would have again seen for a moment the rocky summit of Cynthus beyond Apollo's temple and above the Oikos of the Naxians. Directly upon this axis of view, standing out against the mountain top with its broken stones, the great marble colossus of Apollo stood by the Oikos' north wall. Against the complementary background of the mountain the colossus would have been taking one tense step northward across the western, here probably the entrance, end of his Doric temple. (*Fig. 224*)

Begun around 475 B.C., this is the largest of the three buildings which step back one after the other toward the north and face westward into the altar's enclosure. It was hexastyle and peripteral, with an opisthodomos, so that its rear, toward the secondary enclosure to the east, was columned and penetrated, too. (Some would prefer an eastern entrance here,[62] but the archaeological evidence, though inconclusive, seems against it.) Next to Apollo's temple was a curious, wide building constructed by the Athenians in the later fifth century: Doric and amphiprostyle, it too was oriented westward but had a columned façade on the east. This unusual temple is thrust in between the temple of Apollo and the northernmost building, which is the oldest of the three. Identified as the Porinos Oikos, it dated from the sixth century and had only a pronaos and cella, oriented westward and with no eastern opisthodomos or columns. After the new temple was built it served as a treasury, but it also contained an archaic statue of Apollo and may have been more important during the archaic period. The subtlety of the fifth–century handling of the site now becomes clearer. The placing of the new temple had left a gap between it and the older building. This gap was largely plugged by the Temple of the Athenians, for which, as a matter of fact, archaeologists have otherwise been hard put to find an adequate motive. Placed where it is, it tends to direct the spectator, who may wish to penetrate more deeply into the sanctuary, to turn his back upon Mount Cynthus once more and to walk, with the colossus, northward past the fronts of the temple of Apollo and the other two buildings, which now give back like steps in plan before him. As they step back, the front of the first of a curving row of civic treasuries stands forward in the space ahead and begins to cup a turning movement to the right. Turning then around the corner of the old Oikos, the pilgrim had his way indicated for him by the lively and varied curve of the treasuries, which also define an opening arc of space—despite what would appear to have been some sort of wall which cut across them during part of the sanctuary's life. As related to each other, the first three treasuries begin a gentle curve, which then turns a decisive corner with the sharply tilted fourth treasury, and finally slides rapidly south with the widely spaced fifth treasury, which is like an object snapped off in the whip of a turn. (*Fig. 224*) So directed, the pilgrim turned right in the direction indicated by the treasuries and within the space created by them, and found himself looking along the eastern colonnade of the Temple of the Athenians and of Apollo's own temple with the mighty mass of "craggy Cynthus" directly on axis ahead. (*Fig. 225*) Again the sacred object, lost, was rediscovered. Once more the temple of the young god was seen as a near element against a beetling peak. The other buildings which were added to the south and east of the temple could not have been high enough to block this calculated relationship. They would only have served to define, irregularly as always, the nearer enclosure beyond which the culminating mass is seen. In that enclosure a cluster of altars was found, these apparently of special sanctity and in the optimum position between the temple and the hill. There can be no doubt, consequently, that the buildings of the temenos, especially as worked out by the fifth century, were designed as actors along a labyrinthine way whose second, calculated climax came when the shining columns were seen at last against the sacred hill. Again, Cynthus creates the temenos, as surely as the sacred mountain created the Minoan palace sites, but the relationship is now a classic Greek one: reverent in its hold upon the traditions of the labyrinth and the land, but intellectual and humanly definite in the geometry of its forms, and complex in the meanings and alternatives which it imagines to left and right of the actively balanced, always demanding, Way. Yet, thronged as the Sanctuary is, it still tells us that Delian Apollo is most remote of all. Although his eastern columns are finally made to confront rocky Delos across his innermost altars, he himself will only face away from it toward his destiny, his temple pushing westward of the others in its row as if already setting a course for Delphi across the sea.

Farther west, Apollo was of considerable importance in the colonies, where his embodiment of Hellenic discipline and balance might have been intended to contrast with the undisciplined hysteria of the barbarians. His temple guarded the flank of the acropolis hill of Cumae, at one of the northernmost points reached by the Greeks in Italy. Under it is an echoing cavern, later in antiquity instinctively felt to have been the dwelling of the Cumaean Sybil, an oracle of the goddess, who was to direct Aeneas in his journey to the underworld through the "true" gate, the Gate of Horn.[63] The coastal ridge presses close upon the isolated cone by the sea which Cumae is, and Apollo's temple was so set as to dominate the narrow valley between them, across which barbarian enemies might have been expected to advance. Also in view from the temple, a wide–horned mountain looms eastward behind the nearer ridge. (*Fig. 226*) At Syracuse in Sicily, Apollo's ponderous columns were placed at the point where the island fortress of Ortygia, the first part of Syracuse to be colonized, faced the Sicilian mainland. The god turned his back to that view, however, to face eastward toward Ortygia's acropolis height, eventually crowned by a temple of Athena. (*Fig. 227*) On Ortygia, too, was a grotto, a little like that of Vouliagmeni but much smaller. This was the famous spring of Arethusa, out of which welled miraculous fresh water which was supposed to have flowed under the sea bottom from Greece itself. Apollo's temple was of the deeply sheltering Sicilian type we have already noted in Temple C at Selinus, but it is earlier than Temple C.[64] Its columns were extraordinarily thick and close together and their echini and abaci widespreading, so that the capitals almost touched each other. The mass was thus somber and heavy, a great brooding shape as seen from the mainland, and the exaggeratedly conical shafts and broad capitals of its columns created spaces between them which, though voids, must have read very much as phantom figures of great scale. A play of positive and negative was thus set up, as in Greek geometric vase painting: the lights and the darks, the solids and the voids, moving alternately forward and back in plane as the eye changes its focus. (*Fig. 70*) In the eyes of the aboriginal Sicilians the whole must have bulked huge with ambiguous life.

At Selinus the largest temple of all the many temples there was Apollo's.[65] It was placed upon the easterly of the two hills and would have formed a major feature of the view from the acropolis, a point to which we shall return later. (*Fig. 106*) Like many of the very largest buildings from many cultures, this temple seems to have attempted to combine all possible features: a pseudodipteral colonnade, a columned porch behind, a cella with an opisthodomos, but inside the cella a closed adyton at the end of a double line of interior columns. It is a temple within a temple, with the engulfment we have noted over and over again in Sicily, and yet seeming specifically to attempt rather ponderously what was later to be accomplished so integrally at Bassae: to combine, that is, the interior oracular quality of Apollo with his challenging exterior presence, here forced, in the wide landscape, toward the largest free-standing Doric columns ever designed.

But the temple which was built for Apollo at the site of the Greek victory over the Carthaginians at the Himera river in northern Sicily is perhaps the most expressive and moving of all his colonial embodiments.[66] The victory was won in 480 B.C., and, legend has it, on the same day as the victory over the eastern barbarians at Salamis. The Carthaginians, encamped on the west bank of the Himera near the sea, had been awaiting a reinforcement of cavalry from Selinus, with which they were allied. Having discovered this fact, the Akragantine and Syracusan cavalry advanced toward the Carthaginians and were able to draw quite near the camp before it was discovered that they were not from Selinus. They then charged across the shallows not far from the sea and began a rout which developed into a Carthaginian disaster.[67] This decisive victory freed Greek Sicily from the Carthaginian threat for several generations. The temple which commemorates it was placed just west of the river, not far from the spot where the Carthaginian camp must have been. It was Doric hexastyle, is oriented east, and has an opisthodomos. Though on low, flat ground it features a distinct upward curvature to the stylobate. Standing east of the temple and looking west—looking, that is, both at the temple and along the axis of the cavalry charge—one notices that a strongly conical and cleft mountain, now called Monte San Carlogero, the most distinctive feature of the western horizon, is directly on axis ahead. The high rising stylobate carries one's eye in a rapid trajectory toward it. (*Fig. 228*) Thus the temple, seizing hold, as it were, of the one eye–catching and probably sacred object to the west, seems to cause the observer to experience physically the hurtling velocity of the charge. The great lion head waterspouts, now in the museum in Palermo, which disciplined the anarchic fall of water from the sky, stood out in controlled menace overhead, while the temple of Apollo as bringer of victory celebrated in permanent form the disciplined but desperate act which had won it—to the roar of the *Paean*, the god's name and the war cry.

There are two temples of Apollo which break completely with the easterly orientation so well studied by Dinsmoor and discussed here earlier.[68] In them both Apollo, as he confronted the earth's power, was claimed by it, god of the sun though he might in other circumstances be. Both temples are oriented more or less north and south, that at Thermon with its entrance facing slightly west of south, that at Bassae with its entrance facing slightly east of north. More abstruse theories of celestial orientation, such as those of Penrose, cannot explain their positions.[69] In each case it was clearly the shape of the landscape space, and the presence of features of landscape focus, which dictated such placement. One recalls Megaron A at Thermon,[70] a hairpin megaron of the Bronze Age which was set into the natural megaron of the valley under the Hill of Megalakkou and faced slightly to the right of two conical hills at the south of the valley. (*Figs. 229, 230*) Sometime very early, probably during Late Bronze Age times, an extremely curious long megaron, called Megaron B, was built slightly forward and to the left of Megaron A and with just about the same orientation. This was rectangular, with a deep pronaos and a kind of adyton, but its walls seem to have had an elegant and subtle outward curve. Around it, added later, is an open ellipse of small stones which served in all likelihood as bases for the wooden columns of an at least semiperipteral colonnade, perhaps supporting a single, southern gable. Megaron B, whose uses and dates are alike uncertain, competes with Samos for primacy if its apparent peristasis was truly formed as such. Certainly, as we noted earlier, the site itself would appear to have been very holy, high up as it is within the dizzy cliffs above Lake Trichonis but at the same time enveloped in the secluded valley with its warm springs. In the late seventh century one of the earliest Doric temples was built there. Dedicated to Apollo, it had five columns across the front and a long cella with a single row of columns down the center, like that of the first temple of Hera at Samos. There was no pronaos, and perhaps no rear pediment, but already a deep opisthodomos, which the Ionic Samian temples never had. And here the opisthodomos "faces" a dramatically pyramidal peak far to the north. The columns and entablature were of wood, the latter revetted with terracotta. The temple's elongated shape corresponds to the shape of the valley, and the slight shift of its axis as compared with megara A and B brings its central colonnade directly on axis with the valley's focus in the southern cones. (*Figs. 229, 230*) The temple is thus an integral part of the experience of the closed valley, but it is at the same time itself an exterior, Olympian shape with its peripteral colonnade and its opisthodomos. This fact, coupled with the question of the column bases around Megaron B, might further indicate that it was considered from a very early period important that the Hellenic Apollo should take over by fitting into this gentle fortress seat of the goddess, with its protecting precipices and its warm springs. During the Hellenistic period, when the site, under Apollo's protection, was the rich meeting place of the Aetolian league, two extremely long stoas were built to the south of the temple. These hugged the hill slope closely and thus partly blocked the view of the southern hills from the temple. Instead they directed a long line of vision from the Bouleuterion on the south toward the body of the temple itself, seen in this view at an expressively lively angle. A third stoa was built along the south, and its narrow eastern end served further to direct and focus the view from the Bouleuterion to the temple. In this way attention was in a sense turned inward within the sanctuary rather than outward toward the natural megaron in which it was placed, even though the final ensemble of buildings still clearly respected the valley's shape.

Thermon, though high, is thus enclosed, and has the sweep and violence of Apollo's usual sites only to the north, and in the journey one must make to reach it. The temple of Apollo Epikourios at Bassae, however, is high on a rocky ridge with the most dramatic of views.[71] It was built by the town of Phigaleia which lies far to the southwest of the temple and below it on the wild gorge of the Nedda River. Pausanias tells us that the Phigaleians dedicated this temple to Apollo the Savior after he had delivered them from a plague, and that Ictinos was its architect.[72] Many scholars regard the date of the temple, therefore, as being sometime shortly after 430 or 420 B.C., the dates of the two known plagues of the period. Because the plague of 430 hardly touched this remote corner of Arcadia, and on grounds of style, most prefer the date of about 420–417. The sculpture of the interior frieze of the cella was certainly done about that time. With this dating for the temple as a whole, however, Dinsmoor, who has studied the building in detail, does not agree. He feels that its architecture has many features which recall archaic practice, and that it must therefore date before Ictinos' work on the Parthenon. He also contends, as does Riemann, that the temple was worked on at two different times, and would push the beginning date back toward the middle of the century, regarding Pausanias' statement concerning the plague deliverance as inaccurate, since Apollo, as we saw at the Himera, was also a savior in war and the temple might have been built to him as such at any time, in this remote fastness which must often have served as a military refuge for the Phigaleians.[73] It is not necessary for us to enter in detail into the dating controversy or the question of two campaigns, but a consideration of the temple as designed in its landscape may bring certain points to light. The first point is that anyone in antiquity who wished to visit the temple had to walk or ride to it from Phigaleia. It was as the culmination of this rough route that the temple was intended to be seen. The walk involves a desperate scramble through the gorge of the Nedda and then a long pull up the high draw which leads toward Mount Kôtilon. The horned cleft, in the saddle of which the temple is set, is clearly visible ahead for a long period, but the temple itself is invisible, and only dark and savage mountain masses seem to lie beyond the draw. Finally a cool spring, mentioned by Pausanias,[74] is reached, and shortly afterward the temple appears against the sky, so set that its columns, as clear cylinders of geometrical order, rise slowly, step by step in fact, above the broken rock of the hill and above whatever subsidiary buildings may have flanked them lower down on the west. The temple is so placed as to present a three-dimensional view from the path, and at the same time its entablature exactly continues the line of the hill slope to the north. It is thus of the hill and not of it: built of the same stone, though stuccoed white in antiquity, tied to the hill contours but constructed of the abstract measured forms which, especially in this remote place, speak movingly of human presence. As one mounts higher, approaching the southwest angle, the temple, too, rides higher against the hill, its entablature coming out of the contours at a more dynamic angle, its columned body more aggressively dominating to the eye. (*Fig. 231*) It is the god as savior of humanity making his presence felt in the heart of the wild.

We must now note that if the temple had been oriented east and west it could not have produced the effect we have just described, and that effect is essential to its meaning. We must therefore conclude that the present orientation is not due solely (or perhaps at all) to the fact that it would have been difficult to build out a platform on the hill to receive an east–west temple, but instead derives from the fact that the temple can only act as it was meant to do by being oriented as it is. As one comes closer along the path, and exactly at the point where the contours ease northward to lead the observer along the west flank of the temple, the remains of a rectangular plinth appear by the path. A statue of Apollo, later seen by Pausanias at Megalopolis, may originally have stood here. If so, the statue would have been in an ideal location, because it marks the moment of turning directly into the temple's presence and of coming wholly under the dominance of its mathematically ordered forms. (*Fig. 232*) One moves past the statue base toward the south end of the temple; behind the columns here is the opisthodomos, not the pronaos. (*Fig. 236*) Therefore one must continue along the long west flank, the natural way of movement toward the north entrance. (*Fig. 233*) Looking down the flank, one notes that the temple's entablature seems still to be coming directly out of the hill slope. One notes also that the stereobate and the entablature have no upward curvature, such as we have seen on many temples and such as Ictinos gave the Parthenon. Is its absence here an archaic feature? Or does it mean that refinements were too difficult to carry out in this remote region? The answer to both questions must again be in the negative. As one looks along the west flank, it is apparent that a rise in stylobate and entablature would have ruined the temple's relationship to the northern hill. Because it is close to that hill the temple must seem to come straight out of it, not to leap toward it, as the trajectory of the curve would have made it seem to do. If it had carried the eye rapidly toward the hill it would itself have seemed to be butting meaninglessly against a mass which was too close for such antics; thus it must be made to come straight out of the slope, as we have seen. (*Figs. 231–233*) In accord with this, none of the details of the temple speak of lift or dynamic energy. Though slimmer than the old columns at Corinth and with a slight entasis, these shafts with their trim capitals give much the same effect of simply standing: absolutely quiet, calm and unaffected by the natural tumult round about, disciplined, cool, anonymous as a hollow rectangle of soldiers. (*Figs. 232, 234, 235*) Can their stiffness be considered an archaic or provincial quality? This answer must again be no. This is the way these columns must be where they are.

The route to the temple's entrance has forced us always to the north, and one reason why the pronaos faces north instead of south is again apparent. As he did at the Parthenon, to be considered later, Ictinos has forced us first to experience the exterior of the temple as a whole by moving around it. Similarly, that movement is in a sense forced to continue beyond the northern colonnade itself, since as we move along we begin to see the temple not against its near north hill but against the great view which is opening to east and south. We thus mount the northern hill a little way and, looking back, we see that the temple is carrying our eye in a long perspective toward the bow of the southern hills and beyond that arc to the flat–topped mass of Mount Ithome. (*Fig. 235*) Since we are now seeing the temple from above, we realize that an upward rising curve in stereobate and entablature would not have aided its extension of our view but would indeed have tended to bunch the building up rather than to stretch it out, arrowlike, below us. The long gable ridge, with its two slanted roof planes diminishing in perspective below it, would have reinforced that arrowlike effect. We are now reminded of the long natural megaron of the two goddesses which is above us on the summit of Mount Kôtilon and which has the same view. (*Fig. 182*) As we mount higher, the action of Apollo's temple in the tremendous landscape becomes always clearer and more decisive. Its geometric, abstract form stands out as an expression of human and Olympian order against the chaotic hills. (*Fig. 236*) It rides its own rocky ridge like a perfectly stable boat on the crest of a mountainous wave. To the east of it, beyond the dizzy gorges which give the name, Bassae, to the place; the farther mountains rise themselves like higher, stormy seas. Seen from above on the slopes of Kôtilon near the goddesses' shrines, the temple is poignantly small below the mountains, but it is harder, denser, calmer than they. Its long axis swings again toward Ithome across the distant horns, and as it does so it locks the whole landscape into place. (*Fig. 237*) Temple and landscape are now one architecture, which clearly expresses a double reverence in its form: both for the mighty earth, with all its power, and for man, with the god who champions his lonely acts upon it.

For all these reasons, the north–south direction of its long axis is essential to the temple in this place. But there is much more to the temple here than its exterior landscape relationships. There is an interior experience which—despite the question of a second campaign and another hand—has been made an inseparable part of the whole. (*Fig. 238*) As we approach the north entrance we have the whole panorama of Ithome and the two seas before our eyes. To the left the wild hills of Arcadia are still tumultuously present. As we approach the pronaos we notice that the colonnade at this point, as on the south, is pseudodipteral: that is, there is a deep space between it and the pronaos. (*Figs. 237, 238*) We may or may not consciously notice, but we will certainly unconsciously experience the fact that the northern columns, like those on the south, are thicker than the columns of the flanks. This has been called an archaic holdover, but is it not a conscious device used for a special, illusionistic purpose—to make the already wide space between the columns of the entrance and those of the pronaos seem even deeper than it is by setting up a false perspective of distance. If anything, the device might be called "archaizing," though here the old method is used with new or heightened effects in view. This entrance perspective is then further carried on by the extraordinarily deep pronaos, much deeper than the opisthodomos. (*Figs. 238, 239*) A spatial axis was being created. The worshiper was being drawn toward the inside. As he looked down the exaggerated axis, on those few days when the doors were opened, he would have seen a Corinthian column standing alone at the end of the dark space of the cella. Behind it the light would have been pouring through the unusual east door which was cut into the side of the adyton. (*Fig. 240*) The column, treelike, and the earliest Corinthian column known in Greek architecture, would have been standing against the light on the direct line of sight from the north. It was thus precisely on the spot where the image of the god would normally have been placed in the usual cella arrangement. (*Fig. 239*)

As the worshiper stepped into the dark cella toward the column and the light he would suddenly have experienced something hitherto unknown in Greek temples: an expansion of interior space, an increase in scale. This was caused by the engaged Ionic columns, which were higher than the columns of the exterior colonnade, since they rose up through the space occupied on the exterior by the entablature. (*Fig. 240*) In the temple of Hera at Paestum we have already noted that the columns of the interior were doubled, one row above the other. (*Fig. 98*) This was common archaic and fifth–century practice, and it meant that the scale of the building dwindled on the interior because the upper columns were much smaller than those already experienced on the outside. At Bassae the reverse is true. The scale is set on the exterior and then becomes greater inside. The effect is one of surprise and indeed of spatial release where one had expected the usual spatial dwindling. This effect would not have been accomplished if the Ionic columns had been freestanding in this actually quite narrow space. They would then indeed have seemed to overpower it, which was one reason why single columns had not been used before. Ictinos overcame this difficulty by making the columns part of the wall and by crowning them with Ionic capitals which were treated as chunky, three–sided terminations of thick wall masses rather than as compressed and spreading culminations of columnar jets. It is thus the whole body of the cella which rises up, but which still captures the kind of scale which is possible only through the use of the column. It is true that the seventh–century temple of Hera at Olympia had made use of interior columns set quite close to the wall and with every other column connected to it by a spur of wall, and her second temple at Samos apparently reinforced its mud brick walls with engaged wooden columns. (*Figs. 80, 82*) Again, a device recalling archaic practice can hardly be called archaic here, for now at Bassae the niches formed between the engaged columns were made consciously plastic, and the whole interior became full of richly painted shadows and spatial depths.

It was also an aggressive interior. The columns rose from their spreading bases to their massive volutes and supported a continuous frieze which ran around the interior of the cella walls above the Ionic and Corinthian capitals alike. (*Fig. 240*) The heavy figures of the frieze, the struggling centaurs and lapiths, Greeks and Amazons, clearly derive from earlier works like the metopes of the Parthenon, but most of them are extraordinarily gross, contorted, and exaggerated in form. (*Fig. 241*) These characteristics have often been ascribed to a failure in the provincial execution of a brilliant Athenian design. This may be partly true. At the same time, one need only have looked at the figures in situ and then have gone out again for a moment to look at the landscape in order to understand their appropriately expressive power. (*Fig. 236*) They are like the surrounding mountains brought inside, awkward and thunderous, and they engage in the contest which is one part of the meaning of the temple as a whole: men against the beast power in nature, men against the old ways. The massiveness of the figures must at least partly be ascribed to the architect's desire for certain specific effects— effects which might once again be described as both consciously "archaizing" and consciously "optical." Some of them indeed recall the west pediment of the temple of Zeus at Olympia, now merged with a heavy rendition of the "wet drapery" style of their own period. One may accept the often repeated statement that the frieze, closed in the darkness of the cella, could not normally have been seen by men and was thus primarily an offering to the god.[75] It was an offering, however, conceived in optical terms, as it could best be seen by human beings on the god's feast day when his inner character was revealed. Its heavily modeled figures and exaggeratedly swirling draperies were exactly calculated to catch and dramatize the reflected light from the doorways on those special days when they were solemnly swung open.

The temple therefore makes use, both outside and in, of archaizing devices which are knowingly calculated to create a drama of contrasts, developing effects of space and light which are almost baroque. In this drama the freestanding Corinthian column and the east–lighted adyton behind are the climax. The Corinthian capital is a more fully "mid–space" object than are the other two Greek capitals. The Doric most closely approaches it, but its squared–off abacus is constantly presenting corners to the view; it is thus partially planar. But the Corinthian capital is a pure bell shape; the eye moves always fully around it. And the Corinthian capital at Bassae particularly emphasizes the clarity of its bell and was therefore ideally suited to stand free in space. (*Fig. 240*) The Ionic, on the other hand, is fundamentally a relief capital, with the clearly defined plane of its volutes. It can, if necessary, be made to define a corner by bringing two volutes together at a projected diagonal, and this is done in the three–

sided, engaged capitals at Bassae. It has long been a matter of dispute, however, whether the capitals of the southernmost engaged columns, which flanked the Corinthian column, were Ionic or Corinthian. Opinion, especially that based upon the evidence to be gleaned from Haller's notebooks, now seems to be inclining toward the Corinthian. Dinsmoor also claims to have detected differences in the bedding of the top blocks of the end columns which indicate to him that they had capitals differing from those of the other engaged columns.[76] It is true that the last pair of engaged columns differs from the others in that it is set at an angle to the wall. (*Fig. 238*) This angle is important for the unity of the temple as a whole, since it leads the eye rhythmically from cella to adyton and thus relates those spaces coherently with each other. It therefore seems unnecessary to assume, as some scholars have done, that the diagonal spurs, simply because they are diagonal, necessarily represent later additions to an older temple.[77] All seems to work together in a conceptual unity, but since the end spurs are different from the others it is conceivable that Greek visual logic might have given them different capitals. Such seems especially possible because of the special angle for the corner volutes, differing from that used on all the other capitals, which the diagonal of the spur wall would have required. Thus it is possible that Corinthian would indeed have been preferred to Ionic at that point. Yet, even if Corinthian, the flanking capitals would not have vitiated the central column's freestanding quality, while they would have assisted its own capital in framing the adyton. The essential question for us would thus seem to be not what kind of capital the corner piers had but why the first of all freestanding Corinthian columns was used between them on the central axis of the building. We have perhaps answered the question insofar as it relates to design: a structural support was needed at that point if the adyton was to be connected with the cella by something wider than a door, and a column whose character was uniquely freestanding made the best form for that support. Was there an iconographic reason as well? Here the second quality of the Corinthian column comes to mind, namely that, as it was the most freestanding, it was also, with the rich foliage of its capital, the most naturalistic, the most treelike, of all Greek columns. Why should the architect of Apollo's temple have wanted a tree–evoking capital on the axis of view from the northern entrance? We know that Callimachos, a fifth–century worker in bronze, made treelike metallic forms and was reputed to have invented the Corinthian capital.[78] The latter is thus related both to metalwork techniques and to the evocation of trees. We recall that the Athenians had dedicated a bronze palm tree outside Apollo's temple at Delphi shortly after 460 B.C. and that Nicias donated, in 417 B.C., another bronze tree to the sanctuary of Apollo at Delos. We have already discussed the importance of that tree as a symbol of Apollo's birth. It had been, in Crete, a symbol of the goddess, and Leto had grasped it for support while bearing her divine child.[79] The palm tree in bronze, therefore, was a symbol not only of Apollo but also of those chthonic powers of the goddess which he had usurped. The Corinthian column in stone is a treelike form derived from bronze originals. It is my belief that it is used for the first time at Bassae precisely in order that it should stand as a symbol of the god and, most appropriately at this site, of those earth powers which Apollo had brought under his sway. The answer to the further question as to why such a symbol was needed has been answered, I believe, by our discussion of the necessary orientation of the temple in the landscape, which demanded that the long axis of the building run north and south, as even the earlier temples on the site may have done. Even the adyton arrangement with its eastern door may have been traditional here: so that the god could face toward the east, especially if, as we shall discuss in a moment, it was particularly important that the god should look in that direction from this place. For the arrangement to have worked, the image of the god would have had to be placed in the adyton, facing east away from the main entrance. The classic architects of the temple, Ictinos and his successor or assistant, Callimachos, then had a new and subtle perception: something was needed to stand for the god on the axis of the dramatic entrance view. Their solution was apt: the Corinthian column, the god's tree symbol.[80] (*Figs. 239, 240*)

Yet, if so, why does its capital use acanthus leaves and not something closer to palm, like those of the treasuries of Massalia and Clazomenae at Delphi, whose general shape the bell of the Corinthian capital here recalls? (*Fig. 202*) The answer cannot be certain, but its main lines may be surmised. The Corinthian is both a more solid and a more richly leaflike capital than the palm type. Its drum is more compactly sculptural, while its acanthus leaves have a more articulated edge and are consequently richer in light and shade. Thus the first example of the Corinthian column defined its future. For the interior of Bassae, it was optically more expressive (like the frieze) than the other would have been, and for later centuries, inside or—until the Roman period very rarely—out, was exactly in accord with more pictorial, baroque taste and, as Augustus desired, with an expression of the earth's abundance. Yet its beginnings were with Apollo, and it was appropriate to him, because if it less specifically recalled palm leaves than the other it was clearly much more like a living tree.

Dinsmoor insists, however, that the image of the god stood in the cella at Bassae, in front of the column.[81] There is no evidence whatever for this arrangement in the pavement of the cella, no sign of a base, and it would furthermore have been visually deplorable. It is true that a base could conceivably have vanished without trace, since in all likelihood the cult image it supported was small and of wood, as the primitive xoanon of an old shrine would have been. Cockerell, however, believed the image to have stood in the adyton,[82] but Dinsmoor insists that there is no evidence in the pavement for any base there either. There is not much, but there is something. In the southwest corner of the adyton there is a paving block (*Fig. 238*) which is bonded into the wall and thus still cantilevers out from it at a right angle, contrasting in this way with the other blocks of the pavement which have sunk considerably. Corbett, who first sensed a significance in this specially bonded block, also discovered something else: that from it there is a direct view through the east door toward the peak of Mount Lykaion, the highest mountain in Arcadia, where, as at Ithome, there was the sanctuary of a primitive Zeus to whom human sacrifice was offered. (*Fig. 242*) From no other place in the adyton is Lykaion visible except along the line defined by the block in its southwest corner. Did the old image out of the former shrine stand here, looking out as a primitive Apollo Lykaios, Apollo of the Wolves, toward a wolfish Zeus on Lykaion? Corbett is inclined to think it did, and so am I.[83] We will recall a similar diagonal axis to a distant peak set up in the temple of Apollo's sister, Artemis, at Loutsa. (*Fig. 147*)

The measure of the greatness of the architects at Bassae now becomes clear. From the cool rank of its Doric colonnade to the verdant bell of its Corinthian column the temple makes one splendid unity out of many complex parts and ideas, handling the most ancient and savage of traditions with inspired invention and expert calm. It not only controls the landscape from Ithome to Lykaion but also makes the interior of the Greek temple express, for the first time, a complex psychic structure in the god. It explores to the full the double character of Apollo: its outward aspect, bright and Olympian, its inward aspect, chthonic and dark. Like the dramatists of their Athens, the architects at Bassae created a work of classic art, because they dealt not with a part but with the whole of things.

At the same time, the genius of invention which the temple of Apollo exhibits looks forward, as does much classic art, to the developments of the Hellenistic age. Its manipulation of interior space, its rich handling of light and changes of scale, its expressive reintegration of inside and out for dramatic effect, all find their counterparts there. The later Hellenistic temple of Apollo at Didyma, for example, of the third and second centuries and the Roman period, while it picked up once more the tradition of the great archaic Ionic dipteral temples, still reinterpreted that tradition in terms that one feels would have been comprehensible to Ictinos and Callimachos. The temple stands on a long, low ridge of land well south of Miletos.[84] The way to it winds south from the city through barren, rolling foothills from which the Aegean Sea and the islands of the Dodecanese are visible to the west. After a time the hills open and a plain sweeps ahead to the south, terminated by the ridge near the center of which the temple is placed. The Sacred Way from Didyma's port of Panormus on the Aegean would have intersected the route from Miletos on the ridge. Only three columns of the temple are now standing to their full height, but when the temple was complete it would have appeared like a grove of trees against the sky upon the otherwise barren contour line. It is set in a slight depression between two gentle rises of the ridge, locked into place against the distant views. Beyond the temple, the land, never high, falls off rapidly toward the Gulf of Mendelia, so that the temple stands exposed at the center of a vast landscape: a circle which is defined on the south by the ridge lines across the gulf, on the west by the arc of the Dodecanese beyond Cape Monodendri, on the north by the mighty horns of Mykale's flank beyond Miletos, (*Fig. 243*) and on the east by ranges of hills beyond which rises the fanged summit of Latmos. The light of the sun is blinding in this place, beating down from above, shimmering on the distant water with the islands in the heat haze. In the heat the mountain and island forms spin around the temple like a fixed sun at their center, but the colonnades of the temple itself offer the only coolness and shade within the dazzling circle. It is in fact the sacred grove of the god, his "wooded grove," to which the Homeric Hymn so often refers.[85] Its high and deeply fluted columns make a true forest around the clifflike walls of the open cella. (*Figs. 244, 245*) Entrance to the temple is through the many columns which penetrate the pronaos, but the wide door in the center, from which the oracles of the god may sometimes have been announced, is too high above the pavement to be entered. Through the doorway, from the pronaos, could be seen the shadowed columns of the roofed area behind it, and beyond them, above the unroofed walls of the cella, only the bright blue of the open sky. The way into the grove thus comes to a preliminary climax, announced by the effects of light, but further progress forward is blocked until one leaves the light and heads downward through the body of the temple along either of the narrow, sloping, barrel–vaulted ramps which flank the central door. At the end of their dark tunnel another spot of light beckons, and the viewer finally emerges into the blazing light of the cella court. Here the walls, plastically conceived, are much higher than the columns outside because one has descended so far, and they rise upward toward the sky to define a vast expansion of space. At the same time, their Corinthian pilasters are placed above a dado and are thus kept the same height as the exterior columns, so that the observer has a firm series of reference points with which to link interior and exterior together. Originally, the exterior grove of columns was again recalled and transformed by the grove of trees which, Strabo tells us, was planted in the court around the shrine.[86] A further drama of scale change is still created, however, by the small prostyle shrine which stands near the far end of the court and emphasizes, by contrast, the height of the walls that surround it. The climax seems reached, the finding of the inner shrine in the high, wide, brightly lighted place after having passed through the low and narrow dark. But a further surprise and climax was provided. Movement back from the shrine was confronted by the wide stairway which rose toward the chamber behind the great doorway through which movement from the other side had been impossible. (*Fig. 245*) Engaged Corinthian columns stood splendidly beside the opening at the top of the stairs. The whole drama of the god was revealed. His shadowed grove had now opened up, beyond his dark grottos, to reveal the splendor of his appearance—like his head upon the capitals—as the sun which was also his: where, as it sails through the cosmic dust, "a rich, finespun garment glows upon his body and flutters in the wind."[87] Thus Didyma, like the much earlier work at Bassae, is remarkably complete. The whole fabric of the temple is calculated to set up a baroque drama of basic sensations in the mind of the observer. The emotions so aroused must have made the complex nature of Apollo almost fully comprehensible: shelter and coolness in his grove, the taste of death in the dark restriction of his caves, release from the darkness once again into the trapped sunlight of the court with its whispering leaves. Finally, and unexpectedly, there was, in this place where the raised voice booms in echoes like thunder, the promise of his epiphany above the stairs.

Almost directly north of Didyma, far beyond Mykale and across the Ephesian gulf, lies the site of Apollo's oracular temple at Klaros. Once again the horns of Mykale's flank play an important role in a site sacred to Apollo, just as the mountain's mounded west end served as a focus for the Samian Heraion. (*Fig. 77*) The sanctuary at Klaros was probably very old, as was that at Didyma, but the temple which has now been excavated dates from the third century and contains some Roman work as well, including a propylon of the Hadrianic period which faces directly toward the horns of Mykale across the gulf.[88] (*Fig. 247*) The tiny plain of Klaros, south of the mounded hills of Colophon which held a sanctuary of the Mother of the Gods, is shaped like a hairpin megaron itself, approximately two kilometers deep and several hundred yards wide. North of it the hills close in an arc, and to the south it opens to a curving beach which faces Mykale. The eastern side of the beach is closed by the mounded promontory which was the site of the town of Notium, and from this point Ephesos itself is visible to the east. The temple of Apollo is placed in the natural megaron well back from the beach at a point marked on the west by a conical hill and on the east by a jagged, horned gorge. It is the latter formation which, as was noted earlier, can be seen in the western view from the temple of Artemis at Ephesos. Within it was a cave containing prehistoric and geometric sherds; in all likelihood it was the oldest holy place of the area, although no specific connection of it with Apollo's cult below has yet been found. The temple itself was a large hexastyle Doric structure with three gigantic figures: of Apollo, Artemis, and Leto (Latona) standing on a common pedestal in the cella. Under them was a vaulted cave, reached by two stairways from the pronaos, and designed as a labyrinth of seven turns. This groped its tortuous way to a sacred spring and the final cavern. (*Fig. 246*) The dark and chthonic nature of Apollo was thus fully stressed in this Hellenistic and Roman building, and the old Cretan forms of the natural megaron, the mounded hill, the horned mountain with its sacred cave, the labyrinth, the spring, and the constructed cavern seem most consciously and knowingly to have been used. The propylon, as noted, faces the sea and Mykale's double peaks. (*Fig. 247*) From the propylon the Sacred Way is given a purposefully fluid curve to bring it to the temple exactly on line with the latter's east front. Elaborate votive monuments border the Way on the west and lead sinuously to the temple. On this route, a deeply folded cleft lies dead ahead to the north, but as the front of the temple itself is approached the eye is led across the wide interval between temple and altar toward the jagged gorge to the northeast. (*Fig. 248*) Once again the bright columns would have stood upright in the light against the darkly folded hills, but behind and beneath them lies concealed the god's own darkness and his underworld. (*Fig. 246*) Knowing and elaborate as it is, the sanctuary of Klaros manipulates exterior and interior effects with a suppleness which can again remind us of the experiments of Ictinos and Callimachos. Now, however, the effects achieved seem the result not only of Hellenistic and later antique desires for rather spooky drama, but also of those periods' growing wish to recapture a security which had long gone by. So the Apollo of "know thyself," challenging Hellenic presence as he had been, and still bright sun as well as grove and cave at Didyma, seems at Klaros to be much more of the under than of the upper world. So Hadrian, seeking here as elsewhere the place of ancient mystery and the heart of the myth, faces his propylon across the water, and indeed across the centuries, toward the horns.

Chapter 8

ZEUS

Zeus: whatever he may be, if this name
pleases him in invocation,
thus I call upon him.
I have pondered everything
yet I cannot find a way,
...
Zeus, who guided men to think,..

Aeschylus, AGAMEMNON (Lattimore)[1]

THE CONCEPT OF THE NATURE of Zeus as it was worked out by the fifth century was one of the noblest creations of the Greek mind. Yet even then it was recognized that the elements which had gone into its creation were so varied and interwoven, and had undergone such a complex development, as to defy analytical separation of part from part. The work of scholars such as Cook has shown us how various the aspects of Zeus were and how his character changed over the centuries.[2] He was at once the Indo–European sky and storm god and a child born to the goddess of the earth and nursed in a cave on Crete. To these opposites were joined many others, until his character became itself an embracing syncretism, developing from more primitive concepts to more refined.[3] His cults were everywhere and his attributes innumerable, both male and female. He could be horned or thousand–breasted; his symbol could be the eagle or the snake. He was almost Hestia, goddess of the hearth, whom the Greeks made his most dutiful and retiring sister, so that he was with Hermes the protector of the family cult and of the house, from which he was the averter of his own lighting. He was, with his daughter, Athena, the protector of the city, that grouping of families and of cults. He was also all nature, and had power over all the gods and goddesses who held the earth and sea in trust for him. He himself was in all things: at Megara he was worshiped as the dust.[4] He was at once in cyclical time and outside it: a son who had taken power from his father but a being who had all *telos*, all fulfillment of the whole of things, and thus had always been. Precisely because he had come to represent so many aspects of life and nature he was above all else the god of things as they are. Since he alone knew the future he was also god of things as they would be. He was the facts of all existence, natural and human; his was the power of the fact. All suffering was Zeus, and all illumination. Similarly, it is an indication of the Greek view of

132

the symmetry and essential reasonableness of the universe that the fact of Zeus should have been equated not only with *telos,* fulfillment, but also with *dike,* justice. He was already such for Hesiod, and Themis, his daughter and goddess of Established Justice, soon sits beside him in the Homeric Hymn.[5] It is also a mark of Greek courage that the recognition and worship of Zeus did not bring with it human immortality or merging with him but only knowledge: the recognition of the facts of existence, the knowledge of things as they are. Therefore, human growth in its knowledge of the whole of things, and in its capacity to play out a truly human part in relation to the whole, was the Way to Zeus. So he himself grew: from the savage father who must be propitiated, to the supreme lord of all things, and finally to the just god of the whole who embodies at last the reciprocal balances and the boundaries of power.

As the supreme deity, Zeus was the true successor of the old goddess, from whom, in myth, he had usurped power through marriage and with a certain violence and cunning, as he had also usurped it from his father Kronos. His most important sanctuaries, therefore, were placed in those kinds of sites which had been most sacred to the goddess: the tops of the highest mountains, for example, but also the largest natural megara of the earth. They are not necessarily the sites of the greatest violence and drama—except for the drama of the sky— as many of Apollo's sites are. Their meaning is not struggle but dominion, and their architectural development seems to follow the same course as that of Zeus' character itself, toward an expression of the wholeness of the universe, of grandeur, and of majestic calm far beyond strife. Thus his temples, though no less dependent upon the landscape than any others, often seem not so much to be set in balance with it as, more than others, to dominate it with themselves. It is clear that the building of a temple for Zeus was a project not to be undertaken without the most scrupulous care and reflection. There was clearly an awe and reverence hung about his person such as was associated with that of no other Greek god. Indeed, his special presence often seemed to throw the Greeks off stride, so that monstrous or hybrid constructions resulted, such as the Ionic–planned, Doric–columned Peisistratid project in Athens, the courtyarded temple at Dodona, and the Atlantean–figured colossus at Akragas. Therefore, while Zeus' altars and shrines were ubiquitous, the number of his temples and of sites dominated in person by him without the mediation of other divinities would seem to have been carefully limited, compared, for example, with those dedicated to Apollo.

Zeus' mountain shrines are the most obvious expressions of his power and probably the earliest symbols of it. Mount Olympos itself was his great northern embodiment, rising, many–peaked and bastioned but essentially pyramidal in shape, just beyond the confines of archaic and classic Greece and seeming sometimes to float, detached from its base, as Seltman has pointed out,[6] belonging as much to the upper air as to the land. No sanctuaries have as yet been found on Olympos itself; it was a dominant but remote presence, to be glimpsed from afar. So Zeus assumed the caves of Ida, opening with his birth, of Dikte, his gated citadel, and of Jouctas, his hero tomb. (*Figs. 3, 7, 16*) One also recalls Evans' report of the modern association of the western view of Jouctas with his profile.[7] (*Fig. 21*) In Crete, he must in some way have been associated with the former young consort of the goddess, now come into power on his own. His later association, as Zagreus, with the infant Dionysos would support this view, as would the daimonic kuretes, the Cretan ministrants, who danced and clashed their weapons before his cave to keep his infant cries from the ears of Kronos.[8] In Arcadia, on the other hand, Zeus would seem at first to have been a mature embodiment of barbarous power. At Mount Ithome his human victims were apparently immolated at an open altar under the sky on the summit of the flat–topped mountain which itself resembles a great natural altar. (*Fig. 237*) Ithome is a truncated pyramid, and it has a compact, austere geometry which curiously reminds the modern observer of the forms of the pre–Columbian temple platforms of the Valley of Mexico, such as those of Teotihuacan or Cholula. Like those platforms, Ithome is itself a dense, abstracted mountain form, and like them, too, its rites were bloody. We have seen how Ithome formed the center of a number of landscape axes: toward Taygetus to the east, toward the conical mountain south of Pylos, toward Bassae to the north. The impression from its summit is of being in the center of a wide and varied world. The Messenian plain lies to southeast and north; deep gorges fall off into the site of Messenia itself below. The sea completes the southern arc and the mountains of Arcadia the northern. Ithome therefore occupies a central position and has a form which itself suggests an architecture of exposure to the sky and of sacrifice under it.

On Mount Lykaion, which rises above the plain of Megalopolis in central Arcadia, Zeus apparently had a wolfish aspect and received human sacrifice as well.[9] The complicated mass of Lykaion culminates in a conical peak, (*Figs. 236, 242*) but the open, earth–mounded altar of Zeus, with its twin columns upon which golden eagles perched, was on a slightly lower elevation south of the cone. Between the two heights (clearly visible in the view from the adyton at Bassae) was a depression or saddle, apparently arranged as a hippodrome. The cone of Lykaion's summit itself is visible from Zeus' altar and forms the focus of the view from that point to the north. The goddess' maternal symbol is thus used by the new god, his site defined by its presence. The more decisive the cone, the higher, the more central, so much the more desirable was it as a sanctuary for Zeus and as his symbol. The shape of Mount Oros on the island of Aigina fulfills all these conditions. Its western flank—as we noted earlier from the site of the temple of Apollo and of the neolithic and Mycenaean settlement on Aigina—rises up in two sweeping ridges which enclose the cleft and horned gorges of the lower slopes. (*Fig. 183*) Its upper profiles rise tensely to the pointed summit; the line they make is taut and pure. In this view the mountain is not a static mass but an upward pointing force. It has much the same quality from the south, as seen from Poros, (*Fig. 281*) while from the east and northeast its profile is harsher and more savagely carved. Upon its summit was placed the open sanctuary of Zeus Panhellenios, the Zeus of all Greece.[10] Set as it is in the Saronic Gulf, Mount Oros seems to rise near the center of a beautifully bounded sea. It is the focus of a specifically Greek universe: one of sea and islands clearly limited in a definite arc. Close to the west rise the mountains of the Peloponnesos: the jagged massif of Methane, the clefts and horns of Troezen. After Poros the horizon recedes toward the southeast and east but is kept tangible and definite by the distant profiles of the Cyclades. These swing around toward the north through the sea haze and carry the eye back to the Attic coast. From there, especially, the mountain of Zeus forms a definite focus for the southern view. (*Fig. 357*) Every morning the weather can be tested from Athens by the atmospheric conditions around its cone. When it disappears in haze or cloud, rain may be expected, or a heavy and oppressive haze settles over the land.

When the winds blow cool and clear the mountain reappears in clean profile against the gulf. In this way the sacred object acts as a true focus for the view: indistinct when Zeus' dust or rain turn the solid forms of nature fuzzy, sharp and precise when his power reveals once more the essential precision of the world.

While the mountain of Zeus is in view from Athens it is hidden from Eleusis by the long body of Salamis near at hand. From the horns of Kerata above Eleusis, however, Mount Oros swings up into sight once more and is exactly on axis behind two low, wide, and upward–sweeping saddles of Salamis itself. (*Fig. 249*) Because of this precise relationship across space between Oros and Kerata—and because of the obvious importance of Kerata as the insignia for Eleusis—(*Figs. 121, 122*) it possibly may be felt that Kerata was originally sacred to the goddess and was then assumed by Zeus. (However, a case might be made for Artemis, who guarded the outer gate at Eleusis and held a somewhat similar horned mountain above Sounion, *Fig. 290*, to be discussed later.) Old tradition had it that the highest horn of Kerata had supported the throne of Xerxes when he witnessed the battle of Salamis.[11] It is clear that the tradition was in error but, since its appearance indicated that something was probably to be found on Kerata, the summit was visited by Reichel in 1898.[12] He noted a cutting in the rock which might have suggested a throne to later viewers and a platform which he believed might, or might not, have been man–made. (*Fig. 249*) An examination of the site made by Eugene Vanderpool and myself in April 1958, indicated that the platform was certainly man–made and cyclopean, and that the cuttings which are clearly apparent in its rocks show that some sort of enclosure was formed upon it. Many fragments of archaic roof tiles were found on and under the platform, some Corinthian, others Attic. The building was therefore roofed. No indication of its use could be discovered. It might conceivably have been an Athenian observation post which guarded the route from Megara, as the summit of Kerata was used during the Greek Civil War of 1944–51; Megara itself is clearly in view to the west, as we noted earlier. The use of Kerata's summit as such, however, would not have precluded the existence of a shrine there as well, and the shape of the cutting does not particularly suggest that of a watchtower. Instead, the remains suggest a building constructed in an L–shape, of which one section may have been an open court. The impression is of a rustic sanctuary, and this feeling is heightened by the nature of the site. The horns are violent and full of power; their broken rocks pile up into jagged spires, and just below them, on a knife–edged ridge, the blocks have settled so as to form a natural corbel–vaulted cave. Its form somewhat recalls that of the constructed stone gable of the cave of Herakles on Mount Cynthus on Delos, where the summit was sacred to Zeus. (*Fig. 222*) Large birds of prey, often called generically "eagles" by the ancient Greeks, wheel above the site.[13] Its view to the east embraces the plain and bay of Eleusis and the whole recumbent body of Salamis, and it comes to rest at last far beyond Daphni upon the horns of Hymettos. (*Fig. 249*)

South of that formation, and just below the main summit of Hymettos, was another sanctuary of Zeus. It was located in the southernmost and smallest of a number of bowl–shaped depressions which lie along the mountain's main ridge. Looking across the site toward the east, the horns of Ocha are just visible; to the north lie Pentelikon and Parnes with the horns of Deceleia, and to west and south the whole sweep of Attica, Salamis, the gulf, Aigina with Zeus

Panhellenios, and beyond it the mountains of the Peloponnesos. On a clear day Acrocorinth can be seen. What the excavators believed to have been an altar was so placed as to make the most of this great view to west and south, but from the bowl itself nothing is visible but the sky. A small apsidal building was placed on a cross–axis inside the bowl, but the natural megaron which the depression itself forms has no physical focus in any landscape shape.[14] This fact is especially striking because there is a much larger and beautifully formed depression just east of the one which houses the shrine. There, however, the view is open to the mountain's peak and the space is not only less sheltered than that of the first but also takes on a horizontal direction. It is apparent that the shrine of Zeus was placed in the one depression on the ridge where the space formed could be simply one complete globe: the bowl of the earth, the dome of the sky. The observer is at once protected from the various distractions offered by wind and view and is at the same time so hemmed in by the walls of the hollow that his eye is constantly running up its curving sides to the near and uninterrupted shape of the sky. It has more shape for him than it could have had if he were standing upon a peak, because in that case his eye would have been constantly straying off to the multitudinous shapes of the land. In the hollow there is no escape; the sky is formed and definite. Its shape completes that of the earth. The observer's experience, therefore, can only be single and complete. He is exposed, without ir-relevant distractions, to the largest and simplest of natural realities.

Such expression of the whole of things in their grandest terms is characteristic of Zeus' great-est sites. Among these his oracular shrine at Dodona is one of the simplest and most impres-sive.[15] At Dodona Zeus had married the goddess Dione and thus assumed her oracle. Talking birds, symbols of the goddess, had supposedly instituted the oracle itself. Priestesses always re-mained on the site, and the flight of doves was observed, but the main oracles were interpreted by barefoot priests of Zeus, the Helloi, the "men who sleep on the ground."[16] In consequence, powers of air and earth alike were invoked at Dodona. The site is far north in Epirus, on the very frontier of the Hellenic world. It may be approached from the northeast, on which route a low pass is crossed to reveal the whole length of Mount Tomaros, bounding a long and narrow valley near the center of which, under the mountain's gullied and horned masses, the sanctuary is set. Yet the journey to Dodona taken by the majority of the pilgrims in archaic times, when it was at the first height of its power, would probably have been from the south, and it is when approached from the south that the site can best be experienced. The way north from the Amphilochian Gulf passes through the hills north of the Ambracian plain. Before the pass the great mass of Tomaros begins to rise up on the left, and the way to Dodona winds under its flanks. It passes first through a narrow, winding valley which lies crushed under the outlying masses of the mountain. (*Fig. 250*) The massif rises up in splendidly bare and sweeping terraces to a towering ridge which is crowned by horns. The pilgrim's mind is stunned by the greatness of the landscape scale and by his own smallness. He is made to feel a power far grander than his own, and that power is entirely of the earth, enclosing him, restricting his freedom of movement, directing him with an insistent pressure. The way is narrow, but the whole curve of the passage leads him on. As he moves forward, the mountains begin at once to recede and to soar higher than before, as, in a beautifully rhythmic curve, a long valley opens out before him. He has been compressed, so that now the release, when it comes, is palpably felt. It is definite, and what is experienced is double: the culminating grandeur of the earth, the mighty expansion of the sky. The valley widens and the mountain masses curve up and away from its floor in a way which again, as at Hymettos but now with great scale, causes the eye to travel up along their slopes and then to follow down their ridges, to experience the form of the sky. This time that form does have an axial direction down the valley; the sky is a vaulted ellipse, and as the eye is carried down the shape it sees a long, low mound of earth lying across the valley floor. (*Fig. 251*) The lateral extension of that low barrier emphasizes the width of the plain, so that the sky again is felt as very wide. The mountain slopes to left and right continue past the hillock and hold the sky shape, so that the latter is also seen as a spread canopy which arches over and far beyond the mound. At the same time the profiles of the flanking ridges and the hillock make a widely spreading, doubly curved horn shape. Thus it is in the center of horns, along the near face of the hillock, that the buildings of the sanctuary are placed. The temenos extends forward into the valley, and its propylon is so calculated as to occur at the exact spot from which no further hills of any kind can be seen beyond the hill itself; it is thus totally open under the sky, and the release which began at the head of the valley is now complete.

The main temple lies at a slight angle ahead, oriented well south of southeast toward the valley's entrance. Largely third century in date, it is a megaron in antis, partly embedded in a forecourt with its own propylon and with its interior colonnade omitted on the eastern side where the oracular oak tree grew. (*Fig. 252*) Treasuries stand around it in a loose semicircle. Although apparently casual, their arrangement is in fact exact. First of all, they are organized as an arc, and it is clear what that arc accomplishes: it forms in plan a semicircle which complements the semicircle in elevation which is the valley shape, and it faces southward in order to do so. (*Fig. 253*) In this way a circle is completed, the circle of earth and sky, the globe of the world. Secondly, it is only because the temple and its treasuries are irregularly spaced and oriented along their arc that they have the power so to complete the valley shape and to act in it as well. If they formed a precise arc they would lose individuality and freeze on it, a tight shape in a big valley. They would lose both the power which movement has to attract the eye and the large scale which rhythm gives to movement. In other words, their arc dances against the clear backdrop of the hill and under the ellipse of the sky. Beyond this primary act, the buildings of the temenos also set up complementary rhythmic echoes to the landscape. The axial mass of the temple, for example, carries the eye toward the higher hill along the curving way beyond the entrance to the valley, and emphasizes, by contrast, the decisive horns of the valley opening which lies between them. Similarly, in a line of sight diagonally across the buildings' arc, the temple and the treasuries emphasize the scale of the mountain ridge which flanks them. These echoes become stiffened as one moves past the inadequately excavated hypostyle hall toward the Hellenistic theater. In its shape the concave landscape hollow is purely geometricized. The slope of the theater also picks up and clarifies the slopes of the lower ridges to the north, and its hollow is keenly felt against the massive buttresses to the south. In these views, too, the summit of Tomaros is clearly seen as double-peaked and horned; its rough face furnishes the necessary opposite to the deep and fertile valley, rich in horned cattle—as Hesiod tells us, the "shambling kine"[17]—but, as seen from the arc of the sanctuary, it is less a dominating bulk than the definer of a space.

At Dodona, therefore, the site became holy to Zeus because it not only invoked the old symbols of the goddess but also offered a progression toward wholeness and calm. The old awe and terror of the land, expressed by the mass of Tomaros, the person of Dione, is wedded to the larger grandeur of Zeus' dominion. The buildings themselves are so arranged as to enhance and clarify that expansive potential in the landscape and to link it with human experience. Its meaning is the person of Zeus: the wholeness of things known when the sky and earth are felt as one. The way to it is labyrinthine, hard, and awesome. The culmination is wide and embracing, at once calmer and more grand than might have been expected on the way. (*Figs. 251, 253*) Recognition of the fundamentals is thus achieved through hardship. The place is now:

> Zeus, who guided men to think,
> who has laid it down that wisdom
> comes alone through suffering.[18]

Zeus' most fully expressive sites are therefore not usually to be found on mountain summits, unless in a hollow upon them as at Hymettos. His temples will be so placed as to cause the observer to experience the bowl of the sky. A moment's reflection upon the sites of Hymettos and Dodona can also make us understand how that kind of sky is not felt on a broad and boundless plain, where the sky, however close to the earth, cannot be seen as a definite shape. At night, under the stars, it may sometimes be felt as a dome, but even in optimum daylight conditions, when, that is, it is defined by sailing clouds, it can only be read as a continuous plane which extends horizontally above the earth and never meets it at a convincing boundary. Such a boundless world of continuous horizontal planes, the world of the prairie, was unsympathetic to the Greeks on both aesthetic and philosophical grounds. It is an indefinite ambient of continuous flux and change, the world alike of the horse nomad and of modern history. But in the Greek view the world was by rights bounded and definite, and this is the world they embodied in Zeus.

The setting of the Temple of the Olympian Zeus in Athens is characteristic, using as it does the deepest part of the arc of the valley between the Acropolis and the hills to the east. (*Fig. 254*) We can legitimately consider this temple now since it was laid out on its present foundations in the late sixth century, even though it was not completed until the second century A.D.[19] The Corinthian columns now standing are Hadrianic, as is the entire temenos wall and its propylon. Some large unfluted drums of the sixth-century columns have been found, but no bases, which has led some observers to believe that the original temple, though planned like an Ionic dipteral pavilion, was in fact Doric.[20] With the understanding that the original columns would have been shorter than the present Corinthian ones and that we furthermore have no idea where the original propylon, if any, was intended to be, we can, I think, still treat the arrangement as it now stands as one which had been generally characteristic of Zeus' sites. True, when we enter through the Hadrianic propylon which is placed on an exact cross–axis with the east front of the temple and in a temenos wall which is exactly parallel to the temple's long side, we are taking part in a regularized space experience which was generally uncharacteristic of archaic planning and which may have occurred first in the earlier campaigns of building at the sanctuary of Poseidon at Sounion or at the Temple of Aphaia on Aigina, about 513–500 B.C. Such regularization has special effects and meanings which can best be discussed later. Yet when we move toward the temple as the arrangement now stands we are impressed, I think, by its general appropriateness for the site as a whole. (*Figs. 254–255*) So seen, the east colonnade stands vertically against a long, gentle curve of horizon which rises up with the nearer hill on the east, within whose fold the Panathenaic stadium was contained, and then continues beyond it toward the ridge of Hymettos. As one moves forward, the bulk of the temple, now very much a full grove of Corinthian trees, looms larger, blots out the Acropolis to the west, and is finally seen as complete against the arc of the contours which curve up toward the hill of Philopappos beyond. (*Fig. 254*) The whole gently defined arc from Hymettos and the eastern hills to Philopappos is high enough to block the nearer elements of the long view to the sea. In the distance the mountain cone of Zeus Panhellenios can be seen —and could have been seen from the temple's altar—but the general effect is not toward a horizontal extension of vision but rather toward the cupping of it in a wide bowl. This effect is also strong when the temple is seen from the south. Now the sharp planes of the south and east walls of the Acropolis to the west, north of Philopappos, and the slopes of Hymettos to the east, define the northern horizon in a wide sweep. Indeed, in the eastern view from the temple, the whole long length of Hymettos is visible, (*Fig. 256*) and it can be seen that the long axis of the temple is oriented almost exactly upon the higher of the two conical hills which flank the cleft of Aphrodite at Kaisariani. (*Fig. 257*) As at Dodona, Zeus stands in a volume of landscape which is primarily defined by the horned mountain of the goddess, and here his image faced the sacred natural forms. The temple as a whole seems to expand mightily within a globe of space which is only just large enough to contain it. The eye is constantly being carried toward the shaped sky and measuring the temple against its form. In the view northward along the temple's east front, toward partially marked Lycabettos, similar effects are experienced. The shape of the hill's cone directs the eye upward within the landscape cup in which the temple, fragmentary as it now is, is the only sculptural whole. It is the holy grove of Zeus, planted in the single spot near the Acropolis from which the latter's solid bulk could be subordinated or blotted out and where the earth was so formed as to assert the closeness and tangibility of the sky and the unquestioned dominance of the temple placed beneath it. No mistake need be made; Zeus is lord.

It is therefore Zeus who takes over those natural megara of earth which are at once wide enough to express his dominion and defined enough by curving hills so as to seem roofed by sky. The site of Nemea is especially moving in this regard.[21] The present temple dates from 340, but it replaced a much earlier one upon the spot, which was apparently chosen at a very early period as expressive of the nature of Zeus. It was at Nemea that Herakles killed the lion of the goddess and instituted the panhellenic games in honor of the young Opheltes who had been killed by a serpent. The myths which surround the site thus stress the power of the goddess, her possible malignancy, and her subjugation to the rule of Dorian law. But nothing in

139

the landscape speaks of strife. It has the calm of Zeus' greatest sites. Entrance to the valley is best gained from the east. The road winds among the rolling hills west of the route between Corinth and Argos and comes out finally at a low pass from which a sweep of valley opens. Directly ahead, the hills on the opposite side of the valley dip down to reveal the wild Artemis mountains of the central Peloponnesos, and, in the center of the valley on this axis of view, the columns of the temple can be seen. (*Fig. 258*) The temple is placed upon the only flat platform of valley floor which is visible from this angle, and it is therefore so securely based in its bowl of space as to stand absolutely quiet and to hold the observer's view while the horned mountains thunder behind it. To the left a notched mountain rises up to define the southern confines of the valley, and its large form seems again to emphasize the stillness of the temple. The vertical columns are so abstract and fixed upon their plane of earth as to form, comparatively small as they are, the hub around which the landscape shapes revolve and from which they seem to take their orders. As one moves down into the valley the scene shifts its axis. The far mountains drop out of sight, and the temple begins to be seen against an unexpectedly long and gentle extension of the valley toward the north. From the stadium at the south the sweep of the view is apparent. (*Fig. 259*) One feels released for action; there is space to run and a shape to run in, since the whole long valley has the effect of being a huge stadium itself. Similarly, the wide arc of the hills shapes a wide dome of sky. In this space the position of the temple is critical. It is the element which creates the kind of human scale which is desired here and thereby makes the observer sense the valley's size. Again, the precise verticals of its columns emphasize not only the firmness of its position but also the contrasting wide sweep of curving hills and the horizontal continuity of valley floor. All these impressions are intensified as one comes close to the temple. Its fourth–century Doric columns are high, abstract, and slender. They seem appropriate here, where they rise toward the sky against a far background of complementary curves. (*Fig. 260*) Only one natural object in the northern background stands out clearly as a single whole. It is the mountain which, from Acrocorinth, resembles a crouching lion (*Fig. 171*) but which from Nemea, as from Sikyon, has a shape both flat–topped and geometrically abstract, resembling that of Mount Ithome. Like Ithome it, too, expresses exposure to the sky as the natural altar of Zeus. As the observer approaches the temple's own altar, set before its eastern colonnade at a northerly opening angle, he is made especially conscious of the relationship between the colonnades of the temple in the valley and the truncated pyramid of the hill. It is a contrast in which the special qualities of both objects are emphasized and in which the eye is again carried back and forth between earth and sky.

Inside the fourth–century temple, Corinthian columns were engaged in the cella walls, and there was an adyton or crypt down several steps. The temple consequently evoked the interior world of grove and cavern, concealing it behind the cool precision of its slender Doric colonnades. Release from the darkness and richness of the cella was to the width and clarity of the valley shape and the equally clear and tangible shape of the sky. The standing columns still define the feeling. At Nemea Zeus is a god of peace and calm. His temple there expresses a reconciliation between men and nature through the wholeness of his power and thus asserts the propriety and reverence of human action within the natural order.

Zeus, as Polieus, was the protector of human action in the form of the city.[22] His temples, like those of Athena, were often placed upon the height of the acropolis hill, and the reason for this is obvious. Often, however, his temples in cities were placed on somewhat lower ground in order to carry out the same function of bringing earth and sky together that was central to his other sacred sites. This is the case in the wide valley landscape of Stratos, where his present temple is again late, 321 B.C., but where its effect is so characteristic as to warrant brief mention now. At Stratos the temple is on a low hill which projects forward into the valley to the west of the rather higher hills upon which most of the city is placed.[23] It is exactly on the city wall, which intersects its north and south flanks. Seen from the higher hills, the temple is an object which swings the arc of the mountains across the valley into focus. The wide flood plain of the Acheloos is brought into more graspable scale by this placement, and the sweeping landscape is given the fixed point of reference which makes it permanent and complete. Seen from the valley outside the city the temple has much the same effect. Its projecting hill is not so high in relation even to the farther mountains as to isolate the temple upon a height. Instead, it is like a promontory thrust forward into a wide bowl whose walls are higher than itself, so that it becomes once more the focal object in the center of a globe.

At Cyzicus, on an island almost touching the southern coast of the Propontis, the temple of Zeus was to the west of the city, apparently so that it could be under the most impressive formation of the mountain which, Strabo tells us, supported on its summit a shrine of Dindymene, Mother of the Gods.[24] From the temple the whole full sweep of earth, sea, and sky is formed in an arc from the mountain of Dindymene across the narrow strait which separated Cyzicus from the mainland to the hills of the mainland itself. A long ellipse of sky is formed by the mountains on both sides of the strait, and a perfectly conical promontory hill defines the view as the strait widens to the west toward the open Propontis. The landscape again is one deep bowl of completeness and quiet.

We have already discussed the need which the colonial Greeks in South Italy and Sicily seem to have felt to bring the strange landscape into scale through the placement of their temples and to people it thereby with their gods. The person of Zeus, where the landscape could be made to express his presence, was naturally of considerable importance in this program. At far Cumae,[25] where the temple of Apollo lay upon the flank of the acropolis, the temple of Zeus was placed upon its summit, where, as Polieus, the god not only protected the town and civilized the power of the earth deity in her cavern below but also faced toward the wide inland horns, mentioned earlier. (*Fig. 226*) These now open, as seen from the height, into a calm half circle, expressive again of the wholeness of Zeus' world. Westward from his templed height stretches a sea horizon, bounded by Ischia, where the earliest known Greek settlement in Italy had been made. His temple is thus placed, under the broad but horn–defined sky, so as to bring Italian land and Tyrrhenian water into a balanced Greek view.

At Syracuse the temple of Olympian Zeus had to control a much wider and less definitely bounded landscape. It was placed with great skill in order to accomplish exactly that. It lies well to the southwest of the town and outside it on the wide, low plain through which the Kyane River flows. (*Fig. 227*) Low hills rise behind it and begin a gently protecting but not very extended arc. The temple is backed against this arc and faces directly east across the plain toward the harbor. Its position is just high enough so that the shape of the harbor can be seen:

an oval defined by the horns of island and headland which almost close its mouth. The west end of the temple has a closed adyton in the early Sicilian manner, and the east end the equally characteristic "double front" like an extended porch.[26] It thus definitely "faces" the sea, and its colonnade carries the eye out of the bowl of the western hills toward the bowl in plan of the harbor. Once more, as at Dodona but now in a vast and uninflected landscape, the temple of Zeus occupies a central position around which swings the great circle of the world. From no other position near Syracuse could this effect have been accomplished so well, and the arcs of hill and harbor, since they are the only accents to be seen, are read as visible metaphors which describe the arc of the empty sea horizon toward which the temple's columned porch directs the view. The observer is made in this way to feel a tremendous expansion of sea and sky but one which never escapes into boundless continuity. The actual view is so formed that what might be called the psychic view again has a double experience: on the one hand, of the great blazing wheel of sky over vast and golden Sicily and its sea, and on the other, of the long axis along which the temple points, across the sea void toward Greece.

At Akragas, too, the temple of Olympian Zeus performs a function which has to do with the control of a vast landscape and its covering sky. We have already noted the great size of the partly enclosed bowl of earth which the site of Akragas forms. (*Fig. 103*) From the height of the acropolis on the north, a long ridge sweeps around in a curve to east and south and finally dwindles away into the plain. To the west is another line of hills, but these stand far enough outside the open, lower end of the bowl not to enclose it. The main gates to Akragas on the southwest and west occur low down on the ridge and in the open valley between ridge and acropolis. From either of these gates the eye travels directly to the acropolis across the low ground between, and in both cases the acropolis itself seems far away indeed. The eye may also travel up the southern ridge line, its journey now given rhythm and measure by the temples which are placed along its height. But beyond the last temple, where the ridge dips and then rises again as it begins to swing around toward the northern height upon which the temple of Demeter was located, the eye loses the scale of the enclosure and the definition of its distances. The actual shape which the ridge and the hills make becomes visually unclear because of this lack of definition, and the complementary shape of the sky is thus also confused. The problem is one of scale and distance in a large space, and it is basically the same when viewed from the acropolis itself. The problem now is partly to define the southern ridge—and this is done by the temples along it —but most of all to mark the termination of that ridge so that it will not simply dwindle away into the plain and the whole nearer bowl, which is the city, spill out beyond it toward the empty sea along the tilted plank of the coastal plain. It is this double problem which the temple of Olympian Zeus must have been intended to solve. Its huge bulk was placed exactly at the point where the southern ridge begins noticeably to dwindle away, and it would have been the first large object seen near at hand from either the southwest or western gates. (*Fig. 103*) The present motor road penetrates the wall of the city at the point where the southwestern gate was placed, and this must always have been the main route into the city by road from the sea. As one approached it, the upper portion of the great temple would have been in view for some time against the acropolis hill far to the north. Just inside the gate itself, the whole mass of the temple would have loomed up on the left. Its scale would have been so large as to seem to balance the bulk of the acropolis in the distance and to dwarf the valley interval between them, thereby appearing to bring the acropolis hill closer to hand. A study of the plan of Akragas would also indicate that this effect was exactly intended, since a line of vision drawn from just within the gate along the corner of the temple will be seen to continue precisely to the edge of the acropolis height. A similar effect of reduced scale and distance can be observed if one looks from the temple along the arc of the southern ridge. The latter would have been snapped into space from the mass of the temple, which would have defined its beginning and from which the eye would have sought out the complementary mass to the northeast which terminates the movement: the height, that is, upon which the temple of Demeter was placed. With that height the temple of Zeus was also connected by the cross streets of the town's grid, and it was the only one of the temples along the ridge to be integrated into that system.[26a]

In the opposite view, from the acropolis toward the sea, the temple would have terminated the ridge and prevented it from seeming to die away. It would at the same time have been large enough to be seen itself as a focal object between the acropolis and the sea. Two areas, the cup of the city and the slope of the plain, would have been clearly differentiated but set side by side within the greater arc of landscape which the temple would have drawn into perceptible scale. Zeus once more is placed so as to express the essential wholeness of the world and his engrossing dominion over it.

In all these critical views, the unusual form and details of the temple would have been of considerable importance.[27] (*Fig. 262*) Its size, first of all, was essential. It had to be very large indeed in order to function as it did, especially as seen from the acropolis height. The distance is so great that the other temples along the ridges seem very small, as can still be tested today. From the critical entrance view toward the acropolis, sheer bulk, though helpful, would not have been indispensable, since the temple was seen close at hand. But the huge Atlantean figures which appeared between the columns would certainly have added to the particular effect desired here. The use of these unique figures would seem to have been occasioned first by the temple's size itself. The critical point was the width of the intercolumniations, since, as mentioned before, the parts of the Doric temple were adjusted to each other according to such an abstractly integrated proportional system that they could theoretically attain any size without slipping over into environmental rather than sculptural scale and thus crushing the human observer—any size up to the point where the intercolumniations became so wide as to require an intermediate support for their spanning lintel. Here the lintel had to span between columns whose centers were more than twenty-six feet apart, and it was made, like the columns themselves, of separate blocks of masonry. It therefore required not only iron reinforcing bars but also some intermediate support. The architect could hardly have inserted a continuous vertical element between the columns, rising the whole height between stylobate and entablature, since this would not only have destroyed the whole rhythm of the temple but would also have emphasized the actual size of the main columns and confused their proportional relationships to each other and to the intervals between them. They thus would have been given positive scale by contrast and become in visual fact gross and overwhelming. Whatever support was used, therefore, had itself to be supported upon a cross wall between the columns, which then became engaged in the wall. Not only were the columns made part of the wall but they were

143

also backed by pilasters, so that the whole body of exterior column and interior pilaster was thicker than the wall itself as, therefore, was the entablature. One can imagine the architect as he attempted to determine the nature of the intermediate support for the projecting architrave. It could hardly have been a dwarf column or pier, since either would have involved an impossible relationship between its capital and those of the giant Doric order. The Atlantean figures may have been the only solution, since the bulk and meaning of the temple as a whole would have made Ionic caryatids absurd. The *telamones* are certainly figures of giants, and their faces are those of barbarians. Their use may have been suggested by the victory over the Carthaginians at the Himera, and in style they clearly date after 480 B.C. Most scholars have dated the temple by them, although Dinsmoor suggests the date of c. 510 for its beginning.[28] It is possible that the victory itself and the gangs of dejected Carthaginian prisoners who were then put to work upon the temple may have suggested the final form of the intermediate supports to the architects. Certainly the telamones bring a brutality to the temple which is entirely uncharacteristic of Greek architecture anywhere else. Their introduction into a Doric temple also tends to destroy its abstraction and so limits its intrinsic force, contracting its capacity to suggest both a general civilized order and the specific body of a god through the sculptural manipulation of its own integrally architectural members. Yet the very bludgeoning of the senses which the size of the giant–barbarians would have caused as they were seen just inside the entrance gate would have further reduced the apparent size of Akragas and played its part in forcing the distant acropolis into a comprehensible relationship with the gate. (*Fig. 261*) The whole problem itself, and the means taken to solve it, seem most expressive of the larger dilemma faced by the Greeks in Sicily. It is perhaps a dilemma faced by rich colonial peoples everywhere: how to bring a new and vaster landscape into civilized order without perverting the values upon which that order was based; how to conquer barbarism without becoming barbarized oneself; how, perhaps most of all, to make use of vaster sums of money than had ever been available at home without expressing the power of the money rather than the power of the god.

In the colonies as in Greece, nonetheless, the sites sacred to Zeus were chosen for their capacity to express the wholeness and oneness of the physical and spiritual universe. The Greek view of the nature of that universe and of the human place in it developed rapidly throughout the later archaic period. The Greek mind seems always to have insisted upon a kind of symmetry in the world. During the archaic period that symmetry had been conceived in terms of oppositions: between the old gods and the new, between men and the natural powers. Therefore, the characteristic god of those centuries was, in one sense, Apollo, who, his sites as well as his myths tell us, brought symmetry about by opposing his order, light, and discipline to the dark and shifting forces which raged against him from below. Beyond this, fate governed all. By the early fifth century, however, a deeper and more integral balance was imagined, in which the old and the new, men and nature, were to be interrelated in a harmony. The new order; though men were still fated in it, was nevertheless increasingly to depend for its structure upon human understanding of those interrelationships and upon the difficult choices and moral judgements made by men themselves in accord with that understanding. In this new early classic world the essential god was Zeus, whose law governed nature and man alike, and who alone could "lead men to think," as Aeschylus tells us, and who could thereby bring them to that "knowledge" of the wholeness of things upon which the wisdom of their choices would depend. The great conflicts would now take place, not between men and external things, but within men themselves as they sought perhaps at first to avoid their fate of knowing, and then finally struggled upward toward the knowledge which could alone reveal their part in the whole of things. That part now involved a responsibility. Man could best affect the whole by bringing into it a reasonable and moral comprehension to offset the more blindly implacable facts of things as they are. Thus he could change their total character. That is to say, he could change Zeus. This was the central position of man in Aeschylean tragedy, and it is that human perception of the new harmony of things—a harmony which the old Zeus himself, so Aeschylus indicates, had to be taught to perceive—which is preserved in landscape and in stone at classic Olympia.

We recall the ancient holiness of Olympia as a site.[29] The hairpin megara of pre–Mycenaean times had huddled close beneath the southern flank of the conical hill of Kronos, the old king's tholos tomb, named by Herakles (Pindar, Ol. 10). (*Figs. 263–265*) In the eighth century a temple of Zeus was built beside the hill, as we have seen, and by the late seventh century its several rebuildings had culminated in the present Doric temple. (*Figs. 82, 84*) In myth, Herakles had instituted the Olympic games, from whose historical foundation in the eighth century Hellenic chronology came to be reckoned, and these formed the most important ceremony which brought the Greek world together in truce every four years. The shrine of Pelops, the legendary hero of the land, stood just south of the temple of Zeus. (*Fig. 264*) In his killing of the murderous old king, Oenomaus, and his wedding of Oenomaus' daughter, Hippodameia, Pelops was conceived of as having brought Hellenic order to the Peloponnesos, which took his name. During the sixth century a lively row of treasuries was built along an angled terrace under the hill of Kronos. These overlooked the precinct of the Altis with all the active pressure and alertness of an expectant crowd. Somewhere near the Pelopion and the temple of Zeus, so Pausanias tells us, (though by his time that temple was called Hera's) stood the open altar of Zeus, a great cone of ash whose form echoed that of the conical hill of Kronos itself.[30] Between 465 and 460 the great temple of Zeus was built to the south of the Pelopion. Whether or not it replaced an old shrine of Zeus at that point is impossible to say, but since no remains of an earlier temple have been found, and because what was now to become Hera's temple had originally been his, it may not have done so. The space of its cella was almost filled by the majestic, chryselephantine Zeus of Phidias. Whether the statue was placed in the temple around 460 or thirty years later is a point about which there has also been considerable discussion.[31] The Altis was surrounded by a wall, enclosing the buildings already mentioned and the Prytaneion as well. This was the sacred communal hearth of Hestia, beautifully set back at a retiring angle behind the temple of Zeus, which now, with the building of the new temple, received an altar of Hera before it.[32]

During the classic period the stadium, as Kunze has shown,[33] lay in a long east–west axis at a dynamic angle within the sanctuary itself, overlooked by the treasuries and thus an integral part of the sacred enclosure. (*Fig. 265*) With the increased professionalism of the games in the fourth century, however, the stadium was pushed completely out of the sanctuary to its present position, and the long stoa called the "Echo Colonnade" was built as the western boundary of the temenos. (*Figs. 264, 266*) Other buildings were added later: in the fourth century the tholos of the Philippeion, a memorial to the family of Philip of Macedon, and in the fourth or third century the Metroon, a temple of the mother of the gods which was later reconsecrated to the family of Augustus. In the first century A.D., Nero built a triumphal arch near the south-eastern entrance to the Altis and rebuilt the house of the Hellanodikai, the directors of the games, which stood nearby. In the second century A.D. Herodes Atticus built a large exedra near the temple of Hera. Aside from the damaging exclusion of the stadium and its separation from the site by the Echo Colonnade, all of the other post–fifth–century buildings mentioned, with the exception of the last, can be shown to have consciously respected the classic organization of the Altis. Herodes Atticus may have thought he was doing so as well, but his huge exedra must in fact have injured the site considerably. Other buildings, most of them late in date, and comprising gymnasia, guest houses, and so on, lay outside the Altis, as the shrine of Hippodameia may also have done, although some scholars would like to fill the open space in front of the Echo Stoa with it.[34] Such placement of the Hippodameion now seems unlikely, in view of the fact that this rather dead area in the space of the Altis did not exist until after the exclusion of the stadium. South of the Altis wall lay the group of buildings which made up the Bouleuterion. The two most important units of this, while most likely continuing traditions of the Geometric period, also seem almost to have been intended as references to the Middle Bronze Age forms which underlay the site. They were two apsidal megara, the northern one dating from the sixth century, the other, subtly pointed at its apse and swelling on its flanks, from the fifth. South of the Bouleuterion was another stoa which looked out across the valley of the Alpheios toward the great complex of buildings, including the hippodrome, which occupied that area during antiquity.

For an experience of the classic site we should look first at the landscape setting as a whole. From the hill to the west the long, gentle valley of the Alpheios River can be seen opening along an east–west axis. (*Fig. 263*) The conical hill of Kronos rises on its northern side just east of the point where the smaller valley of the Kladeos River intersects the Alpheios plain. This is the "Alpheios crossing" which Pindar mentions,[35] and the sacred hill occupies the critical point near the intersection. To east and west of this pivotal cone are broad open spaces along the edge of the main valley, and these are cupped by other low ridges which advance into the plain. The site thus opens left and right of Kronos' hill, and, in the eastern enclosure so formed, the stadium was placed, while the major subsidiary buildings outside the Altis were placed along the edge of the western one. The whole site is thus one of absolute order and calm. There is nothing dramatic or startling. It is wide–spreading but completely protected, warm and heavy with cicada song in summer, gentle and edged with wheat and flowers during the winter months. The Altis itself was always deep in trees, planted, so Pindar tells us, by Herakles, in order to protect its "garden, naked of these, from the sun's sharp rays."[36] Upon approaching the site, either through the valley of the Alpheios or that of the Kladeos, the traveler sees first the conical hill of Kronos. (*Fig. 263*) The sacred position is fixed at once by a solid object, and it is only as one comes closer that the volumes of space which are created on both sides of the cone become apparent. Entrance to the sacred enclosure itself is through one of three gates, placed near the northwest, southwest, and southeast corners. Lines drawn across the plan of the site can show a precise relationship between each of these entrances and the major monuments within the precinct.[37] A line between the northwest and southeast entrances will pass through the Pelopion and exactly touch the southwest corner of the temple of Hera and the northeast corner of the temple of Zeus. (*Figs. 264, 265*) The tall pedestal which supported the Nike by Paionios stood upon this line in front of the temple of Zeus. Similarly, a diagonal line from the southwest entrance will intersect the first line at the Pelopion and will touch the northwest corner of the temple of Zeus and the southeast corner of the temple of Hera. It will also continue on directly toward the hill of Kronos, and will fall within the arc of the later exedra of Herodes Atticus. One will note that the later Metroon and Philippeion are kept well away from these lines, (*Figs. 264, 266*) but a further point should be made. A line drawn from the point of intersection of the two main lines in the Pelopion to the southeastern corner of the easternmost treasury—the treasury of Gela, which stands in that view just above the exit from the Altis to the later stadium—will be found to fall precisely upon the southeast corner of the Metroon. One can only conclude that this late and intrusive temple was nevertheless discreetly located with that critical line of sight from the Pelopion in mind. The Pelopion, shrine of the human hero between the temples of the major deities, would thus clearly seem to be the center of the site. And Pindar says of Pelops in his first Olympian ode: "His tomb is thronged about at the altar where many strangers pass. . . ."[38]

It seems reasonable, therefore, to move toward that central point. Three routes are open. The first two are quite direct. From the northwest one passes the beautifully set back hearth of Hestia, heads toward the Pelopion and swings around toward that sanctuary's own propylon on the southwest. All this time one has been very close to the long, low temple of Hera at its opisthodomos end, but has not seen it fully against the hill of Kronos until arriving within the Pelopion itself. The temple of Zeus has been some distance away as a great mass against the sky. The second route is a fuller experience, and it is the Way that Pausanias seems to have used.[39] Entering from the southwest, one has a view directly toward Kronos' hill. (*Fig. 267*) The bulk of the temple of Zeus is close at hand, and the farther hill slope, as Doxiadis has shown, seems to fall just at the line where its entablature was.[40] Ahead, the temple of Hera lies low beneath the hill, and the observer moves directly toward the ramped entrance to the Pelopion with this relationship of Kronos and Hera constantly in view. (*Fig. 268*) The disastrous character of the exedra of Atticus now becomes apparent. It is important that the view should run unimpeded past the edges of the buildings to the natural hill. The exedra, however, much higher than the temple of Hera, cups the view and traps it in a volume of space, thus in a sense removing the Kronion, visible though it of course still is, from direct participation in the architectural organization of the temenos. (*Figs. 264, 266*) It was the Roman method, as fully developed during the early imperial period, to conclude an axis within a protecting and engulfing building shell. This is the opposite of the archaic and classic Greek way, as we have seen, except that certain tendencies in that direction were to be observed in the architecture of the mystery cults. (*Figs. 131, 418, 419*)

Two routes have led us to the Pelopion. There can probably be little doubt that the second one, just described, would have been, for a visitor in antiquity who knew the monuments of the site as a whole, the simplest and best route to the Pelopion, the center of the place. Its ramped entrance lay before him, only slightly to the left of the axis toward the hill. With the relationship of the temples to each other and to the hills clearly in his view, he could have walked almost in a straight line, himself like the Dorian hero, under the shadow of his Zeus toward the goddess and the sacred hill. In this route to the central spot the old labyrinthine way would have largely disappeared in favor of simple and direct action. It is true that a curving detour was necessary in order to enter the Pelopion, and to see the Temple of Hera for a moment as sliding under the hill, but the line of sight which directed the action was straight as an arrow or a line of march, at the end of which, significantly enough, the high and huge Roman exedra was later placed. Equally significant is the fact that, before the fifth-century temple of Zeus was built, Pelop's shrine lay outside the temple of the god and the sacred cone, separate from them. Thus it was the classic Zeus who finally enclosed the hero in the center of the site.

With this in mind, it would still be preferable for us here to follow a more labyrinthine route into the sanctuary in order to grasp for ourselves the full meaning of the experience of the site as a whole, as it can finally be gained from the Pelopion. The southeast entrance was certainly of great importance in antiquity, and Nero built his arch outside it. It, too, would normally have been entered directly from the south, serving in this way not only the vast complex of buildings in the valley but also the Bouleuterion as well. Yet one can imagine a processional route beginning at the northwest of the site and following the wall of the Altis toward the south. Directly ahead across the valley is a gentle cone in the farther ridge, soft and hazy in the sun. It forms an uninsistent focus for movement toward the south. From this route the western pediment of the temple of Zeus rose high up above the Altis wall. Upon it the tangled forms of men and beast—men in strife were calmed by the figure, at once kingly and godlike, of Apollo or Peirithous who appears between them and holds out his arm. (*Fig. 269*) Facing west out of the Altis, the forms of centaurs and lapiths were an expression of the wildness and indiscipline of the natural world before it receives the law. The pediment is in every way like Aeschylean drama. Chorus and protagonist are opposed, individual and group, old law and new. The combatants writhe like the Furies in the *Eumenides* who danced their dark hate around Apollo at Delphi, and the central figure here is much as Apollo must have been there, commanding but still isolated and splendid as a sculptural ʼαγάλμα among them. The pediment also expresses the nature of the sacred truce itself, which enabled the participants in the games to travel to Olympia. The centaurs, outside the law and without self–control, had broken the truce of hospitality at the wedding feast of Peirithous. In this they do violence to nature itself, as they seek to drag away the maidens, whose peploi fall in folds like bark and who are treated as trees in the act of being uprooted and felled. The crime is rape, always one of the first and most horrible manifestations of the breakdown of law and a unique act of double murder, since it seeks to degrade both those who suffer it and those to whom they have given themselves. "But as for me may I be dead," says Hector to Andromache, "and may the earth have covered me / Before I hear you cry out or see you dragged away."[41] Thus the meaning of the pediment, clearly embodied in its form, is of the horrors of uncivilized indiscipline and of that naked force which reigned before the coming of divine kingship and Zeus' law.

With this meaning fully in mind, the participants in the procession would have turned left along the Altis wall with the body of the temple rising above it and the columns marking a disciplined beat of movement toward the east. From the southeastern entrance the cone of the hill of Kronos looms exactly ahead. The way moves at first toward it. We said earlier that a line drawn in plan from the northwestern entrance would fall exactly here, and this is true, but it is also true that the line of actual sight in that direction would at first have been blocked from the southeastern entrance by the large votive monuments which were placed inside it. The worshiper would not have seen the whole at once, but would have had first things first: the conical hill which was the old goddess or Kronos the father. Then, as he moved forward, the brightly stuccoed bulk of the temple of Zeus, standing as it did close by, would have risen higher up as a balancing element to the natural object. Zeus, well out in space away from the hill of his father, opposed his presence to the old way and stood above the route to the stadium where the sacred contests, the *agonai*, were carried on in his name. High in the air, Victory lifted her wreath before him. His temple was large and solemn, precise and avoiding active elements, having no upward curvatures or perceptible entasis. Its bulk was apparently rather inert and heavy: immovable, as it must have been intended to seem in this entrance view. As the worshiper came opposite its eastern ramp and looked up it into the cella, it would have become apparent, on the lucky mornings when the doors were open, that the temple was indeed almost solid mass, since its interior was barely large enough to hold the tremendous image of Zeus which was placed inside it.

Gleaming dully of ivory and gold in the light reflected from the oil–covered black marble floor before it, and with its majestic head high up in the shadows near the roof, this seated Zeus by Phidias must for a time have blotted out all other perceptions. The presence of Zeus diminishes the presence of the chthonic Kronos and the older powers. At this time, too, the temple of Hera can be seen in relation to the hill of Kronos and the temple of Zeus. We said earlier that it was possible that the temple of Hera, though essentially a spatial pavilion, may have taken on a kind of image quality once the classic temple of Zeus was set in contrast with it. This now seems to be the case. In contrast to the high, broad, compact, sculpturally dense form of the temple of Zeus, that of Hera is now seen as purposefully long, low, open, ground–hugging. (*Figs. 270, 83, 84*) At the same time, its close relation to the hill of Kronos now begins to take on special meaning. It seems to hug the hill and to seek its presence, like the goddess holding on to the old way of the earth or the daughter holding close to the father. In contrast to this, Zeus seizes his own space under the sky. His temple stands solidly well away from the hill and out in the void: the new god of the heavens, or the god of human conception, or the son who must challenge the father. Opposites are thus set up, opposites as yet unreconciled and seeming to demand choice between them.

In the east pediment of the temple of Zeus, directly above the worshiper at this time and overlooking the stadium in the classic arrangement, another moment of choice was presented. (*Fig. 271*) It is the taking of the oath by Pelops and Oenomaus before their fatal chariot race. Zeus stands between them but remote from them as a cult image, an 'αγάλμα Διòs, Pausanias was to say. Like the body of his temple as a whole, he does not act, does not warn or admonish. Does he listen, judge, learn? Is he simply there, indifferent to human fate; or, potentially dangerous, is he being changed by what men do around him? Perhaps this last was intended, making the passive figure of Zeus, so unlike the active Apollo on the west, central, as it should be, to the fundamental meaning of the pediment as a whole. To left and right of his person are displayed all the elements of ferocious Dorian myth, now seen in human and complicated terms. Oenomaus stands proudly with his hand on his hip, his whole body expressing assurance, ownership, the mature man, cruel, who has everything he desires and will keep it by force if he can. On the other side of Zeus, Pelops stands with restless awkwardness, hungry and young, his head twisted over and down, his hip-shot torso bony. The women are misplaced in the museum at Olympia. Sterope should stand subdued with folded arms next to her husband Oenomaus, whose life is in danger once more. Hippodameia lifts her mantle proudly as she prepares to ride off with Pelops. After all, they are fighting over her; she is the prize. Those who cruelly have and those who will as cruelly take are set side by side here in the absolute stillness of their most revealing attitudes. Similarly, it was known to all who viewed these figures in antiquity that Pelops had already invalidated his oath by bribing Oenomaus' driver to tamper with his master's chariot, so that in the race Oenomaus was in fact thrown and dragged to death. The viewers know this, but some of the major actors on the pediment do not. Zeus knows, and the old man, the seerlike Teiresias, apparently has a sudden vision of the truth, as with a realism hitherto unknown in Greek art he raises his hand to his cheek in horror and his wrinkled torso quivers with his gasp. As in a contemporary drama, the major actors are thus exposed to the judgment of an audience which knows more about them than they yet know about themselves. A feeling of the total exposure of the human self and of its unique, perilous capacities is almost unbearably present. From the narrow angles of the pediment, nature, in the person of the river god, watches the exposed ranks of men with cold, unwinking eyes. It neither judges nor forgives, having no code nor pity. But the human viewer must judge, and a whole range of choice lies open to him. He may, like Pindar, ignore the profanation of the oath. "Breaking the strength of Oenomaus, he took the maiden and brought her to bed," is all that Pindar says of the contest.[42] But the participant in the games, standing in the presence of Zeus, has in him the knowledge of his own oath which must be taken, his oath of sportsmanship and fair play. He must choose his way of action, and how he chooses may detonate Zeus, or change him, change the nature of things as they will be.[43]

With this crowd of images and values fixed in his mind, and with the diagonal length of the stadium beckoning to action on his right, the worshiper would then normally have continued on his way toward Zeus' altar and to the Pelopion, the center of the site. (*Figs. 270, 268*) He can no longer do so as a simple, conquering hero, approaching the goddess in isolated pride. The awesome presence of Zeus now looms behind him as he turns through the propylon of the hero's shrine with the low temple of Hera and "the lifting hill of Kronos" focused before his eyes. As he reaches the point where all phantom lines meet in the Pelopion's enclosure he will without doubt look eastward, past the massive cone of the altar of Zeus and across the open ground before him toward the stadium, from which, perhaps shortly, the roar of the crowd will rise. From this point he also sees the treasuries, symbols of all Hellas, standing like witnesses upon their terrace. (*Fig. 265*) They generally follow its line, but where its angle turns sharply in one direction the two adjacent treasuries turn slightly in the other. Because of this, and because of the other slight variations in their placement, the individual buildings are not static parts of their terrace platform nor simply space definers of the site, but instead, as always, engaged participants in the ceremonies and actions which take place below. Around the worshiper, too, the site was peopled with hundreds of statues, a great crowd in the space, but all of them, precisely because of their varied sizes and scales and their scattered, not overly regularized placement, remaining active participants who were subordinate to the great forms of the temples, the stadium, and the hill. It comes to the modern observer in the Pelopion, as his eye swings in its one–hundred–and–eighty–degree arc of vision, that he, the individual, has for the first time in Greek site planning been placed at the center of the whole. He is in fact stand-ing in a central position in the space of a calm and ample room. It is a room which is defined on the flat and stable surface of the Altis under the hill by the temple of Hera on the north and the temple of Zeus on the south. (*Fig. 273*) No camera can photograph these two at once from the central position in the Altis. But the eye, while it cannot focus upon them both, can perceive them looming left and right at the very corners of its arc of vision. The long flank of Hera's temple is closer but lower; the bulky columns of Zeus are larger but farther away. Thus a balance is set up between those embodiments of Zeus and Hera which had been per-ceived before as opposites. The hill of Kronos and the temple of Zeus now also balance each other. (*Fig. 272*) A deep, calm relationship can be felt as the eye swings on its arc and tests shapes against each other. It is a visual relationship which may be felt to express profound meanings through the interplay of forms: of the mature reconciliation between the rebellious son and the necessarily overthrown father; between the new god and the goddess whom he had equally overthrown; between the brother Zeus and the sister Hera, husband and wife, whose life together had been, in myth since Homer, a continual and bitter strife. In the calm of the relationship may be felt, therefore, that reconciliation between men and nature, men and women, and between the old gods and the new, which was explored in contemporary Attic tragedy, as, for example, in the *Oresteia* of Aeschylus.

The reconciliation, however, is richer and more active at Olympia than has yet been described. The important point here is the fact that the temples of Hera and Zeus, oriented toward the dawn of their feast days, are not quite parallel to each other. They do, in fact, define a kind of room around the observer placed near the center, and his eye, perceiving this fact from the Pelopion, tries very hard to see what the human mind behind it will always demand: namely, that such definition is clear, obvious, and unthreatened. The mind says that the temples are in fact parallel, as they almost are, but the eye perceives that the temples are not quite parallel and that they are in fact active forces pressing in upon the space between them toward the east. Their relation to each other is thus positive. They are not simply negative space definers either, but presences capable of action. Yet their action does not stop there, since the eye, under the prodding of the mind, is constantly attempting to swing their western ends in toward each other, in order to compensate for the pressure which is being exerted by their eastern ends upon the precious volume of space between them. Visually, therefore, the colonnades of massive Zeus and open Hera loomed and receded in a gentle counter movement, as their bases seemed to swing in and away from each other. (*Figs. 272, 273*) They exerted an attraction upon each other across the intervening space, like the recognition of a contact once made, always re-newable. One is reminded of that moment in the *Iliad* when Hera, the old, familiar wife, stood before her husband transformed. It was the *Hieros Gamos*, the Sacred Marriage, with which came peace and the blooming of the land.[44] It seems, in the deep movement which both creates and breathes life into the calm of Olympia, that the Sacred Marriage is above all else the rite which the classic age imagined there, architecturally embodied. It reconciles all forces in Olympia's gentle light and brings the hero of the Pelopion not into conflict with the powers but to their center, to a space alive, because the masses defining it are so.

The elemental strifes of gods and men, no less than those of being and of void, are stilled; divine kingship in Zeus becomes a partnership of the whole. The law for god and man alike is knowledge and understanding of the ultimate reciprocities. These together bring reconciliation, *Hesychia*, "kind goddess of peace, daughter / of justice . . ."[45]

The full space of the outdoor room between Hera and Zeus then slides eastward with the stadium which expresses, both in its form and placement, the proof of thought by action. Its world of competition is not yet divorced from the contemplation and sanctity of the rest of the site, so that a man could have competed in it with all his force, but in peace and with justice. Therefore the metopes across the top of the pronaos and the opisthodomos of the temple of Zeus, which give its mass depth, clearly answer the awful questions its pediments ask. In them, Herakles, once the violent Dorian slayer, cleans up and civilizes the world through a force as much moral as physical. (*Fig. 274*) He now seems to choose his enforced labors for what they mean; noble, obsessed, and simple, he does his work for Zeus' right. In this his face acquires a radiance which prefigures that of the Christian saints and is calmer than theirs, while the Athena who seconds him has the look of a loving girl.

The mighty oneness which the classic Zeus now was had as an integral part of his nature the concept of limit, of justice. The liberation of the human mind which he himself had guided ("Zeus, who taught men how to think") was paradoxically balanced—as, for example, existentialist liberation and personal acceptance of responsibility is today not normally so balanced—by a sense of active law and of a positive measure of rightness to the whole whereby action itself could be tested.[46] It was against this dimension, this limit, that the whole power of the liberated intellect had to be judged. It might even be said that a fascination with the idea of reasonable limit was one of the factors which most stirred the classic intellect to thought. This is so, I think, in classic tragedy, and it is equally so at the temples of Nemesis and Themis at Rhamnous.[47] These goddesses are not Zeus but they were beyond all others closest to him. The whole development of the experience which the site of Rhamnous suggested is itself a measure of the development of the Greek mind in its search for the whole truth. The original sanctuary at Rhamnous was clearly of some goddess of the earth whose position was later preempted by Nemesis and Themis as powers of Zeus. Its temple was associated with the coastal town of Rhamnous in northern Attica and was meant to be experienced primarily from that place. The town itself occupies a bluff which projects into the sea and is separated from the closely surrounding hills by two precipitous gorges. Looking up from the town, one sees the higher hills as rising in deep folds around a gorge to the arc or horns of their summits. In the arc so formed the temple was placed, and it would have been seen standing out above the town between the protecting summits of the hills. During the Periclean period a great new platform was built across the saddle, and a new peripteral Doric temple of Nemesis was placed upon it. According to Pausanias' account, this temple was connected not primarily with the goddess cult of the town but with the battle which had taken place on the plain of Marathon, well to the south on the eastern coast of Attica.[48] Next to the Periclean temple of Nemesis is a smaller temple, in antis, of Themis. (*Fig. 275*) It is not entirely certain whether the smaller temple is earlier or later in date, but present opinion, based upon its style of masonry and the relation of its foundations to those of the larger temple, tends toward the latter conclusion.[49]

Tradition had it that the statue of Nemesis which stood in the Periclean temple was carved by Phidias from a block of marble which had been brought ashore by the Persians as the raw material for a trophy they had expected to set up after their victory.[50] From this point of view, the temple was intended as a comment upon human *hybris*, and upon the limits which the law of things as they are sets to human pride. In another sense, the Athenian desire to build a new temple for Nemesis at the period of their greatest successes may be conceived of as an apotropaic gesture. Work on it seems to have ceased with the beginning of the Peloponnesian War. It may, therefore, not be entirely incorrect to envision the land journey to Rhamnous as beginning most appropriately at the tumulus which covers the dead on the Marathon plain. From there the way leads north along the plain and mounts the low hills which border it. From these a view is offered backward across the whole sweep: the arc of the bay, the swamps in which the Persians foundered. The way winds among the hills, and the plain of Marathon drops out of sight behind. At the height of the pass a view opens to the north across a long upland valley with the arc of the hills between which the temples are placed clear against the distant horizon. At this distance the larger temple, of luminous Pentelic marble, would, I think, have been just visible above and beyond the bulk of the smaller. But from the valley floor a long mound rises up to block the arc of the saddle from view. The sacred place is thus seen at a distance and lost again, and the way across the flat valley within the circle of the hills is hard. It is hot and unshaded in summer, cold and windswept in winter. Its surface is boggy and difficult to walk upon. After a time the intervening ridge is passed, and the arc of the temple's setting comes into view again, now much closer than before. The sanctuary itself is exactly on the saddle, (*Fig. 276*) and the view from it opens up to include the town of Rhamnous itself far below, the waters of the gulf, and the mountains of Euboea. (*Fig. 279, 280*) Yet there is no impulse to walk down into that view, since the high platform of the temples and the main temple itself so clearly express a limit, an end to movement. This occurs because their axis cuts decisively across the axis of the view. They mark a central place and a barrier. From the platform of the temples the whole bowl of valley to the south (*Fig. 278*) is balanced on the other side by the far sea view, bounded by Euboea. The site is a tightrope stretched between two voids. Its temples are set between two halves of the world upon a platform which seems fixed forever. There is nowhere to go from it, since any movement would mark a fall from clarity and completeness. This spot marks the end, the limit, and the whole.

The placement of the temples in relation to each other upon the platform enhances this effect. (*Figs. 275–280*) Each has a strong individuality because of its contrast with the other, the temple of Nemesis of gleaming white marble, with a pteron of unfluted (never finished) Doric columns, the temple of Themis of grey cyclopean masonry with columns only in antis. The larger temple, that of Nemesis, almost exactly parallels the northern wall of the temenos platform and thus reinforces the former's quality of marking a boundary. The small temple, which probably dates after the Periclean temple, is so placed at an angle to the latter that it seems to turn toward it and, so turning, to be arrested by the other's flank. This blocked movement further emphasizes the quality of barrier which the larger temple and the platform suggest. Similarly, the smaller temple, though supposedly rough and rugged, actually has a very strong rise to its base, especially on its entrance side. The larger temple, while ostensibly more elegant, has no stylobate curve whatever. It is absolutely flat and therefore does not rise or move but draws instead the sharp line of a rigid boundary. It, too, is stretched tight across the saddle between the hills to east and west, and its immovability further dramatizes the impassability of that barrier as it is seen against the smaller temple's lively, upward–curving movement toward it.[51] The immovability of the temple of Nemesis would also have been emphasized by its unfluted columns, which would have given it a solemn, somber weight. Here again, as at Thorikos, Eleusis, and Segesta, one wonders whether an unfinished condition might not have been allowed to remain because it enhanced a specific and appropriate effect.[52]

The placement of the two structures at Rhamnous is clearly calculated to create the effect of an association between two beings that has been frozen into the permanence of timeless immobility. Three further relationships also reveal this fact. First, a line drawn from the northeastern corner of the platform will fall exactiy upon the northeast column of the larger temple's colonnade, upon the southeast anta of its pronaos wall, and upon the southeast corner of the temple of Themis. (*Figs. 275, 280*) Platform, Nemesis, and Themis are thus securely locked together in a tight geometry. Secondly, when standing east of the two temples and looking west between them, one notices that a conical mountain in the distance is exactly on this axis of view. (*Fig. 276*) The cross–axis of the platform and the saddle is thus reinforced by a distant landscape form, and the two temples are so placed as to make the most of that space–freezing and significant object together. Thirdly, from the altar for the two temples, which is placed only in front of the temple of Nemesis, a line of sight falls along the edge of the larger temple's stereobate, between the pronaos columns of the smaller temple and through its door into the southwest corner of its naos. (*Fig. 275*) It was exactly in that unusual place, the corner, that the statue of Themis, now in the National Museum in Athens, had its base and was found. If it had been placed in the center of the cella the common altar would not have been visible to it. One recalls the rather similar diagonal axes used at Aulis and Loutsa. (*Fig. 147*)

The visual facts show, therefore, that the temple of Nemesis, who inevitably punished transgressions of the laws of limit, and the temple of Themis, who was Zeus' justice, are placed together in the exact positions they occupy with purpose and for a meaning. Nemesis and Justice are locked together, since Nemesis is not a horror but a fact: the fact of the wholeness of Zeus and of the balanced measure which is his law. All is visible only from the place where these two forces take their stand. The old landscape of the goddess is infused with human mind, and the symmetry of a classic Zeus falls over land and sea, exactly as, at Olympia, his dominion had led the Greeks, almost without willing it, to shape space itself as a living and palpable thing.

Chapter 9

POSEIDON AND ATHENA

These are the riders of Athens, conquered never;
They honor her whose glory all men know,
And honor the god of the sea, who loves forever
The feminine earth that bore him long ago.

Sophocles, OEDIPUS AT COLONUS (Fitzgerald)[1]

WHEN THE WOMEN of Athenian Colonus praise Poseidon and Athena they invoke them together as deities who will support positive human action. Poseidon, as god of the sea and of horses, was the patron of sailors and horsemen. Athena, as Polias, was protector of the city–state named for her, while as an earth goddess she had endowed Greece, and especially Attica, with the olive tree. Even this is seen as forceful:

> The olive, fertile and self–sown,
> The terror of our enemies
> That no hand tames or tears away—[1a]

Athena was also traditionally associated with horses, and it was her terrible horse, symbol of the Indo–European riders, which breached the walls of Troy. She thus combined the most active qualities of the old goddess and of the young male gods who had partly superseded her, as she embodied the polis, that special Greek setting for the encouragement of competitive activity. Poseidon, like Athena, is associated by the chorus specifically with the destiny of Athens. It hails him for having first bestowed the art of horsemanship, "of the curb and bit," upon the men of Colonus, and he is named "the lover of our land."[2] In the natures of Athena and Poseidon as imagined by Sophocles there are thus two fundamental divergences from, for example, the natures of Zeus or Apollo. Zeus, first, was not primarily a god of actions but of the general state of things and of its law. Secondly, he was Panhellenios and could be claimed with justice by no Greek state over another as special patron. Apollo, similarly, was the whole Greek conquest of the old order and of barbarism, and his way, moreover, was one of discipline and order. This is not to say that knowledge and discipline were unimportant in the developed characters of Athena and Poseidon. Athena, as the daughter of Zeus alone, was indeed the embodiment of wisdom, and the conquest of horses and of the sea was attained through the disci-

155

pline of curb and bit and through the measure of the "long sea—oars in wondrous rhyme."[3] But Athena, as Polias, was the special protector, through thick and thin, of whatever city–state wished to invoke her as it pursued its own indefatigably Greek quest for advantage over others. As, with trickery and deceit and countenancing their use, she had stood behind Achilles, Odysseus, and Herakles, so she would stand by her city, right or wrong. She could in this way be a goddess of positive aggressive action and might best be invoked in this guise by the special city which bore her name. She could thus be a spur to the breaking of boundaries and limits, although her wisdom might be counted upon to direct such daring into projects dictated by intelligence. Similarly, Poseidon, ancient god of nature's violence that he was, still offered in that very character not only the terror and violence of the waves and of stallions, but as well the godlike sense of movement and command which was felt by the horsemen and by the sailor at the tiller in a following sea. Those actions themselves were in accord with Poseidon's special chthonic nature and with the shapes of his sites; they were long and rhythmic with the free roll of the earth, the swell of the sea. They were actions, therefore, that demanded the consent of those nonhuman forces, the horse and the sea, from which their splendid sense of power derived. Sometimes rebellious against Zeus and probably his rival or predecessor long ago, Poseidon was in this way doubly a god of deep pride as well as of danger, a pride which men felt too in his gift to them of collaboration with him. In a related way, Athena, at her greatest, was even more what men could do and make themselves be. Both deities presented a challenge to human beings which could find release only in the courageous action which they required and which their major sites image and demand.

At the same time, it is apparent that both Poseidon and Athena are close to the old deity of the earth. Poseidon, ancient consort of Potnia, the "Mistress," that he was, is named the son of earth by Sophocles,[4] and, like the old goddess and her horned bull, he was the earthquake maker. Athena's snakes and olive trees are obvious. Perhaps she too had been Poseidon's "Mistress" and "Divine Mother" long ago. At Colonus Poseidon and Athena are together at a spot where, as we noted earlier, southern Attica rises up around them like a sea.[5] (*Figs. 118, 119*) The horns of Parnes above Deceleia lie behind Demeter's hill to the north and the horns of Hymettos mark the eastern horizon. Under them Lycabettos is seen with its long ridge streaming behind its southern cone like a mane. Below it the Acropolis slides out across the sloping plain under the bulk of Hymettos, and directly to the south the eye is carried out across the gentle slope to the Saronic Gulf, where the cone of Zeus Panhellenios stands directly on axis across the water. This is the long, releasing sea view of the slanting Athenian plain, from the active, olive–bearing earth across the shore:

> Upon whose lovely littoral
> The god of the sea moves, the son of Time.[6] (*Fig. 145*)

It is true that Poseidon, as Hippios, was also to be found under the wildly leaping hills around Mantineia, far from the sea itself.[7] Yet the flat plain of Mantineia, bounded as it is by the high mountains of Artemis, may also have suggested an inland sea to the Greeks, the unexpected "thalassa" which fulfilled at Mantineia the fatal prophecy which had purportedly been made to Epaminondas.[8] Similarly, a sanctuary of Poseidon Hippios lay at Onchestos beneath the winged sphinx mountain on the southern shore of Lake Copais in Boeotia.[9] (*Fig. 41*) Its wooded grove is mentioned in the Homeric Hymn to Apollo,[10] when Apollo visited there on his way to Delphi: another of the links between the two gods—a link which is strengthened by the fact that Poseidon himself had one of the earliest sanctuaries at Delphi. On one side of Onchestos lay the waters of the lake, on the other the long plain, ideal for horses, which stretches toward Thebes.

Poseidon's sea view itself, as that of a Greek god, is not normally boundless. From Colonus it is Mount Oros and the mountains of the Peloponnesos behind it which focus and define its extent, so that the enclosure made for Athens by its mountain boundaries is half Athena's land and half Poseidon's sea; the land all grey green olive in antiquity, the sea grey blue. Mount Oros also forms the focus of the view across the sea from Poseidon's sanctuary on the northern coast of the island of Poros, the ancient Calauria, to the south of it. The remains of his temple lie below a windy saddle on a rounded hill between two narrow valleys with the ancient town close by to the south.[11] (*Figs. 281, 282*) Below the natural platform the coast is deeply bitten into by the sea, and the waves wash under the north wind on the jagged rocks of the shore. Seen from a ship, the temple would have stood out upon its hill above the arc of the saddle behind it, and the higher hills to east and west would have framed it in a wide V. Approaching by sea, the pilgrim would have had the temple first in silhouette against the much higher mountains of the Peloponnesos beyond Poros, but it would have risen slowly above them as the angle of view increased, until it finally stood alone at the point of the V and against the open sky. The impression would have been of its riding forward and up upon its rising platform above the sea, itself potent as a rearing stallion above the breakers, a revelation of the power of Poseidon both by sea and land. Similarly, approached from its town, the sanctuary opened in a fan of subsidiary buildings to reveal the temple isolated on its headland, lifted against the sky with Mount Oros far across the sea to the north.

Another and especially rich experience of the site could have come about by following the way which winds to it from the port of Poros on the southern shore of the island. This place must have been the main port of the island in antiquity as it is at present. It is set upon two conical hills which are connected with the main mass of the island by a very narrow spit of land. Only a few hundred yards of channel separate the town from the high ridge of the Argolid to the south. To the east of the port lies the open Aegean, extending to the Cyclades which are normally out of sight below the horizon. To the west the bay between Poros and the mainland stretches like an inland lake below the horned peaks of Troezen to the southwest, where the shrine of Aphrodite was placed. Beyond Troezen, as noted earlier, rises the mountain formation which fills the western sky with the colossal image of a woman on her back. (*Fig. 169*) The whole view west from the harbor of Poros is thus enclosed by the power of Aphrodite, dominating sea and human beings alike. From this place of the old goddess a narrow pass mounts toward the ridge of the island. The experience takes on a totally inland character. The port itself, seen from the rising trail, shows no sea around it and seems to lie cradled within the mountains as if it were miles from any water. When the pass is topped the sea appears again, wide now beyond the gentle northern slopes of Poros, and the cone of

Zeus Panhellenios lies directly ahead across it. Eastward lies Poseidon's site, actively rising toward that view. (*Fig. 281*) The eastern slope slants steeply down; two conical hills appear below it; the sanctuary's hillock platform rises upward in a strong and solid curve; the sea cuts under it. A further conical headland takes the eye out to sea, and the eye jumps to the curious rocks which rise in the sea beyond the headland, rocks which look like a ship under sail and are in fact called "Karavi" by the Greeks. From these the eye leaps to the cone of Oros once again, with the void of the sea opening to the right of its bulk. The rocky horns of Moni carry the eye away from the void, however, toward the serrated masses of wild Methane which close the view across the water to the left. Into this mighty but definitely bounded expanse the temple was projected as a focus, its colonnade exerting a counter pull to Oros and Methane by setting up an insistent diagonal axis northeast toward the sea void. At the same time its hill rose wavelike and seemed to lift and carry it sideways toward Oros. Now the earth, engulfing on the other side of the island, is releasing in the rhythm of its forms. Out of that earth—as here most specifically from the twin conical hills to the east of the temple's height— the god is born, and "loves forever / The feminine earth that bore him long ago."[12] But his stoas open out to show his temple rising free, so that he embodies liberated action and thus supplants that Aphrodite who was the dominance of forces upon men.

Another expressive relationship between the old goddess of the sea and Poseidon is set up by the latter's sanctuary on the Isthmus of Corinth.[13] The Isthmus itself is a long strip of land which seems flat from a distance but which has in fact a surprisingly high camber, a little like a ship's deck or the stereobates of some Greek temples. The site as a whole can best be surveyed from the rise above Poseidon's temple. Westward the curve of land, like an expression of the shape of the planet itself, rises toward Acrocorinth, which is hull–down behind it. (*Fig. 283*) Around this dramatic mass horned mountains reverberate like low–lying and fast–moving clouds. The place of Aphrodite rises in this way over the rim of the world, and an irresistible west wind comes from it across the bare and curving surface of the intervening land. This west wind of the Isthmus is one of its most impressive characteristics, and it adds to the unsheltered and violent character which repeated earthquakes also give the place. Turning one's back on the wind, as one is constrained to do, one sees the long slope of land toward the Saronic Gulf. (*Fig. 284*) The hills curve up on left and right, and the land curves away between them, so that the effect here is exactly the opposite of the view to the west. It is of looking across a wide and continuous hollow which slides into the sea rather than across the outer surface of a globe. Exactly at the point in the slope where, from above, the ground seems to flatten out in its seaward slide, the temple of Poseidon was placed. It would have seemed from the high ground like a ship sliding down long ways to a harbor, with the west wind already full behind it. As at Poros, it would also have had the vitality of a certain sideways motion. This occurs because the temple seems to be headed toward the nearer points of the Megarid, which form a kind of bay, while at the same time the long sea void is opening on a diagonal to the right. The contrast of space between the sheltered harbor and the open sea is again measured and made definite in the typical way, by the conical hill which rises near the horizon on the southern tip of the island of Salamis, possibly sacred also to Aphrodite. This is the hill, horned in fact but seen as conical from a distance, toward which Aphrodite's temple on the summit of Acrocorinth was also roughly oriented.

The approach to Poseidon's sanctuary across the Megarid from Attica would have shown the temple first on the low Isthmus with the bulk of Acrocorinth far behind it. From the north, across the Isthmus, high jagged horns of rock stood above the site on the south, but these disappeared from view as one crossed the Isthmus and moved down toward the site. Nearer to, the height of the land and the depth of the gullies which cut into it took the pilgrim by surprise. Acrocorinth also went out of sight, and one was, as at Poros, temporarily engulfed by the earth. The later stadium was placed near the eastern side of the Isthmus, close to the sea but so imbedded in the land that no water could be seen from it, while it was in turn invisible from the temple above. On the slope above the stadium the temple stood in pure profile against the sky. The archaic and classic stadium lay directly below it to the southeast, closely connected with the temple as the early stadium at Olympia had been. The way into the sanctuary came first to a propylon near the southeast corner of the temenos wall. From this direction one had the typically archaic angle view of the body of the temple, framed now in an arc by the curving profile of Mount Loutraki to the north. The nearer, articulated mass of the building would have given scale in this view to the farther, solid mass of the mountain. As one mounted to the stylobate, Acrocorinth would have risen into view above the western sky horizon, as it now does from the temple's altar. From the altar, too, the older stadium slanted off actively on a diagonal southeastward. The altar itself was set exactly at the contour where the level platform upon which the temple was placed falls off in a renewed slope to the water. The participant was thus poised once again between sea and land, with the temple like a ship ready for launching above him, at the edge of the ways into the sea. (*Fig. 285*)

Such dramatization of the movement of the solid earth toward a definitely shaped sea is marked at most of Poseidon's sites. At Cape Monodendri, in Asia Minor, on the low and barren point of land which pushes outward into the water southwest of the temple of Apollo at Didyma, he had an open altar, defined at the four corners by sweeping Ionian volutes like horns.[14] It recalls the horned altars of the Minoan goddess. From it the sea is vast but clearly formed into an almost complete circle by distant islands and headlands; it is an orchestra for the action of a chorus of ships. Southward lies horned Kos; northward Samos and Mykale loom.

East of Samos, below the northern flank of Mount Mykale and its horns and looking northward across the curving arc of the bay of Ephesos, was the site of the Panionion, the central meeting place for the league of the twelve cities of Ionia. (*Fig. 286*) We have already noted how Herodotus wrote that the god worshiped there was Heliconian Poseidon,[15] and he was followed by Strabo, who more or less described the position of the site.[16] The travelers of the eighteenth and nineteenth centuries roughly marked its position, but it remained for Wiegand, shortly before the First World War, to discover the architectural remains of what would appear to have been Poseidon's sanctuary.[17] These consist of a long altar set within a temenos wall on the summit of a low hill which juts forward into the narrow coastal plain before a deep cleft in the mountain. The hill slides forward out of the cleft toward the circle of the great bay. The god is born out of the earth and approaches the sea which floods in below his altar and then stretches in an unusually wide and unimpeded vista northward beyond the farther headlands. The view is one of release and command, but the forces of the earth also pull downward at the site. Below the temenos a profound cavern, now the nesting place of birds, deeply penetrates the hill like a wound made by stabbing, and the seats of an ekklesiasterion are cupped into the slope below it. From the arc of seats the cleft in Mykale is seen beyond a mounded hill to the south, while to southwest and west the higher ridge of the neighboring town with its fortification walls finally falls away to permit a long view across the sea to Samos. It is possible, as we noted earlier, that the Doric temple of Apollo, mentioned by Vitruvius as having been built by the Ionian cities, though not necessarily at the Panionion itself, might have been upon the higher ridge to the west and thus also, like the altar of Poseidon, forward of the great cleft and under the banner of the horns.

The Panionion would seem to have lost something of its earlier importance after the Persian conquest of the Ionian cities in the later sixth century. As a result of that conquest, however, one of the most expressive of all Poseidon's sanctuaries was founded: that at Velia, or Elea, on the western coast of Italy. Herodotus tells us that Velia was settled by the Phokaians, the most daring navigators of the sixth century, after their refusal to accept Persian rule.[18] Their town of Phokaia in Asia Minor—the northernmost of the Ionian towns—had been set within a sheltering bowl of hills that enclosed a double harbor. Natural rock menhirs of great scale stand within the bowl, giving it an extraordinarily monumental dignity, and each harbor is formed into a bowl by its own headlands and its chain of islands. The shapes are all full and encompassing ones. The site at Velia, while still protected by mountains on the land side, is much less enclosing than is that of Phokaia. The surrounding hills make a deep but comparatively narrow pocket which opens to the sea. Down the center of the corridor so formed runs the long spine of a longitudinal ridge. It divides the flat lands of the site in half, leaving only restricted, though still rich, fields for agriculture on either side. The sea in antiquity apparently penetrated more deeply into the lowlands beside the ridge than it now does, and the harbor was tucked into the southern slope of the ridge at the point where it opens into a lateral draw through which entrance to the high ground is gained. The ridge was the acropolis of the town and was eventually protected by walls and by towers near its eastern extremity where the encircling hills come closest to it. Its long summit slants from east to west, toward the sea. As it approaches the sea it dips down into a low saddle and then mounts to a conical hill which is now slightly back from the shore but which, during antiquity, apparently rose directly out of the water. Below the summit of this promontory, and facing inland away from the sea, a temple was placed in the late fifth century.[19] (*Fig. 287*) It is not known to what god the temple was itself dedicated, but its richly curved base moulding indicates that it may have been Ionic though certainly not dipteral. High up on the ridge to the east of the temple, and across the depression which isolates the mass of the hill on which the temple is placed, is another monument: an open altar, dedicated to Poseidon. (*Fig. 288*) This is set toward the eastern, inland side of a broad and level platform. It is so related to the platform that it has today a view in which the edge of the platform masks the depression between it and the western promontory and sets up in this way a line of sight directly from the altar toward the temple on the acropolis whose roof in antiquity would have risen above the summit of its hill. (*Fig. 289*) The angle of view was such that the temple would have seemed to stand above the houses of the town on the far horizon of the sea. No islands were visible, and the arc of the horizon was empty and vast.

The meaning of the experience so shaped seems clear. It was the view now appropriate for the Phokaians—one for exiles, mariners, and men of courage: straight as an arrow toward the open sea. But still, in their unwonted landscape, they so placed Poseidon's altar and their acropolis temple as to focus the sea for the former. In this way they not only dramatized the direction of their site but put their confident mark upon it. Indeed, set upon the sea horizon, their temple became the single solid point of reference between the voids of sea and sky. With it the Phokaians, accepting to the full the force of their god, monumentalized for him the shape-less expanses across which they had sailed, making a statement of permanent humanity on the verge of Ocean.

It is even possible that the temple at Velia, facing the land and the city as it does but also, from Poseidon's altar, claiming the sea for the city, was of Athena, who was with Poseidon at Cape Sounion in Attica and was housed there in a temple which, like that at Velia, may have had an Ionic colonnade. At Cape Sounion there were again two separate sanctuaries: Poseidon's upon the highly rising and dramatic headland, Athena's on a gently mounded hill in the low saddle behind it.[20] North of the two sites the mountains of Attica open up into a deep cleft to frame a pyramidal peak behind them. (*Fig. 290*) A shrine of Artemis was placed, appropriately enough, near the summit here. The westerly of the two nearer horns itself has a double, horned peak. It is clear that the optimum view of the two temples from the sea has them framed by that characteristically sacred formation. The temple of Athena, for example, seen across the two harbors on east and west which bite into its spit of land, would have moved always against the sky or before an indefinite background of hills, until, from the southeast, it fell into axis with the cleft and the horns behind it. In this way it would have presented to the traveler, who began to round Sounion from the Aegean, the characteristic landscape formation which had, since Minoan times, marked the sanctity of the earth: the mounded hill before the horned mountain. Similarly, the temple of Poseidon stands out first against the sky upon its projected headland, (*Fig. 291*) and then, as the ship comes exactly opposite it, falls into place in the beautiful V of the horns. It must have seemed to the Athenians that they had been especially favored by the old goddess, since that point of their land which projected farthest into the sea and which first announced Attica to the seafarer had been so clearly formed as a holy place.

As at the shrine of Athena Pronaia at Delphi the name of the new man–favoring goddess had been given to a place of ancient chthonic power, so at Sounion the name of Athena was given to the landward of the two sanctuaries. In a double sense Athena must also have been a kind of Pronaia here, lying as she does both at the entrance to holy Attica and, from the land side, before the shrine of Poseidon. She was probably an embodiment of the ancient female deity of land and sea alike. Her shrine lies between two seas, but it is at the same time protected and embedded in the land, since it is on lower ground between two heights, those of the moun-tain and the promontory. Moreover, the experience of Athena's site, from the land as from the sea, is an experience of the earth, not of the waters. The fact that this was intended to be so is shown, I think, by the curious, half–peripteral colonnade, possibly Ionic, which was added to her sixth–century temple about 450 B.C.[21] The columns enclosed the east and south sides of the temple and lapped around the west side only far enough to make a firm intersection with the cella wall. This unusual feature, which was mentioned by Vitruvius,[22] indicates that the temple was intended to be viewed from the southeast. It is true that a small temple in antis, possibly of Apollo, stood close to the northern flank of the larger temple, so that a colonnade on that side would have been inordinately crowded. There was plenty of room on the west, however, so that the Periclean builders would have had no difficulty in enclosing the western end had they cared to do so. It is therefore clear that an experience of the shrine from the southeast was the meaningful way. As a ship approached Sounion from that direction the colonnade would have been seen where it was required to be, in front of the landscape horns. The same is true on the site itself. Mounting the hill from the south, the participant would have seen the columns against the natural formation, which, as he came nearer, the colonnade itself would have blocked. As he moved past the temple toward the small shrine to the north of it, the measured rhythm of the near columns would finally have given way to reveal the mountain once more. From this position, in front of the temple in antis, the view is again that exactly chosen one which was at least as old as Knossos: of the gently mounded hill backed by the horns. In this way the old goddess, probably backed by Apollo and Artemis watching the gate and now identified as the special protectress of Athens, sat enthroned in the earth at Sounion, and her symbols must have seemed to guard the Attic land, while, approached from the north, her sanctuary lay before the sea god's shrine.

The experience of Poseidon's sanctuary from the landward side is an entirely different affair. There were earlier temples upon the site of the present Periclean one, and the remains of sixth–century columns have been found at the site of the present propylon, which dates from about the time of the Propylaia on the Acropolis of Athens. We have some reason to assume, then, that the present, regularized and cross–axial organization of the temenos is not so different from that of the sixth and early fifth centuries. It would thus represent, with the temenos of the temple of Aphaia at Aigina, one of the first examples of such regularity in Greek planning. We said earlier that planning of this kind tended to freeze the temple within the temenos, to diminish its sculptural plasticity, and to reduce its capacity to carry the eye toward those landscape features which were normally essential to its desired effect and meaning. For this reason the intervals between solid bodies in the temenos had generally been kept irregular throughout the archaic period. We saw in slightly later organizations, however, as in that of the temenos at Rhamnous, that similar regularity might be used for a special purpose: there, for example, to reinforce the effect of a boundary and an end. Much the same sort of effect would seem to have been desired at Sounion, where certainly the present temple and propylon are Periclean and later, and where the temple itself is believed by Dinsmoor to have been designed by the same architect who built not only the temple of Nemesis at Rhamnous but also the Hephaisteion at Athens, which also uses a regularized placement for a specific purpose.[23]

The temple of Poseidon is a double boundary, a kind of fence, first against the empty sky and the sea and then against the land. It is built upon an extremely high platform. The necessary height of this mass essentially determines the width of the temenos on the landward side. In other words, the temenos had to be wide enough to mask the platform as one saw the temple from the north, so that its columns would seem poised merely upon their stereobate against the sky. The stoa which was later built along the north wall of the temenos further masked the platform but was not essential to that end. Instead it marks the first of two barriers which progressively cut off the participant from the land. He entered the propylon on an exact cross axis with the easternmost columns of the temple's northern side. (*Fig. 292*) The temple was seen in a purely flank silhouette; it was a palisade. Its unusually slender columns, without entasis, and with static echini, prefiguring those of many later, fourth–century temples, were thus made to appear slender so that they would be seen as the posts of a fence rather than as the muscular embodiment of physical force. In them, too, it is possible that something of the sea was felt. Their foamy white marble from the quarries of Agrileza nearby is lightly striped with wavy grey horizontal bands like wind on water. As the worshiper mounted toward the colonnade the stoa opened a perspective to the right toward the island of Patroclus and the horned promontory opposite it, blocked off the land behind it and directed the eye, as did the columns of the temple itself, toward the closely bounded sea view to the west. (*Fig. 293*) Here the promontory and island masses paralleled the participant's movement as he climbed toward the temple ahead of him. He approached the corner columns and had therefore to turn left and right again in order to pass in front of the temple. As he did so the sea view opened to his left, and his eye was carried dramatically toward it by the lower headland to the east which curved jaggedly over to a fall like a petrified wave and thrust up and out to sea from beneath the platform upon which he stood. He arrived then at the whole spread of the sea view at the moment when he was not only directly in front of the temple with Poseidon's image inside it but when the earth itself gave a last great thrust beneath him, a movement like that of Poseidon's earthquake power. (*Fig. 294*) He was now on the edge of a sea cliff, alone with the sea.

The platform is irregular on the sea sides so that the space expands freely beyond the temple. The sanctuary's altar was probably placed on the spot near the edge of the exposed platform south of the temple where a flat cutting can now be seen in the rock. It was directly opposite the propylon and on line with the temple's eastern colonnade, which would have blocked any direct view between the propylon and it. Therefore, in order to arrive at the altar the worshiper was required to skirt the barrier of the temple itself, and arriving at it, was wholly presented to the sea. (*Fig. 295*) Seen from the altar, the temple blocked the view of the sacred land formation which we discussed earlier, and its columns formed a barrier to most of the mainland, marching as they did east toward the Cyclades and west toward Patroclus and the horned promontory. In this direction, toward sunset, the sea gleamed with blinding light, with the horns floating above it. (*Fig. 296*) The rest of the sea view was also clearly defined by the islands in it. Even toward the otherwise empty south the flank of Hagios Georgios lies directly on the horizon. To the east Makronisi, Keos, and Kythnos present another set of long flank forms, seemingly parallel to each other. (*Fig. 294*) Beyond them the further Cyclades may sometimes be seen. In this way the sea seems divided by a number of rather regular barriers, like great steps, echoing from ever receding distances the stepped organization of the landward side of the temenos itself. Appropriately in this place the Sounion kouros once took his stand, like the first man to take a first step toward the sea, with the sea shapes coiling and

163

dusking in his hair, and the sea sounds reverberating in the chambers of his ears. (*Fig. 297*) So the regularized form of Poseidon's temenos as a whole dramatized the human act of walking through it toward exposure to the sea.

When the worshiper turned away from the altar and the sea the forms of the land came into his view once more. (*Fig. 298*) The eastern columns of the temple stood out above the horns, and its stylobate continued the line of the hill below them. The attention of the participant was thus firmly directed back to the mainland, and the first forms which the temple brought into his focus were the symbols of Attica's sanctity. But it was from the sea that Sounion was remembered, as Strabo remembers it suddenly when he describes Mykale.[24] From the sea the promontory of the temple of Poseidon truly seems thrust forward from the horned cleft and born out of it. (*Fig. 291*) To the left the island of Patroclus stands away from it, and the clear horns of the farther promontory rise to its right. In the arc so described, with the sacred landscape forms red–brown or black on its flanks, the temple gleams white against the blue sky on its framed headland above the riffled water. It was the true landfall after the treacherous Aegean, the sign of home and victory.

The regularized organization of temenos wall and temple body at Sounion recall the superficially similar organization of the precinct of the temple of Aphaia on the island of Aigina.[25] This can be dated between 513 and 500 B.C. There are other reasons why the temple of Aphaia should be considered with the sanctuaries of Poseidon and Athena. It is so set as to relate decisively both to land and sea. Aphaia was apparently an Aiginetan name for the old goddess of the whole earth and was specifically related to the Cretan Dictynna, protectress of both sailors and hunters.[26] In myth she was associated with Britomartis, or Artemis, and had flung herself into the water to avoid rape at the hands of Minos.[27] Aphaia's name was taken to mean "the vanishing one," and in a sense she did indeed vanish when her cult was absorbed during the fifth century into that of Athena, who already appears late in the sixth century as the central sculptural figure on the pediments of her temple. Aphaia's sanctuary is set upon an open saddle from which two seas are visible: the open Aegean to the south, the Saronic Gulf bounded by Salamis and Attica to the north. The easterly view is blocked near at hand by the greater height of the hills on that side. To the west are the deep gorges and peaks of the center of the island. The site saw at least three campaigns of building. A megaron without exterior or interior columns—and which may have replaced an older apsidal temple—was built during the seventh century, as was an altar, and the whole was enclosed by an extremely irregular temenos wall. This apparently had a simple propylon near the southeast corner. In the sixth century a temple in antis with interior colonnades and two adyta replaced the old megaron, and the goddess' chthonic aspect was still stressed, since no peripteral colonnade was used. (*Fig. 299*) A larger propylon was built on the southeast and the altar enlarged. Entering this propylon, one would have had a long view to the north, and a typical angle view of the temple, as would also have been the case in the seventh–century arrangement. In the final program of building, of c. 513–500, a much larger, peripteral, Doric temple was built. This had an opisthodomos which was, most unusually, connected with the cella through a door slightly off the center axis; furnished with a metal screen as it also was, the opisthodomos may thus have continued to function as a kind of adyton and by so doing seems to indicate a tenacious conservatism in the cult at this place. The long axis of the temple was set parallel to the edges of the now regularized temenos platform which bounded it on the south, west, and north. (*Fig. 300*) To the east the temenos retained its old slant but a new, large altar was placed exactly parallel to the front of the temple, and a long ramp ran from the latter almost to the altar. An impressive propylon was set on a cross–axis to the temple and would have presented essentially the same view toward the north and of the temple itself as had been created by the older arrangements. The temple, though now peripteral, was still kept compact and short–bodied, with only twelve columns down the flank, so that the six columns of the front possessed, in the given angle perspective, an unusually strong capacity to seize and carry the eye toward the northern view.

We therefore have good reason to believe that the same intentions governed all the programs of building on the site and that the final adjustment was simply a monumental clarification of them. Each program had stressed a northern view, and a consideration of why this was done is of primary importance. The key to the problem seems to lie in the existence of a cave under the northeast corner of the temenos platform. A cistern and offering pit led downward from the temenos itself into the cavern, and near them a high Ionic column, crowned by a winged sphinx, marked their position and stood out against the northern view. It seems logical to assume that the cave itself, like the caves of Ida, Jouctas, and Dikte, was the original sanctuary of the goddess, or, as Thiersch thought, of the hero Aiakos as earth–shaker, and the earliest deposits at the site have been found here.[28] The sanctity of the cave may have been suggested by two special qualities which it possesses: first, its peculiar form, and second and perhaps more important, the view from it. The rock masses which vault its entrance are so split by widely spaced cracks as to give the effect of having been constructed of cyclopean masonry. (*Fig. 301*) The grotto is therefore a natural formation which must have impressed its viewers in early antiquity as having an unusually purposeful form. Secondly, from the cave the eye was caught by a large conical hill on the island of Salamis across the gulf. In this view the hill lies before the central depression of the island and is thus perfectly framed by rising slopes to left and right of it. Directly behind the cone, though visible only in the clearest weather, the horns of Mount Kerata can just barely be seen. From a position slightly forward of the cave another conical mound comes into view in the valley below on Aigina itself. This nearer cone lines up exactly with its counterpart on Salamis, behind which the horns of Kerata lie. (*Figs. 302, 248*) The unmistakable impression of a purposeful arrangement of her symbols must clearly have suggested to the Aiginetans the presence on this spot of the goddess of land and sea.

Thus the fifth–century propylon above, with the eastern columns of the temple also forming and directing the view from it, aimed the worshiper exactly at that same conical hill on Salamis, lying directly on axis ahead. It is not, however, actually seen until the propylon has been passed. (*Figs. 303, 304*) The inference is clear: the temenos was always intended to bring that formation into view, and the last arrangement of propylon and temple achieved this end more simply and directly than had the others. It achieved more than this, however. In the older arrangements the worshiper could have moved directly toward the temple without turning to the right, although he would have faced in that direction eventually upon approaching the altar. In the last arrangement, however, the extension of the ramp toward the east forced him to turn right, that is, northeast with the sphinx column before his eyes, in order to attain the temple itself. As he so turned, his view fell across the altar and was then carried far out across spaces of sea and land toward the horns of Hymettos which rise far off beyond Athens but show marvelously clear against the sky on good days. Another long view toward a sacred symbol was thus made inescapable by the final arrangement. The worshiper then went to the ramp, turned west upon it toward the temple and suddenly had before his eyes to the southwest the great mass of Mount Oros, symbol of Zeus Panhellenios and probably of the goddess before him. (*Fig. 306*) At the present time the view of Oros is blocked by trees until this moment, but it was exactly at this moment that the final arrangement of the temenos forced the participant to turn toward the mountain. It can now be perceived that, upon entering the older, sixth–century propylon, the worshiper would have been exactly on axis between the peak of Zeus and the horns of Hymettos. The later arrangement presented them to him one by one, in progression. As seen from the ramp approaching the temple, the pyramidal shape of Oros is the highest in a series of pyramidal hills which mount like steps toward it, and the series then culminates in the pediment of the temple, highest of all since near at hand.

The form of the temple itself and its regularized placement in the temenos were integral parts of the whole experience. It was set parallel to the temenos walls precisely because it was not intended to be first experienced as an aggressive force itself. It was instead meant to frame the critical view to the north and to stand well back from it, thus also allowing the whole critical shift of the view toward Hymettos to take place. Noticeably, the temenos wall on that side was not made parallel to the others because it was intended not to interfere with the diagonal view across it. (*Fig. 300*) The temple was then meant to withdraw behind the perspective set up by its ramp so that the eye, instead of being stunned by the aggressive immediacy of the temple's presence, would have had time to pick up Zeus Panhellenios and the subsidiary peaks and to mount toward the temple across those great steps in space. (*Figs. 305, 306*) For all these reasons the columns of the temple are slender and cool at a distance, but as one comes close to them one sees that they are full of intense though quiet life. Their profiles slant delicately upward and they have an almost imperceptible entasis, just enough to make the cylinder supple and the line alive. The echinus of their capitals is a subtle adaptation of the contemporary spreading type, tending to lift out of the earlier flatter form. Its profile seems especially appropriate here, since it causes the capitals to open above the slender columns like the buds of flowers and to support, above the crystalline abacus, an entablature which has been carefully adjusted to the column's slight but active powers. The columns stand upon a stylobate which rises upward with equal subtlety toward the center and which carries the eye along the northern flank of the temple toward the hills of Palaeo Chora which frame it on that side. The building is a feminine presence, and the refinements which make it so call up the korai of the later archaic period, like those which joined the palmette as its own akroteria. (*Figs. 303, 305, 306*) Like them, and for the same reasons, the body of the temple seems in fact to breathe with a passionate but secret respiration. This occurs because the surfaces of the sculptured forms are so live that, as the observer himself breathes—transmitting as he does so the rhythm of his breathing to the movement of his eye—that rhythm finds an echo and a redirection in the modulation of the shadows across the surface of the forms themselves. The process then reverses: The eye movement affects the breathing rhythm and both are now directed by the sculptural forms. These therefore seem to expand and contract in a cycle which is that of their own breath. (*Fig. 319b*)

The temple of Aphaia is thus an integrated female body, an abstract image of its goddess, standing vibrant but withdrawn between her mighty landscape symbols and in the center of a great space of land and water. That integration is carried out within the temple as well. (*Figs. 307–312*) The jambs of the door of the cella—now reconstructed but accurately so since the lintel block was on the site—show precisely the same degree of inward slant as do the profiles of the columns before them. The solid cylinders thus seem to step forward in their present shape out of the void of the doorway. In certain perspectives, when one of the columns in antis is seen against the nearer jamb and one of the forward columns of the pteron against the farther, a curiously alive and disconcerting twist of columns is set up. There is a moment when forward and back and left and right seem to shift their relative positions, and when the quiet body of the temple therefore pulses suddenly in its depths like a terrible heartbeat. The order of the temple's axial center than instantaneously reestablishes itself, and the door draws the attention to what is within when it offers its framed void as a counterfoil to the intervals between the columns. The doubled inner columns also have the same slant as the doorway. Within the cella the scale is restricted and elegant, with the upper columns of the colonnade so small as they continue the diminution of the lower range that they create an effect of extraordinary delicacy and precision: in fact, feminine in scale. The interior, as usual, was not conceived as a volume of space which might contain a certain number of people but was instead thought of as possessing the intimate workings of its own perfect organism. Its scale is therefore, in its own terms, personal, and again this is caused by the pure abstraction of the elements which make it up and by their sympathetic proportioning to each other. The interior of the temple completes in this way the statement of the exterior: a lucid and rational description of the goddess herself which recreates her being through an interlocked and integral system of wall planes and columns. (*Figs. 307–312*)

We have said that the temple of Aphaia is gentle and refined in its parts and in its general effect. The first sculptural groups which were placed in its pediments were entirely in accord with that quality. Their forms are delicate and cool, their surfaces closed and gently modulated. Though they deal with the two takings of Troy, the first by Herakles and the second by the Homeric heroes, their warriors seem engaged in an elegant dance rather than a deadly combat. Their subject, the victory of Greeks over barbarians, is thought to relate to the Aiginetan victory over the Samians at Cydonia, of c. 519 B.C.[29] The groups are therefore generally assigned to 513–500 B.C., and the effect they create does seem involved in the rather courtly and mannered elegance of late archaic works of the turn of the century. The figures are not committed to the actions in which they take part; they are splendidly detached and civilized. The Phrygian archer of the west pediment, perhaps Paris, draws his bow with a languid elegance, and his body in its barbarian tunic is a purely closed sheath, smoothly continuous and without the bulges of muscles to disturb its surface. (*Fig. 313*) The striding warrior steps preciously forward to display his beautifully articulated abdomen which is primarily an abstract surface pattern. The rhythm of the figures flows coolly from one to another along a clearly defined two-dimensional plane. The solids of the figures and the voids between them would seem alike to have been integral to the pattern, so that the eye reads essentially not the willed action of individuals but the balanced lights and darks of a flat and harmonious whole. The dying warriors in the corners are so turned as to present a clearly flat profile to the front view. They remain in this way precise silhouettes against the background of the pediment. They do not fall forward or out and are thus carefully restrained from becoming plastically aggressive upon the space before them. The face of their Athena is radiant and smiling, soft–featured and smooth. Though she gestures with shield and aegis her expression is not that of a deity who embodies the meaning of strife but of one who, with a gracious, social smile, takes her part in the figure of the dance. Because of these qualities the two earlier pedimental groups seem to form one of the latest and most articulate expressions of pre–classic, late archaic culture, when the pattern resulting from ancient recognitions had become an elegant, formalized one. The deeply patterned singleness of the sculptures does evoke the dance of a chorus; but there are no protagonists, so that they, like the temple as a whole, seem to belong to a pre–dramatic world, like that which produced the choral odes of Pindar who loved Aigina so well.

Not long after its completion a change was made in the temple. The sculptures of the important east pediment were taken down and arranged in a row along the temenos wall. It is likely that they had been damaged in the raid on the sanctuary made by Nikandromos, c. 487–85 B.C.[30] In their place was put a new group which presents a decisive contrast with the old. Its forms are muscular and aggressive. The individual warriors act; they do not pose or dance. The striding spearman steps forward with a heavy tread to kill. The forms of his body bulge with the function of their action. His stomach and chest muscles create a sculptural surface which is heavily plastic and shadowed. The dying warriors fall with a crash, twisting down and out as they tumble forward like landslides above the head of the worshiper below. The archer, Herakles, draws his bow with a hunch of his shoulders and a long stiff arm. (*Fig. 314*) His face is intent, the lips thin and the eyes focused. His intention is to direct the arrow to its mark, and his form should be contrasted with that of the courtly, posing Paris on the west pediment. His Athena has strong features, like his own, and her face is formed like his from within, radiant with the encouraging calm that arises from understanding. She knows the meaning of what is taking place around her. It is these new sculptures that express the true nature of combat, like that which was soon to take place at Salamis across the water, where the Aiginetans themselves received the prize for heroism.[31] The old simple harmonies are set aside in the exaltation of power and victory. The Dorian spirit of Aigina blazes up in a new way. It is decisive, individualized action which counts now, and an interest in the nature and effect of action which directs the sculptor's hand. The patterns and barriers have burst, and men stride forward in savage pride, fully aware for the first time of the wholeness of their strength. This is the raw material of the classic age, and the fierce moment of its discovery is expressed nowhere so well as in the new east pediment at Aigina. By the time of Olympia, as we have seen, its terrible force was brought into the stillness of early classic order, and into the harmonies of the more complex theology of Zeus. (*Figs. 271, 274*) But at Aigina the mighty figures of the east pediment broke out of the integrated calm of the old goddess and destroyed forever the residue of human innocence under her sway. They smashed the temple's gentle scale and thundered topheavily from its pediment. Their forms struck and fell across the view toward Salamis, and the slender columns and virginal capitals of the temple now supported not the calm pattern of Aphaia–Athena but the flaunted aegis of a true Athena Polias, protector of the city and instigator of action in men.

A moment's reflection will show us that Athena as Polias must normally have had a rather different relation to the landscape than had the goddesses who were more purely related to the earth. The name of Athena, it is true, had been given to the earth deity in many instances; not only at Tegea and Aigina but also at Marmaria by Delphi, at Argos (again with Apollo, *Fig. 53*), at Sounion, and at Colonus. She brought the olive and was attended by the snake, and her sixth–century temple in Athens, as we indicated earlier, was clearly oriented toward the horns of Hymettos, where she may have been associated with the Aphrodite of Kaisariani.[32] (*Fig. 36*) In this way she was the crystalline Attic earth itself, as Hera was heavy Argolis and haunted Boeotia, and Artemis was savage Arcadia and hollow Laconia. But, as Polias, Athena was hardly a deity who was purely or even primarily of the earth. Instead she was the goddess whom men enthroned in their citadels. At first she seems to have been the special household goddess of the Mycenaean princes, and was thus the Lady Mykene, the Lady Athene. As such she was in all likelihood enthroned at Mycenae and upon the Acropolis in Athens, and in the Homeric myths it is her Palladium, her wooden image, which protected the citadel of Troy —a citadel which could not fall until that image, clearly with Athena's own consent, had been stolen out of the town. With the archaic period she sat upon the acropolis of the Greek city as the Maiden who was the heart and spirit of the whole population. As such she crowned the acropolises of archaic Mycenae, Athens, Megara, and of many other places. At Mycenae her temple, which overlay the old palace, was turned so as to be seen from across the plain in pure flank profile against the sky between the mighty horns. (*Fig. 61*) At Sparta she had a Brazen House upon the proudly unfortified acropolis hill;[33] she was not, like Artemis, in the depths of the valley. Her xoanon stood upon its own height and was protected by its bronze–plated temple under the horns, the towering head, and the raised arms of Taygetus. Thus Athena Polias was the goddess who represented the political life of the city, and she went wherever men set themselves up in towns. If the place was traditionally sanctified, probably so much the better, but if it was not she still took her stand upon the highest place and lifted her aegis like a shield over the city and a warning to its enemies, human and divine.

Precisely because they were in the center of generally continuous habitation, comparatively few well preserved temples of Athena Polias have come down to us from earlier antiquity, but enough remain to reveal the basic pattern of their landscape relationship and perhaps of their own special qualities of form. At Assos, on the coast of Asia Minor, the temple of Athena, of c. 540 B.C., almost filled the restricted top of a high and precipitous acropolis hill which rose as a massive and vertical plug at the edge of the sea. (*Fig. 315*) It and the temple of Panionian Apollo mentioned by Vitruvius[34] were the only Doric temples known to have been built in archaic Asia Minor. At Assos the temple crowned a restricted height and could therefore not easily have been conceived as a spreading Ionic dipteral grove.[35] It is clear that at Assos a struggle took place in the minds of the builders between their desire for the Ionic form and their recognition of the necessity for the Doric. The temple is broad, the columns wide spread, to become as grovelike as possible around the typically Ionic cella without opisthodomos. The continuous frieze with which they decorated the architraves of their entablature is also an Ionic feature, like the frieze which is known to have existed upon the architrave of the temple of Artemis at Ephesos or that from the treasury of the Siphnians which can still be seen at Delphi. At the same time the carved architrave at Assos, with its dominant winged sphinxes, must have created certain specific effects appropriate to the presence of Athena hovering closely over the city. That is, the play of light and shadow which it and the upper frieze set up must visually have tended to detach the pediment from any clear relation to the supporting columns below. The pediment, abstract and hard without sculpture, and with its own cornice casting a deep shadow over the upper frieze of triglyphs and sculptured metopes, must therefore have seemed almost to float, separated from the columns by an unusually wide, visually non–structural, and highly decorated zone. This effect must have been especially appropriate to the temple's position exactly upon the summit of its extremely steep and dramatically foreshortened height. In perspective, from the city on the lower plateau and from the hill slopes themselves, the lower portions of the temple, the stereobate and the columns, would probably have been largely masked. The primary impression would have been of the flat capitals seen from below and of the pediment hovering harshly above them beyond the zone of crinkled shadow. It thus culminated its acropolis hill with a special kind of wilful energy and distinguished its natural cone from the many turbulent hills that rose inland, while across the water the mounded mountain of Mytilene with its knobbed summit supplied a complementary sign.

An unusual treatment of architrave and frieze also marks the entablature of the temple of Athena at Paestum, of c. 510 B.C.[36] This temple was not placed near the southern boundary of the city where the two temples of Hera were built, but near the northern edge, where the ground was highest. (*Fig. 90*) We will recall that, seen from the city's longitudinal road on the west, the two temples of Hera carried the observer's eye toward a cleft and conical hill which marked the southern boundary of the nearer range of mountains across the plain. (*Figs. 94, 95, 99, Frontispiece*) The earlier temple had been enneastyle and thus a widely spread, sheltering enclosure, while the later one, built perhaps sixty years after the temple of Athena, was a densely conceived and solemn mass. It expressed in its own sculptural form that permanence and oneness with the land of Paestum and of Argos which its relationship with the conical hill also affirmed. Both the temples of Hera thus sought to celebrate the city's unity with the earth and with its goddess. But the function of the temple of Athena, and, thereby, its relationship with the landscape, was a vastly different one. It has nothing whatever to do with the conical hill, nor does it seek to settle heavily into the land. As one approaches it from the road to the west it is seen from below, standing out against the sky. (*Fig. 316*) The capitals of its southern flank carry the eye toward the summit of the ridge in the distance, but the northern column of its western façade lifts the entablature high above the ridges which fall away below it on that side. The temple is thus raised above the landscape in a challenging relationship to it. This effect is carried further by the form of the temple itself. Its columns are grouped in a tightly knit hexastyle arrangement. They lean considerably inward toward the center, and this quality increases their effect as a closely knit group, uniting to lift. The spreading echini of their capitals tense with the upward lift, and above them the extremely high entablature and pediment seem actively thrust up into the air. The entablature is in fact almost doubled in height by the two rich courses of molding which are introduced above the frieze and the single course which is inserted below it. The architrave itself is kept fairly narrow, so that this upward leap at frieze level is all the more noticeable. Above it the pediment is itself high and, uniquely, has no horizontal cornice. This omission increased both the temple's verticality and its lift, so that the raking cornice, however it should be reconstructed, would have seemed of unusual projection and, most of all, as if taking wing.

So the aegis of Athena was flourished above the city and against the enemies who might creep among the surrounding hills. Similarly, the inward lean of the columns is so pronounced when read against the hill slope that the temple seems actually to rear back and lift its pediment across the void of space which separates it from the mountains, like one of Athena's own stallions in challenge and anger. (*Fig. 317*) In this way the goddess faced the interior of barbarian Italy as an unconquerably raging force. Turning again toward the temple from its altar on the east, one sees the high pediment flourished against the sky and above the sea. (*Fig. 318*) Beneath it and behind the tightly grouped Doric peripteral colonnade, a deeply projecting porch of Ionic columns led inward to a closed cella without opisthodomos. Here again Ionic influence may be felt, and the whole interior organization, with its grove and cave, stresses the counter aspect of Athena, her chthonic power. But most of all, as seen from ships approaching the town, the temple of Athena, on the highest ground and with the most pronounced of upward thrusts, would have stood out more than the other temples against the mountains and stated the fact of the city, the "feelings that make the town."[37] For this reason its form tends to go beyond the more usual embodiment of a timeless state of being to a kind of dynamic action, since it is literally the united action of men which it is intended to embody.

The archaic Athena Polias was therefore not only a fiercely guarding deity but also the embodiment of what the city state might be—the polis which helped to liberate men from their terror of the natural world with its dark powers and limiting laws. As such, Athena held the fortified places, and the remains of her temples are built into churches upon the highest points of Akragas and of Syracusan Ortygia, where her echinus itself boldly rose and flourished. Above all, she held the Acropolis of Athens. There the fifth-century speculation upon her nature and the Athenian will to assert her power created the most important group of buildings constructed during classical times. The image which they created has been especially influential during the modern period in western civilization. One of the reasons for this is much the same as that voiced by Plutarch at the beginning of late antiquity, when he wrote that the buildings of the Periclean Acropolis "brought most delightful adornment to Athens, and the greatest amazement to the rest of mankind . . . ," and their existence "testifies for Hellas that her ancient power and splendor, of which so much is told, was no idle fiction."[38] So the buildings of the Acropolis created what an historian has called the "psychological landscape" of Greece[39] as it was seen in later antiquity and as it has taken shape again in modern times. Yet their effect goes farther than this, since their function was to express the character of an Athena who was whatever the finest minds of fifth-century Athens could imagine the destiny of the human city to be. The ancient goddess was remade at the hands of Aeschylus, Pericles, Phidias, and Ictinos, and it is clear that they made of her something that transcended religion as it had been conceived of before, or, perhaps, as it has been imagined since. She was the Victory of the city state over everything, human Victory all and all. Therefore the works done in her name by the intellectual leaders of the Athenian democracy still stand at the frontiers of human consciousness and can touch the imagination of modern man more intensely perhaps than any other works of art done before his time. Because of this they are never easy to experience or to understand, and they are never old. Plutarch understood this quality well. "Such is the bloom of perpetual newness," he wrote, ". . . which makes them ever to look untouched by time, as though the unfaltering breath of an ageless spirit had been infused into them."[40]

It cannot be our intention to discuss these buildings in detail or to take into consideration the vast bibliography which has gathered around them.[41] But we can approach them as they relate to their landscape setting and to each other in that landscape. Indeed, a consideration of them in that regard is essential to an understanding of their architectural character and of the religious function which they so daringly reinterpreted and extended.

The Acropolis is a defensible limestone mass rising out of the Attic plain and fixing the sweep of view which is defined by the bounding mountains and islands. It is a solid object set in an imperial bowl. (*Fig. 37*) It is lower than the rocky cone of Lycabettos but much broader on top. In the Mycenaean period its summit was surrounded by a cyclopean fortification wall, and the remains of Mycenaean houses have been found in its northeast quarter. There was one entrance to the citadel at that point and another farther west on the north side. We have already pointed out the two column bases which may indicate the position of the megaron of the Mycenaean kings, associated with the name of Erechtheus. (*Figs. 36, 319a*) The western slope of the Acropolis was the least precipitous, and there was a Mycenaean bastion on that side with the main gate nearby. Toward this the entrance way must have wound sinuously below the bastion on the narrow shelf of rock before it. During the sixth century two large temples were built upon the top of the hill, in positions that had probably contained older shrines before them. The so—called Hekatompedon, of about 566 B.C., was apparently under the present Parthenon and seems to have had a certain number of treasuries grouped around it as the century went on. The precise orientation of this temple is unknown, although Dinsmoor proposes one slightly more southerly than that of the later temples on the site.[42] From about 529 to 515 a temple of Athena Polias was built. This occupied the presumed site of the palace of Erechtheus, undoubtedly succeeded an earlier shrine of some sort, and was oriented directly toward the horns of Hymettos with the cones of Kaisariani also in view. Athena here would therefore seem to have been associated, as studies of the cults of the Erechtheion which succeeded this temple have also indicated, with the Aphrodite of that place.[43] Her temple was hexastyle peripteral and had a complicated cella arrangement: one, containing the wooden, traditionally holy xoanon of Athena Polias facing east toward the horns and with Athena's great altar lying before it; the other, probably for Poseidon, facing west behind its own pronaos and with a double adyton, probably for the mythical founders, Boutes and Erechtheus, behind it. There were thus two temples of Athena upon the Acropolis, from a very early period, one in which she was associated as a partly chthonic deity with Aphrodite, with the male sea god, and with the hero founders, the other in which she stood alone. In 490 B.C. a new temple, the first Parthenon, was begun over the old Hekatompedon with an orientation something like that of the later, present temple but in a position slightly to the south of it. This older Parthenon was hexastyle with fifteen columns down the flank, and was therefore a long, narrow rectangle. The Hekatompedon and the first Parthenon do not seem ever to have contained an image conceived of as traditionally holy. Therefore the successive temples built on the south side of the Acropolis hill—unlike those of Athena Polias, and later the Erechtheion, on the north side— may always have had a certain freedom in expressive program. Each of them must always have embodied the most advanced thought of its generation concerning the nature of the human city and of the divinity who was its soul. Deeply tied to the earth as the temples to the north were, the temples on the south, none of them, it should be noted, oriented directly upon the horns, must always have housed a somewhat more immediate and humanly conceived Athena, one whom even Plato was later to call "Our own dear Kore who is among us."[44] She was the Maiden in her chamber, the Parthenos of the Parthenon. During the archaic period her own maidens, her korai, stood around her on the hill, until, like the priestesses who remained with them by order,[45] they were thrown down by the Persians in 480 B.C. (*Fig. 319b*) After that, defiled, they were used by the Athenians as fill.

The second Parthenon was burned by the Persians while still under construction.[46] Its placement is exactly known through its foundations which are still visible under the present building, and the proposed organization of the temenos at that period is therefore clear. The old entrance would seem to have angled up to the Acropolis along a southwest–northeast axis, the way to it following the old narrow and tortuous route below the bastion. That route was then widened by Cimon to about half the width of the later Propylaia by a retaining wall and a filled– in terrace. At the same time he gave the traditional gate a monumental character by building a fairly elaborate propylon for it and by topping the Mycenaean bastion with a temple of Athena Nike, so commemorating the victory at Salamis. Remains of Cimon's propylon can still be seen near the Mycenaean wall at that point, and cuttings for it can be detected inside the later Propylaia. Because of these evidences we can tell how it faced: exactly toward the cone of Lycabettos.

Turning the bastion on the new terrace, climbing then due east and entering at an angle through the propylon, seeing the cone, and then turning to the right, the worshiper would have had the two temples coming forward almost side by side across the top of the hill. One fixed object in the middle distance, the cone of Lycabettos on the left, would thus have served as a foil to the two temples near at hand and have emphasized their sculpturally aggressive character as they loomed over the crest. The base of the older Parthenon would have been somewhat higher than that of the temple of Athena Polias, but that, too, was placed upon an enormously high platform built out across the space where the summit of the Acropolis began to fall off rapidly to west and north. The effect would have been of two large forms, with very little space between them, rising upon the highest contour visible from the propylon. One would have been overwhelmed by the double presence of Athena, but the reiteration might have had a rather redundant quality. The fronts of the temples would have almost lined up with each other, reducing thereby the capacity of each form to be seen as an independent force. The two temples would, however, have been opening slightly toward the west with some effect of fanning actively toward the observer. At the same time they also had the opposite quality of setting up a long, rather tunnel–like perspective toward the east, in which direction they, of course, "faced." As one mounted the hill through the purely negative space between the two temples, one would have come high enough to discover the object of their perspective, the horns of Hymettos, toward which the two buildings would have directed the view of the observer with the velocity of a flung javelin. As one passed beyond the shorter temple of Athena Polias, with the much longer flank of the old Parthenon still emphasizing the perspective toward the horns, one would have seen the complementary shape of Lycabettos rising up once more to the northeast, beyond the great altar of Athena. In this way Lycabettos would again have answered a very definite need by giving some sense of lateral expansion to the longitudinal direction of the Acropolis shape and its focal horns. Such lateral expansion was necessary because the long axis of the temenos was itself visually unsatisfactory for a basic reason: namely, that the temple of Athena Polias, sited for traditionally sacred reasons, was right in the middle of it.

In 480 the Persians burned the temple of Athena Polias and the incomplete Parthenon. The former was apparently dismantled by the Athenians and the west cella reroofed as a treasury, with the sacred image, saved from the Persians, rehoused in a temporary shrine on the site of the later Erechtheion. Cimon then constructed his wall, propylon, and temple of Athena Nike, and built out a great platform beyond the southern edge of the Acropolis, but no further important building seems to have been done on the site until the Periclean program, which got under way in 452 with the beginning of the new Parthenon and eventually involved the Propylaia and the Erechtheion as well. (*Figs. 320, 321*) The construction of the new temples required the annulment of the Oath of Plataia, whereby the Greeks had bound themselves to leave as untouched memorials the ruins of all the temples which the Persians had destroyed. It thus seems doubly clear that Pericles overtly intended his buildings to create a fresh image of Athenian triumph, both that over the Persians and that involved in the formation of the Empire. The key building was obviously the new Parthenon, since everything else stemmed from that. It was octastyle, with seventeen columns down the flank, and was placed partly upon the older temple's platform but farther to the north, so that it edged slightly toward the now open space in the center of the Acropolis and was taken further off axis with the horns. It may be true that its use of eight columns partly derived from a desire on the part of Phidias for a wider interior space than usual in order to house his ivory and gold colossus of Athena. (*Figs. 322, 323*) The cella is certainly broad, and it had an interior colonnade around three sides which framed the image within the shafts of columns more completely than earlier temples had done. Behind it four free–standing columns, probably Ionic, supported the ceiling of the wide room on the west: the Parthenon itself, Athena's treasure house and civic chamber. But all this widening of the interior may itself have been only part of Phidias' and Ictinos' larger intention, which was to widen the whole temple bulk as much as they could. As the cella and the closed treasure house expanded laterally, the pronaos and opisthodomos dwindled in depth, until they became merely the slight volumes created by projecting wall ends. Prostyle colonnades fronted these vestigial spaces and, because their columns were not in antis, they also increased the effect of the temple's lateral expansion and created a grovelike, rather Ionic, ambient, above which the Ionic frieze of the Panathenaic procession was itself stretched. (*Fig. 324*) These effects then culminated in the exterior octastyle colonnades, which stretch the eye of the observer past the point where the façade can easily be perceived as a single whole. (*Figs. 325, 326*)

As noted earlier, recent tests of perception have shown that almost everyone can perceive six of any given units at once, without needing to count them.[47] Most individuals can so perceive seven units. Only the exceptional can perceive eight. The eye is thus always being forced beyond the normal limit of its capacity by the Parthenon's octastyle façades, and this is a critical matter, since the temple, despite its obviously purposeful evocations of Ionic form, is clearly not intended primarily to be an Ionic grove through which the eye is meant to wander but a Doric sculptural body which demands that it be perceived as one. A recent critic has condemned the octastyle façades of the Parthenon more or less on these grounds.[48] Such condemnation seems to me to be in error. The octastyle façades function exactly as they were intended to do; that is, they force the eye to return again and again to the building. The observer is never satisfied; he can never quite take it all in. The conception constantly escapes him; Athena, body and spirit, wisdom and force, the fact of the city, remains always a little beyond his grasp. She can never be fully understood and easily categorized. The importance of this fact in the temple's continuing power to stimulate and move those who see it should not be underestimated. Contrast should be made with a contemporary hexastyle temple, such as the so-called Temple of Concord at Akragas,[49] where the hexastyle grouping has become so tightly organized upon its high base and is so easily perceived as one, that the eye so takes it in at once and then passes on immediately to the landscape—as, of course, it was intended to do at that place. (*Fig. 105*) But the Parthenon cannot be so easily passed by. This also occurs because, while the eye can never tire of its almost hopeless attempt to count eight columns at once, the temple is otherwise an extraordinarily integrated and active whole. (*Figs. 324–326*) The stereobate rises noticeably up with a tensile life which is transmitted through the columns and their steep echini to the entablature and crowning pediment. This action can only be read upwards, like the action of Ionic columns. There is comparatively little feeling of a balancing counterweight pressing down, as in most earlier Doric buildings. At the same time the whole springy force of the temple's body is so clearly bounded across its upper profiles, where the triglyphs slide imperceptibly toward their corner joinings and the pediment expands calmly across the whole, that the temple rises as a contained unit, a sculptural presence which abstracts and culminates the upward forces of its hill. So all details tend to lose projection as they are pulled into the stretch of the whole. Contrast should now be made with the contemporary temple of Hera at Paestum, which was intended to sit in deeply shadowed heaviness upon the plain. (*Figs. 96 ff.*) Out of this active counterplay in the Parthenon between unitary dispersion, upward thrust, and tensile unity the architects somehow managed to create a form which was at once aggressive and calm. Its primary effect is of ampleness. It is big as only the greatest sculpture is big because it acts as a true creature which is itself its own proper scale. It can blaze and brood; it can direct the eye far beyond itself, and it can embrace the eye, drawing it inside, causing it both to attempt to enclose its outer shape and to penetrate its body. It is clearly an accident of its own integral dimensioning that its flutes exactly cup the human back, but as they do so they bring its forceful amplitude into a unique accord with human size.

The Parthenon, therefore, is itself the fullest balance between and synthesis of the two opposed kinds of architecture which we have considered: that in which the building is a hollow, female shell, associated with enclosure by the goddess and by the earth, and that in which the building is an exterior, impenetrable presence, associated with the active force of the male standing out against the sky. All peripteral Doric temples had combined these qualities; the Parthenon pushes each almost to its limit and makes them one. Down to its smallest details, where Doric and Ionic elements are juxtaposed, it embodies the act of reconciliation, and therefore wholly embodies Athena, who was herself both female gentleness and male force, both earth goddess and intellectual will. The material of Pentelic marble is an intrinsic factor in this duality. Its strength now allowed ptera and porches—as in the Propylaia, Erechtheion, Hephaisteion, and other later temples—to be spanned with marble beams and coffered marble slabs, so that, in the areas normally open to men, the material defining the voids of the body above corresponds to that at the sides. Moreover, its hard, white, but luminous surface integrally combined the sanctity of stone with the optical sharpness and abstract clarity which had previously been achieved by covering the stone with stucco. Mass and surface were now one; the body is white all through.

Thus stretching and glowing, calling the eye always back to itself and demanding a new expansion and refinement of perception each time, the Parthenon fulfills its function with its form. Through it the old Aphrodite of the Acropolis becomes fully one with Athena, as desire stretches itself to embrace the whole city, which, like all human groupings, can probably be grasped by an individual only through some direct emotion similar to this. So the praise which is given the Kore in her chamber is couched by the Parthenon in terms of her capacity to inspire love, to give it new dimension, and to cause it to endure. In this way the classic polis, as the essential vehicle for effective human action, is made a physically comprehensible fact.

The Parthenon must be considered in relation to its setting as a whole, both upon the Acropolis and in larger space. From the slopes of Lycabettos to the northeast it stands free against the sea. From the Pnyx to the west it is the central force in an upward thrusting triad which includes Lycabettos and Hymettos. (*Fig. 327*) The most complete view of it, in antiquity as now, was from the hill of Philopappos to the southwest. From the summit there it seems embedded in the northern hills, dominated by Lycabettos' cone. (*Fig. 328*) But from lower down, as from much of the plain, it swings up and away from the earth and stands out against the sky. (*Fig. 37*) From either vantage point a startling fact is instantly perceived: that the Parthenon, though it directs the eye toward the horns of Hymettos, cannot itself be seen in diminishing perspective or as a closed box in space. (*Fig. 37*) In this view its west and south colonnades seem to open away from each other, pivoting upon their southwestern column as on a hinge. The temple therefore opens forward actively. It neither recedes along its flanks nor closes upon itself. This effect takes place for two reasons: first, because of the relation of the building to the wall of the Acropolis below it, and second, because of its octastyle façade. Because the wall is both slanting and changing its angle, the eye of the observer has no fixed element against which to test perspective diminution in the building. Secondly, the octastyle façade seems so broad, especially as the wall slants rapidly away in front of it, that the eye can never quite comprehend the fact that it is not looking at that façade in pure elevation but rather from a perspective angle. Because the eye reads the west front as pure elevation it cannot optically account for the fact that it is seeing the long flank colonnade as well, and since the wall below does not fix this into place, the eye is free to make the flank colonnade move in the only way that seems natural for it: that is, to swing outward as a lateral appendage of the front. (*Fig. 328*) Because of these qualities, the temple is always an aggressive figure which comes forward against its ground; it is never a figure which sinks back away from the observer into the depths of perspective distance.

The method which seems used here is exactly that of red–figured vase painting. As there, the Parthenon, blazing white in its Pentelic marble, floats free and luminous before its ground. (*Fig. 37*) Similarly, when in fifth–century painting chairs, tables, and so on are drawn in perspective their lines, instead of receding toward a fixed point in some void behind them, open out in much the same kind of hinged fan that can be experienced here.[50] Thus they, too, remain aggressive figures brought insistently forward to the observer's attention. Their ground remains void, not a space into which they can diminish and lose their positive forward position or destroy the dark surface across which, as figures lighter in tone, they shimmer. Eventually figures would merge with their environment, vase painting perforce cease, sculpture lose something of potency, temples of force; but not yet. So the white Parthenon detaches itself against the deep blue sky. As it comes forward in the view from Philopappos it seems also, because of the angled wall below it, to be dipping toward the south, turning toward the observer as if alive on its height, like a great ship under weigh. For all these reasons, too, the Parthenon, of all Greek temples, most fully embodies an act, the expansive surge, sea–borne, that was Periclean Athens itself.

From the Piraeus it stands bright upon the Acropolis within the V of the higher mountains behind it. It is visible in Attica as a hub of movement from every quarter, a solid, luminous center for the hollow Athenian plain of land and water. From Colonus, on the route from Thebes, it sails forward of Hymettos, as we mentioned earlier. (*Fig. 119*) But the rising hill of Philopappos arrests that movement, and the Acropolis and its temple, though full of plastic life, remain fixed, forming the truly central object which draws the traveler on. Moving down from Colonus to the Dipylon gate one sees the Parthenon still high upon its platform.

At the Pompeion outside the gate the Panathenaic procession formed, the young men rolling Athena's sacred ship out of the building's propylon and mounting their horses, stepping onto the platform of their chariots and gathering up the reins. The procession made its way to the agora, from which the bulk of the Acropolis loomed up high against the sky and the Parthenon began to dwindle behind the hill's nearer flank, with the voluminous north porch of the Erechtheion and the fragments of the entablature of the old temple of Athena Polias, built into Cimon's wall, standing out as the most conspicuous objects of the view. (*Fig. 364*) The procession then mounted toward the hill under the cave of Apollo, from which the priests watched for the lightning flash of Zeus upon the long summit of Attic Harma to the north.[51] The cave itself creates a natural rock arch which leaps upward to support the precisely rectangular box of the Propylaia's north wing. To the right is the hill of the Areopagus where the Amazons had raised their altars to Ares and the caves of the earth goddesses, the Eumenides, guardians of the Attic land, were to be found. Toward the place of the Eumenides the procession must

CHAPTER 9

have wound during classic times, before the more direct and less rhythmic paved Roman road was put in. Above the dark shadows of their caves the bright bastions of the new goddess' citadel mount in sharp edged forms toward the sky. (*Fig. 329*) The Parthenon has dropped entirely out of sight behind the hill, but as the procession curved around toward the south side its pediment would have slid out above the slanting walls below it. Then it would have disappeared again as the procession left its horses and its chariots and came on foot to Mnesicles' Propylaia.

Here at once other effects of great force and subtlety were introduced. It will be remembered that the old way curved sinuously underneath the Mycenaean bastion at the southwest. It moved northwest and uphill for a moment so that the edge of the bastion was seen against an empty sky. The living rock masses of the hill itself support the rusticated base courses of the walls. Above these the masonry is smooth, and the final contrast is provided by the tiny and elegant columns of Mnesicles' new temple of Athena Nike above them, sounding the keynote of the Acropolis. (*Fig. 330*) It is more than possible, however, that Mnesicles' approach to his Propylaia avoided the older labyrinthine way and mounted directly up the face of the hill toward the enclosing wings. Clearly enough, Mnesicles discarded the old angle of the earlier propylon and aimed his Propylaia directly at the center of the long axis of the Acropolis summit. So turned, his entrance also had an easterly orientation. The sloping poros blocks still to be seen below the northern wing of the Propylaia also seem to indicate that Mnesicles extended the old terrace to the west of his wings and thus intended that such a straight, axial route eastward up the center should begin outside the Propylaia as well. (*Figs. 331, 332*) Perhaps even the stair cuttings to be noted on the sides of the southern bastion, usually dismissed as Roman, may derive from his conception. In this revolutionary directness—leading, one should note, not to a concluding shell but to the axially directed spaces of the Propylaia and beyond it to the ultimate freedom of the Acropolis height—we may perhaps identify another of these inventive reconciliations between ritual and reason which were characteristic of the classic age. Certainly there is no evidence to be seen in the rock at present for the complicated series of ramps up to the Propylaia which Stevens so ingeniously proposes.[52] (*Figs. 320, 321*) Perhaps one was intended to walk straight up, on a revetted embankment or even a stair, mounting directly on one's errand between the great wings with the temple of Athena as Victory poised cool and gleaming on the right hand. (*Fig. 333*)

Cimon's earlier temple of Athena Nike that stood upon this bastion had been a simple prostyle shrine facing south of east and presenting its closed rear to the observer as he mounted the hill. The new temple, built above the older one, was made amphiprostyle, so that a colonnade now faced the entrance view. Moreover, the wall ends on the west were projected past the west wall of the cella, so that at least the optical effect of an entrance, not merely a closed end, was produced. (*Fig. 330*) The tiny and elegant Ionic temple now gives added dimension to the much larger Doric columns of the Propylaia behind it, and as one mounts higher toward the Propylaia, the temple itself comes to stand in precise flank silhouette against the sky. (*Fig. 333*) From the Propylaia's height, the temple, with its widely projecting and purposefully overscaled Ionic capitals, now lends dimension to the long view behind, and the view is the appropriate one: directly toward Salamis, old island of the goddess and historic place of victory.

178

(*Fig. 334*) If one stands at the entrance to the Propylaia and looks back toward Salamis, it will be noted that the double peaks of its highest point, in this view horned peaks, are directly on axis to the west. (*Fig. 335*) A long axis in space thus begins at its horns, moves directly up the Acropolis hill, as one believes Mnesicles must have intended it to do, and penetrates the central void of the Propylaia. Around this void the building distributes its columns and walls in order to open up and define a volume of space within a building mass which, so the remains suggest, Mnesicles apparently hoped to make as symmetrical as possible. (*Figs. 320, 338*)

The Propylaia was a revolutionary building, and the essence of that revolution was its new interpretation of the relationship between solids and voids as it opens around the great landscape axis which penetrates it. Thus the space between its solid elements is no longer merely negative, left over when the solids assume their positions, but is instead positive, the chart of the design, with the solids distributed as necessary to define it. (*Fig. 336*) The ability of the Propylaia to suggest volume where it cannot actually enclose it is equally remarkable. The climb to its entrance is especially impressive because of the enclosure suggested by its wings, whose advance into space was also revolutionary. From the picture gallery in the northern wing the impression of volume is heightened. This room suggests a megaron but uses windows on either side of its door, which has, as at Aigina, the same inward slant as that exhibited by the columns in front of it. From the door the axis of view falls directly across the front of the Propylaia's main colonnade, and from this point can be felt the counterforce of the great column cylinders as they not only mark spatial units but also assert their own sculptural integrity as well. (*Figs. 336, 337*) Against their solemn shapes the taller, leaner Ionic columns, which support the ceiling of the central entrance pavilion, create a true change in scale and a palpable expansion of space. (*Fig. 338*) Their capitals, unlike those of the Nike temple which were intended as strong silhouettes against a distant view, have deeply undercut volutes. When seen from below, as they must be seen in their position, the capitals therefore curl over and back above what is optically perceived as the upward thrust of the shaft of the column. The impression, as at archaic Ephesos, is again of hydraulic forces, which lift the roof in a splendid jet. Under these columns the grey Eleusinian marble of the orthostates of the side wall carries the eye forward toward its grey counterpart in the top step of the short flight which leads to the great doors, behind which are the Doric east porch and the Acropolis height itself. (*Fig. 339*) Above the orthostates the last layer of stone has been chiseled from the wall blocks only in a band around bottom and sides, a band which is kept well away from the wall ends. The effect is of the conscious articulation of each large plane of wall into a panel. This impression is heightened by the fact that the last layer of stone has been entirely removed from the projecting fins of walls between the central and side pavilions. In other words, the creation of a panel upon such a narrow surface would have been nervous and busy. The usual opinion is that the wall was left unfinished by accident because of the expense involved in its surfacing. I would suggest, as noted earlier, that the effect obtained, perhaps accidental at first, became in time the desired one and was certainly used in one way or another in many Hellenistic and Roman buildings. It created an integral paneling in stone and thus contrasted both with the wooden panels of Cimon's propylon and with the panel paintings by Polygnotos and other new masters of figures in space which were removed from it and placed upon the dado of the new picture gallery.

These formed an essential contrast to the hard stone and bright sun of the rest of the Acropolis and, placed where they were, began to function as such collections were later to do most intensely in painting's greatest ages: creating at their own chosen scale a special world of environments and acts, challenging the real with the illusion.

But the great fact of the Propylaia is that it is an interior space which leads from one kind of exterior to another and makes the human being who passes through it a different man entering and leaving it. The spatial axis which runs through it, mounting toward the Acropolis height, carries the eye upward along it through the western range of Doric columns, under the upward leaping Ionic shafts, to the wide central opening in the eastern Doric colonnade. The doors which closed the entrances would normally have been shut. Set as they were deep back in shadow behind the Ionic columns, they dramatized the special secretness of what lay behind them. Swung open into the blinding light of the Acropolis, they revealed the Propylaia's final range of Doric columns, the great statue of Athena Promachos, the Ionic columns of the Erechtheion (for which those Ionic columns already passed under had been a kind of preparation) and, finally, the bulk of the Parthenon looming. (*Figs. 339, 340*)

Yet a view straight ahead between all these forms is up the long axis of the Acropolis, toward a central open area which, though full of activity, has the great forms on its flanks. (*Fig. 341*) Therefore, the center of the Acropolis was free, the flattened top of a great curving arc like that of the earth's surface, with the Erechtheion and the Parthenon seemingly set on its sloping sides and the Athena Promachos standing out above it against the blinding blue sky. The great statue, its spear tip visible from the sea, stood slightly to the left of the central axis. (*Figs. 320, 321*) Behind it stretched the high platform wall of the old temple of Athena Polias, now gone, as even its remodeled opisthodomos probably was by the early fourth century. The axis up the center is crossed by the wall, and behind it, above the irregular but burnished and burning white surface of the Acropolis slope, across which the light also runs with a shimmer like water, nothing can or could be seen but the empty sky. (*Fig. 341*) To the left, partly hidden by the wall and by the statue of Athena, the Erechtheion sets up, from its caryatids to its northern porch, a gentle but insistent counter movement out of the Acropolis space toward the north where, in the distance, the horns of Deceleia can be seen. This was not the dominant view, however, because the eye would inevitably have been caught by the lifting entablature of the Parthenon rising toward the south above the small propylon of its own western precinct which partly blocked it from view. A full view of the Parthenon was also prevented by the projecting hall of the sanctuary of Brauronian Artemis which flanks the Propylaia on the right. Such blocking of the view further prevented, as does the hill slope also, the viewing of the Parthenon in diminishing perspective from this point. Stereobate can not be seen with entablature along enough of its length for a perspective illusion to be set up. The Parthenon here, as from Philopappos, remains an aggressive figure, with its octastyle façade swinging forward across the hill slope. Toward this partially masked and therefore all the more compelling presence, the statue of Athena Promachos itself apparently half turned. The participant is therefore constrained to move forward in that direction with the columns of the Parthenon growing always larger but also becoming progressively more blotted out by the rising shape of its propylon as he climbs toward it.

Exactly upon arriving at the propylon the observer's view is suddenly carried far to the eastward above the terrace walls and lights upon the horns of Hymettos beyond the great altar of
Athena. (*Fig. 342*) After the empty sky, and the falling away of the edge of the world, the
earth suddenly announces its focusing presences once more. The landscape axis is now fully
established: extending from Salamis to Hymettos through the empty center of the Acropolis
and falling directly over the place of the cult act, the altar of Athena, in whose presence the
horns of the sacrificial beasts which had been led up through the center of the Propylaia were
echoed by the horns of the mountain.[53] (*Fig. 320*) The sanctuary of Zeus lay to the right of
Athena's altar on the highest point of the Acropolis. Here the axe which killed the self–
dedicated ox was condemned to death.[54] It is precisely at the moment when these sanctuaries
become visible, with the sacred formations behind them—when the whole space suddenly expands and contact with the earth is regained—that the complete body of the Parthenon explodes
upon the observer at its propylon. (*Figs. 343, 344*) Vast as the world has been found to be it
now fills the world. Its columns stretch and rise, and Poseidon and Athena contend for the
Attic land in the western of the two pediments which Beazley and Ashmole once happily char-
acterized as crashes of unison.[55] Here the two central figures lunged diagonally outward from
the center, brandishing spear and trident, with the olive tree bursting upward behind them
and the horses rearing, like the body of the temple itself, on either side. In the corner the river
god, too, unlike the detached being at Olympia, is swept by the wind of Athena's triumph and
thus participates in it. This was the first climax of the Acropolis: the altars with their beasts
discovered, the land refound, the goddess filling it. So in the diagonal approach to the Parthenon from its propylon—along a line to the center defined by the placement of the cuttings for
votive stelai and sculptural groups—the blocking mass of the Chalcotheca, which so far had
prevented any distant vista toward the south from interfering with the full impact of the
Parthenon's nearness, now falls back just enough to allow the profile of Hymettos to rise up
exactly under the temple's stereobate, so that the scale shifts again, and the ever larger temple
seems placed upon the farthest horizon.

So viewed and approached along the intended diagonal, the temple's body becomes progressively penetrable in all its stages. The eye sees balanced Victory in the pediment, moves
below it to perceive the bodies of traditional adversaries becoming single creatures in the
metopes, then finally slides between the column shafts to see the citizens of a Greek state
placing themselves for the only time upon a frieze. (*Fig. 324*) As they put themselves upon
her body they mark the goddess as purely the Athena of Athens, the city and themselves.
It is almost as if they affirmed that, behind her outermost aspect in the world, it is fundamentally what they do that creates her. Here they are "the riders of Athens," and they are
moving northward toward the central open space of the Acropolis once more. That movement is counter to what appears to be the generally southern pull of the figures in the western
metopes,[56] so that the body of the temple, like the goddess herself marshalling her procession,
first gestures the human participant to itself and then directs him back toward the main axis
and the altars, where the flanks of both Parthenon and Erechtheion set up a decisive perspective
toward the sacred horns. The velocity of that visual connection is now increased by the active
rise of the Parthenon's stylobate and entablature. The Erechtheion, on the other hand, with its

bronze tree inside, not only enforces the axis but also functions as an object which opens up a great landscape space to the northeast and north. (*Fig. 345*) Its articulated asymmetry causes the eye to seek a frame for it, and its own entablatures of various heights indicate what that frame must be: the varied horizon lines of the hills and mountains, Pentelikon and Parnes, far behind them. In this way the asymmetrical Erechtheion both helps define the major axis and gives it a new, broad lateral dimension, so that the unilinear landscape direction can become a landscape volume as well. In this the Erechtheion also calls attention to Lycabettos, which now plays its first role in the final scheme. But the role is critical, as its forceful cone plays off against the horns and cones of Hymettos. Aphrodite, the old goddess deeply embedded in the landscape, balances the gleaming white buildings on the hill.

The Erechtheion, as a complex and elaborately scaled set of interlocked parts, is the only Greek temple which may be said to have been designed wholly in terms of existing conditions and wholly in response to other forms, those both of the landscape and of other buildings. It makes an ideal contrast with the Parthenon, and the courageous decision taken by its architects to unite several separate shrines in a single monumental temple of such unprecedented asymmetry must have been justified by them in part because the result would serve the Parthenon so well. In this way the old earth cults were made to enhance the citizens' Athena. The Erechtheion's irregularity complements the Parthenon's singleness, and its korai enforce the Doric columns' abstract scale. So, too, do its Ionic columns, their capitals now not so deeply undercut as those of the Propylaia, but densely furled like ringlets above the broad bands of decoration like jeweled chokers on the necks of girls. The rich decoration of its cornices, evoking plant life in their forms, and seen against the hills behind them, contrasts with the Parthenon's large simplicities, seen against the sky. Climbing southward up the hill from Poseidon's dark north porch, the Erechtheion also sets up a cross axis within the Acropolis itself, one which intersects the long axis from Salamis to Hymettos. This second axis is culminated by the advancing caryatids who, as they define it, people it as well, and stand out as persons, like the broken korai come to life, against the sacred landscape forms. (*Fig. 346*) Directly opposite the korai is the spot in the rock of the Acropolis in which the image of Gaia was placed as if she were rising out of her own earth.[57] (*Fig. 345*) The resultant cross–axis runs from between the two central caryatids, through the image of Gaia, and comes to rest upon the seventh column of the Parthenon's northern colonnade. At the same time, Gaia is also placed exactly on line between the cone of Lycabettos and the Parthenon's northwest corner. Lycabettos is thereby further tied into the final scheme. (*Fig. 345*) Most importantly, the altar of Athena, whose original position was never changed, lies upon that diagonal axis as well, with Aphrodite's taut hill rising beyond it. Gaia's position thus appropriately marks a spot which is enveloped by the whole composition of temples and landscape. From it architecture and earth are single and engulfing. The body of the Parthenon itself, seen from this side, loses its aggressive swell and becomes, as at Sounion, a long, space–defining colonnade, while its sculptured metopes seem at least to have been intended to form one extensive composition, stretched and framed.

The space so created between the Parthenon and the Erechtheion, in view of the altar of Athena and her consecrating horns, was therefore that of a great room, defined by buildings in conjunction with landscape forms. Out of that room there is only one visual axis which has in it the quality of rapid release. It is the view westward—beyond the vertical shaft of the Athena Promachos who stood before it with her spear—down the long slope toward a point south of the pass of Daphni, where the Propylaia sinks below the western horizon and touches with the profile of its pediment the slopes of Aigelaios. (*Fig. 347*) The eye goes to Salamis here in the long vista to the sea. The splendidly challenging and victorious Athena of the first views of the Parthenon gives way in this vast environment, in which buildings and nature act as one, to an even grander deity whose victory is so complete and all–embracing that there are no true conflicts or oppositions any more. So on the metopes of the Parthenon the bodies of centaur and Lapith, and probably those of the other archetypal antagonists, merge into single organisms: men and animals, Greek and Amazon, gods and giants, the upper and nether modes of life, the slayer and the slain. All is at last one. The spirit which infuses the place is like that of the lines in Sophocles' *Oedipus at Colonus*, when Theseus, witnessing the splendid death of Oedipus below Demeter's Hill, salutes "the earth and the home of the gods above / both at once, in one prayer."[58]

This is the final union of the Acropolis center, between human striving and natural law, both felt to the full. At Olympia, the participant stood in the center of things with the Dorian hero, but on the Acropolis, as we have seen, he first seems to leave the earth and then comes to rest at the heart of a larger universe with Gaia, the earth herself. From this point he is led to Athena's unchanging altar from which all the buildings and landscape shapes are wholly visible at last. As in the courtyards of Minoan palaces, (*Figs. 3, 11*) the center of the sacred place is once again a hollow, within which the human participant has his communion with the land. Indeed, on the Periclean Acropolis the long axis from the horns of Salamis to those of Hymettos passes through his body, and links him personally, running almost due east as it does, with the sky orientation as well. But the force of Athena acts through all, making the void no less than the solids hers. Much more sweepingly than at Olympia, mass–positive and space–positive attitudes and methods are combined and the most effective qualities of each encouraged. It seems appropriate that the reconciliation between old and new ways, and indeed the never quite fulfilled vision of the future which this implies, should have taken place upon the very fortress hill against which the Dorian assault had foundered. So in the asymmetrical, gently scaled Erechtheion the old traditional earth cults are humanized and made extraordinarily articulate, lucid, and civil, while in the Parthenon what might be called the human view of Athena becomes unexpectedly splendid, dominant, and divine.

That human divinity is apparent also when the Parthenon is seen from the east, toward which the Panathenaic procession, like the figures on the frieze, would finally have moved in order to see Athena's inner image of gold and ivory. (*Fig. 349*) From the east the long, high rising stylobate of the temple carries the eye in a rapid trajectory across the void of space to Salamis once more. (*Fig. 348a*) To the right the Erechtheion is hugging the ridge lines of Parnes. (*Fig. 348b*) But the Parthenon rises above that earthbound view like a liberated being. (*Figs. 325b, 349*) It rides now out and away from the tumultuous hills of Attica and seems carried sideways by its Acropolis hill toward the sea. The trident mark of Poseidon under the porch of the Erechtheion and the salt pool there, the salt sea, which was Aphrodite's first and then the male god's, are remembered in this culminating seaward view. At the same time the Parthenon is itself lifting, carried westward by its platform off the highest point of the Acropolis. An exhilaration of command over space like that from the Mycenaean acropolis is felt in the Parthenon's movement, but the human participant in antiquity, as now, must have felt an emotion most rare in human life and one which is not felt at Mycenae: a sense of action with nature's consent, of conquest without folly or guilt, pride without loss of reverence. This was the exact realization of Pericles' program, the solitary expression in human art of total victory. So Athena was born armed among the gods and crowned with victory on the east pediment, and the fresh horses of Apollo and the tired horses of the moon rose and sank in their arc—again the great arc of the earth and the sky—while the earth god, Dionysos, calm, opened his body to the sun, and the earth mothers and Aphrodite sloped downward toward the moon like head-lands upon which the sea foam curdles and subsides. (*Fig. 350*) Below them, in the frieze, the gods sat as if floating on cloud and the maidens advanced with the peplos, while Athena's image, touched by the sun on the dawn of her name day, glowed white and golden from the inner darkness. So the temple's figural sculpture, like its body as a whole, harmonized the most intense will toward abstract structure with the utmost confidence in nature's fugitive appearances and permanent powers. It became in this way what it has remained: the only sculpture which convinces us wholly that our forms house gods and that men and Earth are alike in strength and dignity. Now, before Hymettos' cleft, the mountain and the sea are human.

As the Parthenon rises toward the sea and the sky it indeed seems to imbue the human act with nature's force. (*Figs. 349, 351*) The temple seems to be taking wing, moving forward out of the great hollow formed by Hymettos, Pentelikon, and Parnes, lifting and soaring across space despite its weight, the stones themselves rising as one toward horizons far beyond Salamis. The ptera now become true wings for their "eagle," spanning vast distances, but this occurs because the eye is carried by them to definite landscape objects far away, to hill lines one behind the other, leaping in great stages beyond the plain and the sea. Aigina and the cone of Zeus Panhellenios lie across the gulf to the south, with the mountains of the Peloponnesos rising behind them. Beyond Salamis itself even distant Acrocorinth may sometimes be seen. Now the temple makes one fully see that landscape—so unlike Sparta's landlocked, mountain-stunned Laconia—through which the citizens of Athens were encouraged to daring thought and action in the world: that landscape so complete and expansive but still so measured, definite, scaled to human size, and focused by the sacred forms. In that landscape, "ageless and unwearied,"[59] the Parthenon united the power of the place with that of its state and formed the measure for them both. A bounded body, it yet controlled the whole. Therefore, perhaps in antiquity as now, it called human beings back to itself as seen from the east and invited movement westward once more through its majestic colonnades. (*Fig. 352*) Soon the west porch is reached, (*Fig. 353*) with Attic Harma awaiting the lightning of Zeus to the north, (*Fig. 354*) while the sea stretches from it to the south (*Fig. 355*) and Salamis lies dead ahead on the western bearing. (*Fig. 356*) From this point, with everything to westward falling away below, the Parthenon is indeed more than a ship; it rises onward through an expanding universe, bearing with it the best of human courage and mind. (*Fig. 357*) In it, true enough, the attributes of the active Athena had broadened and deepened until they embraced even the character of the goddess of equilib-rium as Pindar had expressed it: "Hesychia, kind goddess of peace, daughter / of Justice, and lady of the greatness of cities: you who hold the high keys / of wars and of councils . . ."[60] But Athena's presence on the Acropolis goes beyond the Dorian solemnity of Pindar's utterance. The dictates of tradition, though woven deeply into her fabric, are truly forgotten in the final state of the whole. A reconciliation beyond thought between the old and the new, and between the earth and man, her temple is above all else the soundless moment of the opening of a people's heart.

Therefore, the sum of the energy harnessed and the assertions made upon the Acropolis is stillness. In the end the forms in the landscape there cannot be spoken of in terms of action or of time. Because of this it is possible that they cannot be satisfactorily spoken of at all. The sonnet which was the complement to the Renaissance work of plastic art cannot apply here. There are no verbal equivalents for these forms, nor is there any music. Both words and music must be experienced over time, and the observer can only be aware that time stops in this classic art. There is only being and light. Time lies dead in the white and silver light of the outdoor room between the Parthenon and the Erechtheion. It dies upon the Parthenon's white and golden columns, so that Athena takes her one step forward and outward forever. Time stops when centaur and Lapith grasp each other, and as the horses rear upon the frieze and while the amphora bearer lifts his jar. Gods and men alike are radiant in the light. It is the only immortality for human beings, approaching the hazard of the light with the gods. The continuity which had been Minoan, and the separate present moments which were archaic Greek, find their union in this illuminated Instant which is the whole of Time. In the light everything is simple and grave. The relation of the buildings to each other and to the land fuses in the white light. What remains is beyond action, too instantaneous for revery, too deep for calm. It is silence, the sweet deep breath taken. Time stops. Fear lies dead upon the rock. The column is. It stands.

Chapter 10

THE INDIVIDUAL AND THE GODS

*Language, and thought like the wind
and the feelings that make the town,
he has taught himself, and shelter against the cold,
refuge from rain. He can always help himself.
He faces no future helpless. There's only death
that he cannot find an escape from. He has contrived
refuge from illnesses once beyond all cure.*

Sophocles, ANTIGONE (Grene)[1]

THE LIBERATION OF THE INDIVIDUAL which began during the classic fifth century requires a rather more general organization of this final chapter than can easily be subsumed under the name of a single deity. That liberation itself, essential as it was for the formation of the classic age, still led inevitably toward a loosening of the structure of that age. The hold of Zeus upon the individual, which involved the recognition of human limit, could, for example, hardly have been so integrally conceived again; instead, the supreme deity could only become once more largely a threatening power or, conversely, a compromisable one. Nor could the imagination ever have been so gripped by the Olympian gods in many of their aspects or as embodiments of the older communal values. The oracular Apollo, archetypal Hellenic god as he had become, was consulted more and more for answers to personal rather than city problems. Even Athena, after the fall of her Athens through its own obvious *hybris*—by which the balance and peace of Hesychia, acclaimed by Aristophanes as by Pindar, was destroyed—could never again be felt as quite so whole a force as for a time she had come to be. The pattern of city organization did not essentially change, and she could remain Polias, but what she meant as embodiment of the city could probably never again grasp the citizens' imagination so fully. At the same time, a special Greek courage had infused the whole archaic and early classic attempt to seek out the natures of the Olympian gods and to weld them into a system based upon the recognition of fact as it could be ascertained. No personal salvation was promised to the individual in that recognition beyond his growth, with Zeus, in the knowledge of the facts, and, with Athena, in the confidence of being able to act upon them. The individual, however, had still been protected by his close association with a tribal pattern and with that of his polis.

With the falling away of Athena—that is, with the waning of the polis as an engrossing moral force—the individual, now for the first time becoming aware of his isolation as a human unit, seems to have begun to seek for gods who could offer him more in the way of personal security.[1a] The mystery cults lay at hand to answer this need, and their influence continued to increase from the classic period throughout later antiquity. In them the individual was brought back toward a kind of relationship with the land a little like that which had been characteristic of Minoan times, so that in them the splendid classic balance, or tension, between building and landscape, man and nature, tended to relax into a simpler reacceptance of something resembling the old, pre–Greek natural order. Other factors of a different kind were also at work to reduce the balanced tensions of the classic way. Most important among these was probably the growth of philosophical speculation, of which the purely geometrical control of space developed by Hippodamian city planning might be considered the architectural corollary. The grid of Hippodamos offered a wholly abstract method whereby the city could be planned with only minimal regard for topography.[2] As such it was an inevitable product of that part of the Greek mind which sought, apparently with increasing desperation, for perfect conceptual order. It is significant that such "rationalized planning," as it has been called, was initiated in city planning—as in the colonial grid—not our primary topic, rather than in the organization of specifically sacred sites. Yet the long visual axes which such planning tended to create eventually exerted a considerable effect upon the planning of sanctuaries, reinforcing in this way the general movement toward axial organization which we noted earlier in the mystery sites themselves. With the development of the axis, the solids of buildings tended to become, as we noted earlier, more purely definers and modifiers of space, and the temple itself, volumetric, thinned–out, and framed, eventually lost something of its power to act as a free sculptural unit and as an integrally physical embodiment of the qualities of its god. This space–positive attitude eventually reinforced old Italic predilections, produced the axial spatial complexes of the Imperial period, and so moved toward its final, Late Antique and Christian, dominance. But the special classic space of the Zeus of Olympia and the Athena of Athens, brought into being through the active life of its defining presences, was never to be made again.

The character of metaphysical speculation after Socrates should again be cited in relation to all these developments, insofar as it tended to break down the old direct acceptance of the physical embodiment of the deity. Plato's concept of an immortal soul whose being was more significant than that of the body, coupled with his corollary distrust of appearances in favor of ideal, immaterial forms, must eventually have played a part in making such localized embodiment seem overly parochial and perhaps absurd. Conversely, if Plato, despite his deeply conservative instincts, was too imaginative and perfectionist to accept the physical presence entirely, Aristotle, despite his stated love for substance and wonder alike, may be felt to have been too reasonable and empirical to do so. Thus mysticism and rationalism alike ensured the demise of the old, certainly more immediate, perhaps more engrossing, way.

Along with the exploitation of the axis and the drying up of the temple certain other modifications in the relationship between buildings and landscape occurred. The mystery sites, it is true, remained or became ever more imbedded in the earth, and their meaning therefore continued the traditional pattern of their type. But the cities—many of them, especially those of the Hellenistic period, large foundations on new sites—were forced, like some of the early colonies, into devices of an almost picturesque character in order to establish contact with the land. Like the Hellenistic Theocritean Idyll, that relationship, though always based in architecture upon the ancient tradition of sacred landscape forms (now concentrated more upon the comforting cone than the demanding horns), was necessarily a rather self–conscious one. It was often concerned with dramatic or idyllic views at least partly for their own sake, and with effects of visual relief, surprise, and "atmosphere" which were sometimes theatrical, sentimental, or forced. A more complex paraphernalia of building types and planning methods was used to create those effects in sanctuaries as in cities; temples received their constructed environments, as painted figures painted ones. Meanings embodied more simply and toughly before were thus elaborated, qualified, and underscored. A certain awe disappeared, as the post–classic period more obviously manipulated the worshiper's experience of landscape and temple, calling up gods in whom it could no longer always believe with the old intensity, but who were still its link both with the natural world and with "the feelings that make the town." At the same time, a growing desire to divinize the ruler and the hero finally came to produce effects reminiscent of those which had been sought during the Mycenaean age.

All of these changes occurred from the fifth century onward throughout the Hellenistic period, and two essential points should be made: first, that some of them came on with remarkable rapidity, so that few fourth–century sites can be considered in fully classic terms; but, second, that throughout the changes the basic principles of Greek architecture remained unmistakably Hellenic. The architects of the cities, for instance, were clearly concerned that the eye of the inhabitant should be carried, wherever possible, out of the city itself to the land. The conformation of the landscape, despite the grid, was thus always kept as integral a part of the city's architecture as possible. Moreover, while some of the ancient awe may have gone, it had not all disappeared, so that the landscape was never stripped naked of its holiness and the natural shapes of cleft mountain and conical hill could retain their old importance and their meanings. Nor had the eyes of the architects lost their old sensibility, so that in any Greek site of any period a coherent interplay between the built and the natural can always be perceived. The architects of the later period were virtuosi, and the landscape was one of the strings of the complex instrument they played. We should no longer, therefore, too easily allow ourselves to think of the post–classic and Hellenistic periods as a time of architectural decadence. The use of the word itself by modern critics has always revealed a certain naïveté, as if the modern age, in its own hunger for security, had expected the Greeks to be more than men, who "know not what the day will bring," and to have wrested a permanence from life which the Greeks themselves had always clearly stated was not there. The Greek could hardly have been expected to stand at Rhamnous or upon the Acropolis of Athens forever. The positions taken at those places were exposed and demanding ones, more difficult than other ages have been prepared to face or, perhaps, than any modern generation before our own has been conditioned to understand. At the same time, the Greek's will to seek out his destiny which had produced those sites led him in turn away from them, albeit with a certain slackening of heart, and his later architecture has its own Hellenic qualities and its own kind of harmony with the land.

Many of its qualities grow out of the liberated imagination of the classic period. We have already mentioned this fact in relation to the classic temple of Apollo at Bassae and the Hellenistic temples at Didyma and Klaros. Similarly, the Acropolis of Athens was in this sense a proto–Hellenistic complex, with its great Propylaia, possibly staired, its long axis, and its volumetric plan. The Hippodamian grid as well was apparently fully developed in the fifth century. Sometime shortly after the Greek victory at Mt. Mykale in 479, Miletos was replanned upon this system, with great rectangular central agorai, long avenues, and grids of residential areas at both ends. (*Fig. 358*)[3] The city itself might now be conceived of as one balanced, articulated body, but one whose form was more closely related to the conceptualizations of a philosophical system than to the physicalities of a piece of classical sculpture. In a sense the site of Miletos itself called for such treatment. A long, low spit of land with a depression in the middle, which jutted undramatically out from the higher hills into the gulf of the Maeander, its own topography suggests the logic of the Hippodamian three–part division into residential grids on the slightly elevated portions and spacious public areas in the low ground near the harbors in the center. The long avenues, too, could carry the eye out of the town toward the only objects of landscape focus which offered themselves: the hills and islands to the south and west, the horns of Mykale across the gulf to the north, the dramatic mass of Latmos inland to the east. At Miletos the Hippodamian grid may therefore be felt to have liberated the town. Hippodamos himself, apparently surrounded by all the rather theatrical reclame which has remained characteristic of the most successful city planners and sociologists from that day to this, was brought to Athens by Pericles and replanned the Piraeus about 450.[4] Here again there was a commodious community space laid out on the low ground between the two hills, which themselves seem to have received the residential grid. Streets ran directly up from the two harbors with all the splendid disregard for contours which made the hills of the Piraeus, like those of San Francisco now, dramatic heights from which the eye slid uninterruptedly down to the sea. (*Fig. 145*)

It is just possible that the example of Hippodamos had something to do with the placing of the Hephaisteion above the Athenian agora. (*Figs. 359, 360*) The temple of Hephaistos and Athena, begun about 444, was the first Greek peripteral temple so oriented and constructed as to be seen in a frontal rather than a side view or in the older, sculpturally three–dimensional angle perspective.[5] The temple's excellent state of preservation makes it easy to test the obvious truth of that fact at the present day. Seen in any view except from the east front, the temple is surprisingly unsatisfactory. It entirely fails to become an integral sculptural body; its columns are thin and its entablature high, so that the whole breaks up into stiff, unresolved oppositions. (*Fig. 361*) These qualities seem to have been recognized in antiquity, and at some date (probably during the third century B.C.) shrubs were planted at regular intervals around the south, west, and north sides of the building. These had the effect of masking from view the whole of its stereobate and at least part of the shafts of its columns. (*Figs. 360, 361a*) The east end was left open, fronting the platform at the top of the hill, somewhat broader in antiquity than at present, which overlooks the agora. The metopes of the east frieze were carved, as were the first four metopes on each flank. The rest were left blank, and the fourth metope of the sides intersects the frieze across the front of the cella, which is continuous to the exterior colonnade, as the frieze across the opisthodomos on the west is not. Similarly, the columns of the east colonnade are pseudodipteral with the cella, as the columns of the sides are not and as those of the west colonnade are not quite. The temple thus presents what amounts to an open front room to the agora, and the rest of its body, as seen from the exterior and as eventually planted out (and indeed as further screened from the side by a large Hellenistic building) was merely a backing for that front and an envelope to contain the images of Hephaistos and Athena inside it. It is clear that the temple, containing as it did the deities who were the patrons of artisans, was meant to be seen from the agora,[6] and it is extraordinarily effective in that view, set as it is slightly off the axis of the path which originally mounted toward it. (*Fig. 361*) The Augustan rebuilding of the fifth–century temple of Ares—which had originally occupied some other site now unknown—and his angled placement of it in the agora enhanced the rhythm of that relationship.[7]

The way up to the Hephaisteion from the agora clearly involved some sort of ramp or stairway system in a position as restored in the excavators' model, although the remains on the site are scanty.[8] This approach served the temple's form exactly, as the present one does not. It ran directly up to its east front but not to the center of that front. The axis was thereby prevented from becoming rigid, and the only quality of plastic action which this temple could have, that of slipping sideways as a frontal unit, was exploited to the maximum. (*Fig. 362*) Similarly, the stairway so brought the observer to the temple that he had the most complete view of it which was possible from the front and indeed the most complete view that it could support. He came up near the second column from the left, so that he could have both a long perspective down the south pteron and an angle view upward and inward which embraced at once the whole space of the dipteral porch that was presented to him. The thin columns are now positively seen as structural posts creating a space, and the high entablature, so viewed in perspective from below, comes into proportion with them. The optical devices were thus serving new intentions which were to become pervasive in post–classic design: to make the temple seem, not more sculpturally alive, but more statically correct. (*Fig. 363*) Exterior and interior friezes are also seen together, as are the coffered ceiling of the porch and the darker spaces of pronaos and cella behind the antis columns. The experience is essentially volumetric, of bounded space, which the solids are intended to frame. The observer is invited to enter the elegant room of the front porch, to pay his respects to the deities of the workaday world and then to turn within that shelter and look back across the center of the city which is under their protection. (*Fig. 364*) The view from the porch is perfectly defined on the south by the Acropolis, where the gods of the upper city are enthroned in greater majesty, and by the cone of Lycabettos to the northeast. The long body of Hymettos with its horns closes the view to the east, so that the city is seen as lying in a sheltered bowl, formed and contained in its valley by the higher hills.

The reconstructed stoa of Attalos, dating from the second century B.C., bounds the agora proper on the east.[9] (*Fig. 360*) It formed one of several stoas which bounded and subdivided the site from the classical period onward. The stoa as a building type was an invention of the archaic period and seems to have been used first at the Heraion of Samos, as we have seen.[10] (*Fig. 80*) But the stoa itself became the essential instrument of post–classic and Hellenistic planning, and it did so because it answered two basic desires of the period: for regularized boundaries and for protected volumes of space. Stoas as boundaries and as protection were added from the classic period onward to many older sacred sites, such as those of Delos, Delphi, Olympia, Brauron, Ptoon, and others. The stoa is therefore a building designed according to principles in which the space rather than the sculptural solid is the dominant factor. The stoa bounds and regularizes exterior space, which thus itself begins to take on a symmetrical shape, and its solid side and rear walls and its front and interior rows of columns beautifully combine in one simple building the two basic qualities of cave and grove which are in one way or another characteristic of all roofed spaces. (*Fig. 364*) One side is wholly closed, the other wholly open to the space of precinct or agora, though its void is spatially defined by the measured beat of widely spaced columns. Sometimes, as in the South Stoa at Athens, the columns may surround a single longitudinal wall, so defining and serving two exterior precincts. (*Fig. 360*) However modified for special circumstances, the stoa always creates a finely unaggressive shell to contain the positive action of human beings. Therefore, as they become simple structural elements and space definers, the stoa's architectural details, of the kind which had formerly been most sculptural, tend to dwindle to shadows, as do those of many other Hellenistic buildings. This can be felt in the pinched Doric and Ionic capitals of the exterior colonnades of the stoa of Attalos, (*Fig. 365*) while the Ionic columns of the gabled upper floor of the interior retain the water–shaped, palm capitals which had always had the quality of spatial jets. In all these ways the stoa is related both to axial planning and to volumetric design and can serve urban purposes well. It can define, itself sculpturally undemanding, the spaces in which more focal monuments stand, and it forms an excellent viewing platform from which to see them. The views of the Hephaisteion from the reconstructed stoa of Attalos may indeed—as Homer Thompson has frequently pointed out in conversation—be extraordinarily revealing of some of the sources and methods of Hellenistic and Roman picturesque vision. The columns and the dado of the stoa frame, as in Roman wall paintings of the second and fourth Pompeian styles, constantly shifting sets of perspectives of the temple on its hill. (*Fig. 366*) The stoa thus serves a picturesque and pictorial purpose as well as those of regularity and shelter.

The view of the Hephaisteion from the stoa reminds us of earlier uses of temples primarily as definitions of urban space. We had observed the need for such definition in the wide spaces of the western colonies. At Akragas, for example, the chain of temples along the southern ridge was clearly intended to give scale and definition to the vast urban enclosure gridded behind them. (*Figs. 100, 103, 261, 262*) The purpose of those temples, even in the archaic and early classic periods, would thus seem to have been as much urban and even semi–picturesque at it was related to the specific cults which they housed. This seems strikingly true of the late fifth–century temple called of "Concord," which sits tightly near the center of the ridge at Akragas and by which the sweeping views to the acropolis and the sea are defined.[11] (*Figs. 104, 105*) Early colonies, too, had made use of long straight avenues to hold the town visually together. This was apparently the case at Akragas itself, at Cyrene in north Africa[12]—where they connected the town's ridges with each other and with the noble platform of Apollo below the heights—and also at Paestum from the fifth century onward, as we have seen. So at Paestum, for example, the temples, while formed in a coherent cult relationship with the landscape, were set in an urban relationship with each other as well.[13] Those relationships created visual connections between objects both within and outside the town. (*Figs. 90, 91*) The two temples of Hera move ponderously in relation to each other, and their near columns create elements close by against which the temple of Athena far to the north is seen. The town space from south to north is thereby defined. Similarly, from the temple of Athena on its slight elevation, the entablature and ridge line of the second temple of Hera pick up the profiles of the hills which bound the valley far to the south. Incidental perspectives thus supplement the essential religious views, and the town as a whole is given definition both in its own extent and as it is related to the wider horizons of the land.

At Selinus in Sicily, where, as we saw, the whole problem of tying the city to an identifiable horizon had always been a difficult one, the temples which crowned the two hills were clearly intended to form solid reference points for each other. (*Figs. 106, 107*) In the otherwise rolling and fluid landscape, opening on one side to the empty reaches of the sea, the temples gave stability and scale to the town between and behind them. Here the cross–axial avenues of the acropolis hill, creating a regular, semi–grid pattern (*Fig. 106*), seem to be as early as the late sixth century, thus well pre–Hippodamian in origin.[13a] However they date, these avenues set up an extremely successful set of relationships with the temples and the landscape. The main gate to the acropolis is at its north end, and a wide avenue runs from that point south to the edge of the high bluff above the sea. One walked down the avenue toward the blue void of the sky, past the cross streets and the choked habitations which filled the blocks between them. To the left ahead the long flank of Temple D was seen above the houses, with the east end of Temple C first visible beyond its own east end but then dropping out of sight behind it. When the pedestrian came opposite Temple D the west front of Temple C would have risen into view above the domestic buildings below it, and along the same perspective the upper works of Temples A and O would probably have been just visible as they rose above the lower masses of the houses. South of Temple C a great east–west avenue crosses the major north–south road, and at the end of the perspective set up by it the conical hill of distant Cape Sciacca comes into view. To enter the precincts of Temples C and D from that avenue would have been to have their long flanks carry the eye eastward again toward the temples on the second hill across the valley, and these would have set up a nearer and stabler reference point against the hazy hill lines in the distance. All of these relationships across space form a solidly locked landscape against the great void of the sea toward which the north–south avenue first directed the eye. It therefore seems clear that the forms tending to arise early from the special colonial need for firm definition developed during the classic period into the general and fully articulated principles of Hippodamian planning.

We have already mentioned the role of the Greek theater in providing an architectural shape within which the earth's own hollows could be experienced and from which the farther landscape could be sympathetically viewed. (*Figs. 212, 213*) The final form of most Greek theaters dates from the fourth century and later, and they thus constitute another architectural form, invented during the classic period, which was carried further throughout the Hellenistic age because it exactly suited later desires. The fact that the seats of Greek theaters, until Roman times, were rarely if ever reduced to a half–circle and integrated with a scaena wall which was as high as they, has been condemned as a lack of invention by a recent critic.[14] But the Greek theater had not originally been intended to enclose space entirely but instead to present the clearly abstract, man–made patterns of its drama against a separate stage building beyond which the greater scale of the natural landscape could open out to left and right or, from the upper seats, above. It is true that after the fourth–century advent of more trivial, domestically scaled plays stage buildings became progressively higher and were probably painted with their own illusionary perspectives, but the whole development seems always to have been hesitant. The old way retained some force, so that the forms of the drama still balanced, like temples, those of the natural order, and human voices were tested by the landscape's murmurous silence. From much of the early theater of Dionysos at Athens a long view was possible across the nearer swells of land toward the Saronic gulf and the cone of Zeus Panhellenios on Aigina. At Syracuse the theater commanded the low ground of the valley where the major part of the city was placed, and the temple of Olympian Zeus across it would have been in sight.[15] To the southeast the island of Ortygia with its temple of Apollo and its crowning temple of Athena stood out against the sea. (*Fig. 227*) There is thus good reason to include the Greek theater among the elements by means of which post–classic cities projected themselves into the landscape and through which they echoed and complemented distant landscape forms.

This fact seems especially clear and even touching at the site of Megalopolis, in Arcadia.[16] Megalopolis was, as its name indicates, a large city; it was laid out, probably in a Hippodamian grid, after the victory of Epaminondas over the Spartans at Leuctra, in 371 B.C. The town was created through the forced synoecism of forty Arcadian villages, and it was intended as a massive urban center, the headquarters of the new Arcadian League, which might act as a check upon Spartan aggression. The city was therefore a supremely artificial creation, larger than the Greek normally cared to live in, and it was apparently no easy matter to keep it occupied, since its enforced inhabitants were forever slipping away into the hills. Its very name is used by some modern sociological writers to denote an overlarge urban concentration. Set down as it was in the center of a plain without traditions and without ancient sanctity, it seems to have used its theater as the primary device for attempting to bring city and landscape together. The theater, intended to accommodate the crowd at the meetings of the League and therefore overlarge itself, is oriented directly toward the single high conical peak which marks the ridge line to the north.[17] (*Fig. 367*) Near the peak is a cleft in the ridge which might perhaps be interpreted as a rather indefinite pair of horns. Along the general axis of view between theater and mountain cone all the holiest places of the town were laid out. The many–columned hall of the Thersilion, the meeting place of the League, was in front of the theater and indeed connected with it. The sanctuary of Zeus the Savior lay slightly to the left across the river in the wide bowl of the valley, and the temple of Hera Teleia (as goddess of marriage) was on the ridge line to the north, directly on line between the theater and the cone. Its position is marked at present by a chapel and cypress trees. In this way the planners of the town may be felt to have done their best to create the traditionally sacred vista for themselves and to have peopled it with the essential gods in the positions appropriate to them. Similarly, from the agora the concave bowl of the theater, rising above the Thersilion's roof, complemented the mountain cone in the distance and further defined and hallowed the town.

The theater of the Hellenistic and Roman city of Ephesos, southwest of the site of the temple of Artemis and nestled between the mounds of its own hill mass, also had in view the conical hill which was a promontory in the harbor during antiquity and which lies much closer to hand than does the cone at Megalopolis.[18] (*Fig. 368*) Between the theater and the cone lay the agora of the city, as it did also at Megalopolis. The axis of the theater itself does not fall directly upon the cone at Ephesos, but is directed, like that of the Temple of Artemis, roughly toward the part of the ridge across the bay beyond which Klaros lies. But again, the heart of the city is looked across and critical landscape objects are used as foci for the view. This was also true at Sikyon (*Fig. 138*) and at the Piraeus, where the theater on the higher hill faced west across the greater harbor, toward the conical hills beyond it. The importance of the theater in creating sweeping views for Hellenistic cities can therefore not be overestimated, and when they were later shut off from the landscape by totally enclosing stage buildings something classically Greek was finally taken from them, exactly as their new plays had already given up a certain stature. This seems especially striking at Taormina, where the Greeks of Tauromenion, driven from Naxos, set their reconstructions of human fate in front of a gulf dominated by Aetna's smoking cone and containing the peninsula of Naxos itself, where their ancestors had first landed on Sicily. The Romans ruthlessly closed off that stupendous and, in the oldest sense, entirely relevant view in favor of the columned screen of their scaena. (*Fig. 369*) Roman theaters, like those at Orange in southern France and at Aspendos in Asia Minor, were intended, like most Roman buildings, to provide an enclosed experience, totally shut away from the outside world. But the Hellenistic theater, like the sacred architecture with which it was intimately connected, still existed in a reciprocal relationship with nature, despite the more elaborate settings constructed for both.

Some Hellenistic cities were like great theaters themselves, tipped forward upon a height in order to achieve a dramatic view across the landscape. Cassope, on the borders of Epirus, was a town of this kind. We have already noted the relationship between the unidentified temple which lay between the horns outside its gates and the temple of Apollo at Actium far below to the south.[19] Cassope itself had a large theater which looked toward that view, but the town as a whole is shaped like a single theater. (*Fig. 370*) A mighty panorama opens out before it, while the savage mountains press up close behind its northern walls. These are invisible from the site itself, and the whole effect is of the city's command over an entire world of plain, mountains, and sea. The Greek of earlier times drew, as we have noted several times before, a distinct line between men and gods, but after the example of Alexander one could probably never again have been so certain of the inevitability of the distinction. Certainly the Hellenistic inhabitants of Cassope must have felt like gods as they surveyed the world spread out before them. They were clearly in a godly place, on a great height next to the horns, but at last the true political Jupiter, Augustus, dragged them all down into the plain to swell the population of the city of Nicopolis which he founded after gaining his supreme dominion at Actium.[20]

While the Hellenistic planners liked dramatic views they were still clearly Greeks and preferred those views to be focused by some definite, preferably holy, landscape object. We have noted the cones which served that purpose at Megalopolis and Ephesos. If such natural objects did not exist the city was sometimes apparently prepared to construct them. This occurred at Pergamon, where two tremendous tumuli of earth, and two smaller ones, were built in the plain south, southeast, and southwest of the acropolis, and well outside the city's walls.[21] The town of Pergamon lay at the foot of a river gorge at the point where it opens into the north side of a long, comparatively narrow plain which runs roughly east and west toward the sea. The acropolis of the town was on a high hill, really a small mountain,[22] which rises east of the gorge and thus beside, not in, the plain. (*Fig. 371*) The approach to Pergamon from the sea or the coastal road runs up the long axis of the valley, which is guarded toward its western extremity by two isolated natural hills which rise out of it. (*Fig. 374*) From the vicinity of these the acropolis of the town can be seen lifting above the lower hills which flank it along the north side of the valley. The high theater, narrow at the orchestra but fanning out above it between the two major platforms of the acropolis top, makes of the acropolis itself a kind of swinging horn shape, the sacred symbol itself: rising over the lower rounded hills but now packed with men and crowned not only with temples but also with the palace of the prince, as in Mycenaean times. (*Fig. 372*) The theater in this view also seems to dramatize the splendid elevation of the upper town. Its seats funnel down like the gods' power from the temples and the palace above, while at the same time they offer a great stairway which rises steeply from the lower world to the higher. Upon a closer approach to the town three of the tumuli in the plain appear: a small one which is comparatively inconspicuous, and the two large ones. The northern tumulus of these two, vaulted within, may be late in date, but the southern one, which stands near the center of the plain, is considered by the excavators to date probably from the time of the first Hellenistic kings of Pergamon in the late fourth and early third centuries. (*Fig. 373*) This tumulus, though repeatedly excavated, has as yet, unlike the others, revealed no signs of a burial chamber.[23] Whether or not its primary purpose was funerary, it is clear that this tumulus in particular plays an important role in the organization of the site. In the approach to the city from the sea both the great mounds are important. They stand as sentinels in the plain and mark off the great distance to the hill of the acropolis which rises far beyond them.

The importance of their position becomes especially apparent, however, when they are seen from the acropolis itself. This is a high and dramatic elevation with the long axis of its summit extending and rising in several tiers from south to north. It must be climbed from the south side, since the great wall below the theater, savagely buttressed, effectively cuts off any direct approach to the upper height by means of the heavenly stairway itself. (*Fig. 372*) At the same time the major sanctuaries above, as so approached from below and behind, stand out when first seen against a view which is primarily to the west. (*Fig. 371*) On that side loom the slopes of a great mountain which rises to the northwest and sends its lower tiers down in fully rounded, deeply cleft, and aggressive masses upon the west side of the river gorge above which the acropolis rises. Its forms create an exactly appropriate setting for the long sanctuary of Demeter which lies on the south flank of the acropolis and is the first shrine approached from the mounting sacred way. Behind it the rounded shapes of the ridge across the valley create an enclosing background for its own axial enclosure. The view from the entrance way above Demeter's sanctuary also swings west and south, however, to reveal the two natural mounds in the far distance and the two constructed tumuli nearer at hand. (*Fig. 374*) The ceremonial path then mounts the shoulder of the acropolis and turns north toward the higher terraces. The mountain on the left hand is rising always higher, but at the same time the larger of the two tumuli in the plain, the one with the as yet undiscovered burial chamber, now lay exactly on the axis of the path behind the worshiper as he mounted, and far down below him in the depths of the plain to the south. (*Fig. 375*) The axis so defined also falls roughly along the western wall of Demeter's precinct and continues northward up the path to fall exactly along the west front of the altar of Zeus and the west flank of the temple of Athena above it. (*Fig. 371*) That same line may be further extended beyond the precincts of Zeus and Athena to the northeast corner of the later Trajaneum's enclosure and to the angle of the bounding wall of the acropolis beyond it, near where another sanctuary of Zeus crowned the highest point of the acropolis. (*Fig. 377*) A long north–south axis was thus created and was given vast landscape extension by the tumulus in the plain.

The worshiper was, however, then forced to leave that axis as the path turned eastward off it and approached the altar of Zeus through its propylon at the rear. A rhythmic sequence of seeing, losing, and refinding was being set up. So approached, the great altar of Zeus was seen first against the bounding ridges of the high mountain to the west. From the propylon it could also have been observed that the porticoes around the temple of Athena on the terrace above were withdrawn enough on the southern side to allow the upper works of that temple to be perceived as lying on a perfect cross–axis to the great altar below them. (*Fig. 377*) This axial direction was then sensed strongly when the worshiper stood finally in front of the altar of Zeus itself and his eye was carried along it to the tumulus in the plain. He was now exactly between the temple of Athena above and the cone below. An expansive order across space and away from the looming masses to the west was made clear. Yet it had to be left once more as the worshiper was forced to leave the sanctuary of Zeus through the eastern propylon in order to mount the final height near the king's palace and to enter the sanctuary of Athena from its own eastern gate. From here the temple, framed by its stoas,[24] was seen first against the bounding ridges (*Fig. 376*) but then swung away from them as the worshiper walked toward it until it carried his eye across landscape distances to fall upon the tumulus far out and below. (*Fig. 377*) Order was reestablished, and release from confinement was complete. Similarly, the long regulated view across space which the tumulus makes possible is a decisive factor in an appreciation of the dominating height of the acropolis as a whole. The axis of the long promenade which leads to the temple of Dionysos below the steep and themselves dramatic seats of the theater cuts across the extended landscape axis in a long diagonal, so that the interlocking visual directions are mutually enlivened. (*Figs. 378, 379, 380*)

The reason for the tumulus, indeed the necessity for something like it, is apparent. The ridge to the west, though one can see over its lower southern slopes to the sea, tends to push in upon the acropolis, and there is no natural feature in the plain conspicuous or focal enough to distract the observer's eye toward the southerly direction. This the tumulus accomplishes. It gives the necessary dimension to that long axis of the acropolis hill to which it so clearly relates, and it creates a typically baroque fixed point against which the equally baroque drama of finding and losing could be played. The tumulus, like the labyrinthine way itself, is also a profoundly meaningful object in typically Hellenistic terms of nostalgic retrospection, since it invokes not only the kingly tumuli of Lydia and Phrygia but also the conical hill of the goddess herself and the ancient tholos tombs that were built in her image by the hero ancestors whom the Hellenistic rulers now succeed. So at Pergamon the deep past, too, was dramatized, and an essential actor in it not being present, it was built. So the kings worked the site hard to convince their subjects and themselves that, housed among the gods, they were in fact traditionally divine. The whole drama is most appropriately felt from the theater, movement toward whose great stair had originally been blocked from below, so that to sit upon the commanding height of its seats must have been felt as a kind of personal triumph. It is oriented slightly away from the most aggressive shoulder of the western mountain which pushes down like a monstrous animal toward it. (*Fig. 378*) As the arc of the theater swings away it causes the eye to travel along a much lower and curved hill which extends westward above the town and directs the vision toward the northerly tumulus and then toward the two hills in the westerly distance whose shapes now echo those of the two tumuli near at hand. Far out beyond those hills stands the great horned ridge of the promontory above Dikili. At the same time, the eye also travels with the turn of the theater southward toward the southerly tumulus in the plain beyond the town. (*Fig. 380*) A wide turning movement from plastic hill solids close at hand to the hollow of the valley is thus accomplished, with the liberation of the long view toward the sea now a central factor in a dynamic experience.

Nothing has as yet been said of how the eye is directed from the acropolis toward the more easterly reaches of the long cross–axis of the plain. This the later gymnasium and the temple of Hera Basileia accomplished. The long axis of the gymnasium runs nearly east and west, parallel with the plain, but the temple of Hera—a prostylar, axially–approached, podiumed, thus almost Italic, structure of the second century—is oriented south by east across it and exactly upon a fourth tumulus built east of the others in the plain. (*Fig. 381*) The intended experience was now complete, and the acropolis, despite its difficult position at the side of the long valley, had been so treated as to become a place upon which the occupants could feel themselves to occupy the center of the world, dominating a great sweep of mountain, plain, and sea. It was indeed a position from which their whole past history as Greeks was demonstrated for them, as the line ran from Zeus and Athena on the height back downward to the earth mother's mound in the plain.

The splendor and wholeness of Pergamon itself makes it the Hellenistic successor to Athens as an expression of the relationship of the city to the landscape and the gods. But at Pergamon, with the great tombs, the palace, and the theater in the horns, self–aggrandizing human calculations seem perhaps all too obviously to make the city's deity a complex expression of human contrivance. Thus her physical reality was not so firmly embodied as it was at the classic site, where the Parthenon, though already explicitly involved with what men wanted to be, was still a demanding being, uniquely and wholly itself, which gave special meaning to all the other forms and relationships through the terror and wonder of its presence. This was no longer quite the case at Pergamon. The baroque opera of the great altar of Zeus must have thundered with a perhaps satanic power, but the unfluted Doric colonnade of the Hellenistic temple of Athena Polias was slender and tight, with dwindled echini and a flattened pediment above it, (*Fig. 376*) in a further development toward such proportions which we noted in the fourth–century temples at Delphi and Nemea. The wide intercolumniations were twin–triglyphed, like the central void in Mnesicles' Propylaia, so that the temple became a skeletal pavilion without much sculptural force. It could still play its part in the organization of the landscape, and it could bring into the landscape its own expression of cool Olympian order and measure, but Athena as a living

197

physical presence it could no longer be: first, because it was no longer fundamentally conceived of as an active body; second, because the final apparatus of courtyards and axes which framed it and linked it to its larger setting were now not so much in balance with it as dominant over it, compromising its singleness and trapping it in perspective space.

Much the same was true of the temple of Athena Polias at Priene, an Ionic building.[25] Though Ionic, the temple was not dipteral and was therefore much less of an inner landscape or a grove than the archaic Ionic temples had been, or than the temple of Apollo at Didyma was. Instead, it took over Doric compactness but avoided Doric triglyphs.[26] Robertson, following Vitruvius, feels that the problem of placement for the corner triglyph was a serious one, the single most important reason for the eclipse of Doric during the post–classic period.[27] If so, it is clear that the Greeks had not allowed it to worry them much before, since a preoccupation with its fundamental insolubility in terms of rule could only have come about when temples began to be primarily thought of as potentially correct, generalized abstractions rather than as potentially active embodiments of specific kinds of force. Priene's Ionic abstraction stood on a platform above the agora, a platform which seems to have come sliding forward out of the savage cleft to the northwest, so taking up its position before the flatly chopped planes of the dominant acropolis cliff which overhangs the city. (*Fig. 382*) Doxiadis has attempted to show how a view from the public altar in the agora would originally have brought the temple's east front exactly in line with the flank of that mountain.[28] (*Fig. 383*) This would have been the case for the first two hundred years of the life of the city, before the columns of the second–century colonnade which surrounded the fourth–century temple's precinct totally blocked such a view from the agora. On the other hand, it hardly matters if Doxiadis' line of sight from the altar is off a degree or two, since the slender pavilion of the temple was clearly meant, in the first conception, to be seen from below as a foil to the solid mass of the cliff. The eye of the citizen was taken by this means out of the colonnaded order of the agora and focused upon the overwhelming natural formation. Against it stood the temple of his goddess, and its brittle elegance emphasized the proximity of the cliff and the tenacious urbanity of the city under its face. (*Fig. 383*) The goddess as embodied in the temple was at the same time aloof and formalized, not physical, but intellectual and remote, delicately etched against the dark.

The long view south from Priene across the valley of the Maeander, which may have been sea at this point during antiquity,[29] could have been seen best from the upper seats of the theater.[30] (*Fig. 382*) This rose in high vertical tiers out of its lower segment of a circle and looked once more across the whole length of the town toward the long and rather regular line of hills far across the water and beyond Miletos. To the far left in the view rises the jagged mass of Latmos, with the town of Herakleia on the hidden lake below it. From the theater the temple of Athena to the right would have been seen at once against the curve of the hills to the southwest and the shimmer of the open sea beyond them, and the reversal of the dominating northern view would have been complete. There was also a sanctuary of Demeter above the temple of Athena on the flank of the acropolis at Priene, under the steepest part of the cliff. With the development of the calculated double view toward beetling cliff and far distance, the dark goddesses of earth and the deities of the open sky were alike invoked by the city, as the eyes of its citizens were carried beyond the urban area which lay in such dramatic terraces between them.

The dwindling of the post–classic temple to a simple element for the definition of a dramatic view can be seen perhaps nowhere more clearly than at Lindos on the island of Rhodes.[31] Lindos had been occupied since the Neolithic period, and the Hellenic city and its sanctuaries went back to the tenth century. The cult of Athena Lindaia was therefore an old one.[32] Her shrine stood upon a precipitous promontory which rises, caverned, out of the sea and served as an acropolis for the town below it. (*Fig. 385*) The southeastern face of the promontory falls off sheer on the sea side. A tiny circular bay, its narrow entrance concealed from above, lies far below in the hollow of the coastal rocks. So seen from the Acropolis it looks like a strange, land-locked lake (like a smaller Lake Avernus, in fact) and has for many centuries been called, "The Eye of the Sea," on Rhodes. (*Fig. 389*) There can be little doubt that the first goddess at this place, here named Lindaia, was of land and sea, like Aphrodite, and that she probably became associated with Athena when the function of her high place as an acropolis became of primary importance. Older temples had existed on the site, and in the very late fifth century a large propylaia was built on the summit. During the fourth century the older temple, built by Cleobolus in the sixth century, burned and was replaced by a high, narrow, tetrastylar amphiprostyle Doric temple set upon the southeastern lip of the precipice, overhanging the sacred grotto and above the sea with its disquieting harbor. The temple was later framed on the north by the widely extended double wings of a combination of propylaia and stoa. (*Fig. 384*) During the third century a monumental stairway with an even more extensive colonnade was built to increase the splendor of the approach to the summit. The building of a considerable platform upon the narrow summit of the rock was necessary in order to make room for the long colonnades. The temple itself thus became the smallest architectural element upon the hill, if also the tightest, highest, and most compact. The wide stairway, with its several terraces and colonnades, probably inspired by Mnesicles' Propylaia, became the largest element, mounting axially from the northeast through the mass of the platform into the great propylaia with their temple behind them, screened by columns like brush strokes of light.

The way to the height of the acropolis at Lindos was of calculated importance, having to do, as at Pergamon, with seeing, losing, and refinding. The most important view of the buildings on the hill must have been first from the sea, and they would have been lost to sight when the harbor was reached, leaving the acropolis to be climbed before they became visible again. On the inland approach a pass emerges from the hills to show the acropolis height rising potently above the sea with its town clustered below it. (*Fig. 385*) From the town, with the sacred buildings now invisible once more, the path winds up the northeastern face of the cliff and comes, high upon its flank, to the relief of a ship's stern, carved in the living rock and merging into a deeply curved exedra. From here the path turned upward toward the summit of the acropolis and came finally to the foot of the wide stairway. From this point the columns of the stairway's colonnade and of the propylaia stood out against the sky, but the temple was as yet invisible. (*Fig. 386*) Mounting the stairs, the worshiper moved forward toward the center of the propylaia, and the temple itself began to come into view behind the nearer colonnades. So far everything had been arranged along a strict axis. Therefore, as the worshiper came near the head of the stairs and looked toward the temple, his preconditioned sense of direction must have been disturbed by the fact that the temple, presumably the climactic object, was not itself on axis with the propylaia or the stairs. (*Fig. 384*) The eye tries to make it be so, but it becomes obvious that the temple lies somewhat south of the center line and is also angled slightly further northeast–southwest. The whole drama of the approach thus seems rather misplaced, and its climax disappointing, until the very last step of the entrance way is reached. Here the architects persuaded the worshiper to keep exactly to the center of the stairs, despite his previous views of the temple off to the side, by cutting a special smaller step in the middle of the final stair. Upon arriving at this point one's eye level rises well above the top of the acropolis platform, and out across space beyond it a conical pinnacle of rock rises exactly on the axis of view. (*Fig. 387*) Toward this sharp cone the diagonal of the temple also directs the eye. The Hellenistic architect of the approaches thus distinctly worked a trick that was directed toward a reworking of the fundamental Hellenic objective, which had been a balance between the natural and the man–made. Now the architect was clearly attempting to extend architectural space by means of the natural object. Again, we are reminded of Mnesicles' reorientation of the Athenian propylaia up the center of the Acropolis with Hymettos eventually discovered on axis beyond it. The whole approach at Lindos was calculated toward a similar end, and it consciously played, in a way characteristic of baroque art, upon the rhythmic alternation of elaborate preparation, temporary disappointment, eventual climax, surprise, and release. So the large propylaia were finally justified, because they were shown to control a much vaster space than had previously been imagined when only the temple itself had been expected as the farther boundary of the experience.

The temple, similarly, is now almost purely a space definer; it is carefully linear and abstract. Movement within the propylaia (or within the space where the propylaia once was) after the climactic extension of the axis to the southwest, shows that their wings also cup a great space to the south and east which it is the function of the temple to define. Its precise verticals of gleaming white marble make a right–angled shape as they intersect the horizon line of the purely blue and empty sea, which itself makes a sharp line with the lighter blue of the sky. (*Fig. 388*) The modern observer has the impression that the whole visual world has been reduced to the urbane, mathematical pattern of a painting by Mondrian. He will retain that impression until he moves forward toward the temple and sees what lies directly below it: the abyss, the savage rocks, the dizzying eye of the bay, and the depths of the sea. (*Fig. 389*) The architects, again demonstrating their baroque virtuosity, have consciously played off the refined and mathematical refuge of the upper world of the platform with the dangerous realities of the natural world of rock and water. They have counted also upon clear natural formations, the cove to the southwest, the formed and unsuspected harbor below, to make palpable the terror of the voids which separate those worlds. It is now clear why, with such effects in mind, the architects could not have made the temple larger and the propylaia smaller. A large temple, filling much of the space upon the restricted hill, might have stood from a distance as a splendid image of its goddess' physical presence, but in this the architects seem not to have been primarily interested. They desired instead visual and emotional effects of contrast and distance which were possible only from the platform itself and which a large temple would therefore have blocked. What was needed was a small temple to define those distances for an observer who could move around it on the platform according to a directed pattern. This function of direction was served by the stairs and the propylaia. Similarly, a view back from the temple toward the northeast reveals another conical headland rising on that side, approximately upon the axis of the propylon and the southwestern peak, so that a line of sight through the sanctuary is directed and extended in both directions by conical hills. (*Fig. 390*) The second supports a Hellenistic tholos tomb on its summit, supposed to mark the spot where the sixth–century tyrant, Cleobolus, was buried. One is reminded of the use of tumuli at Pergamon and of the intense axes they were used to create. The constructed mound on the summit of the southern horn of Hymettos also comes to mind, as does the tumulus at Eretria. (*Fig. 34*)

The intention behind all these devices at Lindos was therefore still the typically Hellenic one of using natural and man–made forms as complements for each other in order to embody the character of a divinity. Yet, while the meanings of the natural and the constructed had achieved a kind of integral unity in the classic age, the architects at Lindos seem instead to have desired the most striking contrast possible. The naturally rugged and rather frightening landscape which embodied their divinity is made to seem even more so by the sharpness, crispness, and hardness of the constructed forms. One senses the texture of romanticism in this, as if the contrasting effects were being heightened as much as possible for their own sake. The world formed by the architect at Lindos is picturesquely awesome perhaps even more than it is naturally so. Such romanticism at Lindos, despite its subtlety and its continued link with the meanings of its religious tradition, seems akin to that of the "Romantic–Classicism" of the later eighteenth and early nineteenth centuries. In both, there is something cerebral, acrid, and violent. Similar "Romantic–Classic" effects (which, it should be pointed out, have also been heightened through the reconstruction of these sites by Italian architects during the Fascist period) seem apparent at the site of the temple of Apollo on the hill above the town of Rhodes itself.[33] There, above a stadium, stairways lead from both sides of a small theater to a terrace, above which a single broad stair rises to a great flat space across which a dry Doric temple is set directly ahead. The monumental approaches and the broad terrace create the drama of surprise which throws the wide landscape of shore and sea into focus and which requires of the suddenly revealed temple only that it assist its platform in giving scale to the view. Again, as at Lindos, the constructed forms are at once elaborated, desiccated, and axially controlled, but the drama of landscape space is keyed as high as possible and pictorially composed.

In the Hellenistic society of expanded sensations the appeal of the mystery cults became, as we noted earlier, more pervasive than it apparently had been before. Here, too, links with the older, pre–classic and even pre–Hellenic world can be detected. The Mysteries offered a kind of security not promised by the Olympian gods, and security, architecturally speaking, has always demanded a fixed end to any journey. In a society of liberated thought, which demanded more and more of the human intellect and tended to separate it from the life of the emotions, the cults now doubly compensated for the lack by offering an escape from thought into the kind of intuitive knowledge acquired through vision and ecstasy. The planned, "rational" city thus found its necessary complement in the counter sublimation of irrational and mystical experience. The process had indeed been going on since late archaic times, with the acceptance of Dionysos into the Olympian hierarchy. The amalgamation of his cult and that of Orpheus into the Eleusinian Mysteries of Demeter and Persephone has been touched upon earlier, as has the general architectural development of the precincts of both Demeter and Dionysos toward axial organization and fixed conclusions. That development was intensified during the post–classic period.

The sanctuary of Despoina at Lykosoura in Arcadia is significant in this regard.[34] Despoina, the ancient Mistress, Potnia, was identified there with Kore, or Persephone, and her title was "the Savior." Demeter, of whom in a sense Persephone herself is only an aspect, was also worshiped there, as was the Great Mother, of whom Demeter herself was an aspect. The cult was thus a typical one of the old goddess, "Mistress," and "Queen." The site of her sanctuary can be identified from the plain of Megalopolis by a large mounded hill that rises near its western edge with a horned mountain behind it. The way winds through the foothills and comes finally to the eastern end of the precinct. A steep ridge rises on the left and a long stoa closes the view on the right. (*Fig. 391*) The pilgrim is therefore in a long nave, with one of its side walls natural and the other constructed. The temple presents its columned porch directly at the end of the nave and on its axis. Behind the temple rises the acropolis of Lykosoura, its mass completing the enclosure of the site. (*Fig. 392*) Altars of Demeter, Despoina, and the Great Mother stood in front of the stoa, and some sort of monumental altar or building, called by Pausanias the "megaron," crowned the ridge to the left. (*Figs. 391, 392*)[35] Movement within the sanctuary can therefore have been only unilinear: directly toward the widely opening volume of the temple which waited to engulf the worshiper. Within the cella a wide pedestal supported a richly coloristic sculptural group by Damophon, of which one of the outstanding features was a marble cloak, worn by Despoina, upon which women with animal heads danced like the attendant demons of Minoan times.[36] Also recalling Minoan practice, as Lehmann has pointed out, are the steps built into the ridge facing the south flank of the temple, from which a door opens to them.[37] They have been called a retaining wall by others, but this can hardly be the case. Each step is much too deep for that, and it seems obvious that they formed a restricted and partly secret theatral area within which some of the ceremonies of the cult must have been performed. Though the practices at Lykosoura were apparently not secret themselves, like those at Eleusis and elsewhere, still the essential religious intention must have been the same: a continuation and revival of the earth–enclosed ceremonies of the goddess. So the temple itself, enclosed as it is to westward by the slope behind it, also looks eastward along a line of sight which is defined by the stoa and which comes to rest exactly on the mounded hill that had originally announced the sanctuary from the plain. On the side toward the temple the hill is gently cleft. (*Fig. 392*) The site is thus defined and enclosed by the shapes of the earth, and the architectural elements merely fix and complete the long curving way to the place— whether from the plain or the acropolis (*Fig. 391*)—and ensure final engulfment by it.

The second–century reconstruction of the temple at Lykosoura has been criticized for its rather impatient and sloppy character,[38] but to criticize it for this is to judge the temple according to classic and Olympian standards with which it has nothing to do. It is in no way intended to be a solemn physical embodiment of its god but is purely a shell enclosing a certain volume of space. Its fabric, unlike that of classic temples, is thus of little importance, except perhaps for the columns of the façade which announce the end of the journey to it. Otherwise the volume of space to be created is, as in Roman buildings, the determinant of the design. (*Figs. 419, 420*) The fabric, as also in Roman buildings, is itself not holy. The building is precisely that, not a sculpture; it encloses space, although it does not yet, as Roman buildings will do, make a kind of environmental sculpture of that space itself.

The old Great Mother was also associated with Demeter and others in those mystery shrines which were guarded by the demons or heroes called the Kabeiroi. The divinities, female and male, who clustered about the Great Mother at those places were called the "Great Gods" to distinguish them from the Olympians—hardly, one gathers, to the latter's advantage. The cult of the Great Gods, too, though very old, apparently became increasingly popular during Hellenistic times. The shrine of the Kabeiroi outside Thebes[39] is again announced by a mounded hill, backed by a subsidiary semicircle of rounded heights. (*Fig. 393*) Directly across from the mound a beautifully winding way follows the course of a small stream into the rolling, gently opening land to the south. But far to the south, filling the horizon, is the great bulk of Cithairon, which, as we have seen, rose above the Heraion of Plataia. Its central cleft, flanked by the horns of the ridge, is exactly on axis with the mounded hill and with the site of the Kabirion which lies between them. Within the great space so defined by the symbols of the Boeotian goddess, the gently curving dance of the sanctuary's own cross–axis leads to its own enclosed temple, oriented east. This again had a prostyle porch and was associated with the seats of a theater, which here, as at the shrine of Artemis Orthia in Sparta, is Roman in date. The way again penetrated into the earth, here at its softest and most soothing, and came to rest at that place where, in calm and tranquillity, the secrets of the mysteries of life and death could be performed. Issuing forth from the gentle cleft, the worshiper would have had first the mounded hills across the way before his eyes and then, above them to the northeast, the masses of Mount Ptoon where the more awesome aspect of the goddess had long ago been assumed by Apollo. (*Fig. 393*)

The most important shrine of the Great Gods was on the island of Samothrace,[40] whose mighty Mountain of the Moon, Phengari, we noted earlier as rising in the view from sacred Troy, many–peaked and horned, far across the sea beyond the long low mound of Imbros. (*Fig. 27*) As might therefore have been expected, the Great Mother at Samothrace was associated with the great Phrygian goddess and with the Aphrodite who made the flowers of Trojan Ida bloom. The shrine of the Kabeiroi at Samothrace, its ceremonies especially efficacious against the perils of the sea, was located near the western shore of the island at the spot where the deep cleft of a stream bed opens the body of the mountain now called "Hagios Georgios," one of Phengari's outriders. Two long ridges enclose the sanctuary, and above it the slopes rise steeply beyond the cleft to culminate in tumultuous rock masses and serrated ridges. (*Fig. 394*) The heavy precipices above seem in fact to be forcing the cleft apart under their pressure, so that the site is not only engulfed by the body of the earth but is also made awesome by the latter's crushing power and great scale. All the major buildings of the sanctuary are volumetric, space–enclosing, in character. (*Fig. 395*) Among them is the circular Arsinoeion, recalling in plan the old tholos tombs and with small Corinthian columns engaged between the windows of its upper walls. The buildings are not arranged along a strict axis: most appropriately not so, because of the decisive axial restriction of the site itself. Their relationship to each other between the knees of the mountain and under its cliffs is as rhythmic as the figures of a dance.[41] The Hieron, apparently the climactic place, has a double prostyle porch, oriented northward, and an apsidal south end containing a raised platform. (*Fig. 395*) Side benches were arranged along its nave, and these faced in toward the center where a small altar was placed. Offerings could be poured, Lehmann tells us, through a hole in what he calls the "choir" platform in the apse, to fall directly upon the porphyry rock underneath, with which the goddess was associated.[42] The whole organization of the building, with its congregation apparently housed within it and with its apse–like end and sacred altar stone, reminds us very much of that of Christian churches. The old religion of the goddess of the earth thus seems, in the architectural forms of the Hieron, to come very close to the later religion of Christianity.[43] Links with the pre–Hellenic past are also strong at Samothrace. The enclosed and columned altar court alongside the Hieron faces the seats of a theater, and we are once again reminded of the Minoan theatral area. The labyrinthine way has wound itself into the closed megaron of the goddess and poured its offering once again upon her sacred stone. The witnesses of the ceremonies gathered, as at Knossos, upon the steps, but these now mounted high, while the Nike of Samothrace, alighting upon the prow of her war galley, crowned their ridge with Hellenic pride and spread her great wings below the mountain, facing outward toward the sea.

As the Hellenistic Greek turned in part toward the Mistress, the Savior, the Great Gods, and the Mysteries, he turned also toward the Healer. Demosthenes had already discovered among the Athenians of the fourth century that the more liberated the individual was, the more difficult it became for him to accept the tyrannical fact of death. Asklepios, the Healer, was the son of Apollo, and in one version of his myth he had himself been struck to death by Zeus, because he had used his arts to bring a dead man back to life. It is to this crime of the breaking of limits that the chorus in the *Agamemnon* refers as it voices its fears for its king:

> Did Zeus not warn us once
> when he struck to impotence
> that one who could in truth charm back the dead men?[44]

The cult of Asklepios as a god increased in strength from the fifth century onward. It was introduced into Athens itself after the plague of 429 and was installed upon the sunny and cliff–protected south slope of the Acropolis between the precinct of Themis and the theater of Dionysos.[45] During the fourth century its facilities were enlarged by the building of a new portico and temple, each twice as large as those which had preceded them.

It is clear that Asklepios had close contacts with the old goddess. His sacred snake is an indication of this, and the aspirants for his cures slept within his precincts at night, perhaps like the votaries in the megalithic chapels of the goddess on Malta. If fortunate, they were visited by his snake who might touch his tongue to their afflicted parts or communicate the method of their cure to them by nuzzling their ears. The site of Epidauros,[46] where the major shrine of Asklepios was located, itself speaks of the power of the goddess. The way to it from the Argolid is marked by mounded hills, and just before the site itself is reached two rounded ridges open to frame a pyramidal peak between them. This, better perhaps than any other among the several more or less conical peaks which surround the area, may be Titthion, the "teat," mentioned by Pausanias as the mountain upon which the infant Asklepios was suckled by a goat and guarded by the goatherd's dog.[47] (*Fig. 396*) To the south the valley opens, and a cleft and semi-horned ridge, somewhat reminiscent of that above the Heraion at Argos, swings around to enclose it in a full and embracing sweep. Farther along, the enclosing hills begin to angle toward the east, and the theater can be seen lying within their folds. The pyramidal peak now lies directly ahead above the temple of Asklepios himself. (*Fig. 397*)

The approach to the site from the north, which is from the sea and from the old town of Epidauros, is even more expressive. The way winds between barren, tightly pressing and vaguely menacing hills, comes out into the open, climbs slightly, and then turns directly, at the point where the northern propylon to the site was placed, toward the embracing saddle of the southern ridge. (*Fig. 398*) The architectural organization of the site, largely complete before the end of the fourth century, was itself a virtuoso performance in the use of landscape. The sacred way moved forward from the northern propylon up a slight grade toward the level space upon which the major monuments were placed. To the right lay a small temple of Aphrodite, necessary to any cure, and beyond it the higher hills to the west, which had so far restricted the view, begin to fall away. Directly ahead the cleft ridge has come closer, and between this and the propylon a semicircle of monuments, each one a small semicircular exedra itself, swings an enclosing arc to the east which echoes in plan the basic shape in elevation of the ridge beyond them. Behind the arc of monuments the eastern mountain swings back and upward in its own concave arc toward its pyramidal summit. The curve of the monuments thus has its echo and climax there as well. The site, though ample, is thus being progressively enclosed to south and east and expanding toward the west. So the semicircle of the row of monuments brings the pilgrim's eye to the temple of Asklepios which is oriented eastward upon "Titthion" and stands before the open space to the west. The flanks of the temple, itself high, narrow, and elegant, carry the view in that direction toward a large mounded hill which rises in the middle distance. (*Fig. 399*) The temple now seems to stand on a plateau, behind which layer upon layer of hills unfold. Then, past the temple itself on the approach to the great altar at its south flank, the conical hill in the distance is blocked by a similar object close at hand: the circular tholos with its conical roof. (*Fig. 400*) Within its outer ring of Doric columns and the wall of its cella, Corinthian columns rose once again in the tholos like the trees of the goddess or of Apollo growing in the darkness. The natural shape of the hill, with all its traditional associations, is supplanted by the architectural shape, where those associations are consciously invoked in symbolic terms. Farther south, near the altar, so placed as to keep both them and "Titthion" in view, hill and tholos are seen together, the tholos standing in the center of a great spread of sky. Now wide horns lie behind it, formed by the first hill and by another which has come into view to the northwest beyond a flat central ridge.

The whole entrance to the site has been a kind of resurrection itself: out of the narrow way into the soothing valley with the unexpected appearance of the sacred symbols, rising like hope in the opening west. Generally along the line which is defined by these insignia lie the temples of Themis, without whom also there could be no cure, and of Artemis, in all likelihood because it is her wide spreading, bowlike horns that mark the western sky. Entrance to the sanctuary from the south—from the guest house, bath, stadium, gymnasium, and palaestra which served the many functions of the sanatorium—would have led the pilgrim through the southern propylon with the temples of the two goddesses close at hand and the temple and tholos of the god standing beautifully together before the hill mass to the north. (*Fig. 397*) The pilgrim seeking a cure slept in the long portico to the north of the temples, backed by the northern ridge. Across from him then lay the main temple and the tholos, and behind them the southern ridge swept down in a low saddle to rise again toward the pivotal intersection of hills within which the theater lies. In a movement toward the theater from the sanctuary, the stadium comes into view on the west, and its long axis runs with direct finality toward the mounded hill. (*Fig. 401*) So in the theater approach the whole site seems already known and secure, but from the theater itself the full spread, the majesty, and the calm of the landscape can be felt anew. A sanctuary of Apollo stood higher yet, its height offering an even more sweeping view. (*Fig. 402*) But the theater echoes and stabilizes the landscape shapes themselves, so that the view from its seats, as the dramas which searched out the soul were being performed below, must always have formed an important part of the experience for the pilgrim there. The horns of its own shape, swinging as they do well past the half–circle, bring the horns of the landscape to the west into new focus. (*Fig. 403*) The arc of its seats is echoed and extended by the shape of the mountain to the northeast, (*Fig. 402*) and the whole partly enclosed bowl of the valley is crossed by the axis of the theater's own partial bowl. Perhaps the calmest view of all is that directly across the valley toward the break in the northern hills through which the route from the sea passes. (*Fig. 404*) Here the tentative curves of the hills are made definite and sure in the curves of the theater, and the whole visible universe of men and nature comes together in a single quiet order, healed.

Beyond the simple desire for individual security which he answered, Asklepios thus embodied qualities which were more profoundly religious. He is the healer whose compassionate will prefigures something of Christ and whose deep link with the rhythm of the landscape recalls the nature of the old goddess as well. It is clear that the earth itself was considered the most positive agent of his cures. Thus most of his sites are calm and enclosed, medically salubrious, psychologically relaxing. At Akragas his temple is well down in the valley below the town. The sweeping distance and panoramas of the city itself disappear, and the temple inhabits a gently swelling bowl of land. It has no opisthodomos, as his temple at Epidauros does not. Such disappearance of the opisthodomos, though it may refer here to the interior, chthonic side of Asklepios' nature, is also in line with general Hellenistic practice, as we have seen. At Akragas, however, a kind of opisthodomos in relief is indicated, with projected wall ends and two deeply engaged columns.[48] Here is a further step toward the purely pictorial rendering of the old feature which we saw already begun in the shallow opisthodomos of the temple of Ismenion Apollo at Thebes, and in the projected wall ends of the temple of Athena Nike on the Athenian Acropolis. (*Fig. 330*) At Pergamon the site of the Asklepieion, where most of the existing buildings are of Roman date, is again well below and outside the town.[49] The acropolis is in sight from part of it, as is a fairly long view of the plain. But the general effect is of a quiet and enclosed place. The sanctuary is almost opposite the tumuli in the plain but is out of sight of them in the rounded folds of the landscape. (*Fig. 378*) The site is absolutely quiet; it is a place intended to eliminate distractions, scenes, and upsets. There is no sound but the gentle murmur of the healing water which flows through it. The theater, the colonnade, the round temple on its slight rise, and the splendid Roman fountain house below it are all contained in the arms of an earth which seems here, if one may use the only word that applies, understanding. The patient is brought into touch with it, and from the vaulted fountain house, partly underground, he may walk up through a cryptoporticus down the center of which runs the water of the sacred spring. Emerging from the cavern he is at the spring itself and before the theater, with the bulk of the temple above him to his right. Though now a new architectural vocabulary, both Greek and Roman, has created and arranged the forms of the buildings, the observer can still feel himself in touch with a tradition of harmony with the earth that goes back to Minoan times.

The same is true of the Asklepieion at Corinth, where the agora itself, with its fountain house and later temples, shows the Hellenistic–Roman methods by which it was reconstructed after Sulla's destruction of the town. (*Fig. 186*) The buildings of the Asklepieion are all post–classical in date.[50] The site is well forward on the plateau, below the theater and just inside the city wall. It is still high and open to the breezes from the gulf, but the temple on the upper level was protected by a high wall with a colonnade inside it, and the springs themselves welled up from a lower level behind the temple. The organization of the temenos is an excellent example of regularized Hellenistic planning which still retains that sense of actual human movement and of optical and functional fitness which had informed the classic world. (*Fig. 405*) A line of sight from the entrance, for example, will be seen to fall along the northern corner of the altar and the southeastern column of the fourth–century prostylar temple, coming to rest exactly in the southwestern corner of the temenos wall. Entrance, altar, temple, and courtyard, though their relationship is apparently geometrical, have in fact been related to each other so that each element can be seen as a separate whole within the precisely known volume of the enclosure. Similarly, the southern votive base alongside the temple appears at first to be the same distance from the temple's flank as is that on the north. Such is not the case, however, and the base has been placed slightly closer to the temple so that another important line of sight, that which leads to the stairs descending to the fountain court below, may run unimpededly from the entrance to that point. Similarly, the placing of the small columned monument to the left of the entrance is neither haphazard or abstractly geometrical, but instead exactly defines the line of sight from the entrance to the northwestern corner of the enclosure. The whole space is thus clearly defined for an arc of vision from the propylon, and the objects in it are fixed in place at once. Out of this calm enclosure the worshiper moved downward again toward the hollow of the earth and the water of the court below.

Such engulfment by the earth connects the cults of other chthonic deities and heroes with that of Asklepios—who himself began his career as a human hero who suffered death—as do the practices of healing which were sometimes involved in them. The sanctuary of the hero Trophonius at Lebadeia, with its gorge, its snake, and its springs, is, as mentioned before, an example of this relationship. It is also apparent at the sanctuary of Amphiaraus at Oropos,[51] across Boeotia from the Trophonion, on the north coast of Attica near the ancient boundary between Athens and Thebes. Amphiaraus, it will be recalled, was the just prophet who was swallowed up with his chariot outside the walls of Thebes.[52] His cult was certainly connected with the old earth deities of the land and was placed by the Thebans in a deep but gentle gorge which ran into the heart of the mountains bordering the gulf of Euboea. Entrance to it by land would have wound between the hills and come finally to the narrow gorge through which a stream flowed out of the deeper clefts of the mountain and in which a spring rose. Entrance by sea would have involved a more clearly axial, though beautifully winding way for a longer distance. A fan-shaped arc of flatter land pushes out from the gorge toward the gulf, and from this point one would have followed the stream bed up the curving and always narrowing defile. From the northern entrance to the site a long stoa, lined with benches for sleeping pilgrims as at Epidauros, leads the eye directly toward the temple at the far end. (*Figs. 406, 407*) The temple itself, dating from the fourth century, had eight columns across the front and a shallow pronaos, but was otherwise simply a wide volume of space defined by outer walls and divided into nave and side aisles by two rows of interior columns. Offerings may have been made inside it as well as at the great altar in front of it, below which the sacred spring is found. The whole movement from stoa to temple, past the altar, is given rhythmic vitality despite the axis by the position of the altar itself and by the curved retaining wall which framed its western side. The worshiper's journey toward the temple would thus have been endowed with variety and surprise just before its conclusion. Behind the stoa a theater lies at a cross-axis to the site. Its volume opens out the otherwise tight enclosure, and its upper seats offer views not only of the ridge across the way but also of the openings in the rounded hills to the northeast. (*Fig. 408*) Though enclosed, the site is therefore not oppressive or awe-inspiring. It is serene and even soporofic. It is also scaled, much more than is Epidauros, to the individual. Even today, without the ceremonies which added their own dimension to it, the site itself can reduce strain, induce sleep, and perhaps even the long healing thoughts which its intercessor with the gods, its dead seer once a man, gave to his pilgrims in their dreams.

Asklepios, and the influence of his rites, thus brought a new kind of humanity to ancient chthonic practice, to the cult of heroes, and to the old, pre-Hellenic sense of oneness with the land. In his conflict with death he is never victorious but always unyielding, and in this his positive Hellenic pride and his kinship with Apollo as well as with the goddess, are manifest. In him the Greek is of the earth and worships it. But he accepts the power of the earth, not in resignation but as a weapon to battle black fate, death, and, in a sense, even Zeus himself who keeps the law of things as they are. So there are sites sacred to Asklepios which have about them something active, joyous, and daring. At Orchomenos his temple is set above the old Mycenaean town and has, like the Hellenistic city at Orchomenos itself, a long view across the waters of Lake Copais toward the mountain of Ptoon upon which Apollo stands.[53] Similarly, at Piraeus his sanctuary lay on the southern slope of the higher hill with a view toward the cone of Mount Oros across the Saronic gulf. In these ways the cult of Asklepios makes a kind of sum of many Hellenic qualities both in their developed Hellenistic form and in their most traditional aspect. His sanctuary on the island of Kos, largely of the third to the first centuries B.C. and with some later work, can demonstrate this fact.[54] While sacred to him, it celebrated also his most devoted human agent and hero, the physician Hippocrates, who was born upon the island. As seen from Kalymnos, the island rises thunderously out of the water, its peaks jagged against the sky. (*Fig. 409*) At this distance it seems a place holy to Aphrodite, rising, as do her greatest sites, splendidly out of the sea. We recall that Asklepios was associated with Aphrodite at her site of Troezen, and she with him at Epidauros. As a ship approaches the port of Kos on its northeastern shore it must pass close to the shore of Asia Minor. There the outstanding feature of the landscape toward Halikarnassos is a high conical hill which projects from the coast as a conspicuous promontory. From the harbor of Kos itself the cone is especially conspicuous, since it seems to stand almost directly on axis with the entrance to the harbor. (*Fig. 410*) From the town the way toward the Asklepieion turns its back upon the cone across the water and passes through the fertile coastal plain of the island. Upon a closer approach, the sanctuary reveals the traditional nature of its siting. (*Fig. 411*) It lies upon the flank of the first rise of land out of the plain. Beyond it the gently mounded foothills pile up, and directly beyond them in this first view the mountain ridge in the distance opens into a wide pair of curving horns, opening and flaring against the sky. Before the entrance to the sanctuary is reached, the mountain horns drop out of sight and are not seen again from it. They signal its presence and disappear. The sanctuary itself is organized in a series of terraces which ascend the slope. (*Fig. 412*) These too were partly reconstructed under Roman hegemony, both during antiquity and in the twentieth century. A great courtyard, with colonnades on three sides and with fountains in its eventually arcuated retaining wall on the south, forms the first platform. The next platform supports the great altar and several temples, one of them dedicated to Apollo, the other to Artemis. The retaining wall of this level is curved back on one side to form a deep exedra. On the topmost terrace, oriented well to the north, stood the temple of Asklepios, in the partial enclosure formed at rear and sides by the wings of a stoa. A monumental stairway connects the terraces with each other. (*Fig. 413*) At first sight this appears to be regular and axial, but it is soon seen that this is not precisely the case. From the first terrace the view is cut off. Ahead stands the great retaining wall with its arched niches. The courtyard which it defines on that side is a wide but sheltered space full of sun and the sound of water. But the wall ahead is not merely a space definer. It is asymmetrically arched on either side of the stairway (the arches a late addition), which is itself well to the right of its center. As one looked up the stairs the temple of Asklepios would have stood out against the sky, almost on axis ahead. Yet the axis is not a straight one, since in this view it is apparent that the second stairway which leads to the temple is decidedly off line with the first. A curving, cascading motion, like the swelling flow of the mountain's healing waters, is thus imparted to the heavy, monumental forms. They can never become rigid; a breath of action infuses them, and that action marks the more casually rhythmic approach, not the march, of a procession as it mounts toward the temple of the god. At the second level, however, the temple of Artemis, on the west, is set at a stiff cross–axis to the final stairs. But the altar in front of it develops a livelier angle, while the temple of Apollo to the east, Corinthian peripteral and late in date, turns actively upon the platform. Behind it the exedra, its enveloping niche also late, swings in a counter movement to that of the altar and the temple. (*Fig. 414*) The platform is thus regular only up to a point; as altar and temples turn rhythmically upon its surface, it too, in the exedra, begins to take part in the dance. From this platform of altar and temples the view has opened up once again, now across the plain of Kos and the waters of the Aegean toward the mainland of Asia Minor. The conical promontory seen earlier from the sea is again conspicuous, but neither the altar nor the lower stair is oriented upon it. The dance is free and swinging across the as yet unfocused horizon.

The stairs above mount directly to the temple of Asklepios, which stands as a dried–up Doric body, frontal and stiff in the center of the terminal platform, enclosed behind and to the sides by bounding colonnades. The worshiper has come up a freely shifting axis to a defined volume of space which seems to terminate the experience. But the platform of the temple is open to the north, and it can now be seen that both the temple of Asklepios and the nearer stairway below it are oriented directly at the conical hill across the sea. (*Fig. 415*) The god himself faces the sacred object across the vast expanse. The terraces below have fallen out of sight, and there remains only that one splendid relationship across the voids of space between the temple and the cone. The landscape view, against the free arc of which the buildings of the lower platform had swung, is now precisely focused and fixed, made definite and permanent. The meaning of the journey, the process of healing or of seeking to be healed, is now found to lie far beyond the self, as the temple and the landscape reveal it together and show it to lie in the earth's keeping. Now, too, the cone, somewhat as in Mycenaean times, becomes the dominant object of focus, and the shrine of long–lived Nestor is recalled. (*Fig. 50*) The reason seems apparent, because the cone had always been the special symbol of the earth's safety, protection, and rest, rather than, like the horns, of its power. At the same time, as seen from the head of the topmost stairs in front of the temple of Asklepios, the cone causes the counter-movements of the lower ranges of terrace and of the objects upon them to take on new vitality, because the true objective which discreetly controls them has been perceived. (*Fig. 416*) So, too, the temple of Artemis is tied to the final axis and thus to the cone, but the temple of Apollo is appropriately treated as an actively intrusive force. It is still, then, a Greek world on Kos, which the rebuildings and additions of the Roman period respected and, indeed, enhanced. Each part, despite the relative regularization which has taken place, can remain free to act out its own role in an articulate way because the whole is ordered far beyond itself by the securely seen, known, and holy forms of the land. With the horizon so fixed, the eye can then swing freely toward the northwest, sweeping across the horns which rise beyond the cone along the upper ridges of the coastal mountains of Asia. (*Fig. 417*) It can travel far in the northward direction across the sea precisely because it is led to seek out the solid islands that mark the way. So Odysseus had followed the islands home, but now the hero himself is a god. Because the divinity at Kos is Hippocrates–Asklepios, the wholly victorious daimon, divinized man, his immortality secured and his presence elevated on high, above the other gods.

A revealing contrast can be made between the sanctuary of Asklepios on Kos and the Roman Temple of Fortune at Praeneste, seventeen kilometers south of Rome.[55] Here, too, we have returned to the great mother, Fortuna Primigenia, nurse and offspring of Jupiter, who gave his oracles from the rock and whose sacred hill is itself a massive cone.[56] The Temple of Fortune, as finally completed, may be thought of as the first monument of Roman Imperial architecture. (*Fig. 418*) Unlike the additions of the Roman period on Kos, it is wholly Roman in intention. Yet it would be difficult to believe that its architects, of the late second or early first centuries, did not have the example of Asklepios' sanctuary in mind, although their work, in its verticality, its great scale, and its tightly interwoven interior and exterior views, also recalls that at Pergamon. As at Kos, Pergamon, and Lindos, the sanctuary at Praeneste climbs its hillside in a series of terraces but culminates not in a rectangular temple within a colonnaded enclosure but in a great stepped exedra. This was a little like a truncated Hellenistic theater, but it had its own crowning colonnade, above which a high tholos rose. The elements at Praeneste are rigidly symmetrical, as those at the Greek sites are not. The central axis of movement at Praeneste is fixed, and the parts are therefore distributed as the definers of symmetrical spaces to left and right according to an internal spatial principle. That principle, while decisive, is based upon the desire for a kind of security which the Greek had normally been willing to deny himself. The parts on the left echo, that is, the parts on the right, so that it is not the intensity of specific actions in the landscape but the careful orientation of the participant in an interior hierarchical order which determines the placement of the elements of the whole. It is true that Mnesicles' axially symmetrical Propylaia is once again recalled; but that led to an open, active acropolis summit, the opposite of itself. It was not, as here, the whole of the experience, which was there cupped in the end only by Hymettos' mountain horns. Praeneste's complex of massively constructed terraces may itself be conceived of as an artificial mountain, whose two monumental ramps, recalling those of Mesopotamian ziggurats, rise diagonally from left and right above the vaulted, cavelike chambers below and meet in the center of the intermediate terrace. The side approach recalls that at Pergamon, but the ramps stiffen the movement and bring it to a central point. Exedras in the retaining wall, richly screened by columns, are symmetrically disposed off that center. Directly up from it runs the steep stair which leads to the upper terrace where the exedra spread its open arms and the tholos temple lifted climactically behind them on the central axis like a high head. The curvilinear shapes so composed recall those of the megalithic sanctuaries in the shape of the goddess on Malta, (*Fig. 20*) as many later Roman architectural complexes, like the Fora of Augustus and Trajan and parts of Hadrian's villa, (*Figs. 419, 420*) were even more specifically to do.[57] Once more, as in pre–Hellenic, central Mediterranean tradition, it may be a desire for unquestionable security in the body of the goddess which forms the design. But the Roman truth is more than that: insofar as Praeneste and its Imperial progeny create both security and dominion at vast scale, mass scale, in fact, appropriate to the objectives of a military empire and indicating that there are no true alternatives at all for human action but only a single way from which all else, however elaborate, must develop. The old labyrinth is now stiffened into a conceptually abstract spatial pattern.

From the dominating height of Praeneste's exedra, and sheltered by its arc, one may look across an expansive landscape, directly through a wide break in the hills toward the Tyrrhenian sea. It is a view for which the temple provides a magnificent viewing platform, and which its own axis locks securely into the landscape cleft. It completes the natural shape and fans out toward it, so that temple and land are a single unit, like the old cave of the goddess opened outward to embrace the world. (*Fig. 418b*) At the same time the temple complex itself, lucid and rational, is defined by its own internal laws, as logical, self–sufficient, and secure as the disciplines of Rome. Progress through it is a march; the view from it an exercise in directed command, as it opens symmetrically around its axis like the legion deploying. Therefore, and this is the essential point, the difference between Praeneste and, for example, Kos is that

Kos is made up of solid elements which act both separate from, and in a complementary relationship to, each other and the landscape, while Praeneste, because of the very realization of internal and external security which informs it, is a single, highly integrated hollow unit which does not so act. A little like the Cretan palaces, Praeneste and its landscape are a single shape, except that now both are felt wholly as containers—as indeed most Roman and later buildings were to be felt—and no solid landscape object forms the focus of the view. For all these reasons, the complexities explored by the Hellenic investigation of the human relationship to nature are ruled out at Praeneste, as they are in Roman architecture generally and, by extension, in western architecture as a whole until, perhaps, the most recent decades of the modern period.[58] Thus the wider architectural environment, deriving from a larger view of wholeness, is created by Kos, which is still traditionally Greek enough to allow for alternatives and to encourage unexpected discoveries as it makes its reciprocal structure of human action and Olympian fact in relation to the fixed shapes of the natural world. For all its splendidly conceived integration of curvilinear and rectangular construction and geometry, Praeneste, like the work of the great architects of the Renaissance who studied it, might therefore have appeared to the earlier Greeks as at once illiberal, timid, and impious.

Yet Praeneste also documents the ability of the Romans to make a conclusive syncretism out of many disparate Hellenistic elements. In this it recalls the convincing manner in which they developed and instinctively integrated the many special building types of halls, houses, public structures, and so on with which the Greeks had tentatively experimented but for whose special potentialities they seem never to have been able to work up much enthusiasm, perhaps because they were not compulsive builders, as the Romans clearly were, and preferred to be outside rather than in. But it may also be that, in the decline of the classic polis, such types represented a truly half–hearted effort for the Greeks, recreating in fragments what had been so fully embodied when the point of the city's life was wholly stated by the temple and the land.[59]

It is therefore incorrect to say, as some critics have done, that Greek sacred architecture, because of the relative simplicity of its temple form, was itself a rigid and limited one. Instead, the reverse is true, and no architecture before or since has been able to explore the problems of being and action quite so forcefully or with such permanent particularity. That exploration has been central to the life of western civilization and is most cogent to it once again in its present challenged phase. It took place because the Greek was prepared to use his intellect both freely and with reverence upon the traditions of awe, joy, and terror which he had inherited from the pre–rational ages. Expecting, most often, no immortal reward for proper action, he was moved to test the poignancy of human desires against the hard reality of nature's demands, saw both in strong, clear shapes and took nothing from the force of either. Believing himself to be unique, but at his best neither arrogant nor despairing in the circle of the world, he was able not only to conceive of the fundamental oneness, but to face the apparent separateness, of things. So the world he built, strictly selective though its elements were, was the world entire. In this he was aided by the special landscape which was his home, where movement always found its focus and variety its balance: the plain its horned or mounded peak, the sea its islands, the cleft its olive–laden valley, and the mountain height its sea.

The Greek architect therefore dealt with forms both natural and constructed. With them he celebrated his three deathless themes: the sanctity of the earth, the tragic stature of mortal life upon the earth, and the whole natures of those recognitions of the facts of existence which are the gods.

Appendix 1

ADDENDA

IN *The Earth, the Temple, and the Gods* I tried to show that all important Greek sanctuaries grew up around open altars which were normally sited where they are because the place itself first suggested the presence of a divine being. Indeed, its natural forms were regarded as embodying that presence. The temple, when finally built, embodied it also, now in terms of the human conception of the divinity. Between the two kinds of shapes a fundamental counterplay developed, seen most richly in the late archaic and classic periods, which created an architectural balance of tensions between the natural and the man–made. Whole sets of meanings having to do with the facts of existence as they could be physically perceived were developed out of these relationships, since the compositional elements involved were those which most directly expressed the demands of the earth and the aspirations of humanity. The chosen and the constructed forms were alike sculpturally real and powerful, so that the force of the god moves through them both and can, to a certain extent, be felt and analyzed today.

The forms in question are at once general and specific, so that absolute differences of character may be distinguished between them, as is possible only between creatures of the same species. So all temples are built of much the same elements, but each differs in one way or another from all others. With the sites it is the same, and a general set of natural shapes tends to dominate the topography of all those places identified by the Greeks as especially holy. From the Minoan period onward throughout all of Greek antiquity (later and elsewhere, too, I think, but that is another study) the cone and the horns seem to play major roles: the conical hill or mountain, the hornshaped cleft or double peak. With the specific meanings which may originally have been assigned to these shapes during the second millennium when, as in the palaces of Crete and the megara of the Mycenaean lords, they dominated all, I have already attempted to deal.[1] By the Greek archaic period they had clearly come to play only a part, though still a major one, in a more complex and actively varied set of recognitions, embodiments, and relationships.[2]

It has therefore seemed worthwhile to discuss a few more sites, other than the some hundred and fifty or so analyzed or mentioned in this book, where such shapes can be found, but where

This first appeared as an article, "The Earth, the Temple, and the Gods: Greek Sacred Architecture. Addenda," in *Journal of the Society of Architectural Historians*, 23 (May, 1964), 89–99. I wish I might have included, and cannot forebear to mention, the island of Boreas, Tenos, with its single great horn around which the winds divide, while the sanctuary of a goddess is throned in its lee and the bay of Poseidon and Amphitrite, unbroken as a mirror, lies on the southern shore far below it. Across the water, on Delos, the windblown figures on the upper works of the Temple of the Athenians, Boreas among them, were lifted into those very winds from Tenos, while the site itself, protected by the island's shoulder, lay quiet below them.

they are by no means the only factors involved. The sites are widely chosen: the Valley of the Muses with an altar, stoa and theater; the sanctuary of Athena Kranaia at Elateia, with a Doric temple; that of Aphrodite at Ta Messa, on Lesbos, with an Ionic one; finally, Thasos, an entire island town, with a Herakleion and sculptured gates. Unhappily, none of the sites in question can show us the standing bodies of temples in place, so that our perceptions can be only partial, touching perhaps little more than half the whole. But that percentage is not such a bad one; it is much less partial than would be the case if, as has been all too common in the past, we were to consider only the remains of constructions and not the meaningful landscapes in which they lie and with which they were originally intended by the Greeks to form an architectural whole of unprecedented vigor and completeness.

The Valley of the Muses at first recalls Ptoon, which looks westward toward it across Boeotia,[3] but the final atmosphere it creates is very different. Like Ptoon it is high, but the long rising path into it, running beside its stream, the Permessos, is a gentle one. Passing beyond Thespiae, one eventually leaves the main crested ridge of Cithairon behind on the left. Ahead the valley begins to narrow and to climb toward the snows on the flank of Helikon, while the conical hill which is usually identified with Hesiod's Ascra[4] closes in on the right. (*Figs. 421, 422*) Ahead the lifting hollow flows upward in long, gentle, female curves until it reaches the rock ridges, heraldically horned, that press in beyond Ascra toward Helikon's swelling bulk on the left. The whole is like a deep–breathing body lying open to the sky. Only the narrow cleft of the Permessos remains open between the slanting masses. Before it, on Helikon's slope, stands the Muses' open altar[5] (not a temple, as was once thought), poised above the stream and dominated by the cleft and by the split rocks of the cliff. (*Figs. 423, 424*) Here the presence of Apollo is felt, his dark side; the place is dread.

But one naturally turns at the altar, and all is changed, because one had climbed higher than one had realized, so that now the view runs farther out across the plain than could have been believed possible before. (*Fig. 425*) Cithairon is out of sight to the south, but Parnes is seen to its uttermost northern ridges, upon one of which, far off beyond Tanagra and even Oropos, the bright scar of the tiniest of quarries shows clear. One is looking with the eye of a god, telescopically, across all of Boeotia and on into Attica, picking up the snow peaks of Euboea on the way. The earth is a concave bowl, defined at a distance vast but visually precise by its bounding mountains, which shape the sky as well. Now the god is Zeus, as one feels that unstrained dominion and embracing calm which are characteristic of sites peculiarly sacred to him,[6] and remembers that the Muses, Κοῦραι Διὸς αἰγιόχοιο, are his daughters. They would have to be, since, as Hesiod's epithet indicates, it is he who holds the power, and the fulfillment of any action, the Τέλος, is in his hands.

Above the altar the long platform of the stoa thrusts out firmly above the Permessos. (*Figs. 423, 424*) It is beautifully placed to enhance the sense of turning toward bright space from the cliffs and the darkness. Indeed, it swings grandly out under the cleft, while above it the theater rises on the flank of Helikon, a natural hollow and highest of all. Here the view is grander yet. Ascra, a purely conical mound, lies before it more or less on the axis of the altar, while the long slide to the plain opens southeastward away. (*Fig. 425*) Around the theater the whole flank of the mountain is running with springs, opening with inexhaustible abundance, prodigal of power.

From the theater the cleft lies to the left, its crowning horns rising directly above it. (*Fig. 424*) One can easily imagine the Muses issuing forth out of this passage between worlds, this Gate of Horn—one at a time perhaps, rather mincingly, holding out their chitons with *korai* hands. The curving base upon which their images may have stood before the stoa,[7] under the theater, (*Fig. 423*) seems the ideal position for them: the dark cleft of power on their left hand and the whole world to which they sing—falsely, so they claim, as they can, but truly if they will—opening in its concave sweep before them. Bitchy, they address mankind without pity, since the lot which the gods, who are the facts of things, give mortal life is hard:

Ποιμένες ἄγραυλοι, κάκ' ἐλέγχεα, γαστέρες οἶον

Hesiod has them say.

The "shepherds of the wilderness" still stand in their cloaks under Helikon, and the farmers "mere bellies," dig in the plain. But to a few men, as to Hesiod guarding his flock one day, the Muses give, by the will of Zeus of the Aegis, liberation through song. So, too, their valley and its horned cleft: it is the place of inspiration's terror, and of the release that comes when the song flows out in the fulfillment of Zeus at last. So there is no temple, nothing further to embody, only space and music flooding out across all the earth from here.

The northern buttresses of Parnassos (*Fig. 426*) are invoked, above Elateia, by a deity named Athena Kranaia (Dorian "of the springs"). Pausanias, the only ancient writer to mention this sanctuary, makes quite a point of telling us that the climb to the temple from the ancient town of Elateia is a surprisingly easy one until it culminates in "a hill which, though for the most part precipitous, is neither very large nor very high."[8] Pierre Paris, who excavated the sanctuary,[9] takes issue with this statement, and, with some justice, calls the last lap "pénible." It climbs out of a rough, torrent-running gorge up the steep slope of a bald hill, set within a heavy, barren semi-circle of higher ridges. The whole formation, as seen from the plain or from the cascade of gentle foothills upon which the town of Elateia itself was placed, seems to writhe apart to reveal sets of pointed peaks and to poise the temple on its platform within a frame of mountains.

The summit of the temple's hill was built out behind a retaining wall into an artificial platform at two levels, and the temple was pushed hard up against the temenos wall on the north, the highest point in the sanctuary. (*Figs. 428, 429*) It was oriented east and west, though which direction the image faced is impossible to tell. (Paris restores a western facing, which he calls north, being in general a quarter turn of the compass off in his description of the site.) The stylobate was, apparently, somewhat lower than the temenos wall, so that the columns were set tight against it and were masked by it to the height of several feet or so. This curious arrangement emphasized the temple's determined grip on the north edge of its platform; it must almost have seemed as if leaning over the wall. (*Fig. 428*) In so doing, it brought into special prominence the dizzy gorges that fall off directly below it on that side. (*Fig. 427*) Down into these flow precipices of rock, scored by landslides. Northeastward the hillsides are more rounded, but still everything funnels rather frighteningly down. The temple's crowding of the temenos wall thus has special plastic meaning, dramatizing as it does its goddess' contact with the depths below and with the streams that run through them and wear the earth away. In this the setting of the temple at Segesta is recalled and, in its own way, that of Athena at Lindos.[10]

The surrounding hills are blank and smothering, and they cut off almost three-quarters of the view. Only in the southern arc back across the lower slopes of the platform can the vision expand. It goes far down the plain toward Helikon but is caught most of all by Parnassos' splendid flank, rising through cloud in symphonic masses of thrones and horns. (*Figs. 426, 432*) The mountain lifts in two slanting bastions which frame further peaks beyond them. Forward, projecting into the plain, lies a concave mass like a cone hollowed out and cut back, a great chair of hill, behind which the flanking bastions open in their V. Here is the shape of release and power; on the side toward it, Athena's own hill, at a natural platform halfway down, bursts open in a spring. The sense is of victory over clogging, earth–swaddling forces. It does much to explain the identification of the goddess here with Athena rather than, for example, with Artemis, whose presence the severity of the immediate site itself otherwise does much to suggest.[11]

At the edge of her platform, farthest from Parnassos and presenting its flank to the mountain and to its own ranges of dependencies lower down, Athena's temple was a compact Doric body, an active counterforce to the mountain's cones and horns. (*Fig. 428*) The surviving fifth–century capital on the site (*Fig. 430*) was identified by Paris with those of the Hephaisteion in Athens, but he felt it to be slightly earlier than they, because somewhat heavier. In any event, it is ripe and springy; the echinus pushes upward in a steepening profile but is still spread and rounded off enough to embody an expansive muscular force. At the same time, the capital as a whole is thick and blunt, an appropriate form for its graceless, demanding site and entirely expressive of the tenacious Athena who takes her position there. Consequently, its distinction from the capitals of the unassumingly urbane Hephaisteion may be a matter of place, not of time. Like all Greek capitals up through the classic period, it is at once involved in a general formal development and adjusted to the expressive demands of a specific situation. The other details of the temple as restored by Paris, especially the height of the columns, may be open to some question, but the capital itself is enough to show that—again like most archaic and classic temples—the building was conceived of as a potent sculptural body. The other capital on the site, (*Fig. 431*) dating from the fourth century, has an abacus of the same dimensions as the other; it may have been used in some repair of the temple. Whatever the case, it can clearly show us how the archaic and classic conception of bodily energy and sculptural presence had already been largely abandoned by that time.

But the fifth–century temple surely stood on its bluff, stern summit as a physical being, solid and strong. It presented Parnassos across the plain with the image of a force no less intense than its own, but abstractly, thus humanly, formed.

The Temple of Aphrodite at Messa or, rather, in Ta Messa (the interior) of Lesbos, is so placed as to bring into focus the generous sweep of land and water which the center of that island is. It can still do so despite the fact that much of it has disappeared even since Koldewey's time.[12] The outline of the temple can hardly be traced, although its placement is clear. The tiny church of Taxiarchis built upon it is itself an unroofed ruin, but offerings are still made within its shell. One suspects a considerable temenos in the area.

The perimeter of Lesbos makes nearly a perfect triangle, though somewhat rounded off into curves. (*Fig. 433*) The extremities are marked by Mounts Levethimno, Ordymnos and, appropriately dominant, Olympos. But the most obvious internal form which the island possesses is that of a long, hollow ellipse, where the Gulf of Kaloni intrudes deeply into the land and is almost entirely enclosed by it. Aphrodite's temple is placed on marshy ground just beyond the head of the Gulf, exactly at the point from which the landscape's shape as a whole can be grasped most clearly. (*Fig. 434*) Low, gently rounded hills enframe the site on its three landward sides; they begin to swing around in an arc which is picked up by hill profiles at a greater distance and directed southward by them to terminate in the two capes that define the mouth of the gulf. (*Fig. 435*) These prongs of headland are horizontal horns at the limit of visual scale, enclosing the gulf's liquid body. The image of fertility so engendered is in accord with what seems to have been one important aspect of horn symbolism from the earliest period onward.[13]

The whole set of forms, undramatic but very firm, locks perfectly into place only from the point where the temple was built. In other words, it was at this spot that the peculiarly appropriate completeness of the landscape's shape first suggested the presence of a divinely ordering being who might be identified with Aphrodite. The siting and form of the temple then made that presence all the more apparent. Oriented east and west, it at once locked itself firmly into the low cups of hills on those bearings and at the same time picked up with its long south flank the only other straight horizontal line to be seen anywhere about: the mouth of the gulf, where the water is starkly flat between the two gently slanting, sharply terminated headlands. (*Fig. 435*) Each straight line, the natural and the man–made, calls attention to its opposite number. The eye goes from one to the other and is thus forced to be aware of the distance between them; a vast space, or shape, is formed.

Southeastward, Mount Olympos leans over the nearer hills as a great domed mass, flanked by lifting shoulders and eastward by a much smaller subsidiary set of horns. (*Figs. 434, 436*) This is the most violent and dramatic aspect that Olympos offers. From closer at hand, across the famous Gulf of Yera, for example, or on other bearings, its shape is undistinguished, and the rock cone of the summit looks too small for the sprawling mass below it. But from Messa, though far off, it is a looming presence, a thunderhead bristling with the images of power, a true mountain of Aphrodite, like Acrocorinth or Eryx, an unreasonable and irresistible force.[14] And it is the only one of Lesbos' three mountains which is visible from the site itself, though on the approach from the south the sharp summit of Mount Levethimno lies just over the enclosing hill lines to northwestward. Celestial orientation and the landscape shape as a whole worked together to swing the temple eastward away from Olympos, however, so that the cella did not face the mountain directly, as the court of a Minoan palace or a Mycenaean megaron, in their own appropriate locations, would have tried to do.[15] A larger, subtler and more general recognition of natural order is thus, as in most Greek sanctuaries, apparent here.[16]

The temple itself not only indicated the mouth of the gulf but also celebrated the soggy earth from which it rose. Hellenistic in date, of about 280 B.C., it was Ionic, 8 × 14, and pseudo-dipteral: of a type, like that by Hermogenes of Artemis at Magnesia, which was much admired by Vitruvius for its sheltering,[17] spatial qualities. (*Fig. 434*) As such it was a slightly desiccated successor to the great dipteral Ionic temples of the archaic period, among them those of Artemis at Ephesos and Hera on Samos. Like those temples, it was placed on low, marshy ground in such a way as to render a vast arc of land and seascape physically apparent.[18] The mighty circle defined by Hera at Samos comes especially to mind. Like those temples, too, and appropriately on the flat site with its abundant water, the widely spread, slender, Ionic columns tended to form a tree-like grove rather than a compactly massed Doric sculptural body.[19]

Meager, therefore, though the remains on the site now are, the place itself can call up the missing fragments for us and, as the placement of the temple makes us see the whole, can show us Aphrodite, too, as she is embodied in the heart of Lesbos: not as she may be in the taut, tight-pointed rock cones of Sappho's Eressos, but in the stretched-out fulness of land and water, marsh, mountain, and sea, perfectly shaped, engrossing and complete.

Thasos is an excellent example of a colonial site—and a city, not primarily a sanctuary—where the Greek gods had to be imported by the colonist. (*Figs. 437, 438*) A similar problem arose of course in the west, with interesting solutions to it.[20] Ideal for the purpose, though seldom rating the true temple that Thasos gave him, was the hero Herakles, who helped secure the Hellenic world from the more intransigent aspects of nature's force. At Thasos the Herakleion is the most elaborate sanctuary yet discovered. (*Fig. 438*) It is set near the southern edge of the town and faces the great inland ridge of the island, wooded, coned, and horned. (*Fig. 439*) The shapes in question are by no means obscured by their trees, so that an equal clarity may be assumed for related formations on mountains such as Hymettos[21] which, though bare now, were forested during most of antiquity. The profile of the ridge on Thasos strikingly resembles that of Mount Pangaion, close by on the mainland of Thrace, as it is seen from Philippi, seat of Bendis, the Thracian Artemis. (*Fig. 440*) Both ridges feature a pointed cone to the left and low, crumpled horns to the right. Each thus exhibits, like most mountains which define sites sacred to Artemis, both the major symbols of chthonic power.[22] Artemis Polo herself had a sanctuary embedded in the heart of Thasos behind the Agora, but it is the strangely broad, short, widely dipteral Ionic temple of Herakles—very much a shelter rather than a god's body—which faces the ridge, opposing its power or drawing it to itself. Dating, according to its excavator, from about 500 B.C., and curious indeed for that time, it replaced a temple of the Geometric period which seems to have faced north toward the altar, from which the ridge would have been visible over it.[23] The new temple represents a different conception, in which the center of sacrifice lies between the major natural and man-made forms, even though it is also framed in a court by subsidiary buildings. Entrance from the propylon leads directly to the steps of the altar, from which temple and ridge rise high together. Water wells up around the sanctuary, and the most southerly element of it always remained an offering pithos sunk in the ground within an archaic peripteral tholos. In all ways, therefore, the forces of the earth are gripped closely here, like Herakles entwined with a snake.

Southward beyond the pithos were three of the famous sculptured gates of the town, carved with figures in relief.[24] They, too, faced the inland ridge. Opposite the horns, symbols of active force and dominion, sits a throned figure, mutilated, identified by Picard with Zeus, by Bernard[25] with Hera. (*Fig. 438*) King or Queen, the figure is clearly that of a ruler and, itself throned, faces that shape, the horns, which, since the second millennium at least, had always been associated with the lap of the goddess of the earth, the consecrated seat of power.[26] (A house in the way prevents photography here.)

Directly opposite the cone was Herakles, hunched up into a fat Ionian ball, lion-maned, shooting his bow out the gate, as if aiming an arrow at the cone. (*Figs. 438, 441*) But Herakles, now in Istanbul, was not alone at his gate. On the opposite side, recorded only in an amateur drawing, was Dionysos and his maenadic train, waving their vines and entering the town. So from the cone, shaped like the tombs of heroes,[27] and expressive of the earth's more nourishing, if engulfing, forces, the god of resurrection and the vine is welcomed by the polis, which invites him to overwhelm for his season the civil cautions of every day. Herakles may be counted upon to redress the balance and to keep any unreasonably dangerous followers out. The two are plainly regarded as necessary sides to a coin, like the coins of Thasos: Herakles drawing the bow on one side, Dionysos glassy–eyed on the other. (*Fig. 441*)

The next gate to the east carries on the theme, but now it is most closely related not to the far ridge but to two swelling conical foothills that here lie close outside the walls. (*Figs. 437, 438, 444*) Between them, on the lowest slope of one, was set the sanctuary of Demeter and, probably, Persephone.[28] The necropolis of the town was nearby. From this place of burial comes the mysterious figure of Silenus, the old teacher of that kind of wisdom which accepts the earth's rhythmic power. (*Fig. 443*) The wild hope of resurrection may roll in with him, as it may do with his master Dionysos to the west. But here Herakles is outflanked, and the satyr enters unopposed, a monster made free of the town, his left hand groping into the gate. Booted like a countryman, big–bellied and horse–tailed, he lifts his cantharus high before him: apostle of excess, wise, beastly, animal man, here one of the most impressive of his kind.

But the town is a work of calculated human art. Its ultimate divinity is an uncompromising one and neither receives nor wrestles with the anarchy of the earth but has to be seen as rising resolutely above it. So the Temple of Athena Poliouchos was placed upon a massive artificial platform of splendid masonry built out between the twin summits (Pan on one, Apollo probably on the other) of the semicircular ridge that rises east of the town and cups it in its hollow.[29] (*Figs. 437, 438, 444–446*) The temple is so placed before the complementary peaks as to seem to come sailing out from between them, lifted as if upon their wave and flourished between their horns as a counterforce to the shapes of the southern ridge. (*Figs. 444, 446*) Here the goddess must have faced west, not east, because the cross wall behind the west end of the existing foundations of her temple is farther back and thicker than that behind the east end. (*Fig. 438*) It must therefore have had the door to the cella in it. The archaeological criteria involved, which are apparently generally accepted now despite other views expressed earlier,[30] are exactly the same as those which assign a western facing to the Temple of Apollo at Delos, another island site.

Facing westward, Athena overlooked the city, showing it her temple's face in its best three–quarter view, and keeping under the glance of her own cool grey eyes not only the aforementioned ridge with its disquieting forces, but also the Poseidonion and the cup of harbor below her (*Fig. 445*) and, in the distance, the blue hills of barbarian Thrace. From the Agora her presence rises directly overhead. (*Fig. 446*) The Temple of Zeus faces toward her. Victory is carried forward on a gally below her.[31] She thus climaxes all civic functions, monuments, and deities with her incomparable sculptural force.

It would be hard to imagine a more complete interplay between natural and man–made forms than this on Thasos, or one more intelligently conceived. To start with, of course, the topography of the site held potential meaning in religious no less than practical terms. The distinction would have been meaningless to the archaic Greeks in any case; those who make it too strictly now are carrying nineteenth–century positivistic materialism further than is wise to do for the interpretation of a people who never heard of it and whose generous sense of sanctities pervaded all their affairs. For them, Thasos was especially favored with chthonic forces, and they used them all, constructing around them, and in balance with them, the ritual which civic life, to function properly, has to be. So Herakles keeps off the tattooed men and the horrors but seizes the springs of life as well, while that side of wild nature which is most necessary to human sanity is grandly ushered in. Above it all, Athena watches, turning her back on the sunrise for her town.

Appendix 2
THE CAPITALS OF KLOPEDI

SOMETHING OVER AN HOUR'S walk west of the town of Hagia Paraskevi, at a place called Klopedi, on the island of Mytilini (the ancient Lesbos) any moderately energetic tourist may enjoy an experience comparable to those which were so poisonously exploited by eighteenth–century travelers. He can see Greek antiquities of first quality in the rough, because here some of the finest Greek capitals extant have been built into a farmer's stone wall. They are Aeolic capitals as well, of that rare archaic mode which died out by the end of the sixth century. The only other examples of their type which can truly compare with them are those few, now in Istanbul, which were found at Larisa and Neandria in Asia Minor, and on the acropolis of the town of Mytilini itself. Taken as a whole, the temple from which they came, perhaps of Apollo, would seem to have been the masterwork of its style. It was a kind of Aeolic Parthenon, perhaps also the last Aeolic temple ever built. If so, it brought its mode to a grand conclusion: embodying, so its capitals tell us, a passion, splendor, and force comparable to that engendered by the literary generation just past, which had produced Sappho and Alcaeus.

If the Temple of Aphrodite in Ta Messa is the personification of the center of Lesbos, the sanctuary at Klopedi, which may be that of Apollo Napaios, is surely its guardian.[1] From it, as from Aphrodite's neighboring lowlands, the hunched cone of Mount Olympos is in view, and it too looks across the Gulf of Kaloni. Unlike Aphrodite, it overlooks the water from a height, but it does so at a considerable distance, set back in defilade from the shore. It occupies not the summit but the eastern shoulder of an inconspicuous hill, and is backed by the higher masses of Mount Levethimno to the north. Its position is that of a man who wants to see and not be seen and who has no intention of standing silhouetted against the sky except upon the close approach of proven friends.

There were in fact two beings personified on the hill: two temples, facing eastward. (*Fig. 447*) That which its excavator called the earlier in date stood with its flank exactly on the military crest.[2] From it, the earth sweeps generously down toward the south (*Fig. 448*), a concave bowl with few blind spots in it, until it rises to its complementary opposite, an equally wide-

This first appeared as an article, "Capitals of Klopedi," in *The Architectural Review, 135* (February, 1964), 129–134.

spreading, low mounded hill that masks much of the shore. Of this temple only part of the foundations exist, now almost entirely covered over again after Evanghelides' excavation of forty years ago. One must at present largely take the excavator's word for its early date. The broad proportions of the plan recall those of many Hellenistic peripteral temples, but the remains are probably too slight to support any firm conclusions.

The second temple (*Fig. 449*) was set north of the other, almost exactly parallel to it. It lies just below the height of the shoulder, above which it would have risen and across which, to the north, the elegant cone of Mount Levethimno's summit lifts high. The bosses which were to be seen on the stereobate at the time of excavation showed that this temple was never entirely finished, so that it may still have been under construction at the time of the Persian conquest. It would seem to date from somewhere as late as the last quarter of the sixth century, which may perhaps be legitimately thought of as the classic Aeolic period. Like the Doric Parthenon of rather less than three generations later, it had a peristyle of eight by seventeen columns, and was thus extremely long, projecting well westward of the other temple and seen above and beyond it on the approach to the sanctuary from the south. Two of its simply cushioned column bases (*Figs. 450, 451*) were in situ on the stylobate at the time of excavation. From their dimensions it is obvious that the splendid Aeolic capitals found in and around the site belonged to this temple. Koldewey found some, Evanghelides others, so that the fragments of apparently twenty–two or twenty–three are known; though where all the pieces may be now is something of a puzzle. Only the two complete capitals which were transported to the museum of Mytilini have been published, and then only in archaeological periodicals of restricted circulation. They have found their way as illustrations into no general book, where they most richly deserve to be. With the demolition of their museum building (designed by an American architect and reputed to have been of unparalleled inefficiency) they now lie in the open on a bluff under the *Kastro*, near a *pavillon de danse*. Here they are alive in the sunlight and seem to take no harm, being carved from a hard, light grey granite.

Equally tough and unweathered are the two capitals which have been built into the aforesaid wall on the slope just south of the sanctuary at Klopedi itself. (*Figs. 452, 452a*) There are also some column drums (*Fig. 452c*) embedded in this and adjacent walls. Upside down, and symmetrically balanced off a block from the temple which is set between them, the capitals resemble eyes rising out of the ground, and the whole composition calls up the apparition of a monstrous face. There can be little doubt that the farmer in question arranged the effect on purpose and worked hard to get it, perhaps with apotropaic intent, perhaps simply for fun.

The capitals are large. Koldewey (*Fig. 453*) gives the dimensions. For Evanghelides (*Fig. 454*) a human being gives the scale, for us a horse. (*Fig. 455*) They are generous and firm like the site, sweeping out big in the coil. Condis has compared those in Mytilini with other Aeolic capitals, but perhaps a word more may be said.[3] Behind the Aeolic type itself lie fairly close Asiatic, particularly Assyrian, prototypes. After it comes the Ionic mode which some regard as an outgrowth of Aeolic experiments and others as simply an eventually more successful variant from the same or another parent Asiatic stem.[4] Between its precursors and successors, however, the Aeolic exhibits a typically Greek development in itself.

The example from Larisa (*Fig. 456a*) is still treelike, delicate and small in the multiple volutes, elegant and tentative, not geometrically decisive and thus not yet wholly Greek in form. The one from Neandria (*Fig. 456b*) builds up the architectural scale of its volutes and clarifies its structural geometry in a typically Greek way, so creating the more or less canonical Aeolic shape. The coils are still shown as separate each from the other and as plantlike, sap–filled, in character. The example in Istanbul from the acropolis of Mytilini (*Fig. 456c*) approaches in shape and dimension those from Klopedi and was once identified, or confused, with them.[5] Condis has pointed out the main difference, however: that the channel between the coils, indicating space and air between them, is still present in the capital in Istanbul but lacking in those from the temple at Klopedi.

The Klopedi capitals are thus more compact, sculpturally dense, and architecturally firm. In terms of general Greek intentions, they—and not, for instance, the more famous and in some ways freer capitals from Neandria—seem the apogee of the style. There is another related point. The fleshy coil of the volute is framed by a kind of flange both above and below it in the capitals from Neandria and Mytilini alike; those from Klopedi use only the outer flange. The effect of the former system becomes rather confused and over–articulated as the volute coils around on itself and the flanges seem to multiply beyond reason, so breaking up the general bulkiness and unity of mass toward which the capital from Mytilini, for example, seems otherwise aiming. The capitals from Klopedi solve the problem by an adjustment which is already extremely sophisticated in an optical sense (that, too, a classic Greek trait): not two flanges but one, which visually functions enough like two in order to frame the volute as it coils but which does not become so visually obsessive as to destroy the compact force of the sculptural body as a whole or, conversely, to draw attention away from the writhing tentacle of the volute itself.

It is, I think, just this combination of compact mass with generous spread that makes these capitals so effective. They are big and releasing forms. One cannot but think of all the Aeolic capitals as somehow related in feeling to their geographical setting of Aeolic islands and coastal plain and to the topography of the specific sites where they have been found—sweeping sites all: Larisa on its tabletop hill above a vast littoral; Neandria with a view as wide as Troy's, taking in, as Koldewey showed,[6] both the cone of Mount Athos and the horns of Samothrace across the Aegean; finally Klopedi, riding the broad curves of central Lesbos.

On the other hand, the architectural shortcomings of the Aeolic capital are apparent, and the reasons for its eventual abandonment in favor of (or its modification into) the Ionic capital seem clear. What, for one, could it do at a corner?[7] It is purely two–dimensional in conception, fundamentally a relief capital, a bracket. Related to this is the fact that the sides and bottoms of its huge volutes are inert surfaces; the mass becomes flaccid and inactive in them, since they do not respond to the forces that run through the faces, as those of the Ionic do. The latter capital could therefore become, in its own way, an effective principal in the sculptural action of those three–dimensional forces which the late archaic and classic temple was to unite into its single freestanding body. But the Aeolic capitals, with the great drooping pad of the abacus flapped across beetling brows, dramatized not unity of action but separateness of structural parts, here especially the unilinear lateral stretch of the entablature they supported.

Yet they must have made a brave show fronting their temple, and they make one still in their wall. May they be left there forever. They are tougher than the stones that encase them, while at the same time those small rough crystals make their own swelling size and spreading curves seem almost miraculous for stone. Perhaps it always seemed that way to the Greeks, a kind of miracle that the mineral, stone, could be carved so as to embody active, organic kinds of life. The intensity of what can only be called the "reality" of Greek sculpture would seem to indicate that something of the sort was true: not least in these Aeolic capitals, which here at their historical end and climax no longer recall plant forms really, nor ram's horns quite. They are wholly themselves— forces, potencies, and beings: eyed, muscular, octopus–armed. One can believe in the archaic Apollo, dangerous, when one sees them.

LIST OF ABBREVIATIONS

Titles cited seldom or short in themselves have not been abbreviated

(*AJA*)	*American Journal of Archaeology*
(*BSA*)	*Annual of the British School at Athens*
(*AAJdI*)	*Archäologischer Anzeiger* (in *JdI*)
('Α.Δελτ)	'Αρχαιολογικὸν Δελτίον
(*BCH*)	*Bulletin de correspondance hellénique*
('Εφ.'Αρχ)	'Εφημερίς 'Αρχαιολογική
(*Hesperia*)	*Hesperia. Journal of the American School of Classical Studies at Athens*
(*JdI*)	*Jahrb. d. deut. Arch. Inst.*
(*JHS*)	*Journal of Hellenic Studies*
(*JRIBA*)	*J. Royal Inst. of Brit. Architects*
(*JSAH*)	*Journal of the Society of Architectural Historians*
(*MAL*)	*Memorie d. r. Accad. dei Lincei, classe di scienze morali, etc.*
(*Ath.Mitt.*)	*Mitteilungen d. deutsch. Arch. Inst., Athenische Abteilung*
(*Rom.Mitt.*)	*Mitteilungen d. deutsch. Arch. Inst., Römische Abteilung*
(*Mon.Ant.*)	*Monumenti antichi pubbl. p. cura della r. Accad. dei Lincei*
(*Notiz.Scav.*)	*Notizie degli scavi di antichità*
(Πρακτικὰ)	Πρακτικὰ τῆς ἐν 'Αθήναις 'Αρχ. 'Εταιρείας
(*PWRE*)	Pauly-Wissowa's *Real Encyclopädie der klassischen Altertumswissenschaft*
("Εργον)	Τὸ "Εργον τῆς 'Αρχαιολογικῆς 'Εταιρείας

NOTES

Chapter 1, LANDSCAPE AND SANCTUARY:

1. Sophocles, *Oedipus at Colonus*, 16, trans. by Robert Fitzgerald, copyright, 1941, Harcourt Brace and World, Inc. Now in *The Complete Greek Tragedies*, 4 vols., ed. by David Grene and Richmond Lattimore, Vol. 2, Chicago, The University of Chicago Press, 1959. Most of the translations from Greek tragedy used in this book are, unless otherwise indicated, from this admirable series. I am grateful, as to other sources acknowledged below, for permission to quote from it.

2. Karl Lehmann, "The Dome of Heaven," *Art Bulletin*, 27 (1945), 1–27.

3. Otto von Simson, *The Gothic Cathedral* (New York, 1956), pp. 8–11, and passim.

4. Bruno Zevi, *Architecture as Space*, trans. Milton Gendel (New York, 1957), pp. 76–78. (Originally, *Saper vedere l'architettura*, 4th ed., Torino, 1953.) Zevi experiences architecture as a true Italic. He wants to be inside, and speaks—in relation to Greek temples in Sicily, thus rather inaccurately—of "the Italic peoples," in their concern for interior space, as "attempting to broaden and humanize the closed formulations of their Hellenic heritage." Ibid., p. 78. Carpenter, who notes that he derives his criteria from Geoffrey Scott's appreciation of Italian Baroque architecture, takes a related view. Rhys Carpenter, *The Esthetic Basis of Greek Art* (Bloomington, 1959 [1ˢᵗ ed. 1921]), pp. 132–133, note 18. Cf. Geoffrey Scott, *The Architecture of Humanism*, New York, 1914.

5. Carpenter, p. 106. A. W. Lawrence, *Greek Architecture*, in *The Pelican History of Art*, (Har-

mondsworth and Baltimore, 1957), pp. 293–295. Although, as noted later, I disagree with a number of the opinions expressed in this book, it is still a useful and readable one, with some excellent photographs of details and an unusually heavy concentration of data on the Neolithic and Bronze Ages. See the same author's early and shrewd review of the objectives and development of Greek sculpture in his *Classical Sculpture*, London, 1929. Also, idem, *Later Greek Sculpture*, London, 1927.

6. For later antiquity, see the formulas of Vitruvius during the Augustan period: Books III, IV, M. H. Morgan translation, Cambridge, 1914. The desire for abstract perfection in the modern period begins with the Romantic–Classicism of the later eighteenth century, as in Stuart and Revett, *Antiquities of Athens*, 4 vols. (London, 1762–1816), suppl., 1830, who did not perceive the curves of stylobate and entablature in the Athenian temples. Such curves were not seen until the 1830's, entasis in columns about 1810. When perceived, the curves were often ascribed to settling or to an attempt to make the profiles appear straight; the concept of sculptural action was avoided. These critical phenomena are described in W. H. Goodyear, *Greek Refinements: Studies in Temperamental Architecture* (New Haven and London, 1912), pp. 2–26 and passim. For the effects upon modern architecture of this view of Greek form see my *Modern Architecture: The Architecture of Democracy, c. 1789–1960*, New York, 1961.

7. Edith Hamilton, *The Greek Way* (New

York, 1930), pp. 201–202. Also, Auguste Choisy, *Histoire de l'architecture* (Paris, 1899), p. 409: ". . . les temples grecs valent autant par le choix de leur site que par l'art avec lequel ils sont construits . . ." In general, Choisy insists both upon the relevance of the site to Greek temples and upon their calculated relation to each other; but he does not put the two concepts together in a broad enough context and sees the latter in purely compositional, "picturesque" terms, as intended to form balanced *tableaux.* Idem, pp. 409–422. See note 20 below.

8. Robert Scranton, "Group Design in Greek Architecture," *Art Bulletin, 31* (1949), 251.

9. Karl Lehmann–Hartleben, "Wesen und Gestalt griechischer Heiligtümer," *Die Antike, 7* (1931), 11–48, 161–180.

10. Paula Philippson, "Griechische Gottheiten in ihren Landschaften," *Symbolae Osloensis Fasc. Supplet.,* 9, Oslo, 1939. In this work, with sixteen excellent landscape photographs, Philippson treats the following sites in which she attempts to describe the nature of the earth mother and the daimon hero as the place and its associated myths suggest them to her: Delphi, Tanagra, Orchomenos, the Trophonion at Lebadeia, Ptoon, Delos, Argos (Hera Argieia), Demeter in Boeotia and at Enna and Thera, Nemesis at Rhamnous, Athena in Attica, Zeus (and Dione) at Dodona. She does not identify any specific forms or develop the problem architecturally. See also Philippson, *Untersuchungen über den griechischen Mythos,* Zurich, 1944, where the frontispiece is of the Valley of the Muses under Helicon.

11. A. von Gerkan, *Griechische Städteanlagen* (Berlin and Leipzig, 1924), passim, esp. pp. 27, 28. Now see also von Gerkan, *Von antiker Architektur und Topographie. Gesammelte Aufsätze,* ed. by Erich Boehringer, Stuttgart, 1959.

12. Lehmann–Hartleben, pp. 162–165.

13. Lawrence, *Greek Architecture,* p. 153.

14. Ibid., p. 151.

15. K. A. Doxiadis, *Raumordnung im griechischen Städtebau,* Heidelberg and Berlin, 1937. For the problem of axial organization within the temenos see also G. Bruns, "Zur Frage der Richtungsbezogenheit in der Grundrissen griechischer Kultbauten," *Fest. K. Weickert* (Berlin, 1955), pp. 137–152.

16. Doxiadis, p. 141.

17. Richard Stillwell, "The Siting of Classical Greek Temples," *Journal of the Society of Architectural Historians, (JSAH),* 13 (1954), 5.

18. R. D. Martienssen, *The Idea of Space in Greek Architecture,* Johannesburg, 1956. This book is too sustained and serious an attempt to arrive at first principles to be grouped with the slighter articles noted below, although Smithson (note 20) has some sound perceptions.

19. J. Needham, "The Siting of Greek Buildings," *Journal of the Royal Institute of British Architects (JRIBA),* 60 (1953), 180–185.

20. Peter Smithson, "Space and Greek Architecture," *The Listener,* Oct. 16, 1958, 599–601; also: "Theories Concerning the Layout of Classical Greek Buildings," *Architectural Association Journal,* 74, No. 829 (1959), 194 ff. Includes comments by other architects. Smithson specifically questions the validity of Choisy's concepts as defining a Greek compositional mode, but this study would indicate that, aside from their topographical limitations and picturesque bias, they were fundamentally correct in their perceptions. See note 7, this chapter, and note 19, Chapter 4. Interestingly enough, they have since been assigned a basic role in the formation of twentieth–century architectural theory. Cf. Reyner Banham, *Theory and Design in the First Machine Age* (New York, 1960), pp. 32–33. See note 53, Chapter 9.

21. I attempted to present my view of the limitations of the morphological and iconological methods in dealing with works of art, and especially with works of classic art, in a paper read in the symposium, "The Nature of the Classical," held at the joint meeting of the American Archaeological Association and the American Philological Society, Philadelphia, December, 1956. Published as: "The Nature of the Classical in Art," *Yale French Studies,* Nos. 19 and 20 (1958), 107–124.

22. Walter F. Otto, *Die Götter Griechenlands: Das Bild des Göttlichen im Spiegel des griechischen Geistes,* 2 vols., Frankfurt am Main, 1947; trans. by Moses Hadas, *The Homeric Gods: The Spiritual Significance of Greek Religion* (New York, 1954), p. 287.

23. Written after 1857. Herman Melville, *The Complete Works,* 16 (London, 1924), 287.

24. Jay Leyda, *The Melville Log,* 2 vols. (New York, 1951), pp. 549–552.

25. Otto, *The Homeric Gods,* p. 170.

26. Homeric Hymn XXX "To Earth the Mother of All," 1–17, Loeb edition, translated by H. G. Evelyn–White (Heinemann, London, and the Macmillan Co., New York, 1914), p. 456.

Chapter 2, THE GREAT GODDESS:

1. Euripides, *Helen,* 1301–1302, trans. by Richmond Lattimore, Vol. 3, Chicago, 1959.

2. For the geography of Greece, the work of Alfred Philippson is indispensable. A complete bibliography of his writing may be found in Ernst Kirstein, *Die griechische Polis als historisch–geographisches Problem des Mittelmeerraumes,* Colloquium Geographicum, Bd. 5 (Bonn, 1956), 15–25. There is now appearing under Philippson's editorship, together with E. Kirstein and H. Lehmann, an encyclopedia of Greek geography under the general title, *Die griechischen Landschaften, eine Landeskunde,* Frankfort, 1950 ff. Also: *Atlas of the Classical World,* Van der Heyden and Scullard eds. (London, 1959) pp. 9–90.

3. See Rudolph Stampfuss on paleolithic finds in Boeotia, in *Zeitschrift für deutsche Vorgeschichte, 34* (1942).

4. Notably by G. R. Levy in her brilliantly conceived work, *The Gate of Horn, a study of the religious conceptions of the stone age, and their influence upon European thought,* London, 1948. See now also Johannes Maringer, *The Gods of Prehistoric Man,* ed. and trans. by Mary Ilford, New York, 1960.

5. Levy, pp. 3–28, 54–63, 128–138, 213 ff.

6. Sir Arthur J. Evans, *The Palace of Minos at Knossos,* 4 vols. (London, 1921–1936), *1,* 151–163, and A. B. Cook, *Zeus, a study in ancient religion,* 3 vols. (Cambridge, 1914), *1,* 157–163. For a conflicting opinion, see Martin P. Nilsson, *The Minoan–Mycenaean Religion and its Survival in Greek Religion* (Lund, 1950), pp. 461–462.

7. Levy, *The Gate of Horn,* pp. 167–177. The recognition of this tradition by the Hebrews and the dialogue which takes place between it and their developing concept of Jehovah is well attested from the Bible, as in Psalm 121: "I will lift up mine eyes unto the hills: whence cometh my help? . . . My help cometh from the Lord, which made heaven and earth." Also Jeremiah II: "Truly in vain is salvation hoped for from the hills, and from the multitude of mountains; truly in the Lord our God is the salvation of Israel."

8. Evans, *The Palace of Minos, 1,* 159–160.

9. Evans, *2,* 159–160. See also Nilsson, *The Minoan–Mycenaean Religion,* pp. 165–193.

10. Strabo, *Geography* 10.4.8, Loeb edition, trans. by H. L. Jones, 8 vols. (London, 1917–1932), *5,* 128, note 4. Knossos in earlier times was called καίρατος, but this was Casaubon's conjecture for κέρατος, "horned," in the actual text.

11. Evans, "Mycenaean Tree and Pillar Cult," *Journal of Hellenic Studies* (*JHS*), 21 (1901), 135–138. And see W. Gaerte, "Die Bedeutung der kretisch–minoischen 'Horns of Consecration,'" *Archiv für Religionswissenschaft,* 21 (1922), 72–98.

12. Walter J. Graham, "The Central Court as the Minoan Bull–Ring," *American Journal of Archaeology* (*AJA*), 61 (1957), 255–262. For an earlier opinion, see Nilsson, *The Minoan–Mycenaean Religion,* p. 374, and Nilsson, *The Mycenaean Origin of Greek Mythology* (Berkeley, Calif., 1932), p. 176.

13. Lawrence, *Greek Architecture,* p. 34.

14. Such harmony has been romantically sought by many writers and architects in one way or another since the beginning of the whole divorce from nature which marks modern times. It is for this reason, I think, that there is such a curiously close and triple relationship between the plan of the palace at Knossos as excavated, its details and frescoes as reconstructed by Evans, and the contemporary, early twentieth–century design of Art Nouveau architects or of Frank Lloyd Wright. I have elsewhere attempted to demonstrate Wright's use of Minoan and related orientations and forms for similar meanings. Eventually, like the peoples of the Ancient East, he even built his own sacred mountain in the Beth Sholem Synagogue, of 1959. This recalls the coned, horned altar of Artemis at Byblos, published by Evans. Vincent Scully, Jr., *Frank Lloyd Wright* (New York, 1960), pp. 28 ff., figs. 96, 97, 102–120, 125–127.

15. Cf. Paolo Graziosi, *Palaeolithic Art* (New York and London, 1960), pp. 96–97. Reference is to schematization of ibex forms, viewed frontally, which, through a series of engravings on bone, can be seen to be progressively abstracted or reduced to a system of V–shaped signs which stand for the horns. This V–shaped symbol for the horned animal may in turn be related to the V–shaped or triangular genital region of so many mother goddess figurines. Cf. plates 2, 4, 5, 9, 11, 12, (mother goddess figurines); plate 82a (accentuated V–cleft); plate 99d–g (progressive schematization of ibex). Also refer to page 103, where mention is made of small, cone–shaped figurines decorated with V–signs and zig-zag lines, symmetrically

placed, with a triangular mark near the base. These objects have been interpreted as phalli, as birds, and also schematized female figures. The latter interpretation is the most generally accepted. Graziosi cites the following: 1) Th. Volkov, "Nouvelles découvertes dans la station paléolithique de Mézine (Ukraine)," in *Congrès Internat. d'Anthrop. et d'Archéologie Préhistoriques*, XIVe session (Geneva, 1912), *1*, 415–428. 2) P. P. Ephimenko, "Kamennije orudija paleoliticeskoi ctojanki v s. Mesine Cernigovskoi gub.," in *Èjegsdnik Pysskogo Antropologhiceskogo obscestva nri S.–Peterburskom universitete*, *4* (St. Petersburg, 1913), 67–102. These objects were found in the Ukraine. Photos originated in E. Golomshtok, "The Old Stone Age in European Russia," *Transactions of the American Philosophical Society*, new series, 29, Part 2, (March, 1938), 189–468. They are illustrated in Graziosi, pl. 101 a–j.

16. For the tradition of the goddess' lap as the king's throne, for the throne as mountain, and for female symbolism in general, albeit in rather cabalistic terms, cf. Erich Neumann, *The Great Mother*, trans. by Ralph Manheim, Bollingen Series XLVII (New York, 1955), esp. pp. 98–100, 273–292. For genital triangle as prominent symbol of the mother goddess: pls. 6–14, 16, 17, 23, 25; figs. 2, 10, 22, 23, 25. See also ibid., pl. 4, where Seti I, XIX Dynasty, is shown sitting on the lap of horned Isis. In this connection it may be significant that the enclosed cup of the Valley of the Kings, used for pharaonic burial primarily during the second millenium, has a nippled pyramidal peak on one side and a pair of mountain horns on the other.

17. Excavation report: L. Pernier, *Il Palazzo minoico di Festos*, *1* and *2*, Rome, 1935, 1951.

18. Cook, *Zeus*, 2, 932–939, and Nilsson, *The Minoan–Mycenaean Religion*, pp. 64–67.

19. Pernier, *1*, 287 ff.

20. For a review of excavations at Agia Triada, see L. Pernier and L. Banti, *Guida degli scavi italiani in Creta*, Rome, 1947.

21. Excavation report: F. Chapouthier, J. Charbonneaux, and R. Joly, *Fouilles executées à Mallia*, 10 vols., Paris, 1928–1953.

22. Cook, *Zeus*, *1*, 148–154, and *2*, 927–932; Evans, *Palace of Minos*, *1*, 151–163; Nilsson, *The Minoan–Mycenaean Religion*, pp. 458–460.

23. Pierre Demargne and Hubert Gallet de Santerre, "Exploration des maisons et quartiers d'habitation (1921–1948)," premier fasc., *Fouilles executées à Mallia*, 9 (1953), 1–21.

24. Excavation report: H. B. Hawes, et al., *Gournia, Vasiliki, and other Prehistoric Sites on the Isthmus of Hierapetra, Crete*, Philadelphia, 1908.

25. The extraordinary symmetry of the earth's enclosure at Gournia and the rounded forms which define it create in the modern art historian the curious feeling that he is standing inside a negative impression of a vaulted Roman building. It is possible, of course, that the religious impulses and psychological necessities which created the symmetries and vaulted volumes of Roman architecture were not so different from those which led the Minoans to choose the enclosed site of Gournia and to orient their palace and "agora" toward the doubly mounded hills. Kaschnitz–Weinberg has brilliantly attempted to show that Roman buildings continued or revived earlier Mediterranean desires for rounded, symmetrical enclosure, and the chosen landscape of Gournia may be regarded as related to that same tradition. G. F. von Kaschnitz–Weinberg, *Die mittelmeerischen Grundlagen der antiken Kunst* (Frankfurt am Main, 1944), passim, esp. pp. 39–66.

26. William Stevenson Smith, *The Art and Architecture of Ancient Egypt*, in *The Pelican History of Art* (Harmondsworth and Baltimore, 1958), p. 227, pl. 166a.

27. Sir T. Zammit, *Prehistoric Malta*, London, 1930; "Prehistoric Remains of the Maltese Islands," *Antiquity*, 4 (1930), 55–79; J. D. Evans, *Malta* (New York, 1959), p. 31 and passim. Kaschnitz–Weinberg, figs. 36, 37, 39, for these and related monuments.

28. For discussion of this evolution, see especially the following: A. J. Evans, "The Prehistoric Tombs of Knossos," *Archaeologia*, 59 (1905), 391–562; *The Shaft–Graves and Bee–Hive Tombs of Mycenae and their Interrelation*, London, 1929; N. Valmin, "Tholos Tombs and Tumuli," *Skrift. Sven. Inst.*, 2, 1932.

29. Evans, *Palace of Minos*, *1*, 154–156; Cook, *Zeus*, 2, 939; Nilsson, *The Minoan–Mycenaean Religion*, p. 71.

30. Evans, *4*, 964–978, 992–1002.

31. For discussion of Hittite kingship and rituals pertaining thereto, see especially G. R. Levy, *The Sword from the Rock* (New York, 1953), pp. 19–35, and O. R. Gurney, *Myth, Ritual and Kingship in the Ancient Near East and in Israel*, ed. by G. H. Hooke (Oxford, 1958), pp. 105–121.

32. Evans, *Palace of Minos*, *4*, 202–215.

33. Ibid., *3*, 68, fig. 38, and 135–144, fig. 91.

34. Ibid., *2*, 396–413.

35. Ibid., *2*, 312–325. From the evidence which Evans offers it is possible to assume that the particular liability of the site of Knossos to earthquakes may have been one of the determining factors which originally led the Minoans to develop the palace there. Existing in a state of harmony with and trust in nature, the Minoans exploited the site not only in terms of its relation to the cardinal landscape formations but also with respect to the chthonian character of the place which, as an earthquake center, seemed to manifest the power of the goddess, or of her creature, the horned bull—perhaps the King as Poseidon—as "Earth–shaker."

36. For Seskoulo, see A. J. B. Wace and M. S. Thompson, *Prehistoric Thessaly*, Cambridge, 1912, and H. D. Hansen, *Early Civilization in Thessaly*, Baltimore, 1933.

37. For Malthi, see M. N. Valmin, *The Swedish Messenia Expedition*, Lund, 1938, and M. N. Valmin, *Études topographiques sur la Messénie ancienne*, Lund, 1930.

38. For Dystos, see T. Wiegand, "Dystos," *Mitteilungen d. deutsch. Arch. Inst., athenische Abteilung (Ath. Mitt.)* 24 (1899), 458–467.

39. For Dimini, see also Wace and Thompson, and Hansen.

40. For Lerna, see J. L. Caskey, "Excavations at Lerna," *Hesperia*, 23–26, 1954–1957.

41. For Asine, see O. Frödin and A. W. Persson, *Asine, Results of the Swedish Excavations, 1922–1930*, Stockholm, 1938.

42. Ibid., pp. 33–38.

43. Ibid., pp. 151–192, 194–198, 356–358.

44. Caskey, *Hesperia*, 23, 23–27; 24, 37–41.

45. The following are the most important works on Troy:

H. Schliemann, *Troy and its Remains*, London, 1875.

Idem, *Ilios: the City and Country of the Trojans*, London, 1880.

Idem, *Troja: Results of the Latest Researches and Discoveries on the Site of Homer's Troy*, London, 1884.

W. Dörpfeld, et al., *Troja und Ilion*, 2 vols., Athens, 1902.

W. Leaf, *Troy, a Study in Homeric Geography*, London, 1912.

C. W. Blegen, "Excavations at Troy," *AJA*, Vols. 36–43, 1932–1939.

C. W. Blegen, J. L. Caskey, and M. Rawson, ed., *Troy, excavations conducted by the University of Cincinnati, 1932–1938*, 4 vols., Princeton, 1950–1958.

Friedrich Matz, *Kreta, Mykene, Troja; die minoische und die homerische Welt*, Stuttgart, 1956.

Note should be taken of the fact that many of the Trojan megara had projecting side walls at the rear, probably for the weather protection of that side. Such is visually, though not in intention, a precursor of the Greek opisthodomos. Noted most recently by Lawrence, *Greek Architecture*, p. 272, figs. 5, 6.

46. "So she came to many–fountained Ida, the mother of wild creatures and went straight to the homestead across the mountain. After her came grey wolves, fawning on her, and grim–eyed lions, and bears, and fleet leopards, ravenous for deer . . ." Homeric Hymn V, "To Aphrodite," 68–74, Loeb, p. 410.

47. See especially Cook, *Zeus*, 2, 313–316. Also L. R. Farnell, "Kabeiroi," in *The Encyclopedia of Religion and Ethics*, ed. by J. Hastings (Edinburgh, 1914), 7, 628–632, and R. Pettazzoni, "Le origini dei Kabiri nelle isole del mar tracio," in *Memorie d. Accad. dei Lincei, classe di scienze morali, etc. (MAL)*, Serie Quinta (Rome, 1909), *12*, 635–740.

48. The sequence of construction of Stonehenge in particular is reviewed in R. J. C. Atkinson, *Stonehenge* (London, 1956), pp. 58–94.

49. Levy, *Gate of Horn*, p. 148.

50. Atkinson, pp. 84–85, 177–178.

51. Ibid., pp. 96–98.

52. Though this analogy seems to be farfetched, and Atkinson, note 51 above, is hard on it.

53. The word is used by Gordon Childe, who spoke also of "Megalithic Saints" in *The Prehistory of European Society*, Penguin Books, 1958, and is cited by Glyn Daniel, *The Megalithic Builders of Western Europe* (London, 1958), pp. 127, 128, who finds the term perhaps too extreme and specialized. Still, the concept it embodies is an appealing one which the existing monuments do much to encourage.

54. Atkinson, *Stonehenge*, p. 52.

55. Ibid., pp. 14–18.

56. This is especially apparent to the photographer. It will be noted that the major axes of Minoan palaces can be recorded in one frame, but most Greek sites demand many or, ideally, composite views for even a minimal record.

Chapter 3, THE GODDESS AND THE LORDS:

1. Aeschylus, *Agamemnon*, 1125–1128, trans. by Richmond Lattimore, Vol. *1*, Chicago, 1959.

2. Evans, *Palace of Minos*, 1, 27–28, and 2, 344–346. R. W. Hutchinson, "Minoan Chronology Reviewed," *Antiquity*, 28 (1954), 155–164.

3. Nilsson, *The Minoan–Mycenaean Religion*, pp. 485–491.

4. For the Hittite mother goddess carved in the rock, see O. R. Gurney, *The Hittites* (Penguin Books, 1952), pp. 135–144. In general, see L. Franz, "Die Muttergötter im vorderen Orient und in Europa," *Der alte Orient*, 35, No. 3, Leipzig, 1937.

5. M. G. F. Ventris and J. Chadwick, *Documents in Mycenaean Greek; three hundred selected tablets from Knossos, Pylos and Mycenae . . .* Cambridge, England, 1956. The observations about Mycenaean divinities which follow derive generally from John Chadwick, *The Decipherment of Linear B*, Cambridge, 1958. This fundamental work has also been excerpted in *Natural History*, 70, March, 1961, 8 ff., and April, 1961, 58 ff.

6. See the following recent survey in V. Müller, "Development of the Megaron in Prehistoric Greece," *AJA*, 48 (1944), 342–348.

7. K. A. Rhomaios discusses Thermon in Ἀρχαιολογικὸν Δελτίον, ('Α.Δελτ.), 1 (1915), 225–279. But see also, E. J. Bundgaard, "A propos de la date de la peristasis du Megaron B à Thermon," *BCH*, 70 (1946), 51–57.

8. For the collectivism of bees in connection with the mother goddess, see H. M. Ransome, *The Sacred Bee in Ancient Times and Folklore* (London, 1937), pp. 61–64, 92, 94, 95.

9. W. Dörpfeld, *Alt–Olympia, Untersuchungen und Ausgrabungen zur Geschichte des ältesten Heiligtums von Olympia*, 2 vols. (Berlin, 1935), pp. 73–94; fig. 3, p. 76; fig. 9, p. 83.

10. Ibid., pp. 108–112.

11. C. W. Blegen, *Korakou, a Prehistoric Settlement near Corinth*, Boston and New York, 1921.

12. J. L. Caskey, "Excavations at Lerna," *Hesperia*, 23–26, 1954–1957.

13. For an excellent account of the site and its publication as a whole see W. Wrede, "Thorikos," Pauly–Wissowa's *Real Encyclopädie der klassischen Altertumswissenchaft* (*PWRE*), 2 (Stuttgart, 1936), 338–339.

14. Dinsmoor, *Architecture of Ancient Greece*, p. 196.

15. Homeric hymn II "To Demeter," 123–128, Loeb, p. 296.

16. Robert Graves, *The Greek Myths*, 2 vols., Penguin Edition (Baltimore, 1955), 24:14.

17. For Spata see *Ath. Mitt.*, 2 (1877), 82–4, 261–276; and *Bulletin de correspondance hellénique* (*BCH*), 2 (1878), 185–228.

18. See Chapter 6 for Brauron, pp. 85–89.

19. The shepherds also claim that the Germans attempted to take the lion away during World War II but that, as they lifted it, it sank ever further into the ground.

20. Eugene Vanderpool and I examined this cave in March, 1958.

21. This monument was also examined by Vanderpool and myself. The Erechtheion is oriented directly upon it.

22. Cf. Chapter 6 for Kaisariani, p. 94.

23. The problem of the column bases is considered by the following: W. Dörpfeld, "Der alte Athena–Tempel auf der Akropolis," *Ath. Mitt.*, Vols. *11, 12, 15*, and *22*, 1886–1887, 1890, and 1897, especially *11*; P. Kavvadias and G. Kawerau, *Die Ausgrabung der Akropolis* (Athens, 1906), p. 84; Nilsson, *The Minoan–Mycenaean Religion*, pp. 474–475.

24. Whitman's point concerning the importance of such continuity in Athens seems especially well taken. C. H. Whitman, *Homer and the Heroic Tradition* (Cambridge, Mass., 1958), pp. 46–64, esp. pp. 47, 51–54, 57. See also O. Broneer, "What Happened at Athens," *AJA*, 52 (1948), 112.

25. K. Kourouniotis and G. Mylonas, Ἐλευσινιακά, Athens, 1932.

26. A. W. Persson, "Der Ursprung der eleusinischen Mysterien," *Archiv für Religionswissenschaft*, 21 (1922), 287–309; K. Kourouniotis, "Das eleusinische Heiligtum von den Anfängen bis zur vorperikleischen Zeit," *Archiv für Religionswissenschaft*, 32 (1935), 52–78; Nilsson, *The Minoan–Mycenaean Religion*, pp. 468–470.

27. For Megarian Minoa see *Ath. Mitt.*, 29 (1904), 79–100. An article on the topography of this area is being prepared by Colin Edmonson.

28. Pausanias, *Description of Greece*, Loeb Classical Library, 4 vols. (London and New York, 1918–35), I.39.5. In general see Sir John Frazer, *Pausanias's Description of Greece*, 6 vols., London, 1898.

29. A. D. Keramopoullos, "θηβαικά," 'Α. Δελτ., Vol. 3, 1917.

30. Pausanias, IX.12.1–3.

31. Pausanias, IX.16.5, was indeed told that the palace of Cadmus became the temple of Demeter.

32. Pausanias, IX.10.2.

33. Pausanias, IX.26.2.

34. Pausanias, IX.24.3; 25.4; 26.1; 27.6; 27.8; 32.2; 32.4; 34.5; 38.6.

35. Pausanias, IX.19.3.

36. Pausanias, I.34.1–2 and IX.8.3.

37. Pausanias, IX.19.4. All of these formations rise above the western horizon when viewed from the rhythmically flowing contours of the site of Tanagra itself. Here, too, Philippson sensed the presence of the earth goddess. Cf. Chapter 1, note 10.

38. Ptoon and its mantic shrine of Apollo are discussed in Chapter 7. Pausanias, IX.36.6.

39. Reports on Orchomenos include H. Schliemann, *Orchomenos*, Leipzig, 1881, and H. Bulle, "Orchomenos," *Abhandlungen der münchner Akademie*, Vol. 24, 1907.

40. Strabo, IX.416; *PWRE*, *1* (1894), c. 1183.

41. Pausanias, I.44.7 and IX.34.5–8. Also Graves, *The Greek Myths*, 70: passim.

42. For Gla see A. Ridder, "Fouilles de Gla," *BCH*, *18* (1894), 271–310.

43. For an association of Gla with the Homeric Arne, see F. Noack, "Arne," *Ath. Mitt.*, *19* (1894), 405–485.

44. Pausanias, IX.24.1–2.

45. Nilsson, *The Minoan–Mycenaean Religion*, pp. 303–306.

46. See among many examples a terra cotta of Hera enthroned, so welded to her throne as to make a chair of welcome herself, in an example from Paestum, in *Archaeology*, 7 (1954), 212, fig. 10.

47. Pausanias, III.19.9.

48. Nilsson, *The Minoan–Mycenaean Religion*, pp. 471, 529–530. Excavation conducted by British School at Athens, reported in *Annual of the British School at Athens (BSA)*, 15 (1909), 108–116. Also Toynbee, *JHS*, 33 (1913), 246–275.

49. Cf. Chapter 6 for Artemis Orthia, p. 81.

50. Cf. Chapter 9, p. 169.

51. Pausanias, III.1.3; 10.8; 16.2.

52. Pausanias, IV.36.1–3.

53. C. W. Blegen, "Excavations at Pylos," *AJA*, Vols. 43, 57, 59, 60, 61, 62, 1939, 1953, 1954, 1956, 1957, 1958.

54. Blegen, *AJA*, 62, 175, 176.

55. Blegen, *AJA*, 63, 570–575.

56. The initial date of trullo construction should not be confused with that of Alberobello, founded in the sixteenth century. The trulli are clearly rural, reflecting a pre–urban, pre–feudal, system of small landholding which may be very ancient in Apulia. For one marked with a horn and snake symbol see G. Pagano and G. Daniel, *Architettura rurale italiana* (Milan, 1936), p. 90. For some African conical huts as breast shapes, with entrances biomorphically treated and horned, see *L'Habitat au Cameroun*, Office de la Recherche Scientifique Outre–Mer (Paris, 1952), esp. pp. 33–39, 45.

57. Graves, *The Greek Myths*, 169:0; Pausanias, IV.3.4; *Odyssey*, IV.209.

58. Pausanias, II.17.1–7; C. Waldstein, et al., *The Argive Heraeum*, 2 vols. Boston and New York, 1902–1905; C. W. Blegen, *Prosymna, the Helladic Settlement Preceding the Argive Heraeum*, 2 vols., Cambridge, Mass., 1937.

59. P. Friedländer, "Die Frühgeschichte des argiv. Heraions," *Ath. Mitt.*, 34 (1909), 69–79, and Nilsson, *The Minoan–Mycenaean Religion*, p. 480.

60. Pausanias, II.24.1.

61. Plutarch, *CLEOM.*, 17.21, and *PWRE*, *2* (1896), c. 1734.

62. A. Boethius, "Zur Topographie des dorischen Argos," *Strena philologica Upsaliensis' Festskrift tillägnad Per Persson*, Upsala, 1922, and W. Vollgraff, "Fouilles d'Argos," *BCH*, *31* (1907), 138–184; 44 (1920), 219–226.

63. Pausanias, II.25.7. Reports on Tiryns include: G. Rodenwaldt, et al., *Tiryns: Die Ergebnisse der Ausgrabungen*, 4 vols., Athens, 1912–1930; H. Schliemann, *Tiryns: the Prehistoric Palace of the Kings of Tiryns*, New York, 1885, and London, 1886; G. Karo, *Führer durch Tiryns*, 2nd ed., Athens, 1934.

64. Pausanias, II.19.3–7; 38.4.; Strabo, VIII. 6.9.; Herodotus, II.171.

65. I am informed that there is also a small cave near the horns upon which the megaron is oriented.

66. C. Robert, "Die Hera von Tiryns," *Hermes*, 55 (1920), 373–387. A contrasting opinion in Nilsson, *The Minoan–Mycenaean Religion*, pp. 478–479.

67. K. Bittel, *Die Ruinen von Bogazkoy*, Berlin, 1937.

68. The reverent character of Danaus as treated by Aeschylus in *The Suppliants* is in harmony with this interpretation.

69. Evans, *Palace of Minos*, *1*, 159–161, figs. 115, 116; 3, 140–143, figs. 91, 93.

70. Pausanias, IX.39.1.

71. Apollodorus, *The Library*, II.4.4–5.

72. Nilsson, *The Minoan–Mycenaean Religion*, pp. 485–501.

73. Pausanias, II.16.3 ff.

Reports on Mycenae including the following:

H. Schliemann, *Mycenae: a Narrative of Researches and Discoveries at Mycenae and Tiryns*, New York, 1880.

G. Karo, *Die Schachtgräber von Mykenai*, 2 vols., Munich, 1930–1933.

A. J. B. Wace, *Mycenae*, Princeton, 1949.

F. Matz, *Kreta, Mykene, Troja: die mi-* noische *und die homerische Welt*, Stuttgart, 1956.

G. E. Mylonas, *Ancient Mycenae, the capitol city of Agamemnon*, Princeton, 1957.

74. Nilsson, *The Minoan–Mycenaean Religion*, p. 304, note 71. See also Neumann, *The Great Mother*, pl. 26, figs. 11, 12.

75. H. Frankfort, *Art and Architecture of the Ancient Orient* (Baltimore, Md., 1953), pls. 125a, 128.

76. Graves, *The Greek Myths*, 128.

77. Pausanias, VIII.22.7.

78. Cf. Chapter 6, pp. 83–84.

79. Henry Miller, *The Colossus of Maroussi* (San Francisco, 1941), pp. 85–95.

80. Pausanias, II.15.4.

81. Aeschylus, *Agamemnon*, 1125–28 ff.

Chapter 4, THE TEMPLE. HERA:

1. In the *Odes of Pindar*, trans. by Richmond Lattimore (Chicago, The University of Chicago Press, 1947), p. 111.

2. S. Marinatos, "Le Temple géometrique de Dréros," *BCH*, 60 (1936), 214–256.

3. L. Pernier, "Tempii arcaici sulla Patela di Prinias," *Ann. Scuol. Ital.*, *1* (1914), 18–111; "New Elements for the Study of the Archaic Temple of Prinias," *AJA*, 38 (1934), 171–177.

4. F. Hiller von Gaertringen, et al., *Thera, Untersuchungen, Vermessungen, und Ausgrabungen in den Jahren 1895–1902*, 4 vols., Berlin, 1899–1909.

5. Hermes was fundamentally an ancient folk god of guile, magic, and luck—a paradoxical deity of householders and sharpers, travellers and thieves. Connected with the earth and sometimes dangerous, he still had no mysteries. Though his boundary stones and phallic herms stood everywhere, and one of the latter guarded the entrance to the classic Acropolis of Athens, he was most of all a traveller, wing–footed, never in one place long. Thus he seems to have had many shrines but few temples, none of them surviving as of now. Cf. Otto, *The Homeric Gods*, pp. 104–124.

6. Simone Weil, "The Iliad, or the Poem of Force," trans. by Mary McCarthy, *The Mint*, 2, 1948. (Originally published, *Cahiers du Sud*, 1940–41; reprinted, ibid., No. 284, 1947.)

6a. For seventh–century houses on Chios resembling early temple plans, see *JHS*, 75 (1955), *Suppl.*, 21. For the classic house, courtyarded and very different in type: ungabled, clearly not monumental but purely environmental in intention, see those of Dystos and Olynthus, as in Lawrence, Figs. 135, 136. The exploitation of the megaron as a palace at Larisa on the Hermos during the sixth century and later is clearly Medizing, not Hellenic, in intention. Lawrence, Figs. 134, 138. Still, Mycenaean forms are apparently more tenacious in Asia Minor than elsewhere, as a fourth–century house at Priene may indicate. Lawrence, Fig. 139. D. M. Robertson, et. al., *Excavations at Olynthus*, Vols. 7, 8, Baltimore, 1938, 1946. L. Kjellberg and J. Boehlau, *Larisa am Hermos, die Ergebnisse der Ausgrabungen*, *1*, 1902, Stockholm and Berlin, 1940. For Priene see Chapter 10, note 25. Despite all this, the only buildings that truly have the same plan, fully developed, are the megara of the Mycenaean lords and Greek temples. But for the development from the house in the early Cretan temples, like those at Prinias, see G. Zinserling, "Kultbild—Innenraum—Fassade," *Das Altertum*, 3, 1957, 18–34.

7. W. B. Dinsmoor, "Archaeology and Astronomy," *Proceedings of the American Philosophical Society*, 80 (1939), 95–173. Dinsmoor's brilliant and sustained demonstration of his theory, involving as it does considerable astronomical knowledge and mathematical skill, would be very difficult to refute. Its refutation, however, is not necessary

to our argument, since the sky orientation can be accepted as one of the many factors which the Greeks seem to have tried to bring into harmony at any one temenos.

8. H. Payne, *Perachora, the Sanctuaries of Hera Akraia and Limenia*, Oxford, 1940.

9. Ibid., pls. 87.4, 88.5 and 15.

10. Ibid., pp. 110–122.

11. E. Buschor, "Heraion von Samos frühe Bauten," *Ath. Mitt.*, 55 (1930), 1–99; O. Reuther, *Der Hera Tempel von Samos* Berlin, 1957, Zeichnung 2, for the reconstruction of the façade reproduced here. The reconstruction of the mass of the capital between the volutes (of which fragments were available) seems disturbingly thin in elevation, giving the capital as a whole a flattened, flaccid appearance. This—coupled with the conjectural entablature which seems derived from that of the fourth–century temple of Athena at Priene, admired by Hermogenes and Vitruvius alike— lends the temple a tentative air.

12. Pausanias, VIII.23.5.

13. Etruscan temples widely overhung their roofs without supporting columns, but here again the reason for doing so would seem to have been more ritual than material. So overhung, the roofs defined a certain area of space around the temple and created the typically Italic enclosure rather than the self–contained and sculptural form which was Greek. Vitruvius (III.3.5) calls such temples "heavy headed."

14. Recent psychological studies have shown that there is a limitation in the human capacity to comprehend numbers of objects in a rapid glance. It has been demonstrated that human beings can assimilate up to seven objects without reference to the tedious counting process, but eight is on the very limit of that capacity and beyond it for many. This factor is important in assessing the aesthetic significance of six or eight columns, e.g. the canonical Doric or the Parthenon, on a Greek temple façade. See G. A. Miller, "The Magical Number Seven, plus or minus two," *Psychological Review*, 63, No. 2 (1956), 81 ff.; E. L. Kaufman, et al., "The Diminution of Visual Number," *American Journal of Psychology*, 62 (1949), 498–505.

15. Cf. W. Andrae, *Die ionische Saüle, Bauform oder Symbol*, Berlin, 1933. For Larisa, L. Kjellberg, "Das äolische Kapitell von Larisa," *Skrift. Sven. Inst.*, 2, 1932. Also Robertson, pl. IIb. For Neandria, R. Koldewey, *Neandria* Berlin, 1891. Also Robertson, fig. 23.

16. Pliny, *Natural History*, XXXVI.16–23.

17. Doxiadis, *Raumordnung*, pp. 98–105, especially plans in figs. 44–48.

18. Stillwell makes the general point that the intervals between buildings, themselves symmetrical, are normally irregular and asymmetrical in archaic temene. "The Siting of Greek Buildings," *JSAH*, 13 (1954), 4, 8. Choisy had made the same point. See following note.

19. See Chapter 1, note 4. Smithson also opines that space was simply void to the Greeks, but he gives the impression that such represents a restriction in their perceptions. Chapter 1, note 20. I have tried to elaborate upon the distinction between "mass–positive" and "space–positive" planning in my *Modern Architecture*, New York, 1961. Choisy, *Histoire*, p. 419, approached a similar view: "Chaque motif d'architecture pris à part est symétrique, mais chaque groupe est traité comme un paysage où les masses seules se pondèrent."

20. E. Curtius, F. Adler, et al., *Olympia: Die Ergebnisse der vom deutschen Reich veranstalteten Ausgrabungen*, 5 vols., Berlin, 1890–1897.

21. W. B. Dinsmoor and H. Searls, "The Date of the Olympia Heraeum," *AJA*, 49 (1945), 62–80.

22. C. Waldstein, et al., *The Argive Heraeum*, 2 vols., Boston and New York, 1902–1905.

23. Pausanias, II.38.2.

24. Homeric Hymn XII "To Hera," Loeb, p. 437.

25. W. Vollgraff, "Fouilles d'Argos," *BCH, 28, 30, 31*, 1904, 1906, 1907.

26. Herodotus, I.31; Pausanias, II.20.2.

27. Cf. T. J. Dunbabin, *The Western Greeks*, Oxford, 1948. Also D. Randall–MacIver, *Greek Cities in Italy and Sicily*, Oxford, 1935.

28. P. Z. Montuoro and U. Zanotti–Bianco, "Heraion alla foce del Sele," *Notizie degli scavi di antichità (Notiz. Scav.)*, 62 (1937) 206–354. Two volumes of the publication, *Heraion alla foce del Sele*, Rome, 1958, are now available. Volume 3 is in preparation.

29. R. Koldewey and O. Puchstein, *Die griechischen Tempel in Unteritalien und Sicilien*, Berlin, 1899. F. Krauss, *Paestum, Die griechischen Tempel*, Bildhefte antiker Kunst, Heft 8, 2nd ed., Berlin, 1943. Idem. "Paestum, Basilika. Der Entwurf des Grundrisses," *Festschrift für Karl Weickert*, Berlin, 1955, pp. 99–109.

30. P. C. Sestieri, "Antiquities of Paestum," *Archaeology*, 7 (1954), 206–213; "Iconographie

et culte d'Hera à Paestum," *Revue des Arts*, 5 (1955), 149–158; *Paestum, Guida della libreria dello Stato*, No. 84, 3d. ed., 1955.

31. Sestieri, *Paestum, Guida*, pp. 14–15, states that the whole sanctuary was dedicated to Hera Argiva, the goddess of fertility, and that the second temple of Hera was the more important.

32. On these points see now A. Trevor Hodge, *The Woodwork of Greek Roofs*, Cambridge, 1960. For his suggestion of the term "slotted," see especially pp. 101 ff. "Battened" might also be used. On Greek materials and methods of working in general see A. K. Orlandos, Τα 'Υλικὰ Δόμες τῶν 'Αρχαῖων 'Ελλήνων, 2 vols., Athens, 1955, 1958. See also Robert Scranton, "Interior Design of Greek Temples," *AJA*, 50 (1946), 39–51, for many plans and a discussion of walls and columns as compositional elements.

33. Cf. H. Kähler, *Das griechische Metopenbild*, Munich, 1949.

34. Cf. W. H. Goodyear, *Greek Refinements, Studies in Temperamental Architecture*, New Haven, 1912, especially figs. 25, 26 for the outward bulge of the flank cornices at Paestum.

35. Herzfeld notes the sacredness of the gable shape in the ancient Orient as in Greece and Rome and connects it with mountain symbolism. E. Herzfeld, *Archaeological History of Iran* (London, 1935), p. 16. This point is made and elaborated upon by Phyllis Ackerman, "The Symbolic Sources of Some Architectural Elements," *JSAH*, 12 (1953), 3–7.

36. Aristophanes, *The Birds*, 999.

37. Lawrence, *Greek Architecture*, p. 149, still attempts this, but earlier articles would seem to have settled the question: Cf., C. Gottlieb, "Date of the Temple of Poseidon at Paestum," *AJA*, 57 (1953), 95–104.

38. Louis I. Kahn in personal conversation. See also *Perspecta, The Yale Architectural Journal*, 4 (1957), 2. For the importance of the column in Kahn's architecture see my *Modern Architecture*, New York, 1961, Part 2.

39. For another analysis of the classic temple at Paestum, see Max Raphael, *Der dorische Tempel*, Augsburg, 1930. Also, for temple form in general, see Karl Weickert, *Typen der archaischen Architektur in Griechenland und Kleinasien*, Augsburg, 1929. A collection of rather dramatic photographs of temples in various lights and a poetic association of Greek texts with their forms may be found in F. Cali, *L'Ordre Grec*, Paris, 1958.

40. For Croton, see P. Orsi, "Croton," *Notiz. Scav.*, Vol. 36 (1911), Suppl. Also, E. C. Semple, *The Geography of the Mediterranean Region, Its Relation to Ancient History* (New York, 1931), p. 632; and pp. 613–637 on "the templed promontories of the ancient Mediterranean."

40a. G. Schmiedt and R. Chevalier, "Caulonia e Metaponto, applicazione della fotografia aerea in ricerche di topografia antica nella Magna Graecia," *L'Universo, Rivista bimestrale del' Istituto Geografico Militare*, 39, 1959. F. Castagnoli, "La Pianta di Metaponto, ancora sull' urbanistica ippodamea," *Rendiconti dell'Accademia Nazionale dei Lincei*, Series 8, *vol. 14* (1959), 49–55.

41. P. Griffo, *Ultimi scavi, ultime scoperte in Agrigento* Agrigento, 1946, and P. Marconi, *Agrigento*, Rome, 1933.

41a. See F. Castagnoli, *Ippodamo di Mileto e l'urbanistica a pianta ortagonale*, Rome (1956), 22–23, Figs. 7, 8.

42. Cf. Goodyear, *Greek Refinements*, on "Perspective Illusion," pp. 139–154; especially figs. 79, 81, 84, 85, for temples of "Hera" and "Concord."

43. E. Gabrici, "Acropoli di Selinunte," *Monumenti antichi pubbl. p. cura della r. Accad. dei Lincei (Mon. Ant.)*, 33 (1929), 60–111, and J. Hulot and G. Fougeres, *Sélinonte, colonie dorienne en Sicilie*, Paris, 1910.

44. Dinsmoor, *The Architecture of Ancient Greece*, p. 80.

45. Extended porches, long, continuous spaces, an engrossingly maternal environment. I tried to trace the development of these forms in *The Shingle Style. Architectural Theory and Design from Richardson to the Origins of Wright*, New Haven, 1955, and to generalize upon their significance and effects in *Frank Lloyd Wright*, and in *Modern Architecture*, Part 1.

45a. I. Marconi Bovio, "Scavi à Selinunte, la scoperta della città prima della sua distruzione nel 409 A.C.," *Urbanistica*, 27 (1958), 76–80. Idem, "Le più recente scoperte dell'archeologia della Sicilia Occidentale, con particolare riguardo agli scavi di Selinunte," Atti, VII, Congresso Internazionale di Archeologia Classica, 2 (1961), 9–30.

46. Herodotus, IX.61, trans. by George Rawlinson, *The Persian Wars*, with an introduction by Francis R. B. Godolphin, Modern Library Edition (New York, Random House, 1942), p. 687.

47. Pausanias, IX.3.1–9.

48. Herodotus, IX.62.

Chapter 5, DEMETER:

1. Homeric Hymn II "To Demeter," 270–272, trans. by H. G. Evelyn–White, Loeb, p. 308.

2. Euripides, *Helen,* 1301–1307, trans. by Richmond Lattimore, Vol. 3, Chicago, 1959.

3. Ibid., 1323–1326.

4. For an exhaustive account of these complexities, see L. R. Farnell, *The Cults of the Greek States,* 5 vols. (Oxford, 1896–1909), Vol. 3, Chapts. 2–4 and notes.

5. Herodotus, IX 57, 62, 65, 69, 101. For a study of the topography of Plataia, see W. K. Pritchett, "New Light on Plataia," *AJA,* 61 (1957), 9–28.

6. Homeric Hymn II "To Demeter," 1, Loeb, p. 288.

7. Pausanias, IX.16.5.

8. Herodotus, VII.200.

9. Herodotus, VII.204–233.

10. Herodotus VII.104. "Law is the master whom they own and this master they fear more than your subjects fear you," Demaratus to Xerxes. Trans. by Rawlinson in Modern Library Edition.

11. For a recent discussion of the island of Thera as a whole, see Z. Durazzo–Morosini, *Santorin, die fantastische Insel* Berlin, 1936.

12. F. Hiller von Gaertringen, et al., *Thera, Untersuchungen, Vermessungen, und Ausgrabungen in den Jahren 1895–1902,* 4 vols. Berlin, 1899–1909.

13. *Les Guides Bleus, Grèce,* Paris, 1956, has composite plan after von Gaertringen and shows votive column to Artemis near the temple of Apollo at Thera, p. 554, plan p. 553. Despite some errors, (See Chapter 8, note 51) the *Guide Bleu* is the most useful readily available guide; the French edition is superior to the English, especially in the number of plans.

14. Homeric Hymn II "To Demeter," 123–128, Loeb, p. 296.

15. Graves, *The Greek Myths,* 24:14.

16. Dinsmoor, *The Architecture of Ancient Greece,* p. 196.

17. J. I. Hittorff and L. Zanth, *Architecture antique de la Sicile: Recueil des monuments de Ségeste et de Sélinonte* Paris, 1870, and Koldewey and Puchstein, *Die griechischen Tempel in Unteritalien und Sicilien* (Berlin, 1899), pp. 132–136, pl. 19, for Segesta, and passim.

18. Cf. Chapter 4. See also H. Johannes, "Die Säulenbasen vom Heratempel des Rhoikos," *Ath. Mitt.,* 62 (1937), 13–51.

19. Cf. Chapter 6. See also H. C. Butler, et al., *Sardis,* II.1 (Princeton, 1922), fig. 11, p. 20, and H. C. Butler, "The Elevated Columns at Sardis and the Sculptured Pedestals from Ephesus," *Anatolian Studies W. M. Ramsay* (Manchester, 1923), pp. 51–57.

20. See W. L. Cushing and W. Miller, "The Theatre of Thoricus," *Papers of the American School of Classical Studies in Athens,* 4 (1885–1886), 23–34, and P. E. Arias, "Il Teatro di Torico in Attica," *Historia,* 7 (1933), 55–64.

21. This is discussed by Jane Harrison, *Prolegomena to the Study of Greek Religion,* 3rd edition (Cambridge, 1922), Chapters 8 and 9.

22. Harrison, pp. 416, 548–551, and Farnell, *The Cults,* p. 177.

23. General reports on Eleusis include the following:

F. Noack, *Eleusis, die baugeschichtliche Entwicklung des Heiligtums,* 2 vols., Berlin and Leipzig, 1927.

K. Kourouniotis, *Eleusis, A Guide to the Excavations and the Museum,* Athens, 1936.

G. E. Mylonas, "The Temple of Demeter at Eleusis," *AJA,* 46 (1942), 120, and *The Hymn to Demeter and her Sanctuary at Eleusis,* St. Louis, 1942.

J. Travlos, "The Topography of Eleusis," *Hesperia, 18* (1949), 138–147.

See also K. Lehmann–Hartleben, "Wesen und Gestalt griechischer Heiligtümer," *Die Antike,* 7 (1931), 161–180.

24. Cf. Chapter 6, note 47, for the sanctuary of Aphrodite and Eros. The Eleusinion is now being fully excavated for the first time. Cf. Homer A. Thompson, "Activities in the Athenian Agora: 1960," *Hesperia,* 29 (1960), 327–368.

25. Sophocles, *Oedipus at Colonus,* 42–43, trans. by Robert Fitzgerald, copyright, 1941, Harcourt Brace and World, Inc.

26. Ibid., 1586–1667.

27. Ibid., 1600–1601.

28. Pausanias, I.1.4.

29. Cf. Chapter 3, p. 29, and fig. 38.

30. Pausanias, I.39.5; I.40.6; I.42.6.

31. Euripides, *Helen,* 1346–1352.

32. See excavation reports of the sanctuary of Aphrodite in Πρακτικὰ (1938), pp. 28–34, and (1939), pp. 39–41.

33. *Guide Bleu, Grèce,* p. 220, well summarizes the information from the above.

34. Homeric Hymn X, "To Aphrodite," 5, Loeb, p. 434.

35. Pausanias, VIII.15.7.

36. Sophocles describes Salamis as "blessed" and "visible to all around," making use of the word, περίψαντος, which, when used of sculpture, means a free–standing figure that can be seen from all sides. *AJAX*, 596–599. I am indebted to Kenneth Happe for bringing this to my attention.

37. Herodotus, VIII.83–95. See also W. K. Pritchett, "Toward a Restudy of the Battle of Salamis," *AJA*, 63 (1959), 251 ff.

38. Levy, *Gate of Horn*, p. 297. Virgil, *Aeneid*, VI, 893–894: "Sunt geminae somni portae, quarum altera fertur / Cornea, qua veris facilis datur exitus umbris." See also Cook, *Zeus*, 2, 36–45.

39. Graves disagrees with the usual philological interpretation, but the topographical evidence is against him. Graves, *The Greek Myths*, 24:6: "Eleusis seems to be a worn–down form of *Eilythuies*, '[the temple] of her who rages in a lurking place.'"

40. The Roman propylaea are discussed in the following:

G. Libertini, "I Propilei di A. Claudio Pulcro ad Eleusi," *Annuario della Scuola Italiana*, 2 (1916), 201–217.

H. Hörmann, *Die inneren Propyläen von Eleusis*, Berlin, 1932.

W. Zschietzschmann, "Die inneren Propyläen von Eleusis," *Archäologischer Anzeiger; Jahrb. d. deut. Arch. Inst.*, (*AA JdI*), 68 (1933), c. 336, fig. I, c. 337.

O. Deubner, "Zu den grossen Propyläen von Eleusis," *Ath. Mitt.*, 62 (1937), 73–81.

41. Cf. note 23: Noack, Kourouniotis, and Mylonas.

42. Harrison, *Prolegomena*, pp. 548–551; Levy, *Gate of Horn*, pp. 295–299; P. M. Cruice, ed., *Philosophoumena* (Paris, 1860), p. 170.

43. Euripides, *Helen*, 1358–1367, trans. by Lattimore, Vol. *3*, Chicago, 1959.

44. In general see Noack, note 23 above. Also J. Travlos in Ἐφημερίς ἀρχαιολογική (Ἐφ.Ἀρχ), (1950–51), p. 3. This shows the Mycenaean shrine.

45. Pausanias, I.39.5. Cf. Πρακτικὰ, (1934), pp. 48–50.

46. Pausanias, II.4.7.

47. Pausanias, II.5.1.

48. Pausanias, II.36.6–8; II.37.2.

49. Cicero, *The Verrine Orations*, II.iv.48–49, Loeb Edition, translated by L. H. G. Greenwood (London, 1935), pp. 106–110.

50. Strabo, 256.

51. Cicero, II.iv.48, p. 106: "umbilicus Siciliae nominatur." See Philippson, "Griechische Gottheiten..." pp. 58 ff.

52. This monument is discussed in the following:

P. Marconi, "La Gronaia a protomi leonine del tempio di Demetra a Girgenti," *Bollettino d'Arte*, 6 (1926–1927), 385–403; *Agrigento, topografia ed arte*, Florence, 1929; *Agrigento*, Rome, 1933.

P. Griffo, *Ultimi scavi e ultime scoperte in Agrigento*, Agrigento, 1946.

53. Pythia 12, 1–3, in *The Odes of Pindar*, trans. by Lattimore, Chicago, 1947.

54. The wheel–shaped or round altars of both the temple of Demeter and the Sanctuary of the Chtonian Gods are described in the following: P. Marconi, "Girgenti, ricerche ed esplorazioni," *Notiz. Scav. 51* (1926), 118–148; "Agrigento arcaica," *Atti e Memorie della Società Magna Grecia* (1931), pp. 35, 102–108.

55. Chronology reviewed in Dunbabin, *The Western Greeks*, p. 310. See also Marconi, *Notiz. Scav.* (1926), pl. 24.

56. This monument is described in E. Gabrici, "Il Santuario della Malophoros a Selinunte," *Mon. Ant.*, 32 (1927–1928), cc. 5–406.

57. Ibid., fig. 27, bis. c. 47, cc. 46–48.

Chapter 6, ARTEMIS AND APHRODITE:

1. Homeric Hymn XXVII "To Artemis," trans. by H. G. Evelyn–White, Loeb, p. 403.

2. Euripides, *Hippolytus*, 2–5, trans. by D. Grene, Vol. *3*, Chicago, 1959.

3. A good account of the interlocked character of the Artemis and Aphrodite cults is given by Farnell, *The Cults*, 2, 425–761. I shall not deal
with the early sixth–century, gorgon–pedimented, octastyle, pseudo–dipteral temple of Artemis on Kerkyra, since I have not had the opportunity to visit the island for long enough to study its siting adequately. It would seem, however, to have been a looming presence—with its short columns, massive entablature, wide gable, and watchful gorgon

—and to have been characteristically placed in a kind of saddle between higher hills, oriented SE toward the arc between them. See especially, F. Versakis in Πρακτικὰ, 1911, pp. 164 ff.; W. Dörpfeld, *Ath. Mitt.*, *39*, (1914), 161 ff.; Hans Riemann, "Zum Artemistempel von Korkyra," *JdI*, *58* (1943), 32–38.

4. The epiklesis Limnaia for Artemis in Sparta is of uncertain significance. Pausanias, III.14.2 identifies Artemis Limnaia with Britomartis; but in describing Sparta he derives the appellation simply from the marshy Limnaion region of the city, III.16.7. Artemid. Oneikr., II.35, identifies Limnaia–Limnatis as a fish goddess.

5. See R. M. Dawkins, et al., *The Sanctuary of Artemis Orthia at Sparta*, (Suppl. Papers Soc. Prom. Hellenic Studies, V), London, 1929.

6. See especially Pausanias, III.16.7; Plutarch, *Inst. Lac.*, 239C; Philostratos, *Vit. Apoll.*, VI.20; and the discussion by Ziehen, *Sparta (Kulte)*, in *PWRE*, zweite reihe III, bd. 2, cc. 1466–68.

7. Cf. Dinsmoor, *Architecture of Ancient Greece*, pp. 280, 366.

8. See especially E. Dyggve–Poulsen, *Das Laphrion, der Tempelbezirk von Kalydon*, Copenhagen, 1948.

9. See Robertson, 2d ed. (1943), p. 138, note 4, where he observes that a northerly or southerly facing is common in early temples. This is true, but such orientation is not confined to early work. Note discussion at beginning of Chapter 4.

10. Pausanias, II.7.6; Charles H. Skalet, *Ancient Sicyon* (Baltimore, 1928), p. 3. For the theater: E. Fiechter, *Antike griechische Theaterbauten*, (Stuttgart, 1930 ff.), Heft 3, *Sicyon*. This series of studies of individual theaters by Fiechter follows his, *Die baugeschichtliche Entwicklung des antiken Theaters*, Munich, 1914. For Sicyon see also, Πρακτικὰ, 1934, p. 116; 1937, p. 94; 1952, p. 388.

11. Homeric Hymn XIX "To Pan," 31, Loeb, p. 245; Homeric Hymn IV "To Hermes," 1–2, Loeb, p. 363.

12. Graves, *The Greek Myths*, 2, 120–21.

13. Pausanias, II.25.3.

14. Pausanias, II.24.5 and commentary by Frazer, *3*, 210.

15. G. F. Hill, *Br. Mus. Cat. of Greek Coins of Phoenicia*, (London, 1910), p. 102 and pl. XII, 13; cf. A. Evans, "Mycenaean Tree and Pillar Cult," *JHS*, *21* (1901), pp. 135 ff., fig. 21, p. 138.

16. Beyond Mukhli the whole Arcadian plain of Tripolis, in antiquity of Mantineia and Tegea, seems dominated, despite the many gods and god-

desses who had their temples there, by the encircling presence of Artemis in the hills. A tented peak like that at Stymphalia rises north of Mantineia beyond the large conical mound which the Mantineians called the tomb of Penelope, and a temple of Artemis lay near it. A shrine of Aphrodite's was also in that area, and the tomb of her lover Anchises was supposed to have been placed nearby. Cf. Pausanias, VIII.12.5–9.

17. There may also have been a relationship between the temple at Tegea of the local goddess Alea, later identified with Athena, and the peaks of Mount Artemision to the north of it. The fourth–century structure at Tegea had a northern as well as an eastern entrance, and this double orientation recalls, as do the engaged Corinthian columns of the interior of the cella, the earlier temple at Bassae, to be discussed later. A pool of water lay along the north flank of the temple, and it and the distant but strikingly clear horns of Artemision would have been in view at the same time from the side door. C. Dugas, J. Berchmans, M. Clemmensen, *Le Sanctuaire d'Aléa Athéna à Tégée au IVe siècle*, (Paris, 1924), *1*, 57–8. The shrine of the mysterious goddess Alea, the root of whose name implies the idea of refuge and protection, dates back to late Mycenaean times. The earliest sanctuary was no doubt a simple enclosure and altar, but these, like the archaic temple mentioned by Pausanias, have completely disappeared. The excavators suggest that the materials from an older temple were re–used in the fourth–century building, and they account for the absence of earlier foundations by supposing the later temple to have exactly occupied the site of the former. C. Dugas, et al., 1–5; also, C. Dugas, "Le Sanctuaire d'Aléa Athéna à Tégée avant le IVe siècle," *BCH*, *65* (1921), 335 ff.

18. See Pausanias, I.1.4; Xenophon, *Hell.*, II.4.11 ff.; W. Judeich, *Topographie von Athen*, 2d ed. (Munich, 1931), pp. 431, 452. Artemis here replaced an older goddess, see U. v. Wilamowitz–Moellendorf, *Glaube der Hellener*, *1* (Berlin, 1931), 123, 182 ff.

19. Cf. Lolling, "Das Artemision auf Nordeuböa," *Ath. Mitt.*, 8 (1883), 7–23.

20. Dystos in Euboea (my Fig. 25) where, of course, no temple of Artemis has been found, should also be mentioned here, since it has at once a central cone, a tented ridge, and a lake, like Stymphalia. Like that site too, it is heavy, enclosed, and secret. For Dystos, see K. Bursian, *Geographie von Griechenland*, 2 (Leipzig, 1872), 428 ff.,

and T. Wiegand, "Dystos," *Ath. Mitt.*, 24 (1899), 458–67.

21. Cf. Τὸ Ἔργον τῆς Ἀρχαιολογικῆς Ἑταιρείας, (*Ἔργον*), (1956), pp. 33–37; Ibid. (1958), pp. 53–60; *AJA*, 61 (1957), 283 ff.

22. Pausanias, IX.19.6–7.

23. For Loutsa, see Ἔργον (1956), p. 31; ibid. (1957), pp. 20–25. For the exacavations of Papadimitriou at Brauron, see Πρακτικὰ (1946–48), pp. 81–90; ibid. (1949), pp. 75–90; ibid. (1950), pp. 173–187; Ἔργον (1956), pp. 25–31; ibid. (1957), pp. 20–25; ibid. (1958), pp. 30–39. Also *AJA*, 63 (1959), 280, pl. 73, figs. 1, 2.

24. Euripides, *Iphigenia in Tauris*, 1448–61, trans. by Witter Bynner, Vol. 3, Chicago, 1959. Copyright by Witter Bynner.

25. Ibid., 1459–61.

26. Pausanias, I.26.1.

27. As by Graves, *The Greek Myths*, 116.5; *Oxford Classical Dictionary* (1949), 104.

28. Euripides, *Iphigenia in Tauris*, 1462–67, trans. by Witter Bynner.

29. Pausanias, I.32.3.

30. Pausanias, I.33.1.

31. See Euripides, *Iphigenia in Tauris*, 1466; L. Preller, *Griechische Mythologie*, 4th ed., *1* (Berlin, 1894), 314. For a general survey of Artemis' role as protectress of childbirth, see M. P. Nilsson, *Geschichte der griechischen Religion*, *1* (Berlin, 1941), 463–66.

32. On Hera as Eileithyia, see O. Jessen, "Eileithyia," in *PWRE*, *11*, bd. 2, esp. cc. 2204–07.

33. Here many beautiful reliefs of the fifth century and later have been found in the most recent excavations. Cf. *AJA*, note 23 above.

34. Acts, XIX:34. The supposed residence and death of the Virgin at Ephesos have never been officially recognized by the Church; see *Catholic Encyclopedia*, *15* (New York, 1912), 470.

35. There is simply not enough evidence for us to be sure of anything here. The temple was burned by a madman in the fourth century, and the archaic temple must be reconstructed from fragments found under the Hellenistic rebuilding which has itself left incomplete clues as to its form. See J. Wood, *Discoveries at Ephesus*, London, 1877, and D. G. Hogarth, *Excavations at Ephesus*, London, 1908. For later restorations see A. E. Henderson, "Excavations at Ephesus and Restoration of the Croesus Structure," *J. Royal Inst. of Brit. Architects*, 3d sec., 16 (1908–09), 538–540, and idem, "The Hellenistic Temple of Artemis at Ephesus," *JRIBA*, 3d sec., 22 (1914–15), 130–134. For

restoration without eastern door, see F. Krischen, "Das Artemision von Ephesos," *Wilhelm Dörpfeld Festschrift* (Berlin, 1933), pp. 71 ff.; followed by B. H. Grinnell, *Greek Temples* (New York, 1943), pp. 5–7, pl. 6. See also B. L. Trell, "The Temple of Artemis at Ephesus," *Numismatic Notes and Monographs*, No. 107, 1945, and F. Miltner, *Ephesos, Stadt der Artemis*, Vienna, 1958.

36. Charles Picard, *Manuel d'archéologie grecque*, La Sculpture IV, Period Classique–IVe siecle, Pte. IIe (Paris, 1954), pp. 108 ff., pl. III and figs. 56–58.

37. See C. Humann, "Die Tantalosburg im Sipylos," *Ath. Mitt.*, *12* (1888), 22–41, and E. Brandenburg, "Bericht über eine Reise in Anatolien im Sommer 1906," *Memnon*, *1* (1907), 34–36, figs. 25, 26. Cf. Pausanias, VIII.2.7.

38. Strabo, XIV.1.40. refers to the temple of Magnesian Artemis as far superior architecturally to that at Ephesos, and inferior in size only to the temples of Ephesos and of Didymaean Apollo in all of Asia. Hermogenes, whom Vitruvius admired (III. 3.6–9) and seems most closely to follow in his theory, worked in the second half of the second century. His pseudo–dipterality at Magnesia, in which the temple became primarily a porch, was exactly in accord with Italic taste. Indeed, Vitruvius approvingly notes that a crowd caught in a shower would thus have "a wide, free space in which to wait." III.3.9 (Morgan). See C. Humann, et al., *Magnesia am Maeander: Bericht über die Ergebnisse der Ausgrabungen der Jahre 1891–93*, Berlin, 1904, and W. Hahland, "Datierung der Hermogenesbauten," *Bericht über den VI. internationalen Kongress für Archäologie*, Berlin, 1940. Vitruvius (III.3.6–8) also praises Hermogenes' "eustyle," that is, "good" system of column placement in his temple at Teos, about which, as about his temple at Magnesia, Hermogenes wrote an explanatory book, now lost.

39. Euripides, *Iphigenia in Tauris*, 127, trans. by Witter Bynner.

40. See especially H. C. Butler, *Sardis* (*Publ. of Am. Soc. for Excavation of Sardis*), Vol. 2, pt. 1, "The Temple of Artemis," Leyden, 1925. The new excavations at Sardis, directed by George M. A. Hanfmann and A. Henry Detweiler, have had preliminary publication in *Archaeology*, *12* (1959), 53–61, and *14* (1961), 3–11. I am extremely grateful to Professor Hanfmann for generously allowing me to use his as yet unpublished photograph of the site as an illustration here.

41. Strabo, XIII.4.5.

42. Butler, *Sardis*, 85, 92–93.

43. Herodotus, I.84.

44. The Near Eastern goddess Astarte–Ishtar, who is usually identified with Aphrodite, exhibits a striking dualism in her attributes. She is worshipped both as goddess of love and procreation, and as patroness of war and the chase. See A. Jeremias, *Handbuch der altorientalischen Geisteskultur* (Leipzig, 1913), pp. 253–63, and S. Langdon, *Tammuz and Ishtar* (Oxford, 1914), pp. 98–108.

45. Homeric Hymn V, "To Aphrodite," 100–03, Loeb, p. 413.

46. Strabo, X.3.22.

47. On the cult of Aphrodite and Eros at Athens see I. Bekker, *Anecdota Graeca*, *1* (Berlin, 1814), 317, and H. K. Usener, *Götternamen* (Bonn, 1896), pp. 267 ff. For the excavation of the shrine, see O. Broneer, "Eros and Aphrodite on the North Slope of the Acropolis in Athens," *Hesperia*, *1* (1933), 31–55.

48. For Kaisariani, G. Lampolus, "'H Μονὴ Καισαριανῆς," Παρνασσος, 5 (1881), 645–58.

49. G. W. Elderkin, "The Cults of the Erechtheion," *Hesperia*, 10 (1941), 113–24.

50. Homeric Hymn V, "To Aphrodite," 257–58, Loeb, p. 425.

51. See Chapter 5, note 32.

52. See G. Welter, *Troizen und Kalaureia*, Berlin, 1942.

53. Pausanias, II.32.4; E. Meyer, "Troizen," in *PWRE*, zweite reihe VII, bd. 1, cc. 630–31.

54. Welter, *Troizen und Kalauris*, pp. 37, 38, pls. 21, 22a.

55. Strabo, VIII.6.20.

56. Strabo, VIII.6.21; Pausanias, II.5.1; cf. Blegen, et al., *Acrocorinthus* (*Corinth: Results of Excavations Conducted by the American School of Classical Studies at Athens, III, pt. 1*), Cambridge, 1930.

57. Strabo, VIII.6.21; Blegen, et al., *Acrocorinthus*, 31–60.

58. Apollodorus, ii.5.I; Valerius Flaccus, i.34; Diodorus Siculus, iv.II.

59. Greek authorities trace the establishment of the temple and cult of "Aphrodite" back to mythical times: Strabo, XIII.1.54, to Aeneas; Diod. Sic., IV.83, to Eryx, both sons of Aphrodite. The identification of the native goddess with Aphrodite was current at least as early as the fifth century B.C.; see Thucydides, *The Peloponnesian War*, VI.43.3.

60. See S. B. Platner and T. Ashby, *Topographical Dictionary of Ancient Rome* (London, 1929), pp. 551–552; Strabo, VI.2.5.

61. See O. Richter, *Antike Steinmetzzeichen* (Berlin, 1885), pp. 43 ff.

62. See F. W. Kelsey, *Excavations at Carthage 1925*, Prel. Rep. (New York, 1926), pp. 33–51, on the precinct of Tanit. The tradition of the sacred forms was clearly not confined to Greece; it was obviously widespread, possibly universal, and offers a field for further research. It was certainly Asiatic, as the settings of Sardis and Phoenician Carthage and the many other traditions of sacred mountains, referred to earlier, would indicate. Later: the Hindu mountain–temple and the Buddhist stupa.

63. R. V. Scaffidi, *Tyndaris*, Palermo, 1895, and rev. by Lupus, *Berl. Phil. Woch.*, 16 (1896), cc. 1109–10; *PWRE*, 2d. ed., 7 (1948), c. 1787; Biagio Pace, *Arte e Civiltà della Sicilia Antica*, 3 (Genoa, 1945), 546. R. Ross Holloway, "Tyndaris: Last Colony of the Sicilian Greeks," *Archaeology*, *13*, No. 4 (1960), 246 ff. Tyndaris was not colonized by Greeks until 396 B.C., and then by exiled Messenians who brought the name with them.

64. P. Marconi, "Cefalù—Il Cosi detto 'Tempio di Diana,'" *Notiz. Scav.* (1929), pp. 273–95.

65. Ibid., pp. 293–5.

66. Homeric Hymn V, "To Aphrodite," 68–73, Loeb, p. 411.

67. See R. Koldewey and O. Puchstein, *Der griechische Tempel in Unteritalien und Sicilien*, p. 132 and pl. XIX; and D. Serradifalco, *Antichità della Sicilia*, *1* (Palermo, 1835), 109 ff., pls. II–XII.

68. Dinsmoor, *Architecture of Greece*, p. 112. But see now A. Burford, "Temple Building at Segesta," *Classical Quarterly*, 55 (1961), 87–93.

69. Pausanias, VIII.41.10; K. Kurouniotis, in Πρακτικὰ (1902), 75 ff.; 'Εφ.'Αρχ. (1903), pp. 151 ff. See also E. Meyer, "Phigaleia," in *PWRE*, *19*, bd. 2, cc. 2708–09.

70. Pausanias, IV.33.1; Frazer ed. of Pausanias, *3*, 437.

71. Pausanias, IV.9.4 f.

Chapter 7, APOLLO:

1. Aeschylus, *Eumenides*, 150, trans. by Richmond Lattimore, Vol. *1*, Chicago, 1959.

2. The character of Apollo has been heavily romanticized by a number of modern writers from Winckelmann on. Cf. Otto, *The Homeric Gods*, pp. 61–80.

3. For this reconstruction see Fiechter in *JdI*, *33* (1918), 107–245, and Buschor and von Massow in *Ath. Mitt.*, *52* (1927), 1–85.

4. Homeric Hymn XXI, "To Apollo," 2–3, Loeb, p. 447.

5. Homeric Hymn III, "To Delian Apollo," 143–45, Loeb, p. 335.

6. See F. Stählin, et al., *Pagasai und Demetrias*, Berlin and Leipzig, 1934.

7. Homeric Hymn III, "To Delian Apollo," 22–24, Loeb, p. 327.

8. For early excavations of this site see T. Wiegand, *Priene* (Berlin, 1904), pp. 25 ff. For a short report of current excavations see M. J. Mellink, "Archaeology in Asia Minor," *AJA*, *62* (1958), 103.

9. Herodotus, I.148.

10. F. Hiller v. Gaertringen, et al., *Thera, Untersuchungen, Vermessungen, und Ausgrabungen in den Jahren 1895–1902*, 4 vols., Berlin, 1899–1909.

11. Vitruvius, IV.1.5. He had already said (IV.1.3) that Dorus, King of Achaea, had built a shrine, "which chanced to be of this order, in the precinct of Juno at Argolis." (Morgan.)

12. Strabo, XIV.1.36.

13. Vitruvius, IV.1.6.

14. Vitruvius, IV.1.7–8.

15. See above, Chapter 4, note 15.

16. For Naucratis see W. M. F. Petrie and E. A. Gardner, *Naukratis*, 2 vols., London, 1886–1888, and E. Gjerstad, "Studies in Archaic Greek Chronology, i, Naucratis," *Liverpool Annals of Archaeol. and Anthropology*, *21*, 1934.

17. W. A. Oldfather, "Lokroi," *PWRE*, *13* (1927), c. 1289–1363, and E. Petersen, "Tempel in Lokri," (*Rom. Mitt.*), *5* (1890), 161–229.

18. Strabo, VII.7.6.

19. "Archaeology in Greece, 1954," *BSA*, Vol. *49*, 1955. The association with Artemis is only my conjecture.

20. G. Welter, *Aigina*, Berlin, 1938; see also below, Chapter 9, note 25.

21. Farnell, *The Cults*, *1*, 62.

22. Pausanias, I.37.3.

23. Pausanias, I.44.9–10.

24. See the excavation reports of the American School at Athens *Corinth* (Cambridge, Mass., 1932 ff.), especially *1*, chapt. ii by R. Stillwell, pp. 115–134.

25. C. H. Morgan, "Excavations at Corinth I, 1936–37," *AJA*, *41* (1937), 539–552; "Excavations at Corinth II, 1938," *AJA*, *43* (1939), 255–267.

26. A. D. Keramopoulos, in 'Α Δελτ, Vol. *3*, 1917.

27. The bibliography of the temple at Ptoon includes: A. K. Orlandos, "Ο ναος τοῦ Ἀπόλλωνος Πτώου," 'Α Δελτ, *8* (1923), 1–51; and P. Guillon, *Les trépieds de Ptoion*, 2 vols., Paris, 1943.

28. Pausanias, IX.26.2–4.

29. Philippson's description of the awesome character of Ptoon is most striking. *Griechische Gottheiten*, pp. 24–30.

30. Hesiod, *Theogony*, 420 ff. The most recent study of Hecate is by Theodor Kraus, *Hekate*, Heidelberg, 1960. Reviewed by Nilsson, *AJA, 65*, No. 1 (1961), 78–79.

31. G. M. Richter, *Kouroi* (New York, 1942), chapt. X, "Ptoon 20 Group," pp. 213–46.

32. For the site of Delphi see especially *Fouilles de Dèlphes*, École française d'Athènes, Paris, 1923 ff., and P. de la Coste–Messelière, *Dèlphes*, Paris, 1943.

33. Homeric Hymn III, "To Pythian Apollo," 230 ff., Loeb, p. 341.

34. Ibid., 281–85.

35. Ibid., 516–21.

36. Ibid., 300–04.

37. Ibid., 363.

38. Aeschylus, *Eumenides*, 170 ff., trans. by Richmond Lattimore, Vol. *1*, Chicago, 1959.

39. Ibid., 22–24.

40. See note 32, above.

41. Pieske in *PWRE*, xii, c. 1048 ff.

42. Pausanias, IV.39.5 ff., and Strabo IX.2.38.

43. Homeric Hymnn III "To Pythian Apollo," 382–85, Loeb, p. 351.

44. *Les Fouilles de Dèlphes*, École française d'Athènes, especially ii, fasc. iii and iv, 1923–25.

45. Discussed below, Chapter 10, pp. 203–4.

46. Pindar, Nemea 6, in *Odes of Pindar*, trans. by Lattimore.

47. Pausanias, IX.15.4–5; Pierre Amandry, "Notes de Topographie et d'Architecture delphiques," *BCH*, *78* (1954), 295–315.

48. Aeschylus, *Eumenides*, 193 ff., trans. by Lattimore.

49. P. Amandry, *La mantique apolliniènne à Dèlphes* (Paris, 1950), pp. 196–200.

50. Aeschylus, *Eumenides*, 22 ff., trans. by Lattimore. Sophocles in the *Antigone* connects Dionysos with the "double–crested rock" (of Parnassos), and Euripides in the *Bacchae* (lines 305 ff.) says "You shall see Dionysos on the Delphic rocks leaping with torches upon the twin–peaked plain."

51. Kolbe in *PWRE* xix, c. 973 and C. D. Buck, "Discoveries in the Attic Deme of Ikaria," *AJA*, 5 (1889), 154–181.

52. Diogenes Laertius, III.56; Horace, *Ars Poetica*, 275 ff.

53. See Dinsmoor, *Architecture of Ancient Greece*, p. 361, for a complete bibliography of this precinct.

54. See in this respect K. Lehmann, *Die Antike*, 7, 172–175.

55. R. B. Richardson, et al., "Excavation at Eretria," *AJA*, 7 (1891), 371–389; 10 (1895), 326–337; 11 (1896), 152–175.

56. Pausanias, I.31.1.

57. For Zoster, ʼΑ Δελτ, 11 (1927–28), 9–53.

58. T. Homolle, et al., *Fouilles de Délos*, 17 vols., Paris, 1902–1939. But see especially R. Vallois, *L'Architecture héllénique et héllénistique à Délos*, 2 vols., Paris, 1944, 1953.

59. Homeric Hymn III "To Delian Apollo," 66–76, Loeb, p. 320.

60. Ibid., 14–18.

61. Plutarch, *Theseus*, 21; Pausanias, VIII.48.3; Farnell, *The Cults*, iv, pp. 287 ff.

62. Cf. *PWRE*, 4 (1901), 2470.

63. Virgil, *Aeneid*, vi.42 ff.

64. R. Koldewey and O. Puchstein, *Die griechischen Tempel in Unteritalien und Sicilien*, pp. 62–66, pl. 7. G. Cultrera for restoration of the temple in *Rivista del R. Istituto d'Archeologia e Storia dell' Arte*, 9, 1942. M. Guarducci, "L'iscrizione dell' Apollonion di Siracusa," *Archeologica Classica*, 1 (1949), 4–10.

65. E. Gabrici, "Acropoli di Selinunte," *Mon. Ant.*, Vol. 33 (1929), cc. 61–112; "Per la storia dell' architettura dorica in Sicilia," *Mon. Ant.*, Vol. 35 (1933), cc. 137–250; J. Hulot and G. Fougéres, *Sélinonte, colonie dorienne en Sicile*, Paris, 1910. Speaking of the Temple of Apollo, Robertson (p. 86) suggests a possible conflict "between art and religion" in the general abandonment, resisted on Sicily, of adyton for opisthodomos; that is, priests may generally have wanted the adyton and here got an inner shrine to replace it.

66. P. Marconi, *Himera, lo scavo del tempio della Vittoria e del temenos*, Rome, 1931.

67. Herodotus, VII.165 ff.

68. See again Dinsmoor's "Archaeology and Astronomy," in *Proceedings of the Amer. Philos. Society*, 80 (1939), 95–173.

69. F. C. Penrose, "On the Orientation of Certain Greek Temples and the Dates of their Foundation," *Proc. of the Royal Soc.*, 53, 61, 65, 68, 1893–1901, and *Transactions of the Royal Soc.*, 184, 190, 196, 1893–1901.

70. For Thermon buildings see K. A. Rhomaios in ʼΑ. Δελτ, 1 (1915), 225–229, and also his article on Thermon in Πρακτικὰ, (1931), 61–70; also H. Payne, "On the Thermon Metopes," *BSA*, 27 (1926–27), 124–132. See also J. A. Bundgaard who explores the question of date for the peristylar column bases around Megaron B: "À propos de la date de la peristasis du Megaron B à Thermon," *BCH*, 70 (1946), 51–57.

71. For reports of this site see K. Kourouniotis on the excavation in ʼΑ. Δελτ (1903), pp. 153–88, and his discussion of the temple of Apollo in ʼΑ. Δελτ (1910), pp. 271–332; also K. A. Rhomaios on the peculiarities of the temple in ʼΕφ. ʼΑρχ (1914), pp. 57–70, and his later treatment in ʼΕφ. ʼΑρχ (1933), pp. 1–25.

72. Pausanias, VIII.41.7–10. However, see Riemann who, like Dinsmoor as noted below, believes the temple shows two campaigns of building and two different hands. H. Riemann, "Iktinos und der Tempel von Bassae," *Fest. Zucker* (Berlin, 1954), pp. 299–339.

73. For the arguments of Dinsmoor see "Temple of Apollo at Bassae," *Metropolitan Museum Studies*, 4 (1933), 204–227; *Architecture of Ancient Greece*, pp. 154–57; "The Lost Pedimental Sculptures of Bassae," *AJA*, 43 (1939), 27–47; and a further note in *AJA*, 47 (1943), 19–21.

74. Pausanias, VIII.41.10.

75. See Dinsmoor in *Met. Mus. Studies*, 4 (1933), 213.

76. Dinsmoor, *Architecture of Ancient Greece*, p. 157 ff.

77. W. Hahland, "Der iktinische Entwurf des Apollontempels in Bassae," *JdI*, 63–4 (1948–49), 14–39. I personally can detect no evidence in the junction of the diagonal walls with those of the cella which would indicate that a change had ever been made at that point.

78. Vitruvius, IV.1.9 ff.

79. Homeric Hymn III "To Delian Apollo," 115–16, Loeb, p. 333.

80. The possibility that the column on axis stood for an image of the god was first suggested to me by Margaretta Magannini. The author realizes that the consideration of the Corinthian column as a tree symbol by the architects at Bassae and its association with Callimachos reinforces the argument that the building shows two campaigns and that the second was carried on by Callimachos himself. Yet the temple's conceptual unity is so impressive that it seems unnecessary to disassociate the only architect mentioned in an ancient source, Ictinos, from any part of it. See also Robertson's views on the character of the Corinthian capital. 2nd ed. (1954), p. 141.

81. Dinsmoor, *Architecture of Ancient Greece*, p. 156.

82. C. R. Cockerell, *Temples of Jupiter Panhellenius* [sic] *at Aigina and of Apollo Epicurius at Bassae* (London, 1860), pls. 11–12 and pp. 55–56.

83. This opinion was expressed to the author in conversation by Mr. Peter Corbett of the British Museum. I am grateful for Mr. Corbett's permission to record it, as well as for his many kindnesses to me at the Museum.

84. E. Pontremoli and B. Haussoullier, *Didymes, fouilles de 1895 et 1896*, Paris, 1904, and H. Knackfuss, *Didyma, I, Die Baubeschreibung*, 3 vols., Berlin, 1941. A von Gerkan, "Der Tempel von Didyma und sein antikes Baumass," *Wiener Jahreshefte*, 32, 1940; also: "Der Naiskos im Tempel von Didyma," *JdI*, 57, 1942; both now in *Von antiker Architektur . . .*, pp. 204–226.

85. Homeric Hymn III, "To Pythian Apollo," 235, 245, etc.

86. Strabo, XIV.1.5.

87. Homeric Hymn XXXI "To Helios," 13–14, Loeb, p. 459.

88. Pausanias, VII.3.1 and VII.5.4. For excavation reports of the site see L. Robert, *Les fouilles de Claros*, Limoges, 1954; and for more recent progress on the site *AJA*, 60 (1956), 236–7; 61 (1957), 381–82; 62 (1958), 98–99.

Chapter 8, ZEUS:

1. Aeschylus, *Agamemnon*, 1914–40, trans. by Richmond Lattimore, Vol. *1*, Chicago, 1959.

2. See Cook, *Zeus*, passim.

3. A good short account of the origin and syncretistic growth of Zeus is given by M. P. Nilsson, *Geschichte der griechischen Religion, I* (Munich, 1941), 364–400.

4. Pausanias, I.40.6.

5. Homeric Hymn XXIII, "To the Son of Kronos," 2–3, Loeb, p. 449.

6. C. Seltman, *The Twelve Olympians and their Guests*, rev. ed. (London, 1956), pp. 14–16; Cooke, *Zeus*, *1*, pl. IX.

7. A. Evans, *The Palace of Minos at Knossos*, *I*, 153–59. For a recent investigation of the site of the "Tomb of Zeus" on Mt. Jouctas, see P. Faure, "Le Mont Iouktas, Tombeau de Zeus," *Minoica* (Berlin, 1958), pp. 133–148.

8. The many ancient sources are assembled by Schwenn, "Kureten," in *PWRE, 11*, bd. 2, esp. cc. 2204–07.

9. Pausanias, VIII.2 passim.

10. Cook, *Zeus*, 2, 894 ff, and *PWRE, 35* (1939), cc. 1175–1177.

11. Plutarch, *Themistocles*, 13.

12. A. Reichel, "Ein angeblicher Thron des Xerxes," *Festschrift für Otto Bendorf* (Wien, 1898), pp. 63–65.

13. Curiously, not hawks but vultures seem to have been most frequently confused with eagles by ancient Greek writers, e.g. Aeschylus, *Prometheus Bound*, 1022. See D'A. W. Thompson, *A Glossary of Greek Birds*, new ed. (London, 1936), p. 5.

14. For the excavation report see Rodney Young in *AJA*, 44 (1940), 1–9. For the sanctuary on the summit see *PWRE*, 23 (1924), cc. 41, 42.

15. C. Carapanos, *Dodone et ses Ruines*, Paris, 1878. For Dakaris' reconstruction of the temple and peribolos as renovated after 219 B.C., see now: *AJA*, 65 (1961), 301.

16. Strabo, VII.7.10–11.

17. Hesiod, *Catalogues of Women and Eoiae*, XCVII, Loeb, p. 215.

18. Aeschylus, *Agamemnon*, 176–78, trans. by Lattimore.

19. See L. Bevier, "The Olympieion at Athens," *Papers of the American School of Classical Studies at Athens*, *1* (1882–3), 181–212, and G. Welter, "Das Olympieion in Athen," *Ath. Mitt.*, 47–48 (1922–23), 61–71.

20. Dinsmoor, *Architecture of Ancient Greece*, p. 91 and note.

21. See C. W. Blegen and B. H. Hill, *Nemea, Excavations Conducted by the University of Cincinnati* (in preparation), and R. Vallois and M. Clemmensen, "Temple de Zeus à Némée," *BCH*, 49 (1925), 1–20.

22. G. Kruse, "Polieus," in *PWRE*, 21 bd. 2, cc. 1376–78, with complete collection of instances of the appellation; Nilsson, *Geschichte, 1*, 390–96.

23. See A. K. Orlandos, on Stratos in 'A. Δελτ., 8 (1923), 1–51, and C. Picard and F. Courby, *Recherches archéologiques à Stratos d'Arcarnanie*, Paris, 1924.

24. Strabo, XII.8.11.

25. For Cumae see E. Gabrici, "Cuma," *Mon. Ant., 12*, Nos. 1 and 2, 1913–1914.

26. For the Olympieion of Syracuse, see P. Orsi, "L'Olympieion di Siracusa," *Mon. Ant., 13*, 1903.

26a. See note 41a, chapter 4.

27. Dinsmoor's projected monograph, "The Olympieum at Acragas," which he promised for the *Memoirs of the American Academy at Rome*, 20, seems never to have appeared. For full bibliography see his *Architecture of Ancient Greece*, pp. 381–82.

28. Dinsmoor, p. 101, note.

29. See among others the following:

    E. Curtius, et al., *Die Ausgrabungen zu Olympia*, Berlin, 1876–81.

    E. Curtius, F. Adler, et al., *Olympia: Die Ergebnisse der vom deutschen Reich veranstalteten Ausgrabungen*, Berlin, 1890–97.

    H. Schlief, *Die neuen Ausgrabungen in Olympia und ihre bisherigen Ergebnisse für die antike Bauforschung*, Berlin, 1943.

    J. K. Smith, "A Restoration of the Temple of Zeus at Olympia," *Memoirs of the American Academy at Rome, 4* (1924), 153–168.

    E. N. Gardiner, *Olympia, its History and Remains*, Oxford, 1925.

30. Pausanias, V.15.8–11.

31. See C. Morgan, "Pheidias and Olympia," *Hesperia, 21* (1952) 295–339. Also, for contrary opinion see G. M. Richter, *Sculpture and Sculptors of the Greeks*, new rev. ed. (New Haven, 1950), pp. 215–33.

32. Lawrence, *Greek Architecture*, p. 153, speaks of the Prytaneum as "slewed at a strange angle behind the temple of Hera."

33. E. Kunze and H. Weber, "The Olympic Stadium, the Echo Colonnade, and an 'Archaeological Earthquake' at Olympia," *AJA, 52* (1948), 490–96.

34. Pausanias, VI.20.7, 8.

35. Pindar, Olympia I, 92.

36. Pindar, Olympia III, 17–34, trans. by Richmond Lattimore, in *The Odes of Pindar*, Chicago, 1947.

37. Doxiadis, *Raumordnung*, pp. 67–76.

38. Pindar, Olympia I, 92–95, trans. by Lattimore.

39. Pausanias, V.10.1 ff. and V.14.4.

40. Doxiadis, p. 74.

41. Trans. by Mary McCarthy from the original translation by Simone Weil, "The Iliad . . . ," *The Mint, 2* (1948), 95.

42. Pindar, Olympia I, 88, trans. by Lattimore.

43. Even Pindar may perhaps be taken to suggest something of the kind, but this is probably stretching his simpler statement of human felicity too far: "the winner the rest of his lifetime / keeps happiness beside him sweeter than honey / as far as the games go; but the good that stays by day and abides with him / is best that can come to a man." Ibid., 97–100.

44. On the concept of the *Hieros Gamos*, see Nilsson, *Geschichte, 1*, 402–05. The optical effect of counter swing in the two temples was first called to my attention by James Jarrett.

45. Pindar, Pythia VIII, 1, trans. by Lattimore. Copyright 1942 by New Directions.

46. Jean–Paul Sartre in *Les Mouches* and Albert Camus in *L'Homme Révolté*, Paris, Gallimard, 1951, have directly invoked Hellenic support for their conception of the human condition. Sartre's Orestes specifically defies the nature of things which is Zeus, but Camus would revive a sense for the objective reality of the non–human world and of the laws of balance and measure which bind human action to it.

47. A. K. Orlandos, "Note sur le Sanctuaire de Nemesis a Rhamnonte," *BCH, 48* (1924), 305–320; and W. Zschietzschmann, "Der Tempel von Rhamnus," *Archäologischer Anzeiger*, in *JdI*, Vol. 44 (1929), cc. 441–451. W. H. Plommer, "Three Attic Temples," *BSA, 45* (1950), 66–112.

48. Pausanias, I.33.2.

49. See Orlandos, in *BCH, 48* (1924), 306–07, 318; Zschietzschmann, *AA (JdI)*; W. B. Dinsmoor, "The Temple of Ares at Athens," *Hesperia, 9* (1940), 52.

50. Cf. Pausanias, note 48 above.

51. The first excavators, who thought the Themis temple was earlier, could only account for the angle of the larger temple by suggesting that its builders hoped by this means to subordinate the smaller so that it might all the more easily be allowed to fall into decay. J. P. Gandy, *Unedited Antiquities of Attica*, Society of Dilettanti (1817), pp. 41 ff. The plan used in the *Guide Bleu* brings the logic of neoclassicism even more doggedly to bear by eliminating the angle and making the two temples parallel. *Guide Bleu, Grèce*, pp. 210–212, plan p. 211 after Orlandos; see also Orlandos, *BCH, 48* (1924), pl. VIII.

52. Augustus, for example, could have finished the temple when he had it rededicated, rather appropriately, to Livia.

Chapter 9, POSEIDON AND ATHENA:

1. Sophocles, *Oedipus at Colonus*, 1068–1071, trans. by R. Fitzgerald. Harcourt Brace and World.

1a. Ibid., 698 ff.

2. Ibid., 714–15.

3. Ibid., 719.

4. Ibid., 1070.

5. See Honigmann in *PWRE*, xi, c.1114.

6. Sophocles, *Oedipus at Colonus*, 712, trans. by Fitzgerald.

7. Pausanias, VIII.10.1.

8. Pausanias, IX.11.6.

9. Pausanias, IX.26.3.

10. Homeric Hymn III "To Pythian Apollo," 229–30, Loeb, p. 341. But see also Strabo, IX.2.33, who says of it: "it is bare of trees . . . even though the poets call it a grove."

11. S. Wide and L. Kjellberg, "Ausgrabungen auf Kalaureia," *Ath. Mitt.*, 20 (1895), 267–326, and G. Welter, *Troizen und Kalaureia*, Berlin, 1940.

12. Sophocles, *Oedipus at Colonus*, 1070, trans. by Fitzgerald.

13. O. T. Broneer, "Isthmia Excavations, 1952," *Hesperia*, 22 (1953), 182–195, and a series of articles in *Hesperia* thereafter. Idem, "Isthmian Sanctuary of Poseidon," *Archaeology, 8*, 1955.

14. Restored by A. v. Gerkan, *Der Poseidonaltar bei Kap Monodendri*, Berlin, 1915, Band I, Heft 4; in T. Wiegand et al., *Milet; Ergebnisse der Ausgrabungen und Untersuchungen seit dem Jahre 1899*, Berlin, 1906 ff.; reproduced by Lehmann in *Die Antike, 7* (1931), 26.

15. Herodotus, I.148.

16. Strabo, XIV.1.20.

17. For bibliography, see above, Chapter 7, note 8.

18. Herodotus, I.162–167.

19. A. Maiuri, "Velia, prima ricognizione ed esplorazione," *Atti e Mem. Soc. Magna Grecia*, 1926–27, and P. C. Sestieri, "Greek Elea—Roman Velia," *Archaeology, 10* (1957), 2–10.

20. See A. K. Orlandos, on the temple of Poseidon at Sounion in 'Α. Δελτ 1917; V. Stais, Τὸ Σούνιον καὶ οἱ ναοὶ τοῦ Ποσειδῶνος καὶ Ἀθῆνας, Athens, 1920; W. H. Plommer, "Three Attic Temples," *BSA, 45* (1950), 66–112.

21. Vitruvius, IV.8.4; Robertson, p. 332.

22. Vitruvius, IV.8.4.

23. Dinsmoor, "The Temple of Ares at Athens," *Hesperia, 9* (1940), 47; also see W. H. Plommer in *BSA, 45* (1950), 94–109.

24. Strabo, XIV.1.12–13.

25. A. Furtwängler et al., *Aegina, das Heiligtum der Aphaia*, 2 vols., Munich, 1906. H. Thiersch, "Äginetische Studien," *Nachr. d. Gesellschaft und Wissenschaften zu Göttingen, Phil-Hist. Klasse* (1928), pp. 135–194, and G. Welter, "Aeginetica," *AAJdI, 52* (1938), cc. 480–540.

26. "Diktynna," *PWRE, 4* (1905), cc. 584–588.

27. C. Iulius Solinus, 11.8 (Mommsen ed.); Pausanias, II.30.3.

28. Thiersch, "Äginetische Studien," pp. 140–50.

29. Herodotus, III.59, and also Thiersch, p. 167 ff.

30. See on this point also, Thiersch, pp. 167–94.

31. Herodotus, VIII.93.

32. G. W. Elderkin, "The Cults of the Erechtheion," *Hesperia, 10* (1941), 113–124.

33. Pausanias, III.17.2.

34. Vitruvius, IV.1.5.

35. J. T. Clark, F. H. Bacon and R. Koldewey, *Investigations at Assos*, Boston, 1902–21, and F. Sartiaux, *Les sculptures et la restauration du temple d'Assos en Troade*, Paris, 1915.

36. F. Krauss, *Paestum, Die griechischen Tempel*, Bildhefte antiker Kunst, Heft 8, 2nd ed., Berlin, 1943; C. Lamb, *Die Tempel von Paestum*,

Leipzig, 1944; Dinsmoor, "The Greek Temples at Paestum," *Mem. Am. Acad. Rome*, 20, 1950; now Krauss, *Die Tempel von Paestum*, 1, Berlin, 1959.

37. Sophocles, *Antigone*, 354, trans. by E. Wyckoff, Vol. 2, Chicago, 1959.

38. Plutarch, "Perikles," 12.1.

39. H. Focillon, *The Life of Forms in Art* (New York, 1948), p. 14.

40. Plutarch, "Perikles," 13.3.

41. For this bibliography see primarily Dinsmoor's list in his *Architecture of Ancient Greece*, pp. 357–60, as well as *Hesperia* thereafter. A review of recent work in Athens is to be found in Ida C. Hill, *The Ancient City of Athens, its topography and monuments*, Cambridge, Mass., 1953.

42. "The Hekatompedon on the Athenian Acropolis," *AJA*, 51 (1947), 109–151.

43. See above note 32.

44. Plato, *Laws*, 796; also referred to by Levy, *Gate of Horn*, p. 275. The distinction between the two temples in terms of siting is reinforced by the argument of C. J. Herington, based largely on philological studies: *Athena Parthenos and Athena Polias; a study in the religion of Periclean Athens*, Manchester, 1955.

45. As stated, perhaps falsely, in the late inscription of disputed date, purporting to record the Athenian order of battle of 480, recently discovered by Jameson at Troezen. Cf. Michael H. Jameson, "A Decree of Themistokles from Troizen," *Hesperia*, 29 (1960), 198–223.

46. Herodotus, VIII.53.

47. See above, Chapter 4, note 14, on contemporary studies of perception.

48. Martienssen, *The Idea of Space in Greek Architecture*, pp. 81–2.

49. See G. Patricolo, "Il Tempio della Concordia in Girgenti," *Studi e documenti relativi alle antichità agrigentine*, Palermo, 1887, and P. Marconi, *Agrigento*, Rome, 1933.

50. See John White, *Perspective in Ancient Drawing and Painting*, London, 1956, pp. 9–42.

51. See E. Pfühl, *De Atheniensium pompis sacris* (Berlin, 1900), pp. 3 ff.

52. G. P. Stevens, "The Periclean Entrance Court of the Acropolis of Athens," *Hesperia*, 5 (1936), 443–520, and "Architectural Studies Concerning the Acropolis of Athens," *Hesperia*, 15 (1946), 73–106. See also J. A. Bundgaard, *Mnesicles, a Greek architect at work*, trans. by I. Nixon, København, 1957.

53. It is interesting that the visual importance of the central axis from sea to mountain in the architecture of the Acropolis was first noted by the greatest, and in a sense most Hellenic, twentieth-century architect, after he had visited the site himself and studied the incomplete plans of Choisy. He confused the place names. "The axis of the Acropolis runs from the Piraeus [sic] to Pentelicus [sic], from the sea to the mountain." LeCorbusier, *Towards a New Architecture* (London, 1927), pp. 173–74. (First edition, *Vers une Architecture*, Paris, 1923.) I have attempted to show how LeCorbusier's life work embodies the attempt to reassert Hellenic values in contemporary terms through the relationship between sculpturally humanistic buildings and their natural settings, in my *Modern Architecture*, New York, 1961, Part 2, passim. See above notes 7 and 20, Chapter 1.

54. "They set barley mixed with wheat on the altar of Zeus Polieus, and keep no watch; and the ox which they keep in readiness for the sacrifice goes up to the altar and eats of the grain. They call one of the priests the Ox-slayer, and here he throws away the axe . . . and flees away; and they . . . bring the axe to trial." Pausanias, I.24.4. (Frazer)

55. Sir John Beazley and Bernard Ashmole, *Greek Sculpture and Painting* (Cambridge, 1932), p. 49.

56. P. E. Corbett, *The Sculpture of the Parthenon* (Middlesex, 1959), p. 12, says that the movement is generally "right to left." I assume he is speaking of the figures' own right and left; if of the observer's the question would be in dispute. Seven metopes seem to move southward as against two north and five neutral or unreadable. In general cf. A. H. Smith, *The Sculptures of the Parthenon*, London, 1910.

57. Pausanias, I.24.3.

58. Sophocles, *Oedipus at Colonus*, 1653 ff., trans. by R. C. Jebb.

59. So Sophocles hails the earth in his Ode to Man. *Antigone*, 333 ff., trans. by E. Wyckoff, Vol. 2, Chicago, 1959.

60. Pindar, Pythian 8, 1–3, trans. by Lattimore. New Directions.

Chapter 10, THE INDIVIDUAL AND THE GODS:

1. Sophocles, *Antigone*, trans. by E. Wyckoff, Vol. 2, Chicago, 1959.

1a. Dodds, in his brilliant essay, sees this largely as a progressive loss of faith in reason from the classic period onward. E. R. Dodds, *The Greeks and the Irrational*, Berkeley, 1951.

2. G. Cultrera, "Architettura ippodamea, contributo alle storia dell' edilizia nell' antichità," *MAL* Ser. V, *18* (1924), 357–603. See also A. von Gerkan, *Griechische Städteanlagen*, Berlin, 1924; Roland Martin, *L'urbanisme dans la Grèce antique*, Paris, 1956; F. Castagnoli, *Ippodamo di Mileto e l'urbanistica a pianta ortagonale*, Rome, 1956. Archaic grid: J. M. Cook et al., "Old Smyrna, 1948–1951," *BSA*, *53–54* (1958–59), 1–181.

3. B. Haussoullier, *Études sur l'histoire de Milet et du Didymeion*, Paris, 1902; O. Pontremoli and B. Haussoullier, *Didymes*, Paris, 1904; T. Wiegand et al., *Milet; Ergebnisse der Ausgrabungen und Untersuchungen seit dem Jahre 1899*, Berlin, 1906 ff.

4. Cultrera, in *MAL*, pp. 361–371.

5. W. B. Dinsmoor, *Observations on the Hephaisteion*, Cambridge, 1941; W. H. Plommer, *BSA*, *40* (1950), 66 ff.; D. B. Thompson, "The Garden of Hephaistos," *Hesperia*, 6 (1937), 396–425.

6. Lawrence, *Greek Architecture*, p. 176, also makes this observation, coupled with an excellent analysis of the column—entablature relationship.

7. W. B. Dinsmoor, "The Temple of Ares at Athens," *Hesperia*, 9, 1941. The surviving details of this temple seem to resemble those of the Hephaisteion.

8. T. L. Shear, et al., "The American Excavations in the Athenian Agora," *Hesperia*, 2–18, 1933–1949, and H. A. Thompson, "The Buildings on the West Side of the Agora," *Hesperia*, 6 (1937), 396–425.

9. *Hesperia*, 26 (1957), pl. 30, and Homer A. Thompson, *The Stoa of Attalos II in Athens*, Princeton, 1959. Photography by Alison Frantz. For reconstructed plans of Athens in all its metamorphoses to 1959 A.D. See now John D. Travlos, Πολεοδομική Ἐξέλιξις Τῶν Ἀθηνῶν, Athens, 1960.

10. Its early appearance there is used by Doxiadis, *Raumordnung*, pp. 98–101, 127 ff., 137, to reinforce his contention that Ionic sites tended to seek more positive enclosure than did Doric sites.

11. G. Patricolo, "Tempio della Concordia in Girgenti," *Studi e documenti relativi alle antichità*, Palermo, 1887.

12. Martin, *L'urbanisme*, pp. 83–84.

13. See notes 27 and 28, Chapter 4.

13a. For the recent publications which have established the early date of the grid plan in the Greek colonies of South Italy and Sicily, see Chapter 4, notes 40a, 41a, and 45a.

14. Lawrence, *Greek Architecture*, p. 294. For the development of the theater in general, see M. Bieber, *The History of the Greek and Roman Theater*, Princeton, 1939.

15. C. Anti, *Teatro antico di Syracusa*, Syracuse, 1948.

16. Strabo, VIII.7.3; VIII.8.1. E. A. Gardner, R. W. Schultz, et al., *Excavations at Megalopolis*, London, 1892. For the theater see E. Fiechter, *Antike griechische Theaterbauten* (Stuttgart, 1929 ff.), Heft 4, *Das Theater in Megalopolis*, Stuttgart, 1931. For the Thersilion: E. F. Benson and A. G. Bather in *JHS*, *13* (1892–93), 319–328.

17. Ibid., p. 69.

18. W. Dörpfeld, "Über das Theater in Ephesos," *AAJdI*, *28* (1913), 37 ff.

19. In Chapter 7, notes 18, 19.

20. Pausanias, V.23.2; VII.18.8,9; X.38.4.

20. For Pergamon and its monuments in general, see A. Conze, et al., *Die Ergebnisse der Ausgrabungen zu Pergamon, vorläufiger Bericht, 1880–1886*, 3 vols., Berlin, 1880–1888. Also: Staatliche Museen zu Berlin, *Altertümer von Pergamon*, Berlin, 8 vols., 1885—in progress. Recently: Martin, *L'urbanisme*, pp. 57–60, 127–146, etc.

22. Strabo, XIII.4.1.

23. W. Dörpfeld, "Die Arbeiten zu Pergamon," *Ath. Mitt.*, *32, 33*, 1907, 1908. See Dörpfeld also for the temple of Demeter, *Ath. Mitt.*, *35*, (1910), 355–384, and Ibid., *37* (1912), 235–256.

24. The archaic Greek temple at Pompeii was eventually framed in much the same way during the Roman period, there by a V–shaped enclosure, the "Triangular Forum," which opened from its northern entrance in a fan shape to show the temple standing out at an angle above the valley and against the mountain masses to the south. Phyllis Lehmann makes the point that the Temple of Athena at Pergamon was not so framed until the second century and thus originally stood free. The

same was the case at Priene. See note 28 below. Lehmann's article approaches the subject of Hellenistic religious architecture with great sensitivity to problems of space, scale, and setting; it refers to some sites (Herakleia, Lagina, Apollonia, Antioch) not treated here and promises a much needed book to come. Phyllis W. Lehmann, "The Setting of Hellenistic Temples," *JSAH, 13* (1954), 15–20.

25. T. Wiegand and H. Schrader, *Priene. Ergebnisse der Augrabungen und Untersuchungen in den Jahren 1895–1898*, Berlin, 1904; and W. Wilberg, "Zum Athena–Tempel in Priene," *Ath. Mitt., 39* (1914), 72–82. A. von Gerkan, "Zum Gebälk des Athena tempels in Priene," *Ath. Mitt., 49*, 1924.

26. Pytheos, the architect of this temple, was commended by Vitruvius, who cited his book in relation to the triglyph problem: I.8.1; VII. Pr. 12; IV.3.1. Cf. Dinsmoor, *The Architecture of Ancient Greece*, pp. 272–275; also, Robertson, pp. 114–115.

27. Robertson, pp. 106–112. Vitruvius, IV. 3.1–2.

28. Doxiadis, *Raumordnung*, figs. 36, 37.

29. Strabo, XII.8.17. Pausanias, VIII.24.11.

30. A. von Gerkan, *Das Theater von Priene*, Munich, 1921. W. Dörpfeld, "Das Theater von Priene und die griechische Bühne," *Ath. Mitt., 49*, 1924.

31. C. Blinkenberg and K. F. Kinch, *Lindos, fouilles et recherches, 1902–1914*, Berlin, 1931.

32. Strabo, XIV.2.11.

33. C. Jacopi, "Il Tempio e il teatro di Apollo Eretimi," *Clara Rhodos, 2* (1932), 77–116.

34. B. Leonardos, in Πρακτικὰ, 1896, pp. 93 ff., pl. 1 for temple and stoa. For Megaron, see Kourouniotes, in Ἐφ. Ἀρχ (1912), p. 107. For spring house, see Orlandos, in Ἐφ. Ἀρχ (1911), p. 201.

35. Pausanias, VIII.27.6.

36. G. Dickins, "Damophon of Messene," *BSA, 12* (1905–1906), 109–136 and I. C. Thallon, "The Date of Damophon of Messene," *AJA, 10* (1906), 302–329.

37. K. Lehmann–Hartleben, *Die Antike, 7* (1931), 31, 32, fig. 30, p. 30.

38. Cf. Dörpfeld, *Ath. Mitt., 15* (1890), p. 93.

39. P. Wolters and G. Bruns, *Das Kabirenheiligtum bei Theben*, Berlin, 1940.

40. A. Conze, et al., *Archäologische Untersuchungen auf Samothrake*, Vienna, 1875; *Neue archäologische Untersuchungen auf Samothrake*, Vienna, 1880; K. Lehmann–Hartleben, "Excavations at Samothrace," *AJA, 43*, 1939; *44*, 1940; *45*, 1941; *53*, 1949; *Hesperia, 12*, 1943. Now: idem, *Samothrace, 1*, New York, 1958, and *2*, New York, 1961.

41. Like the frieze of dancing maidens from the propylon of the sanctuary excavated by Lehmann. Cf. Karl Lehmann, *Samothrace; a Guide to the Excavations and the Museum* (New York, 1955), fig. 31.

42. Ibid., p. 66.

43. The unfinished temple of Zeus at Lebadeia also had an apse, as did many later Roman temples. Such re-use of forms reminiscent of the old apsidal megara and the movement toward Christianity itself thus reflect related aspects of a general later antique development. J. A. Bundgaard, "The Building Contract from Lebadeia," *Classica et Mediaevalia, 8* (1946), 1–43, and A. Choisy, *Etudes épigraphiques sur l'architecture grecque* (Paris, 1884), p. 174.

44. Aeschylus, *Agamemnon*, 1022–1024, trans. by Richmond Lattimore, Vol. 1, Chicago, 1959. A complex study of Asklepios as a divinity, including a topographical description of some of his sites, is presented by C. Kerenyi, *Asklepios*, trans. by Ralph Manheim, London, 1960.

45. G. Allen and L. D. Caskey, "The East Stoa of the Asclepieum at Athens," *AJA, 15* (1911), 32–43, and P. Girard, *L'Asclepieion d'Athènes d'après de récentes découvertes*, Paris, 1881.

46. A. Defrasse and H. Lechet, *Epidaure, restauration et description des principaux monuments du sanctuaire d'Asclépios*, Paris, 1895; and P. Kavvadias, *Fouilles d'Epidaure*, Athens, 1893.

47. Pausanias, II.26.4.

48. P. Marconi, *Agrigento* (Florence, 1929), pp. 146 ff.

49. O. Deubner, *Das Asklepieion von Pergamon, kurze vorläufige Beschreibung*, Berlin, 1938.

50. Carl Roebuck, "The Asklepieion and Lerna," *Corinth, 14*, Cambridge, Mass., 1951, and Robert Scranton, ed., *Ancient Corinth, a guide to the excavations*, 6th ed. (1954), pp. 75–81, fig. 5.

51. F. Versakis, "Der Tempel und die Stoa im Amphiaraeion bei Oropos," *Ath. Mitt., 33* (1908), 247–272.

52. Pausanias, I.34.2–5.

53. H. Bulle, "Orchomenos," *Abh. Mün. Akad.*,

24, 1907, and Schliemann, *Orchomenos*, Leipzig, 1881.

54. R. Herzog, et al., *Kos, Ergebnisse der deutschen Ausgrabungen und Forschungen*, Berlin, 1932. (Vol. 1, *Asklepieion*, by P. Schazmann)

55. F. Fasolo and G. Gullini, *Il Sanctuario della Fortuna Primigenia a Palestrina*, Rome, 1953; H. Kähler, "Das Fortunaheiligtum von Palestrina Praeneste," *Annales Universitatis Saraviensis*, Philos.–Lett. *1* (1958), 189–240.

56. Cicero, *De Divinatione*, II.5.

57. Here again Kaschnitz–Weinberg's theory concerning the continuation of Mediterranean traditions in the enclosing forms of Roman architecture seems especially cogent; one might, probably wrongly, be almost tempted to think in terms of highly conscious revivals: *Die mittelmeerischen Grundlagen der antiken Kunst*, pp. 39–60.

58. See above, Chapter 8, note 46; and Chapter 9, note 53.

59. The progressive development of later Greek art away from its initial and pervasive sculptural principles (Friedrich Matz, *Geschichte der griechischen Kunst*, 2 vols., Frankfurt–am–Main, 1950; and now Rhys Carpenter, *Greek Sculpture, A Critical Review*, Chicago, 1960) toward more pictorial methods, seems significant here as part of a general post–classic movement away from the "real" (the solid figure free–standing in actual space and natural light) toward the illusion (the painted figure, modeled in controlled light and fitted into perspective space)—all of this, too, integrated into an embracingly "illusionistic" system by Rome. (Doro Levi, "L'Arte Romana," *Annuario della Scuola Archeologica di Atene*, 24–26 (1950), 229–303; and, in general, Otto J. Brendel, "Prolegomena to a Book on Roman Art," *Memoirs of the American Academy in Rome*, 21 (1953), 9–73.) The effect upon architecture, which had always been the central agent in the full experience of the real, has been observed throughout. See above, pp. 2–3, 5, 46, 126, 128, 177, 179–180, 187–188, 191, 192, 198–199, 201. When, finally, by the Late Antique and Early Christian periods, both the physical body and the natural world had lost religious significance—and the figure in painting or mosaic could achieve, where desired, a new, otherworldly, supra–reality through frontality, optically hypnotic dazzle, and the elimination of perspective depth—free–standing sculpture almost disappeared and architecture sought purely transcendental, interior, space–positive, mass–negative values. See above, pp. 4, 53, 64, 65, 71, 79, 112, 151–152, 154, 182–183, 187, 202–203, 211.

Appendix 1, ADDENDA:

1. See above, pp. 9–40, and Figs. 1–69.

2. See above, pp. 43–47, and passim.

3. See above, pp. 105–18, and Figs. 191–96.

4. Pausanias, IX.29.2.

5. G. Roux, "Le Val des Muses et les musées chez les auteurs anciens," *BCH*, 78 (1954), 22–48.

6. See above, pp. 132–54, and Figs. 250–63.

7. Pausanias, IX.30.1.

8. Pausanias, X.34.7. (This is Frazer's translation.)

9. P. Paris, *Elatée. La Ville. Le temple d'Athena Cranaia*, Paris, 1892.

10. See above, pp. 97–99, 199–201, and Figs. 176–81, 384–90.

11. See above, pp. 80–93, and Figs. 133–65.

12. Robert Koldewey, *Die antiken Baureste der Insel Lesbos* (Berlin, 1890), pp. 47–61, pls. 18–26. For the sanctuary of Apollo Napaios in the Hills above Ta Messa and for its splendid Aeolic capitals, some of them built into a farmer's wall on the site, see Appendix 2.

13. See above, p. 14.

14. See above, pp. 93–99, and Figs. 164–74, 283.

15. See above, pp. 9–40, and Figs. 1–4, 8–11, 13–18, 36, 46, 48–50, 50–57, 68.

16. See above, pp. 44–46.

17. Vitruvius, III.3.9.

18. See above, pp. 49–53, 89–91, and Figs. 77–81, 156–69.

19. See above, pp. 50–53, and Figs. 77–81; pp. 60–66, and Figs. 95–99.

20. See above, pp. 57–59, 141–44, 160–61, and Figs. 88–109, 261–62, 287–89.

21. See Figs. 34–37, 145, 342, 346, 364.

22. See Figs. 59–69, 143–45, 149–52.

23. Marcel Launay, *Le sanctuaire et le culte d'Heraklès à Thasos*, Études thasiennes, *1* (Paris, 1944).

24. Charles Picard, *Les Murailles, I. Les portes sculptées à images divines*, Études thasiennes, 8 (Paris, 1962).

25. Cf. G. Daux, "Chronique des fouilles et découvertes archéologiques en Grèce en 1961," *BCH, 86* (1962), 945.

26. See Figs. 1–6, 59–62.

27. The conical hill was probably the inspiration for the tholos and is certainly connected with it in meaning. See Figs. 3, 50–51, 60, 67, 390, 393, 415.

28. F. Salviat, "Décrets pour Epie fille de Dionysios: déesses et sanctuaires thasiens," *BCH, 83* (1959), 362–97, esp. 382–90, figs. 3–6; also Daux, in *BCH, 85* (1961), 930.

29. Daux, in *BCH, 83* (1959), 392–93, 781–82, Fig. 14; *84* (1960), 864–66.

30. Picard, in *Comtes rendus de l'Académie des Inscriptions et Belles–lettres* (1912), pp. 210–11.

31. Roland Martin, *L'Agora, I.*, Études thasiennes, 6 (Paris, 1959).

Appendix 2, THE CAPITALS OF KLOPEDI:

1. Apollo Napaios is mentioned by the Scholiast on Aristophanes. *Clouds,* 144. Koldewey thought he had found this temple at a place he called Kolumdado, near a church named Taxiarchis, as is that at Messa. He was deceived, however, by remains from Klopedi built into the church. Robert Koldewey, *Die antiken Baureste,* pp. 44–46, pls. 16, 17.

2. The excavation of the sanctuary was incomplete, but the remains of the two temples were laid bare. Δ. Εὐαγγελίδου, in Παραρτ. ᾿Αρχ. Δελτ., 9 (1924–25), 40–44; and Idem, in Πρακτικὰ ᾿Αρχ. ᾿Ετ. (1928), pp. 126–137. Also, *BCH, 51* (1927), 497–98.

3. J. D. Condis, "Capitello Eolico di Eresso," *Annuario,* 24–26 (new series 8–10) (1946–48), 25–36. Reference here is to a curious capital where the two volutes do not approach each other but run straight down the sides of the capital. The volutes from Klopedi do not touch either, though they slant toward each other. Condis feels, probably rightly, that such lack of contact means that they must have had an echinus, else they would simply have bled into the column shaft. Cf. Fig. 425c.

4. Cf. W. Andrae, *Die ionische Saüle.*

5. By Schefold, who was taken to task by Condis but who may have had a point, in so far as it is just conceivable that the same temple could have used several variations of capital and one of them, though with much labor, might have been transported to Mytilini for any number of reasons. The possibility is a little farfetched, however. K. Schefold, "Das äolische Kapitell," *Ost. Jahresh., 31* (1939), 42–52.

6. Robert Koldewey, *Neandria,* Figs. 2 and 2a. For the view west from Troy, see the watercolor by Edward Lear in the Gennadeion Library in Athens, reproduced here, Fig. 27.

7. Schefold, in *Ost. Jahresh.,* Figs. 19–20, shows a corner fragment of a temple model from Larisa where an Aeolic capital is simply used frontally at a corner. No adjustments, like the Ionic use of a diagonally projecting volute, seem to be made in it.

INDEX

Athena (*cont.*)

temple of Athena Polias, 174, and of Athena Nike, 174; old temple of Athena Polias, 177; Mnesicles' new temple of Athena Nike, 178, and earlier temple of, 178, and capitals compared with Propylaia's, 179; old temple of Athena Polias, 180; at Pergamon, 196–97; at Priene, 198; on Acropolis (Athena Nike) projected wall ends as pictorial rendering of opisthodomos, 206. For temple of Athena and Hephaistos, *see* Hephaisteion

Athenian order of battle (480), 235 n. 45

Athens: evidence of early habitation, 21; Mycenaean site of, 28, and megaron, 30; site as sacred, 31; Athenian grave monuments (9th and 8th c.) as embodiments of new Greek attitude, 43; sanctuary orientation, 44; archaic Athens, altar placement, 45; procession to shrine of Demeter, 74; sea gate to, 84; Athenians' placement of Artemis site, 85; relation to Artemis' temple site at Loutsa, 88; women of Athens worshiped Artemis at Brauron, 88; Athens–Eleusis, Sacred Way, 103; mentioned, 108; route to Delphi from, 109; Athenian treasury on Way to Delphi, 112; shrines of Athens on Delos, 118; mountain of Zeus (Mt. Oros) seen from, 134–35; temple of Zeus at, and temple–landscape description, 138–39; Athenians, and temple of Nemesis at Rhamnous, 153; National Museum, 154; and Poseidon and Athena, 157; orientation of temple of Athena in, 169; fall of, 186; and Hellenistic Pergamon, 197; and cult of Asklepios, 204

Atkinson, R. J. C., cited, 24

Atreus, House of, 38

Attalos, stoa of, bounding Athenian agora, 190–91

Attic Harma, a mountain, 177, and seen from Parthenon, 184

Attica: landscape, 9, and description of land, 27; view toward Eretria, 116; view of Parthenon from, 177

Augustus, at Actium, 194; temple of at Olympia, 146; and Livia, 234 n. 52

Aulis, cult of Artemis at, 39; temple of Artemis at, 85; orientation compared with Loutsa, 87; arc of hills compared to Brauron, 88; axis compared with Rhamnous, 154

Avebury, 22–23

Basilica, Early Christian, 79

Basilica of the Black Virgin, at Tyndaris, 97

Bassae: temple orientation, 44; altar placement, 45; Artemis at, mentioned, 84; sanctuary of Artemis and Aphrodite, 99; earliest use of Corinthian capital, 111; temple compared with Apollo's temple at Selinus, 120; temple of Apollo, orientation, 121, 123–24, dating, 122–23, interior experience of, 125–26, frieze relation with landscape, 126, placement of image, 128, temple–landscape relationship, 129; compared with Didyma, 130; and Ithome, 134; view of Lykaion, 134; temple of Apollo as classic, 188. *See also* Columns, Corinthian

Beazley, J., and Ashmole, B., cited, 181

Biton, 55

Boeotia: landscape of, 9; plain, visible from above Erythrai, 29, described, 30, mentioned, 109; effect of Cithairon in southern Boeotia, 68; great goddess of, 107; and Hera, 169

Boghaz–Köy. *See* Hittite Hattusas

Bouleuterion, on Way at Delphi, 110; at Thermon, 122; and hairpin megara at Olympia, 146

Boutes, 172

Brauron: evidence of early habitation, 21; site, 27; temple of Artemis, 85–87, approach to, 88, site, 89; addition of stoa, 90

Bromius, as Dionysos, 114–15

Bronze Age: ritualization of traditions in Crete, 11; habitation in Greece, and use of landscape, 21; palace at Lerna, 21; ritual circles in southern England, 22; religious practice and landscape use outside of Greece, 22; at Troy, 22; purveyors of southern tradition to north, 23; monuments of English downs, 24; Middle and Late in Greece, 25; Middle, house type description and sites, 26; lords as hero–ancestors, 26; Middle, landscape brought into human focus, 27; Early, settlement at Brauron, 27; other sacred formations related to sites, 27; Middle, megara at Olympia and Korakou, 31; Late, megaron at Pylos of Nestor, 33; habitation in plain of Argos compared to Minoan settlement, 34; world of the goddess, 41; Middle, relation of hairpin megara to early Greek temple, 47; holiness of sanctuary at Samos, 49; megara at hill "of Kronos," 54; megara of Troy compared with temple of Hera at Olympia, 54; Megara A and B at Thermon and archaic temple of Apollo, 121; Middle, forms underlying Olympia site, 146

Bull dance at Knossos, 13

Cadmus, palace at Thebes, 29; site of palace, 71

Calauria. *See* Poros

Callimachos: and Corinthian capital, 127; at Bassae, 127; mentioned, 129, 131

Calydon: sanctuary orientation, 44; Artemis' site, 81; temples of Apollo and Artemis, 82; wings of mountain compared to formation at Mukhli, 84

Calypso's island and cavern, 18; island compared to Delos, 117

Camus, Albert, 233 n. 46

Cape Monodendri, 129; altar of Poseidon at, 159

Cape Sciacca, conical hill of, seen from Selinus, 192

Cape Sounion: sanctuaries of Athena and Poseidon, 161; approach to Poseidon's sanctuary, 162; approach to shrine of Athena, 162; Kouros, 163; Athena at, 169

Cape Zoster, and legend of Apollo's birthplace, 117

Capitals. *See* Columns

Carthage, site of, and temple of Tanit (Aphrodite) at, 96; site of Greek victory over Carthaginians the

FIG. A. Mt. Taygetus above Sparta

FIG. B. The stadium at Delphi

SKETCH MAP: I. Greece and Asia Minor

SKETCH MAP: 2. Greece. Detail

AEGEAN SEA

NAXOS

PAROS

MYKONOS
SANCTUARY
DELOS
ORTYGIA

MELOS

ANDROS

TINOS

KARYSTOS

MT OCHA
DYSTOS

MARATHON
RHAMNOUS
THALAE
BRAURON
HORIKOS
SOUNION

ZOSTER

AMPHIARAION
OROPOS
MT PARNES
DEKELEIA
ATHENS
PIRAEUS
DAPHNI
APHAIA
AIGINA
MT OROS
SANCTUARY OF POSEIDON
CALAURIA (POROS)
METHANE
TROEZEN
ASINE

EUBOEA

CHALKIS
ERETRIA

AULIS
TANAGRA
HYPATOS
THEBES

BOEOTIA
MT PHAGA
MT KITHAIRON
PLATAIA
MT KERATA
ELEUSIS
MEGARA
SALAMIS
MT GERANIA

CAPE ARTEMISION
ARTEMISION

GLA
ORCHOMENOS
MT PTOON
LAKE COPAIS
LEBADEIA
MT HELICON

PERACHORA
LOUTRAKI
ISTHMIA
CORINTH
NEMEA
SIKYON
STYMPHALIA
MT KYLLENE
MYCENAE
HERAION
ARGOS
MT EUBOEA
MT ARTEMISION
MIDEIA
TIRYNS
NAUPLION
LERNA

A R G O L I S

EPIDAUROS
APOLLO

MT OSSA
PAGASAE (VOLOS)
DIMINI
SESKOULO
PELION

THESSALIA
PENEOS

THERMOPYLAI
MT OETA

PHOCIS
MT PARNASSOS
DELPHI
ITEA

AMPHISSA
OZOLIAN LOCRIS
THERMON

ACHELOOS RIVER
LAKE TRICHONIS
CALYDON

AETOLIA
STRATOS

PINDOUS RANGE

DODONA
MT TOMAROS
CASSOPE
AMBRACIAN GULF
ACTIUM

ITHACA

KEPHALLENIA

ZAKYNTHOS

A C H A I A

ELIS

OLYMPIA
ALPHEIOS RIVER

ARCADIA
MANTINEIA
MT LYKAION
MEGALOPOLIS
TEGEA
LYKOSOURA
BASSAE

MESSENIA
MT ITHOME
MESSENE
MALTHI
NESTOR'S PALACE
PYLOS
MT MATHIA

MT PARNON

LACONIA
SPARTA
MENELAION
AMYKLAI
MT TAYGETUS

SKETCH MAP: 3. South Italy and Sicily

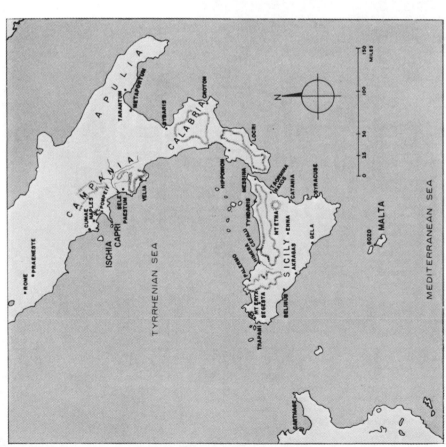

SKETCH MAP: 4. Crete

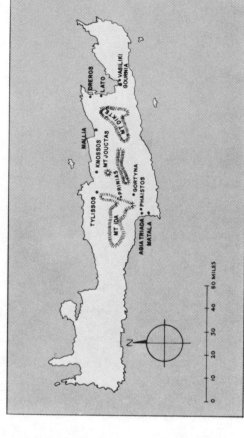

FIG. 1. Mt. Jouctas from ancient harbor of Knossos

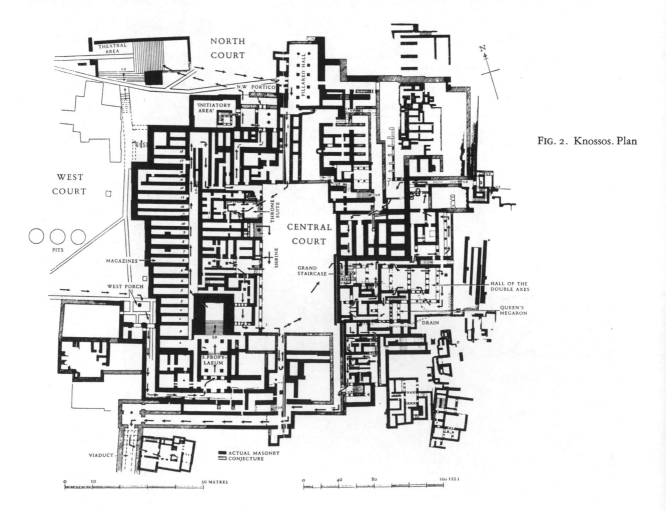

FIG. 2. Knossos. Plan

FIG. 3. Knossos. Central court and Jouctas from northern entrance

FIG. 4. Knossos. South Propylaia with façade horns and Mt. Jouctas

FIG. 5. (*above*) Knossos. a. Fresco, shrine. Reconstructed
b. Fresco, Bull Dance. Reconstructed

FIG. 6. Isis with the Pharaoh, Temple of Seti I, Abydos,
XIX Dynasty

FIG. 7. Phaistos. a. (*above*) Mount Ida from the palace hill
b. (*below*) Palace from the northwest with the Valley of the Mesara

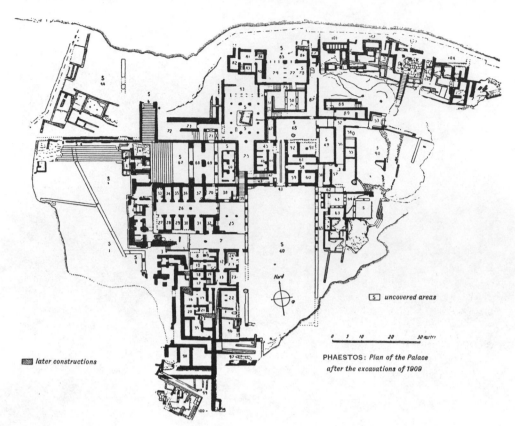

FIG. 8. Phaistos. Plan

later constructions

uncovered areas

PHAESTOS: *Plan of the Palace
after the excavations of 1909*

FIG. 9. Phaistos. North stairs with Mt. Ida

FIG. 10. Phaistos. Theatral area and propylon

FIG. 11. Ida from central court at Phaistos

FIG. 12. Agia Triada. Arc of view from Ida to Paksimadhia

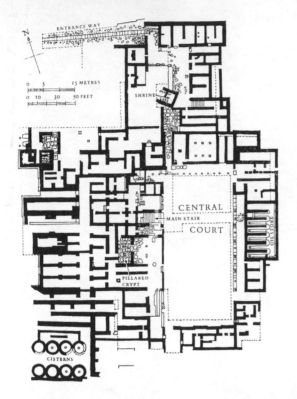

FIG. 13. Mallia. Plan

FIG. 14. Mallia from the west

FIG. 15. Mallia from northern entrance way

FIG. 16. Mallia. Court from the northwest with Mt. Dikte

FIG. 17. Gournia

FIG. 18. Gournia. View south from palace across "agora"

FIG. 21. Jouctas from Herakleion, showing "Head of Zeus." Watercolor by Edward Lear, 10 May 1864

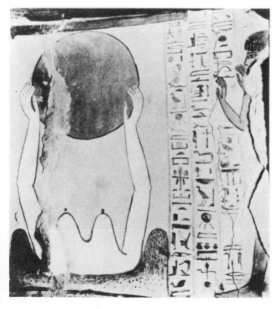

FIG. 19. The Goddess of the Horizon, XIX Dynasty

FIG. 20. Malta. Gigantea on Gozo. Model, Museum, La Valetta

FIG. 22. Knossos. Royal Temple Tomb

FIG. 23. Knossos. From "High Priest's" tomb

FIG. 24. Knossos. Royal Villa and view

FIG. 27. View toward Samothrace from citadel of Troy. Watercolor by Edward Lear, 30 Sept. 1856

FIG. 25. Dystos, Euboea

FIG. 26. Dimini. Citadel from the gate

FIG. 28. Avebury

FIG. 29. Mound of Silbury

FIG. 30. Avebury. "Sanctuary" with mound of Silbury

FIG. 31. The Downs.
Stonehenge in center distance

FIG. 32. Stonehenge from above

FIG. 33. Stonehenge. Sunrise

FIG. 34. Mt. Hymettos. South horn with tumulus, East Attica, and Euboea

FIG. 35. Mt. Hymettos. From south to north horn. Pentelikon in distance

FIG. 36. Acropolis, Athens. Temple of Athena Polias with Mycenaean column bases and horns of Hymettos

FIG. 37. Acropolis, Athens, with horns of Hymettos and conical hills at Kaisariani

FIG. 38. Minoa from Scironian cliffs. In distance: center, horns of Salamis; left, horns of Kerata

FIG. 39. Thebes from the north, with Mt. Cithairon beyond

FIG. 40. Thebes from the south. Mt. Hypatos right. Lion mountain and Ptoon left

FIG. 41. Mt. Phaga, Sphinx Mountain, with Mt. Ptoon, from Lake Copais

FIG. 42. Mt. Akontion and Orchomenos

FIG. 43. Orchomenos from Lake Copais

FIG. 44. Gla,
from slopes of Mt. Ptoon

FIG. 45. Sparta.
Menelaion with Taygetus

FIG. 46. Sparta. Menelaion from the east with Taygetus and the Valley of the Eurotas

FIG. 47. Sparta. Taygetus and Amyklai from Mycenaean Sparta

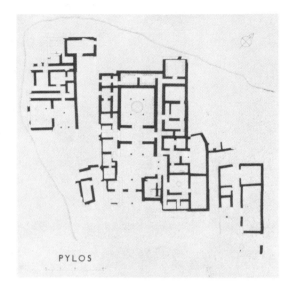

FIG. 49. Palace of Nestor. Plan

PYLOS

FIG. 48. Pylos. Megaron, Palace of Nestor, looking south

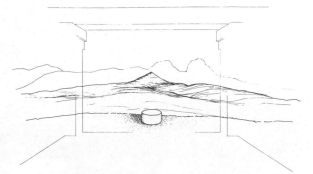

FIG. 50. Palace of Nestor. Orientation of shrine and altar. Schematic drawing

FIG. 54. Tiryns.
a. Citadel from the north
b. Northern Enceinte
c. East gate and entrance ramp
d. Corbel vault

FIG. 51. Pylos. Tholos tomb

FIG. 52. Trulli near Alberobello, Apulia

FIG. 53. Cone of Argos from Aspis. Foreground: Mantic Sanctuary of Apollo and Athena

a

b

c

d

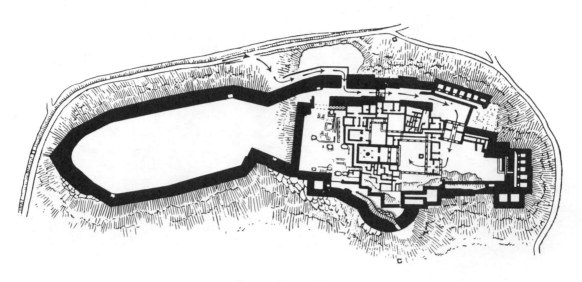

FIG. 55. Tiryns. Plan

FIG. 56. Tiryns. Propylon, courtyard, megaron, and Heraion of Argos

FIG. 58. Mideia from the north

FIG. 57. Tiryns. Megaron and Palamedes above Nauplion

FIG. 59. Mycenae

FIG. 60. Mycenae. Tomb "of Agamemnon"

FIG. 61. Mycenae from below the citadel

FIG. 62. Bull's head from Knossos

FIG. 62a. Mycenae. Lion Gate. Detail

FIG. 63. Mycenae. Lion Gate
with Mt. Zara on approach

FIG. 65. Minoan seals. Goddess with lions and as column

FIG. 64. Mycenae. Lion Gate
with Mt. Zara, from below

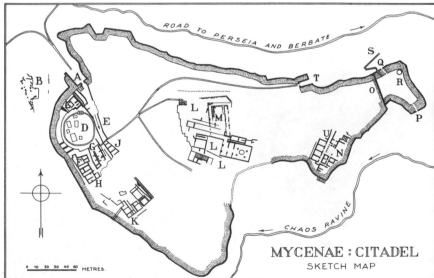

FIG. 66. Mycenae. Plan of the citadel.
A. Lion Gate; B. Prehistoric Cemetery
outside walls; C. Granary; D. Grave Circle; E. Ramp; F. House of Warrior Vase;
G. Ramp House; H. South House; J. Hellenistic Chambers; K. Tsountas' House;
L. Palace; M. Temple foundations; N.
House of Columns; O. Original northeast
wall; P. Sally port; Q. Drain; R. Hellenistic Cistern; S. Secret Cistern; T. Postern
Gate; U. Mycenaean Terrace Wall.

FIG. 67. Mycenae. Grave circle with cone of Argos, tomb of Agamemnon, and Mt. Artemision

FIG. 68. Mycenae. Megaron's court looking west toward Mts. Kyllene and Sciathis above Stymphalia

FIG. 69. Mycenae. View south from height of citadel

FIG. 71. Perachora, dead ahead. Mt. Gerania, right

FIG. 70. Neck Amphora. Kerameikos Cemetery,
Dipylon Gate, Athens. Geometric Period

FIG. 72. Perachora. Model of apsidal temple

FIG. 73. Perachora. The sacred formation

FIG. 74. Perachora. Goddess. Terracotta

FIG. 75. Perachora. Hera Akraia

FIG. 76. Perachora. Sixth–century temple

FIG. 77. Samos. Heraion and the straits.
Mt. Mykale to the right

FIG. 78. Samos. Heraion with hills
to the west

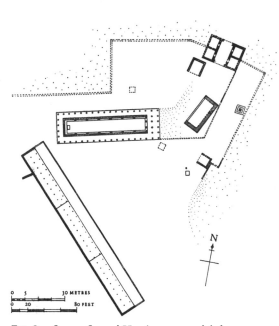

FIG. 80. Samos. Second Heraion as remodeled
and early sanctuary, restored

FIG. 79. Samos. Heraion and cleft to the north from the stoa

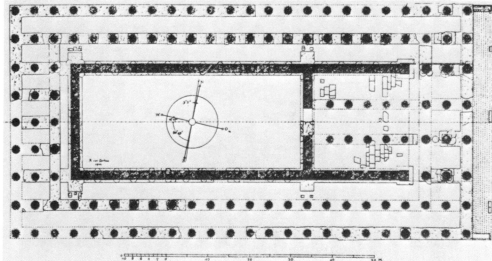

FIG. 81. Samos
a. Plan of Polykrates temple
b. Polykrates temple. Reconstruction drawing of East Front.
Partly conjectural

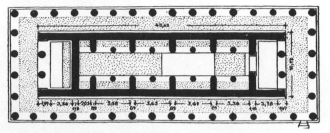

FIG. 82. Olympia. a, b: First Temple of Hera. c: Third temple. Plan

FIG. 83. Olympia. Final Temple of Hera. (Third with interior fins of wall removed)

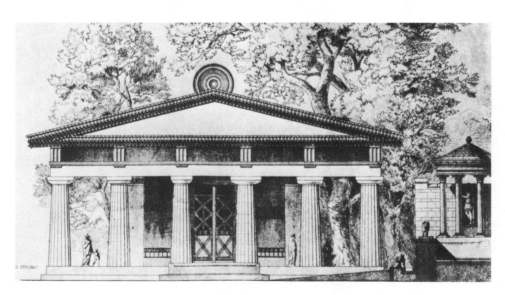

FIG. 84. Olympia. Temple of Hera. Reconstruction drawing

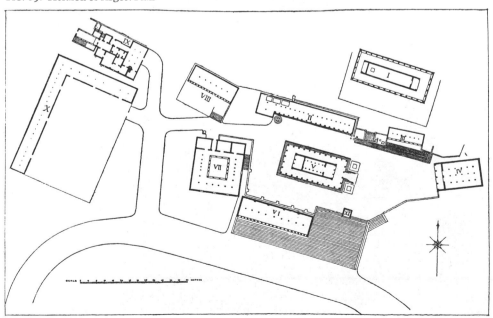

FIG. 86. Heraion of Argos. View from below with Mt. Euboea

FIG. 85. Heraion of Argos. Plan

FIG. 87. Heraion of Argos.
View across the Argolid

FIG. 88. Metapontum. Temple of
unknown dedication, possibly of Hera,
looking inland

FIG. 89. Silaris. Temple of Hera
and Valley of the Silaris

FIG. 90. Paestum. Temple precincts. Air view

FIG. 91. Paestum. View south toward two temples of Hera

FIG. 92. Paestum.
First Temple of Hera.
a. (*right*) Exterior from the west
b. (*below, right*) Interior

FIG. 93. Paestum.
First Temple of Hera. Columns

FIG. 94. Paestum.
First Temple of Hera
with conical hill

FIG. 95. Paestum.
Second Temple of Hera
from the west

FIG. 96. Paestum. a. Second Temple of Hera. Detail. b. Second Temple of Hera. South pteron and cleft

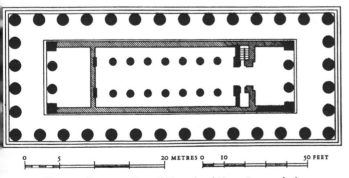

FIG. 97. Paestum. Second Temple of Hera. Restored plan

FIG. 98. Paestum. Second Temple of Hera. Interior

FIG. 99. Paestum.
Second Temple of Hera.
Entablature curve and
conical hill

FIG. 100. Akragas.
Temple of "Hera Lacinia."
From the southeast.
Acropolis of the town beyond

FIG. 101. Akragas. Temple of
"Hera Lacinia." From the city

FIG. 102. Akragas. Temple of "Hera Lacinia" from the northwest

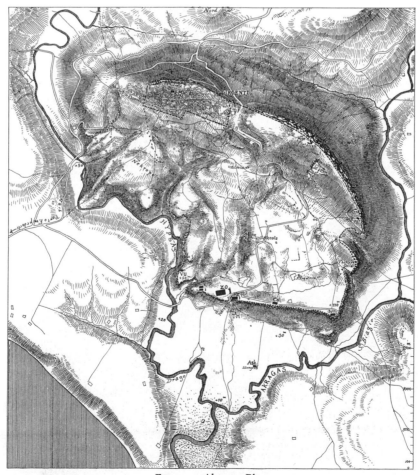

FIG. 103. Akragas. Plan

FIG. 104. Akragas. Temple of "Concord" from Temple of Hera

FIG. 105. Akragas. Temple of "Concord."
    a. (*left*) From the east
    b. (*above*) From the west
    c. (*right*) North flank

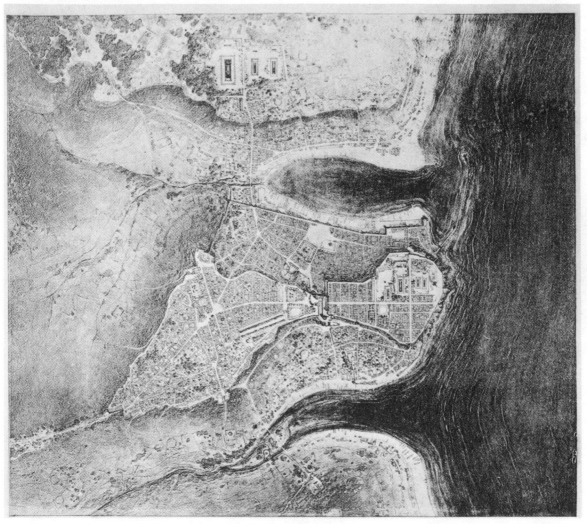

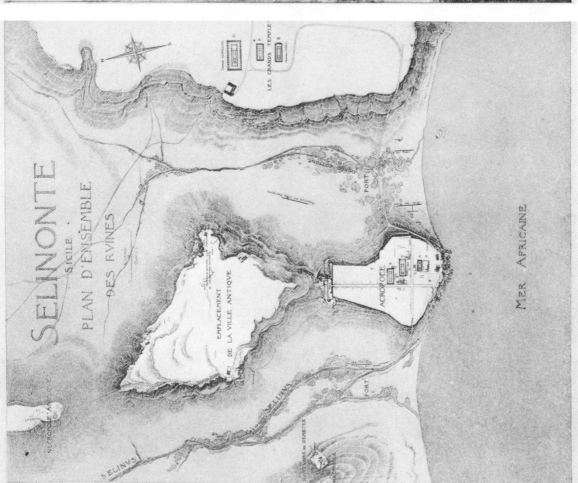

Fig. 106. Selinus. a. Plan. b. Restored plan

FIG. 107. Selinus. Temples on the eastern hill

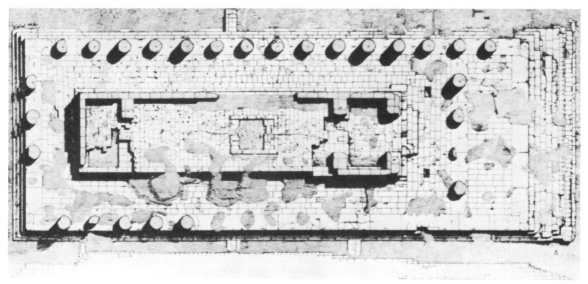

FIG. 108. Selinus. Temple C. Plan

FIG. 109. Selinus. Temple C. Reconstruction drawing by Jean Hulot

FIG. 110. Plataia. Mt. Cithairon from the Sanctuary of Demeter near Plataia. Heraion of Plataia to the right

FIG. 111. Plataia. Cithairon from vicinity of the Heraion

FIG. 112. Mt. Hypatos from Plataia

FIG. 113. Thermopylai. Mt. Oeta from the pass near Anthela

FIG. 114. Thera, Shrine of Demeter and Persephone

FIG. 115. (*above left*) Thorikos. View from southwest, across valley with Sanctuary of Demeter and Kore

FIG. 116. (*above*) Thorikos. From the south. Mycenaean settlement on summit, Theater on slope

FIG. 117. (*left*) Thorikos. Theater. Seats and orchestra

FIG. 118. (*below left*) Colonus. View eastward. Hymettos and Lycabettos

FIG. 119. (*below*) Colonus. View to the southeast. The Acropolis of Athens

FIG. 120. Sacred Way.
a. (*left*) Shrine of Aphrodite with horns of Salamis
b. (*above*) Salamis from Eleusis Bay

FIG. 121. Sacred Way. Mt. Kerata above Eleusis

FIG. 122. Eleusis. Kerata from the acropolis

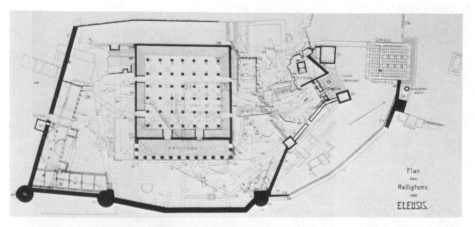

FIG. 123. Eleusis.
a. Composite plan of Sanctuary
b. Periclean project.
Reconstruction drawing

FIG. 124. Eleusis. Propylaia, Grotto
of Hades, and Processional Way

FIG. 125. Eleusis. Telesterion. Detail

FIG. 126. (*left*) Relief of Demeter, Persephone, and Triptolemus

FIG. 127. (*below*) Eleusis. Telesterion and Salamis

FIG. 128. Akragas. Temple of Demeter from west

FIG. 129. Akragas. Temple of Demeter from east and chthonic altars

FIG. 130. Akragas. View east from
Temple of Demeter. Water sanctuary below

FIG. 131. Selinus. Sanctuary of
Demeter Malophoros. Swaying axis from propylon

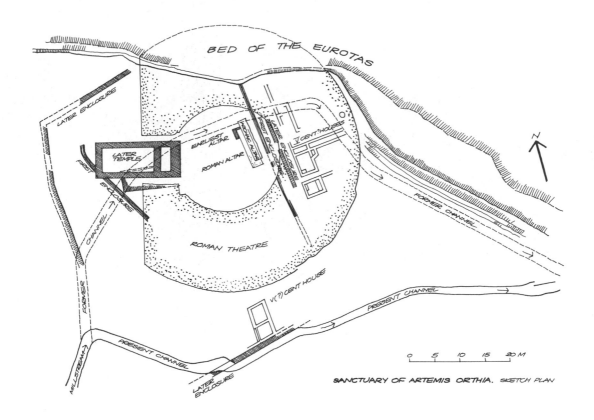

SANCTUARY OF ARTEMIS ORTHIA. SKETCH PLAN

FIG. 133. Sparta. a. (*above*) Sketch plan
b. (*below*) Temple from the southeast

FIG. 132. Bronze hydria: Artemis
as Mistress of the Beasts

FIG. 134. Mt. Ithome.
Temple of Artemis.
Mt. Taygetus in distance

FIG. 135. Promontory,
Mt. Varassova, at mouth of
Gulf of Corinth. Calydon
under ridge in background

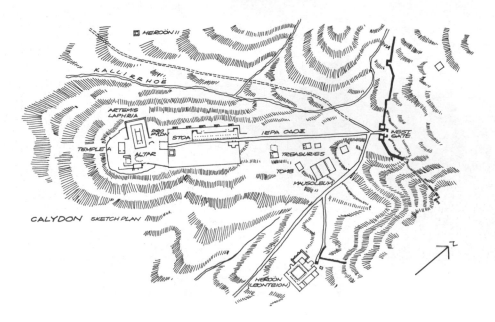

FIG. 136. Calydon.
Sanctuary of Artemis
Laphria. Sketch plan

FIG. 137. Calydon. Promontory from Sanctuary of Artemis

FIG. 138. Sikyon. Temple of Artemis. Two views from the theater

FIG. 139. Stymphalia. Entrance to site from the north

FIG. 140. Boeotian amphora. Mother of the Beasts. 7th century

FIG. 141. Stymphalia from pass into Argolis. Sciathis left, Kyllene right

FIG. 143. Mukhli. View south from cleft: the cone between the horns

FIG. 142. Mukhli. View north: Winged cleft and Mt. Artemision

FIG. 144. Cone of Astarte in horned enclosure, Temple Court, Byblos, on coin of Macrinus

FIG. 145. Piraeus. View showing Phaleron, Hymettos, and Athens

FIG. 146. Aulis. From the south

FIG. 147. Loutsa–Halae.
Temple of Artemis Tauropolis,
with horns of Mt. Ocha on Euboea

FIG. 148. Loutsa–Halae. Temple from the east, with horns of Hymettos

FIG. 149. Brauron. From the Bay. Southern horns of Hymettos in the distance

FIG. 150. Brauron. Mt. Perati seen on way to sanctuary

FIG. 152. Brauron. The sanctuary from the west

FIG. 151. Brauron. Approach to the sanctuary from the west

FIG. 153. Brauron. Plan of Sanctuary of Artemis

FIG. 151. Brauron. Approach to the sanctuary from the west

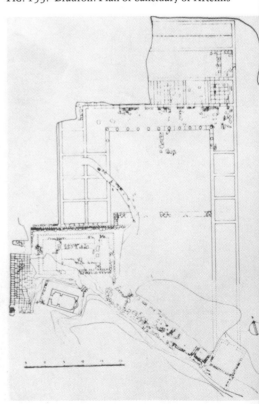

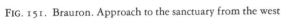

FIG. 154. Brauron.
The cleft

FIG. 155. Brauron.
Temple and cleft

FIG. 156. Ephesos. View from
west toward Temple of Artemis.
(Position roughly marked by
grove of trees in center distance)

FIG. 157. Ephesos. Archaic Temple
of Artemis. Reconstruction drawing

FIG. 158. Ephesos. Temple of Artemis.
Reconstruction drawing of central axis

FIG. 159. Ephesos. Temple of Artemis. Archaic Ionic capital

FIG. 160. Magnesia. Axial view of Temple
of Artemis Leucophryene, looking west

FIG. 161. Sardis. Acropolis with Mt. Tmolus

FIG. 162. Sardis. Tumuli, Acropolis, and
Mt. Tmolus from tumulus of Alyattes

FIG. 163. Sardis. Temple of
Artemis–Cybele from the
southwest

FIG. 164. Sardis. Temple of
Artemis–Cybele from the east

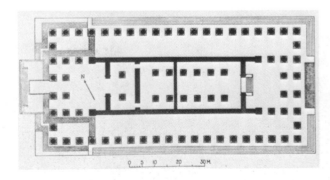

FIG. 165. Sardis. Temple of Artemis–Cybele.
a. Plan. b. Eastern entrance

FIG. 166. Kaisariani and Lycabettos

FIG. 167. Kaisariani. View toward Daphni

FIG. 168. Troezen

FIG. 169. Poros (Calauria) and the "Woman on Her Back"

FIG. 170. Acrocorinth. From the north

FIG. 171. Acrocorinth. Temple of Aphrodite. Panorama south and west

. Panorama north and east

FIG. 173. Tyndaris. From the south

FIG. 174. Cefalu

FIG. 175. Cefalu. The water sanctuary,
"of Diana," on the shoulder under the peaks

FIG. 176. Segesta. The temple

FIG. 178. Segesta. Temple from the theater

FIG. 184. Aigina. Temple of Apollo with
the sea and the promontory of Methane

FIG. 185. Corinth. Temple of Apollo
with Acrocorinth. From the east

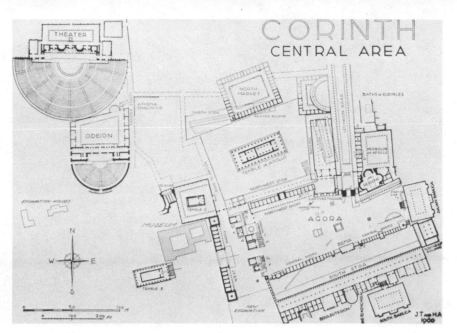

FIG. 186. Corinth. Plan

FIG. 187. Corinth.
Temple of Apollo from the stairs

FIG. 188. Corinth.
Temple of Apollo from the east

FIG. 189. Corinth.
Temple of Apollo. The columns

FIG. 190. Corinth.
Temple of Apollo from
the Fountain of Glauke

FIG. 192. Mt. Ptoon. Site of Sanctuary of Apollo Ptous. Temple under horn, right

FIG. 191. Mt. Ptoon from Lake Copais.
Right: horns of the mountain. Center: cleft at Agraiphnion

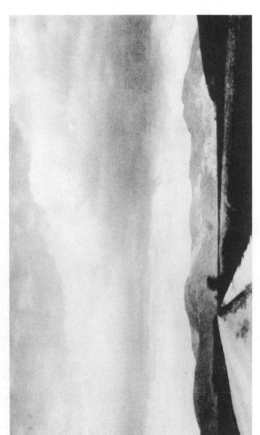

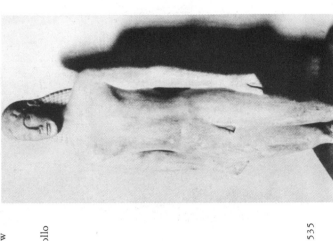

FIG. 193. (*above, left*) Mt. Ptoon. Lake Trikeri. From cleft below the Sanctuary of Apollo. Heraion of Plataia in the distance

FIG. 194. (*above, right*) Mt. Ptoon. Approach to Temple of Apollo from the west and below from shrine of the hero, Ptous

FIG. 195. (*left*) Mt. Ptoon. Temple of Apollo. View westward toward Helicon and Parnassos

FIG. 196. (*right*) Kouros from Sanctuary of Apollo at Ptoon, c. 535

FIG. 197. Delphi. Mt. Parnassos
on route from Itea

FIG. 198. Delphi. a. View from
near Sanctuary back toward Itea
b. (*below, left*) Horns of the Phaedriades

FIG. 199. Delphi. Temple of Apollo under the horns

FIG. 200. Delphi. Opening of Parnassos, with Telphusa, left

FIG. 201. Delphi, Marmaria. Sanctuary of Athena Pronaia, with Telphusa

FIG. 202. Delphi, Marmaria. Treasury of Massalia, restored   FIG. 203. Delphi, Marmaria. The tholos looking west

FIG. 203a. Delphi, Marmaria. Tholos. Detail

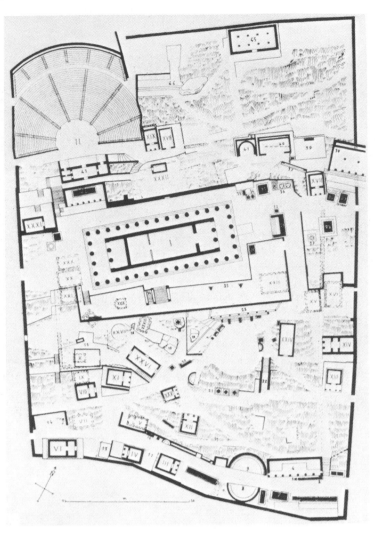

FIG. 204. Delphi.
Plan of Sanctuary of Apollo. Restored

FIG. 205. Delphi. Temple of Apollo
from entrance to the Sacred Way

FIG. 206. Delphi. Athenian Treasury

FIG. 207. Delphi. Sacred Way and smaller horns

FIG. 208. Delphi. Portico of the Athenians, polygonal wall, and Temple of Apollo with the cliff

FIG. 209. Delphi. Temple of Apollo
after the second turn of the Way

FIG. 210. Delphi. Temple of Apollo. Altar of Chios left; Prusias monument right

FIG. 211. Delphi. Temple of Apollo with the Phaedriades

FIG. 212. Delphi. Theater with
the cliffs

FIG. 213. Delphi. Theater and
Temple of Apollo with mountains
across the valley

FIG. 215. Delphi. Athenian Treasury and Valley, of the Pleistos

FIG. 214. Delphi. Temple of Apollo from above

FIG. 216. Dionyso (Ikaria). Mt. Ocha
from Sanctuary of Apollo

FIG. 217. Eretria. Temple of Apollo
from the south, with acropolis and
flanking mountains

FIG. 218. Eretria. Temple of Dionysos.
Southeast corner with theater and acropolis

FIG. 220. Cape Zoster. View from Vouliagmeni

FIG. 219. Cape Zoster. Temple of Apollo from the south

FIG. 221. Delos from Sacred Lake

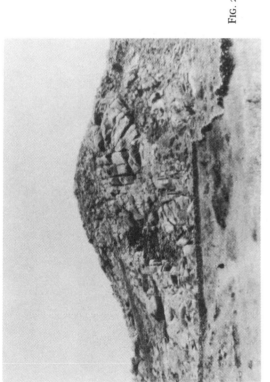

FIG. 222. Delos. a. (*left*) Mt. Cynthus, with Grotto of Herakles
b. (*below, left*) Grotto of Herakles and Altar
c. (*below*) Sanctuaries and Harbor from Cynthus

FIG. 223. Delos. Temple and Altar of Hera
with Mt. Cynthus

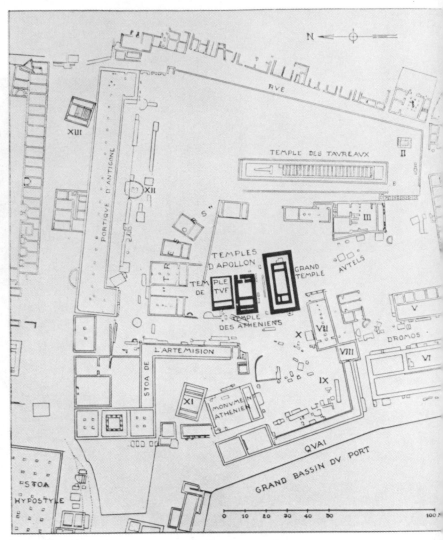

FIG. 224. (*right*) Delos. a. Sanctuary of
Apollo. Plan: VII, Oikos of the Naxians; VIII,
Propylon; IX, Bronze palm tree; X, colossal
kouros; XI, Temple of Artemis; Monument
Athénien=The Keraton. b. (*below*) Central
area. Plan

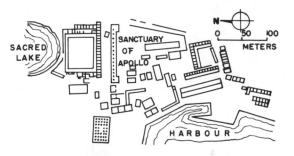

FIG. 225. Delos. Eastern ends of Temples of
Apollo with Mt. Cynthus

FIG. 226. Cumae. Temple
of Apollo looking northeast

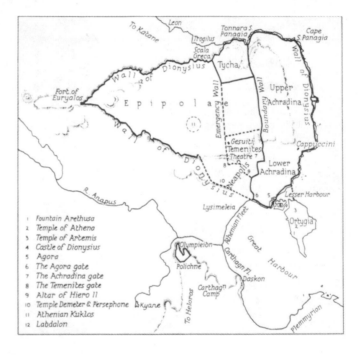

FIG. 227. Syracuse. Plan. For
Temple of Artemis, read Temple
of Apollo

1   Fountain Arethusa
2   Temple of Athena
3   Temple of Artemis
4   Castle of Dionysius
5   Agora
6   The Agora gate
7   The Achradina gate
8   The Temenites gate
9   Altar of Hiero II
10 Temple Demeter & Persephone
11 Athenian Kuklos
12 Labdalon

FIG. 228. Himera. Temple of
Apollo. Looking west along the
south colonnade

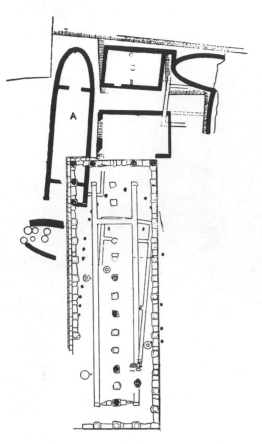

FIG. 229. Thermon. Plan, showing Megara
A and B and archaic Temple of Apollo

FIG. 230. Thermon. View south showing Megaron A, foreground,
and Temple of Apollo

FIG. 231. Bassae. Temple of Apollo. Southwest angle

FIG. 232. Bassae.
Temple of Apollo. From the turn

FIG. 233. Bassae.
Temple of Apollo. West flank

FIG. 234. Bassae.
Temple of Apollo. West
pteron looking south

FIG. 235. Bassae.
Temple of Apollo. From
the north with Mt. Ithome

FIG. 236. Bassae.
Temple of Apollo.
From Mt. Kôtilon

FIG. 237. Bassae.
Temple of Apollo.
North front

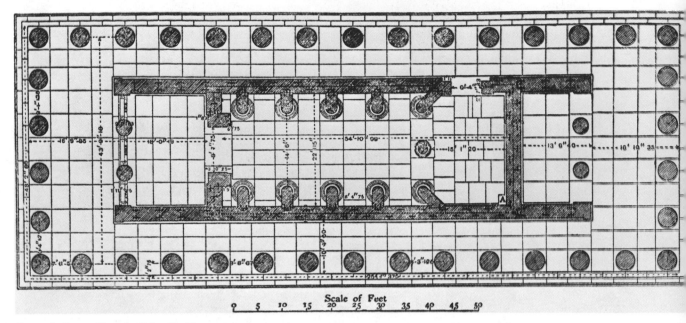

FIG. 238. Bassae. Temple of Apollo. Plan

FIG. 239. Bassae. Temple of Apollo. Interior from the adyton

FIG. 240. Bassae. Temple of Apollo. Reconstruction drawing of interior from north

FIG. 241. Bassae. Temple of Apollo. Detail of frieze

FIG. 242. Bassae. Temple of Apollo. Line of sight from wall–bonded slab
in the southwest corner of the adyton to the summit of Mt. Lykaion

FIG. 243. Didyma. Temple of Apollo with horns of Mykale to the north

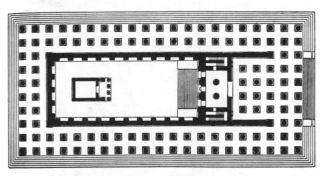

FIG. 244. Didyma. Temple of Apollo. Plan

FIG. 245. Didyma. Temple of Apollo. Cella. View eastward from shrine toward stairs

FIG. 246. Klaros. Temple of Apollo. The labyrinth and the cleft

FIG. 247. Klaros. Temple of Apollo with horns of Mykale.
Hadrian's propylon under tree clump, left rear

FIG. 248. Klaros. Temple of Apollo.
East front and gorge

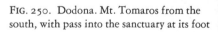

FIG. 249. Mt. Kerata. Sanctuary. Salamis and Oros right. Salamis center. Eleusis, Daphni, and Hymettos left

FIG. 250. Dodona. Mt. Tomaros from the
south, with pass into the sanctuary at its foot

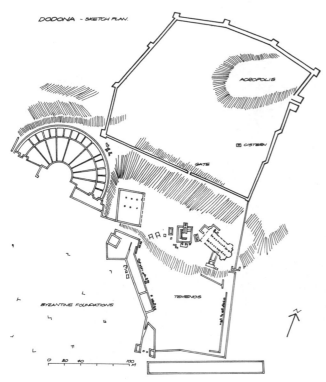

DODONA - SKETCH PLAN.

ACROPOLIS

CISTERN

GATE

BYZANTINE FOUNDATIONS

TEMENOS

0   20   40   100
                    M

FIG. 252. Dodona. Sanctuary of Zeus. Sketch Plan

FIG. 251. Dodona. Sanctuary from the south

FIG. 253. Dodona.
Sanctuary from the north

FIG. 254. Athens. Temple of the Olympian Zeus. From the Acropolis

FIG. 255. Temple of the Olympian Zeus. The propylon

FIG. 256. Temple of the Olympian Zeus. From the southwest

FIG. 257. Temple of the Olympian Zeus.
Axis toward Hymettos

FIG. 258. Nemea. The valley from the east.
Temple of Zeus center

FIG. 259. Nemea. The valley from the south. Temple of Zeus left

FIG. 260. Nemea. Temple of Zeus. a. From the east.

b. From the south

FIG. 261. Akragas. Temple of Zeus. Telamone and acropolis

FIG. 263. Olympia. From the west. Hill of Kronos, Altis, Valleys of Alpheios and Kladeos Rivers

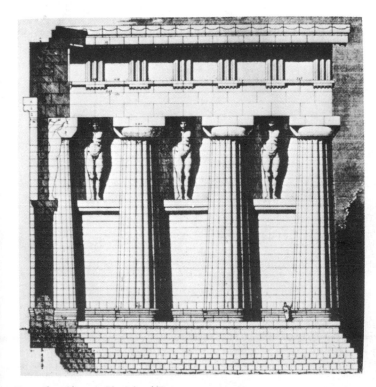

FIG. 262. Akragas. Temple of Zeus.
Restoration

FIG. 263a. Olympia. Hill of Kronos and
Hellenistic stadium

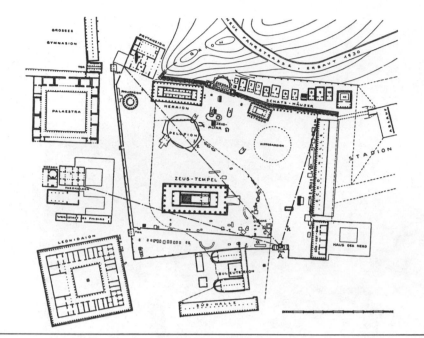

FIG. 264. Olympia. Plan in later antiquity, and with Bronze Age megara. Hippodamaion conjectural

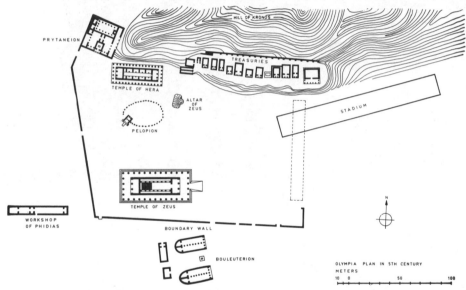

FIG. 265. Olympia. Plan in the fifth century

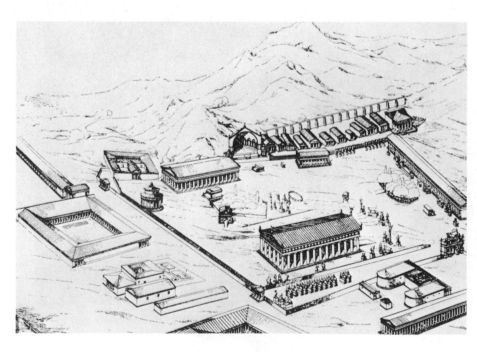

FIG. 266. Olympia in later antiquity. Reconstruction drawing, Hippodamaion conjectural

FIG. 267. Olympia. View from
southwest of Temple of Zeus,
Pelopion, Temple of Hera, and
Hill of Kronos

FIG. 268. Olympia. The proplyon
of Pelopion and Temple of Hera

FIG. 269. Olympia. Temple of Zeus. West pediment

FIG. 270. Olympia. Temple of Hera as seen from east of Temple of Zeus

FIG. 271. Olympia. Temple of Zeus. East pediment

FIG. 272. Olympia. Zeus, Hera, Hill of Kronos

FIG. 273. Olympia. Hera, Pelopion, and Zeus

FIG. 275. Rhamnous. Town and Temples of Nemesis and Themis. Sketch Plans

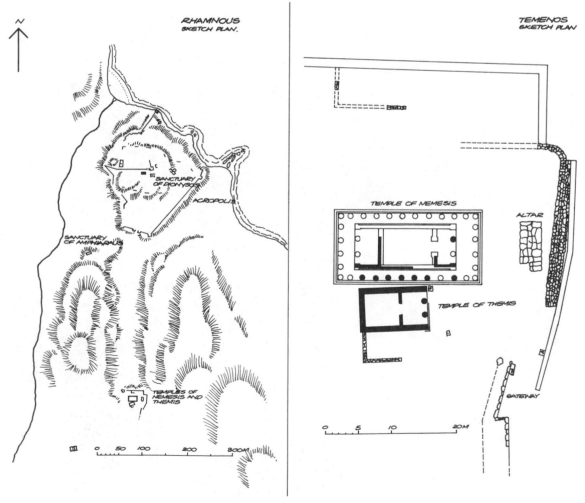

FIG. 274. Olympia. Temple of Zeus. Metope of the
Stymphalian Birds

FIG. 276. Rhamnous. Temples of Nemesis and Themis
from the east

FIG. 277. Rhamnous. The two temples from the west. Detail

FIG. 278. Rhamnous. The two temples. View southeast into Attica

FIG. 279. Rhamnous. The two temples, the gulf, and Euboea

FIG. 280. Rhamnous. Along governing
diagonal southwest to northeast

FIG. 281. Poros (Calauria). Sanctuary of
Poseidon. View from the south: Aigina
straight ahead, Methane far left. Temple
on mounded hill, right, near tree on summit

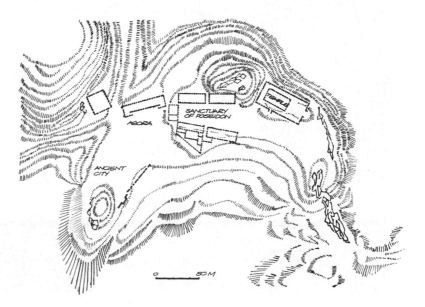

FIG. 282. Poros (Calauria). Sanctuary of
Poseidon and ancient town. Sketch plan

FIG. 283. Isthmia. Above Sanctuary of Poseidon.
View westward toward Acrocorinth

FIG. 285. Isthmia. Temple of Poseidon, looking east

FIG. 284. Isthmia. View eastward across the Sanctuary of Poseidon from above

FIG. 286. Mt. Mykale and bay from the east. Site of Panionion under horns

FIG. 287. Velia (Elea). Hill
of the temple from the agora
of the town. (Temple to the left
of medieval tower)

FIG. 288. Velia. Altar
of Poseidon. From the north

FIG. 289. Velia. Altar
of Poseidon. View seaward

FIG. 290. Sounion. View north from Sanctuary of Poseidon. Sanctuary of Athena on mounded hill, right, in loop of road

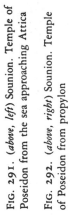

FIG. 291. (*above, left*) Sounion. Temple of Poseidon from the sea approaching Attica

FIG. 292. (*above, right*) Sounion. Temple of Poseidon from propylon

FIG. 292a. (*far left*) Sounion. Temple of Poseidon from the northeast

FIG. 293. (*left*) Sounion. Propylon and stoa. Looking west

FIG. 294. (*below, left*) Sounion. View east from Temple of Poseidon

FIG. 295. (*below*) Sounion. Altar from temple

FIG. 296. Sounion. Temple of Poseidon. View west from altar

FIG. 297. Kouros from Sounion, c. 600. Detail

FIG. 298. Sounion. Temple of Poseidon. View between the columns toward the land

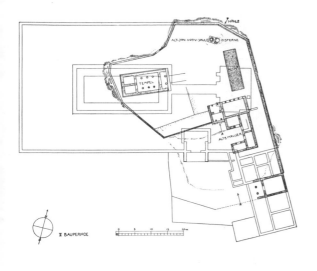

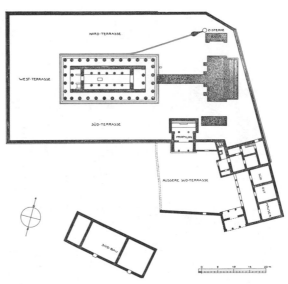

FIG. 299. Aigina. Sanctuary of Aphaia in mid–sixth century. Plan

FIG. 300. Aigina. Sanctuary of Aphaia c. 500. Plan

FIG. 301. Aigina. Sanctuary of Aphaia. Cave below

FIG. 302. Aigina. View from cave toward conical hill on Salamis

FIG. 303. Aigina. Sanctuary
of Aphaia. Approach to propylon

FIG. 304. Aigina. Temple of
Aphaia and conical hill on Salamis

FIG. 305. Aigina. Temple of
Aphaia from altar

FIG. 306. Aigina. Temple of
Aphaia and Mt. Oros, from the
east

FIG. 307. Temple of Aphaia (1)

FIG. 308. Temple of Aphaia (2)

FIG. 309. Temple of Aphaia (3)

FIG. 310. Temple of Aphaia (4)

FIG. 312. Temple of Aphaia (6)

FIG. 311. Temple of Aphaia (5)

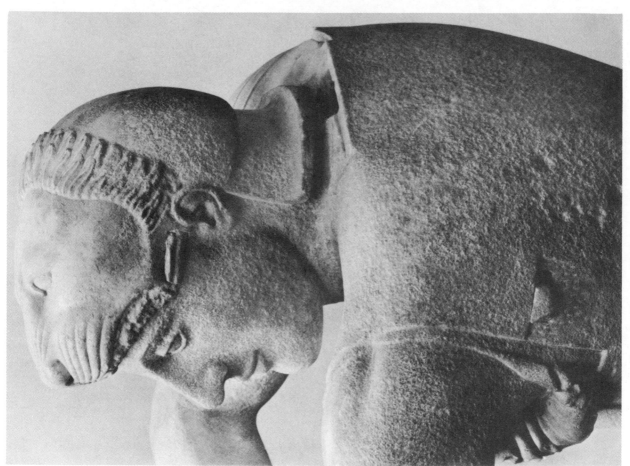

FIG. 314. Temple of Aphaia. Herakles, east pediment

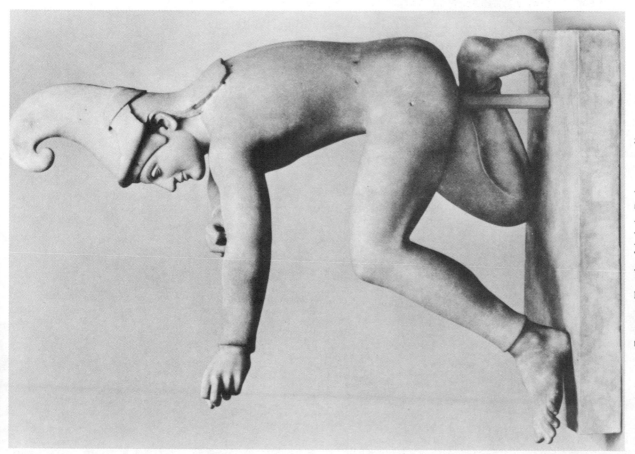

FIG. 313. Temple of Aphaia. Paris, west pediment

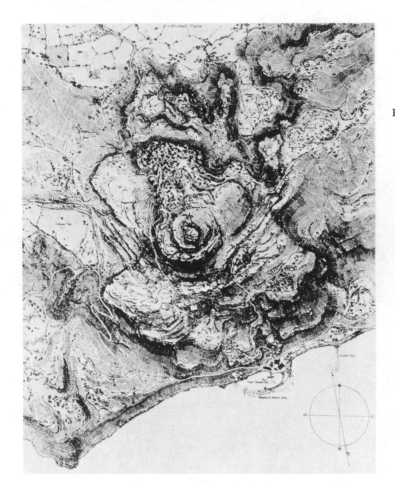

FIG. 315. Assos. Contour Map

FIG. 316. Paestum. Temple of Athena from the southv

FIG. 317. Paestum. Temple of Athena with mountain range

FIG. 318. Paestum. Temple of Athena from the east

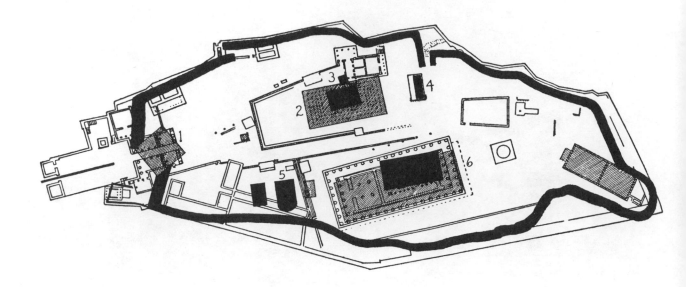

FIG. 319. a. (*above*) Athens. The Acropolis
showing pre–Periclean structures. Plan.
b. (*left*) Acropolis. Kore wearing peplos,
c. 540–530

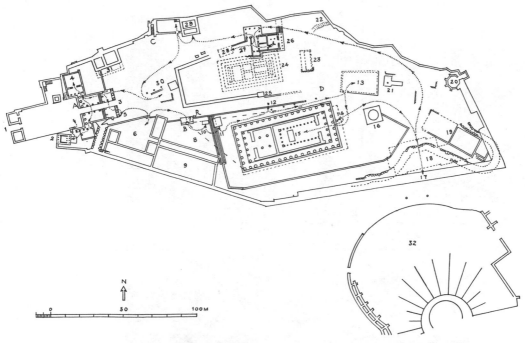

1. Beulé's Gate. 2. Nike Temple. 3. Propylaea. 4. Pinakotheke. 5. Statue of Athena Hygieia. 6. Sanctuary of the Brauronian Artemis. 7. Propylon. 8. Court. 9. Chalkotheke. 10. Votive Bull. 11. Monument of Athena Ergane(?). 12. Inscription of Ge. 13. Precinct of Zeus Polieus. 14. Statue of Iphikrates. 15. Chryselephantine Statue of Athena in the Parthenon. 16. Temple of Roma. 17. Votive Group of Attalus. 18. Modern Museum. 19. Work Shops. 20. Modern Belvedere. 21. Boukoleion. 22. Mycenaean Steps. 23. Great Altar of Athena. 24. Old Temple of Athena. 25. Propylon (*I.G.*, I², 4). 26. Erechtheum. 27. Court of the Pandroseum. 28. Temple of Pandrosus. 29. Dwelling of the Arrephoroi. 30. Group of the "Promachos." 31. Service Building(?). 32. Theatre of Dionysus.

FIG. 320. Acropolis. Plan as developed during and after Periclean period

FIG. 321. Acropolis.
Reconstruction drawing

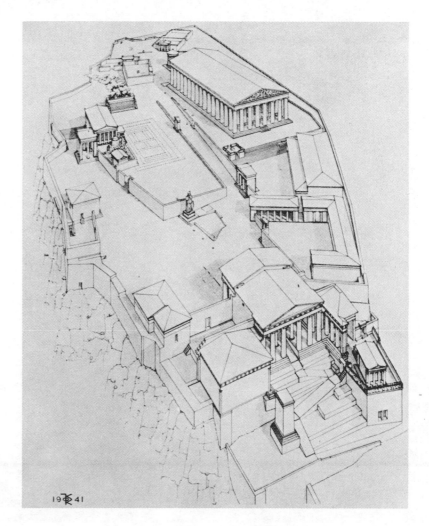

FIG. 322. Parthenon.
Interior looking west

FIG. 323. Parthenon.
Interior looking east

FIG. 324. Parthenon. West front. Detail

a. Parthenon. Southwestern corner   b. Erechtheion. North porch. Detail

FIG. 325. Parthenon. a. (*above*) From the west. b. (*above on facing page*) From the east

FIG. 326. Parthenon. From the northwest

FIG. 327. Parthenon. From the Pnyx

FIG. 328. Parthenon.
From summit of Philopappos

FIG. 329. Acropolis from
"Cave of the Eumenides"

FIG. 330. Athena Nike.
From the southwest,
showing "false front"

FIG. 331. Turn of old
Sacred Way below bastion
toward Mnesicles' Propylaia

FIG. 332. Propylaia and stairs

FIG. 333. Athena Nike (in snow)
from the Propylaia. Piraeus beyond

FIG. 334. Athena Nike and
Salamis from the Propylaia

FIG. 335. Propylaia,
central axis and Salamis

FIG. 336. Propylaia.
Interior looking toward
picture gallery

FIG. 337. Propylaia. Looking toward picture gallery from south \ Ionic column to right

FIG. 338. Propylaia. Ionic column

FIG. 339. Propylaia. North wall of central pavilion, showing gray orthostates and "paneled" wall treatment

FIG. 340. Propylaia. Central and south doors

FIG. 341. Acropolis height. View from the Propylaia

FIG. 342. Reappearance of horns of Hymettos on approach to Parthenon's propylon

FIG. 343. Northwest corner of Parthenon
from its propylon

FIG. 344. Parthenon from its propylon. Reconstruction drawing

FIG. 345. Lycabettos and Erechtheion from northwest corner of Parthenon. Site of figure of Gaia
marked by metal railing on line with Lycabettos

FIG. 346. Caryatids with Hymettos from old Temple of Athena Polias. Altar of Athena ahead

FIG. 347. View westward toward Salamis from center of Acropolis

FIG. 349. Parthenon and Erechtheion from the east

FIG. 348. a. Parthenon. North Flank.
b. Erechtheion and Parnes from northeast
corner of Parthenon

FIG. 350. Parthenon. East Pediment. Dionysos; Leto, Dione and Aphrodite

FIG. 351. Parthenon. South flank looking westward

FIG. 352. Parthenon. North pteron moving westward

FIG. 353. Parthenon.
West porch from its northeast
corner

FIG. 354. Parthenon.
West porch looking north
toward Mt. Harma

FIG. 355. Parthenon.
West porch looking south
toward Saronic Gulf

FIG. 356. Parthenon.
West porch looking west
toward Salamis

FIG. 357. Parthenon. West front looking south. Hill of Philopappos right, with Mt. Oros on Aigina (Zeus Panhellenios) beyond

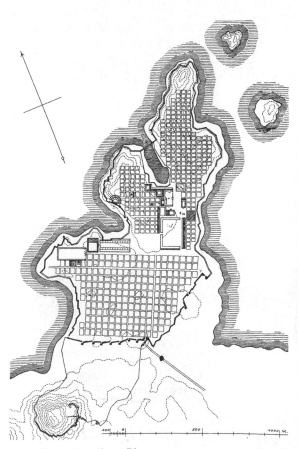

FIG. 358. Miletos. Plan

FIG. 359. Athens. Agora from north slope of Acropolis. Hephaisteion, left. Sacred Way and reconstructed Stoa of Attalos, right

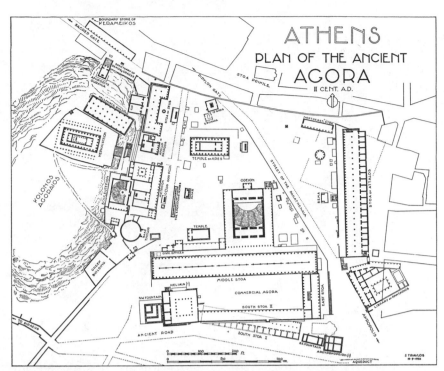

FIG. 360. Agora, Athens.
Plan in second century A.D.

FIG, 361. a. Hephaisteion. South flank.
b. Hephaisteion. From the Agora

FIG. 362. Hephaisteion.
Approximately as seen in
ancient frontal approach

FIG. 363. Hephaisteion.
South pteron and east porch

FIG. 364. a. Hephaisteion. View from east porch.
b. (*below*) City of Athens with reconstructed Stoa of Attalos. Areopagus right

FIG. 365. Stoa of Attalos. Exterior details

FIG. 366. Stoa of Attalos. Hephaisteion from upper floor

FIG. 367. Megalopolis. Theater. Thersilion columns middle foreground.
(Sanctuary of Hera marked by evergreens on hill)

FIG. 368. Ephesos. Greek and Roman theater,
view west across bay

FIG. 369. Taormina. Theater with Roman scaena. Naxos and Aetna beyond

FIG. 370. Cassope. The town. View south toward Actium

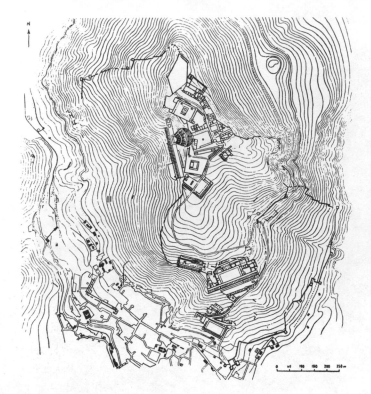

FIG. 371. Pergamon. General plan

FIG. 372. Pergamon. Reconstruction drawing

FIG. 373. Pergamon. Acropolis
from southern tumulus

FIG. 376. Pergamon. Temple of Athena
from its propylon. Reconstruction drawing

FIG. 374. Pergamon. Plain from above
Sanctuary of Demeter. Northern tumulus
(with vaulted tomb) far left. Natural mounds
farther west, in the valley toward the sea

FIG. 375. (*below, left*) Pergamon. Southern
tumulus from entrance way between Sanctuary
of Demeter and Altar of Zeus

FIG. 377. (*below, right*) Pergamon.
Regulating line from upper, northeast corner
of acropolis, showing axis through upper
Sanctuary of Zeus, Temple of Athena,
Altar of Zeus, and southern tumulus

FIG. 378. Pergamon. Theater looking west. Asklepieion in fold far left, middle distance

FIG. 379. Pergamon. Theater with Temple of Dionysos. Looking northwest

FIG. 380. Pergamon. Theater and two tumuli showing diagonal axis of theater terrace

FIG. 381. Pergamon. Temple of Hera
Basileia above Gymnasium. Orientation on
easternmost tumulus

FIG. 382. Priene. Reconstruction drawing

Fig. 383. Priene. The Temple of Athena as
originally seen from altar in agora

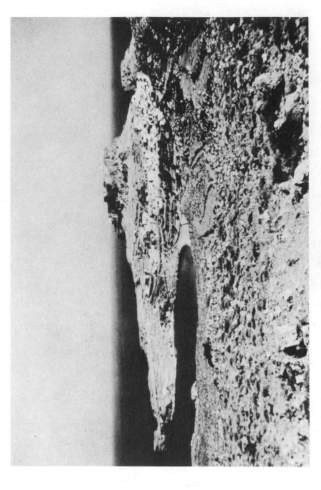

FIG. 385. Lindos. View of town and acropolis from the north

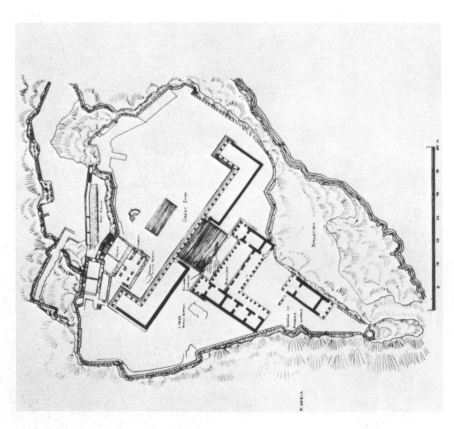

FIG. 386. Lindos. Stairs and propylaia

FIG. 384. Lindos, Rhodes. Sanctuary of Athena Lindaia. Plan

FIG. 388. Lindos. Temple of Athena. From southern end of propylaia

FIG. 390. Lindos. Conical promontory on northeast with "Tomb of Cleobolos"

FIG. 387. Lindos. Axis of view southwest from propylaia

FIG. 389. Lindos. Temple of Athena. View downward

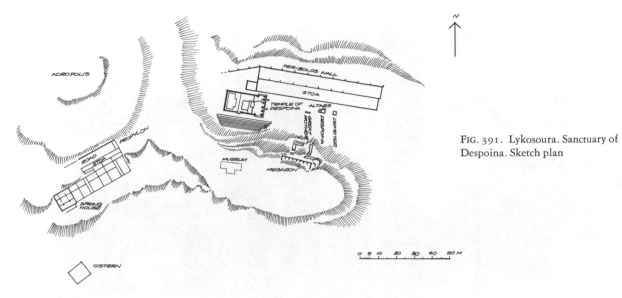

FIG. 391. Lykosoura. Sanctuary of
Despoina. Sketch plan

FIG. 392. Lykosoura. View down
axis of sanctuary from acropolis

FIG. 393. Thebes. Kabirion. View
north from sanctuary toward
mounded hill and Ptoon

FIG. 394. (*above*) Samothrace. Sanctuary of the Kabeiroi. Columns of the Hieron

FIG. 395. (*right*) Samothrace. Sanctuary of the Kabeiroi. Plan. A. Anaktoron; B. "Sacristy"; C. Rotunda of Arsinoe; D. Temenos; E. Hieron; F. Hall of Votive Gifts; G. Altar Court; H. Theater; I. Nike Fountain; J. Stoa; K. Propylon of Ptolemy II; L. *Ruinenviereck*

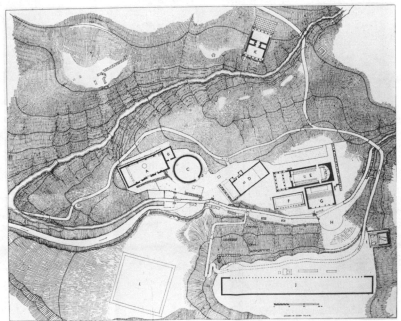

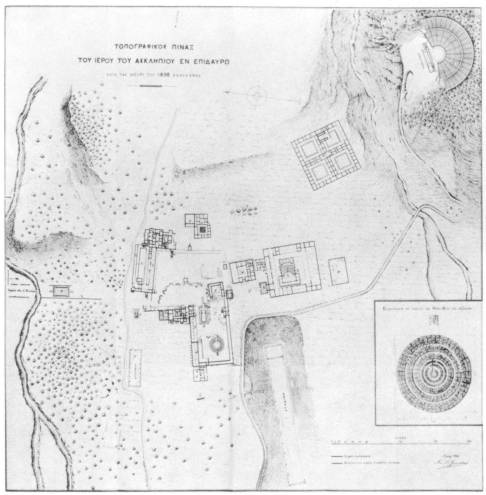

FIG. 397. Epidauros. Sanctuary of Asklepios. Plan

FIG. 396. Epidauros. "Titthion" (?) rising above Sanctuary of
Asklepios on route from Argolid

FIG. 398. Epidauros. Southern ridge from northern propylon

FIG. 399. Epidauros. Temple of Asklepios from the east

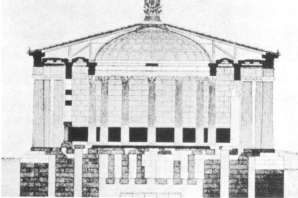

FIG. 400. Epidauros. Tholos. Elevation and section

FIG. 401. Epidauros. Stadium from the east

FIG. 402. Epidauros. Theater
with "Titthion." Sanctuary of
Apollo above

FIG. 403. Epidauros. Theater.
View northwest across Sanctuary
of Asklepios

FIG. 404. Epidauros. Theater. View northward

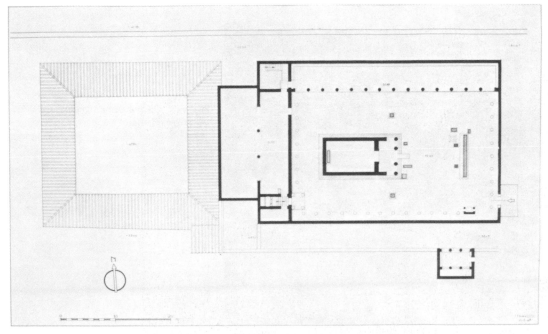

FIG. 405. Corinth. Asklepieion. Plan

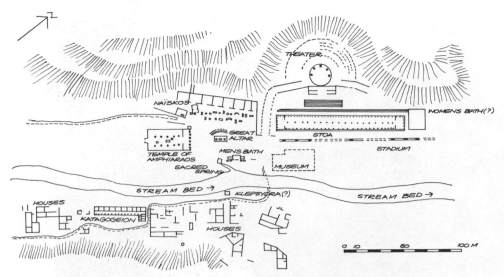

FIG. 406. Oropos. Amphiaraion. Sketch plan

FIG. 407. Oropos. Amphiaraion. Stoa.
Looking toward temple

FIG. 408. Oropos. Amphiaraion. Theater.
View toward altar

FIG. 409. Kos. As seen from Kalymnos at dawn

FIG. 410. Kos. Harbor, with conical promontory of Asia

FIG. 411. Kos. Site of Asklepieion as seen from coastal plain

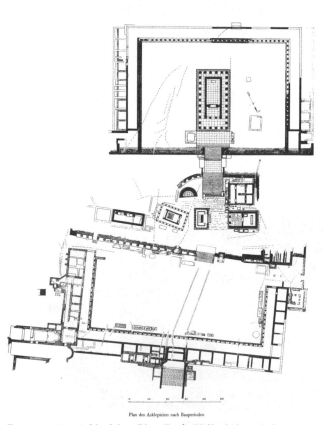

FIG. 412. Kos. Asklepieion. Plan. Dark, Hellenistic period. Light, Roman period

FIG. 413. Kos. Asklepieion. Lower terrace from its entrance

FIG. 414. Kos. Asklepieion. Second terrace, altar, Temple of Apollo and exedra

FIG. 415. Kos. Asklepieion. Temple of Asklepios and conical promontory

FIG. 416. Kos. Asklepieion.
View north from head of stairs

FIG. 417. Kos. Asklepieion.
Temple of Asklepios from above

FIG. 418. Praeneste. Temple of Fortune.
    a. (*right*) Isometric reconstruction.
    b. (*below*) View with Colonna–
       Barberini Palace

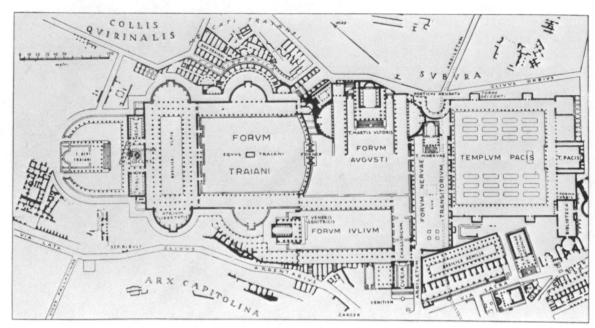

FIG. 419. Rome. Imperial Fora. Plan

FIG. 420. Tivoli. Hadrian's Villa. Small Baths

FIG. 421. Boeotia. Valley of the Muses. Ascra, the conical hill at right. Mt. Helikon at left

FIG. 422. Boeotia. Valley of the Muses. Sanctuary on slope of Helikon, left center distance

FIG. 423. Boeotia. Valley of the Muses. Reconstruction as in second century B.C., by P. Bernard

FIG. 424. Boeotia. Valley of the Muses. Altar and stoa

FIG. 425. Boeotia. Valley of the Muses. View from theater. Ascra to left, stoa and altar between, and Thespiae in the distance

FIG. 426. Mt. Parnassos from Elateia

FIG. 427. Temple of Athena Kranaia, near Elateia, looking west

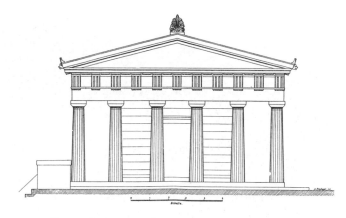

FIG. 428. Temple of Athena Kranaia. West elevation, conjecturally restored

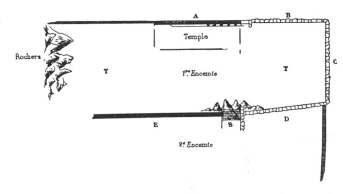

FIG. 429. Sanctuary of Athena Kranaia. Plan

FIG. 430. Temple of Athena Kranaia. Doric capital of fifth century

FIG. 431. Temple of Athena Kranaia. Doric capital of fourth century

FIG. 432. Sanctuary of Athena Kranaia. Retaining wall of temenos.
Mt. Parnassos in distance

FIG. 433. Sketch map of Lesbos

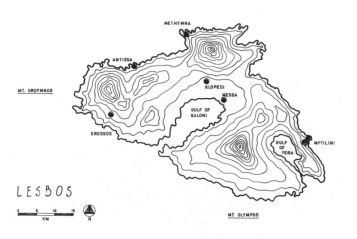

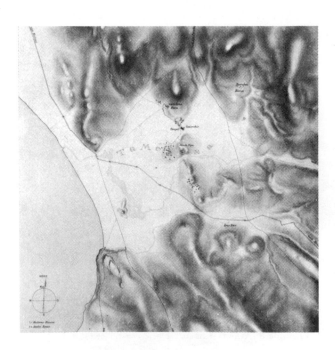

FIG. 434. Ta Messa, Lesbos. Temple of Aphrodite. Site plan and
reconstructed perspective

FIG. 435. Ta Messa, Lesbos. Temple of Aphrodite (now Church of Taxiarchis). The mouth of the Gulf of Kaloni in the distance

FIG. 436. Ta Messa, Lesbos. Temple of Aphrodite and Church of Taxiarchis from the west. Mt. Olympos in the distance

FIG. 437. Thasos. Town below the double-peaked hill at left. Conical hill of Demeter in center. Main ridge of the island rising to right

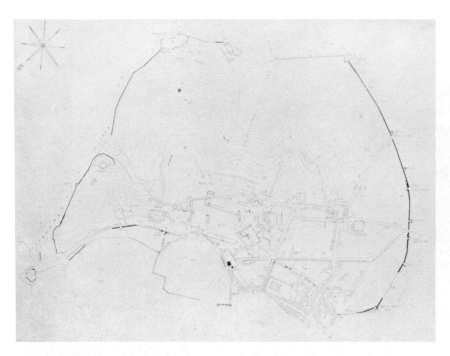

FIG. 438. Thasos. Plan. Sanctuary of Demeter at upper right. Temple of Athena Poliouchos in upper center

FIG. 439. Thasos. The Herakleion looking south along the west flank of the temple past the propylon toward the inland ridge

FIG. 440. Thrace, Mt. Pangaion in
distance, as seen from Philippi

FIG. 441. Relief of Herakles from Thasos,
now in Istanbul, and coin of Thasos with
Herakles and Dionysos

FIG. 442. Thasos. The cone from the Gate
of Herakles

Fig. 443. Thasos. Gate of Silenus

Fig. 444. Thasos. Platform of the Temple of Athena Poliouchos from the northern summit. Conical hill of Demeter below

FIG. 445. Thasos. Agora and harbor from the Temple of Athena Poliouchos

FIG. 446. Thasos. Temple of Athena. Platform from the Agora. Base of Victory in the foreground. Sanctuary of Artemis Polo near the building under trees at left. Passage of the Theores in the middle ground at left

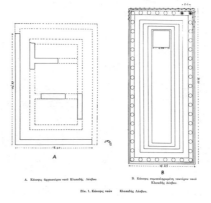

FIG. 447. Klopedi. Conjectural plans, by Evanghelides, of the two temples. A is thought to be the earlier temple, B the unfinished later one

FIG. 448. Klopedi. View south from the first temple (A on plan)

FIG. 450. Aeolic capital from Klopedi, now in Mytilini where it was exhibited in a since-demolished museum

FIG. 449. Klopedi. North flank of second temple (B)

FIG. 451. Second capital from Klopedi in Mytilini with, background left, what is probably an echinus

a. Left hand capital seen right way up

b. Right hand capital seen right way up

c. Column drum also built into the wall

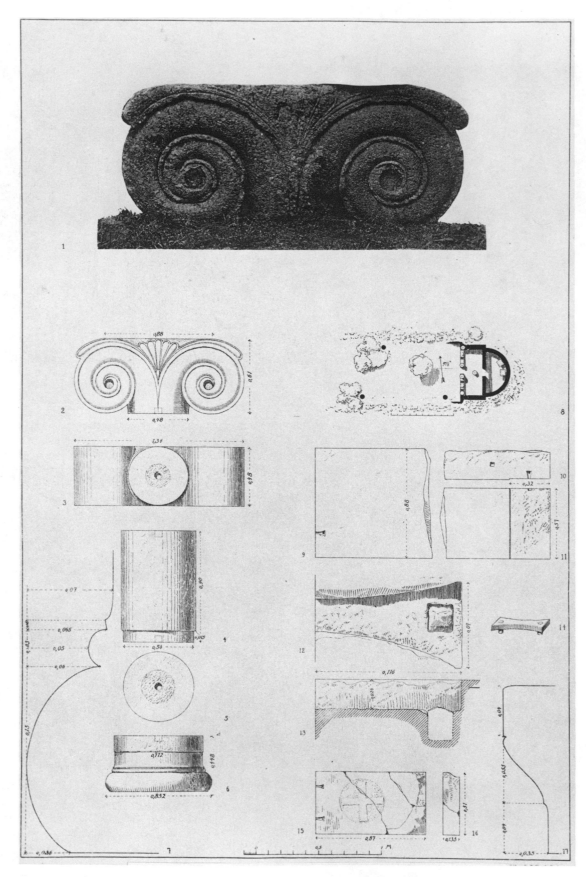

FIG. 453. Koldewey's drawings of one of the two capitals from Klopedi, now in Mytilini

FIG. 454. Scale of one of the capitals from Klopedi at Mytilini

FIG. 455. Klopedi. Capital and horse

FIG. 456. Three other examples of Aeolic capitals, now in Istanbul:

a. from Larisa

b. from Neandria

c. from the Acropolis of Mytilini